Ronan Fitzgerald
Gillian Goggin
01458100

Cannnn **HDE DipT&D MEd ATSD** is Managing
Director of Carole Hogan Associates, a management consultancy firm
with over 20 years' experience specialising in Leadership,
Management Development and Adult Learning, particularly within
the electronic, pharmaceutical and financial sectors. She is a
graduate of the National University of Ireland and Sheffield
University. Carole's research interests include Management
Development Centres, Management Strategies and Training &
Development initiatives. She is presently reading for a Doctorate in
Human Resource Development with the University of Leicester.

**Amanda   Cahir-O'Donnell   MEdMgt   DipPersonnelMgt
GradCIPD** joined AIB Capital Markets as Head of Training &
Development in March 2000. She has established a leading-edge
T&D function through her commitment "to create and embed a
culture of Continuous Learning." In 1989, Amanda qualified as a
Primary Teacher. Her career in management consultancy
commenced in 1994, specialising in Organisational, Team and
Individual Development. She has worked with many diverse
organisations in Ireland and the US. Amanda holds a First Class
Master's Degree in Education Management from Trinity College,
Dublin.

MAKING TRAINING
TRAINING
&
DEVELOPMENT
WORK

A "Best Practice" Guide

Thomas N Garavan
Carole Hogan
Amanda Cahir-O'Donnell

www.oaktreepress.com

OAK TREE PRESS
19 Rutland Street, Cork, Ireland
http://www.oaktreepress.com

A catalogue record of this book is
available from the British Library.

ISBN 1 86076 276 X pb
ISBN 1 86076 289 1 hb

CONTENTS

FIGURES

PREFACE

The essential purpose of this book is to describe and explain a number of core concepts concerned with the role and effectiveness of training and development (T&D) in organisations and to identify and describe the skills necessary to be an effective trainer. We are conscious that T&D practitioners are busy people and are unlikely to read large amounts of theory. With this in mind, each chapter provides an integrative summary of the implications of current research findings on T&D and identifies practical steps that you can take as a trainer to implement best practice.

The book focuses on five major topic areas:

- The core concepts that underpin the subject area of T&D
- The steps and decisions that need to be considered when establishing a T&D function and in identifying T&D priorities
- The process of designing T&D activities and formal events, and the contribution that learning theories can make to effective training design
- The delivery of T&D activities, including the contribution that psychological concepts can make to effective training delivery
- The costing of training activities, their evaluation and the calculation of return on investment.

This book concentrates on the priorities of the T&D specialist. It goes beyond existing training books in a number of ways by:

- Concentrating on summarising the implications of current theories and research for the practices that trainers can adopt
- Articulating clearly the best practice issues that should demand the attention of the practising trainer
- Providing, at the end of each chapter, a set of best practice indicators
- Focusing on various levels of analysis (intra-individual, inter-individual, team and organisational levels) and the factors that are relevant to better understand training effectiveness from these different levels or perspectives.

This provides a strong theoretical-driven foundation, in addition to a practitioner orientation to the book.

The book emerged from a realisation that many practitioner-focused training texts tend to place too much emphasis on the practice without sufficiently explaining the relevant theoretical foundations in practitioner-type language, or tended to be primarily theoretical with a strong strategic focus. We fully understand the need for T&D to think in strategic terms. However, in this book, our primary objective is to focus on the operational realities that the trainer experiences. Our intended audience is practitioners in the field of T&D. They may be internal or external consultants or specialists and are likely to hold such job titles as Training Manager, Training Specialist, Instructional Designer and Direct Trainer. In many larger organisations, responsibility for T&D activities are differentiated between training specialists and line managers. Although the principles set out in this book apply to both, to the extent that the training and development of employees is more likely to be concerned with fundamental practices such as the assessment of T&D needs, formal and informal instruction, and training design and evaluation, this book will prove more helpful to individuals working as specialists within the field.

This book owes its existence to numerous sources of inspiration and support. In particular we wish to recognise the invaluable contribution of our students, colleagues and peers, who have shaped our thinking and contributed to the concepts developed and explained here. The book is given added colour and texture through the case scenarios that we derived from our combined experiences as practitioners and teachers of training and development.

Thomas N Garavan
Carole Hogan
Amanda Cahir-O'Donnell
November 2003

ACKNOWLEDGMENTS

We are fortunate to have the full support of our respective organisations, the University of Limerick, Carole Hogan Associates and AIB Capital Markets.

We would also like to acknowledge the support of a number of leading exponents of T&D in organisations, including Pat Salisbury and Ciara McClusky, Fexco Ireland; Paul Ennis, Eugene Dalton, Mick Loughnane and Jim McCabe, Electricity Supply Board; Aidan Laurence, HP Ireland; Des Moore, Blanchardstown Institute of Technology, Dublin; John Mullen, CEO, Thurles Credit Union; John Conway, HR Director, AIB Capital Markets; Pat Casey, HR Director, Dell Computers; Professor Joyce O'Connor, Julie Byrne and Grace O'Malley, National College of Ireland; Dr Nancy Sullivan, Director of Curriculum and Instruction & Professional Development, Easton Public Schools, MA, USA; Dr John R Sullivan, Executive Director of the New England School Development Council, USA; Professor JV Rice, Trinity College, Dublin; Dr Alma McCarthy, National University of Ireland Galway; Dr David Kearney, Director OPDC; Ineke Powell, Director, OPDC; Paul Dunn, P3 Training Ltd; Damian Lenagh, HR Director, Aer Rianta; Supt Pat Murphy, Director of Quality, Garda Training College, Templemore; Con Egan, HR Director, SPS Shannon; John Mangan, HR Manager, Kostal Ireland; Breda Flaherty, HR Director, Alps (Electric) Ireland Ltd; Pat Costine, Pat Costine & Associates; Michael Barry, Manager, FÁS, Waterford; Noreen Clifford, Consultant; Judy Kinnane, Consultant; Harris Sheike, Consultant; Ann Bollard, Director of Training and Development, Headway Ireland; Conor Clarke, Director of Training and Development, Organon Ireland; Christy Cooney, Assistant Director General, FÁS; Professor Máirtín Ó Fathaigh, University College Cork; Anna Cunningham, Philip Smyth, Joe McDonald and Kate O'Connell, Shannon College of Hotel Management; Hugh Fisher, Director, Training Connections, Dublin; Zeita Lambe, Training Specialist, IBM Ireland; David Goggin, Training Specialist, eircom.net; Alan Grey, Wyeth; Aine O'Reilly Doyle, Consultant; Helena Downey, Consultant; Maurice Kearney, Principal, Ratoath NS.

We are delighted that CIPD Ireland are associated with this book and acknowledge the leadership of Michael McDonnell, Director, CIPD Ireland.

The authors would like to thank the following at the University of Limerick, AIB Capital Markets and Carole Hogan Associates for their support and encouragement: Roger Downer, President, University of Limerick; Professor Noel Whelan, Vice President, University of Limerick; Professor Donal Dineen, Dean, College of Business; Joseph Wallace, Head, Department of Personnel and Employment Relations; colleagues Paddy Gunnigle, Patrick Flood, Mike Morley, Sarah Moore, Sarah McCurtin, Tom Turner, Daryl D'Art, Claire Gubbins, Helena Lenihan, Juliet McMahon, Fergal O'Brien, Noreen Heraty, David Collings, Linda Edgeworth, Eoin Reeves, Eoin Devereux, Tom Kennedy, Eamon Collins, Michael Gaffney, Christine Cross, Bridie Barnicle, Dave McGuire, Claire Murphy, Ronan Carbery. Elizabeth Switzer, Naoise Blake, Eilis Moylan, Jeannie Colvin, Deirdre Gray, Sinead Gaynor, Kathleen Murphy; Colm Doherty, MD, AIB Capital Markets; Avril Farrell; Anne Kiely; Helena Downey; Denise Banks; Grace Doyle; Faye Doherty; Niamh Hurley; Maurice McCrum; Kieran Browne; Anne Wasylyk; Kieran Corcoran; Cathy Murphy; Colette Brennan; Denis Culligan; Andrew Rogals; Libby Thornton; Michelle Carter; Michelle Murphy; Karen Nicholson; and Gerard Manning.

The authors' heartfelt thanks go to Kim O'Mahony, University of Limerick, who typed the manuscript and who kept track of the numerous edits and changes made to the book as it evolved.

Finally, thanks to Brian O'Kane and all at Oak Tree Press for their continued support and their professionalism in preparing this book for publication.

DEDICATIONS

Thomas

To my parents, Thomas and Margaret, my brothers, Jim, Gerard and PJ, and my sisters, Mary B. and Rita, for their continued love and support.

Carole

To my husband, Martin O'Donoghue, and my sons, Hugh and Brian, for their love, good humour and tolerance. I would also like to thank my parents, Kitty and Pat Hogan, and my brothers and sisters.

Amanda

Thanks to my husband, Keelan, for his unwavering support, interest and enthusiasm. Thanks to my parents, T.J. and Carmel, for inspiring my love of learning; and to all my family and friends for their encouragement. Finally, a special welcome to my son Conor.

CIPD is Ireland and the UK's leading professional body in the field of personnel & development. There are over 118,000 members throughout the UK and Ireland. Membership of CIPD is widely accepted by employers as a requirement of practice, as it demonstrates a commitment to high standards of professionalism and to continuing professional development (CPD).

CIPD Ireland is enjoying phenomenal growth, from 400 members to 5,000 members in 25 years. The Institute was awarded Chartered Status in July 2000 in recognition of its role in promoting "the art and science of the management and development of people for the public benefit". Full members of CIPD gained individual chartered status on 1 October 2003. The chartered title identifies our members as qualified professionals who are committed to constantly updating their skills and knowledge and understand the wider business environment in which they work.

Members have access to a comprehensive range of services to assist them at all stages of their careers.

FOREWORD

In today's tough business environment, the message is quite simple: if it cannot be measured, it is not worth doing. This sharper focus on performance calls for a new approach to training and development. Far too much expenditure on T&D fails to deliver results for organisations. This creates a serious credibility issue concerning the value of investing in T&D. It often results in the training budget being amongst the first to get cut when times are hard. It does not have to be that way. *Making Training and Development Work: A Best Practice Guide* explains how an organisation can design and deliver training and manage the T&D function to ensure that T&Dis of continued relevance to competitiveness even in times of economic downturn.

I particularly like the fact the authors have chosen to call this important new book "A Best Practice Guide". While there are those, both academics and practitioners, who may question the term "best practice" as it implies an ultimate state of perfection, I beg to differ. In the context of this publication the authors describe "best practice" as adhering to a core set of principles based on leading-edge research, theory and practice, and this is as it should be.

The book will be an invaluable guide for practitioners and students alike. It appears at exactly the right time, when the importance of knowledge as the basis of competitive advantage is becoming obvious.

This is the age of the learner and the training and development of people is essential for any organisation seeking to create and sustain competitive advantage. The challenge for trainers is to choose the most appropriate approach, as clearly the old notion of "one size fits all" no longer applies. Here is one of the great strengths of the book, in that it helps the reader to make those choices that are most appropriate to their particular organisational settings. It describes the emerging trends in e-learning, blended learning, action learning and accelerated learning processes in a clear and accessible way. It also highlights one of the most neglected and overlooked facts that so much learning takes place informally in organisations. The authors describe how to recognise this and maximise the learning outcomes for the benefit of the individual and the organisation.

The practical knowledge that the authors bring to their work is evident from their appreciation of the challenges facing those responsible for implementing training at organisational level. They clearly understand that training policy can be greatly influenced by such things as the strength of the organisation's learning culture, the professionalism of the HR practices and the general level of support for training particularly at senior management levels. The book describes how to deal with these challenging issues, thus ensuring that it will occupy a prominent place on any serious trainer's bookshelf.

I believe this is a unique book because it is aimed at the practicing trainer – or those training to be trainers – yet written by authors who are at the top of their game in terms of serious academic research. As such, it is destined to have a major impact on training and development at organisational levels in all sectors of the economy.

Michael McDonnell BBS MSc Chartered FCIPD
Director – CIPD Ireland

INTRODUCTION

The impetus to write this book comes from a realisation that significant differences in perspective and focus exist between those who research training and development (T&D) as an organisational activity (academics) and those who are practitioners (trainers, managers and learners). Academics are often preoccupied with the bigger picture, with identifying trends and with generalising their findings. Practitioners are primarily concerned with design, implementation and action. They are required to be both proactive and reactive in how they perform their tasks. They are also expected to interact on a day-to-day basis with key stakeholders, internal and external to the organisation. This is a challenging task. Much of the current crop of T&D books does not speak particularly to the practising trainer. We write this book primarily from the viewpoint of the practising trainer, and for individuals who have responsibility for T&D as part of their wider role – for example, as managers. Our primary task is to analyse the research on T&D and identify its implications for the practising trainer. Throughout this book, we continually provide guidelines for practice that may be implemented in organisations. We are conscious that not all of what we recommend can be implemented directly. It may need to be customised to fit the culture, strategic requirements and characteristics of the organisation. How well these practices are implemented, therefore, depends on your skill as a trainer.

We see this book making three important contributions:

- It is a book about T&D practice and seeks to help you make quality decisions about the best learning options to select when you are faced with specific problems
- It will be of value to trainers who are studying Certificates in Training Practice or certificate level courses in Personnel Practice, of which T&D is a core subject
- We also see the book as an important companion piece to *Training and Development in Ireland: Context, Policy and Practice* (Oak Tree Press). This more academic text focuses on the process of developing human resources and the management of the T&D function in organisations. A new edition will be published in 2004.

UNIQUE CHARACTERISTICS OF THIS BOOK

The field of T&D as a set of organisational practices is both exciting and challenging at this time. There is evidence that organisations place a much stronger focus on, and commitment to, the development of people. Organisations are more committed to training and developing human resources, primarily to create and sustain competitive advantage and to ensure that high performing staff are retained. Organisations are more likely to experiment with new approaches to training design and delivery, including E-learning, action learning, accelerated learning processes, and blended learning solutions. Organisations are concerned with the continuous, rather than *ad hoc*, development of human resources. We know that T&D practices vary considerably from one organisation to another. There is lots of evidence to indicate that organisational characteristics such as strategic goals, culture, work processes and characteristics of employees will impact on the training design and delivery decisions you will be required to make. It is clear that one approach no longer fits all situations. T&D practices must be sensitive to organisational changes. To be an effective trainer, you are continuously challenged to choose the most appropriate approach and set of practices – one that will work given the circumstances and context that you find yourself operating in. You are required continually to make choices.

We have written this book, therefore, to assist you in making five core decisions:

- To define the best approach to take to T&D in your organisation, given its characteristics and strategies
- To select the most appropriate delivery strategy
- To select training methods that will achieve your learning objectives
- To select a style of delivery that best matches your skill level and personal characteristics
- To make effective decisions about how best to evaluate your T&D activities and to calculate a return on your organisation's investment in training.

The choices you make as a trainer should be firmly embedded in everyday experience. The realities of your workplace must determine the types of decisions that you can make. You must be conscious of the need to implement good training design principles. However, you must also have a sense of realism concerning issues such as current levels of organisational support for training, the strength of your organisation's learning culture, the sophistication of human resource practices implemented in your organisation, and your current skill level as a trainer. This book will assist you in dealing with all of these issues.

THE CENTRALITY OF LEARNING FOR INDIVIDUALS & ORGANISATIONS

Learning is central to what you do as a trainer. It is a process that can be very enjoyable, but it is also a process that is sometimes difficult and, for some learners, it is the source of failure. Irrespective of whether it is an enjoyable or more painful experience, it is a central issue for individuals and organisations in our contemporary world.

The practices that you implement as a trainer are central in the notion that learners have the potential to increase their contribution to organisations, communities and societies. Many of the activities that you are likely to be involved in will be associated with formal training. However, a lot of learning takes place informally within organisations. You need to recognise this. It is unhelpful to consider learning as simply derived from the training courses that you deliver. Your task as a trainer is to maximise the learning ability of your learners, through encouraging and supporting both individual and collective learning.

We consider learning to be a process rather than simply an outcome. As a training specialist, your explicit role will be to contribute to the effective design of formal learning events and to ensure that there are appropriate planned outcomes. There is a large amount of research available concerning learning. Learning is now likely to embrace the following ideas:

- Learning is not just about knowledge. It is also about skills, insights, beliefs, values, attitudes, habits, feelings, wisdom, shared understandings and self-awareness
- Learning outcomes can be incremental (building gradually on what has already been learned) or transformational (changing ways of being, thinking, feeling and acting)
- Transformational learning, for some learners and for some organisations, may be a struggle, may take time and may involve conflicts over aims and outcomes
- By its very nature, learning is essentially individual, but it can also be collectively generated in teams and organisations
- There is no one right way to learn for everybody and for every situation
- We can learn from any experience – failure, success, having our expectations confirmed or having them confounded
- Learning processes can be conscious (which helps us exercise our control over the process) or unconscious and serendipitous
- Learning processes can be both planned and opportunistic. If you can combine the strengths of both, it will enhance learning effectiveness

- Learning outcomes can be desirable or undesirable for learners and for others – learning always has a moral dimension
- Learning (both as a process and an outcome) can be both a cause and a consequence of change. There is no learning without change, though there can be change with insufficient learning
- Questioning, listening, challenging and enquiring are crucially important to effective learning
- The learning process occurs inside the person, but making the outcomes explicit, and sharing them with others, adds value to the learning
- When the learning process is self-managed, it becomes more effective
- Learning as a process can be subject to obstacles (such as lack of resources or self-confidence). Nonetheless, the desire and ability to learn is hard to suppress
- Wanting to learn, and seeing the point of learning, is often critical and makes it more likely that unexpected opportunities to learn will be exploited
- Your mood as a learner influences the quality of learning. While not a prerequisite, enjoyment of the learning process is a significant enabler.

We consider the articulation of clear learning objectives to be a central feature of effective formal learning design. Learning objectives identify the training design agenda and determine the types of design decisions you will have to make. Learning objectives have the potential to provide your learners with an understanding of what you are trying to accomplish. More effective learning is achieved if, at the beginning of a training activity, you let your learners know where they should focus their attention. There is considerable controversy about how specific these learning objectives should be. However, for now, we argue simply that they are important. Therefore, at the beginning of each chapter, we will identify the key learning objectives that we intend to focus on, indicating what you will learn by reading the chapter.

Following a statement of the learning objectives, we will provide a practical example designed to stimulate you to think about the issues we intend to discuss in each chapter. At the end of each chapter, we will highlight the key learning points that the case example highlights. In line with our focus on implementation and action, we will provide a set of action points on best practice that you should consider implementing in your organisation or professional context.

WHY IMPLEMENT BEST TRAINING PRACTICES?

We have called this book a "best practice guide". Some academics and practitioners may consider this to be an inappropriate title for a book. For us, best practices are understood as adhering to a set of core principles that are well established through training research, theory and practice. We are conscious that your organisational context will influence how these principles are applied. We use the term "trainer" in its most generic sense, to include the following individuals who may have a T&D dimension to their organisational roles; full-time trainers, line managers, instructional designers and human resource specialists. We are fully aware that context is of vital importance in explaining the effectiveness of training.

Why an organisation should implement best training practice is a question that is frequently asked. It is a question that we believe can have positive answers for both individuals and organisations. Learning has many benefits for individuals, including:

• Learning is the key to developing your identity and your potential

• Learning to learn is the key to effective learning

• Learning enables individuals to meet the demands of change

• The capacity to learn is an asset that never becomes obsolete

• Embracing learning helps you to understand that learning is a great deal more than just formal education and training

• Learning increases the range of your options. Learning about your past can help you understand the present, and prepare for the future

• Learning expands the horizons of who we are and what we can become

• The continuing desire to learn fuels curiosity and progress.

For organisations, we consider the potential benefits of learning to be:

• Regular and rigorous use of learning processes increases everyone's capacity to contribute to the success of the organisation

• Conscious use of learning processes enables the organisation to be more effective in meeting its goals and satisfying its stakeholders

• Learning from, and with, all stakeholders enhances and helps clarify purpose, vision, values and behaviour

• A focus on learning – planned and unplanned, formal and informal – produces a wider range of solutions to organisational issues and problems

• Learning helps achieve a better balance between the pressures of long-term effectiveness and short-term efficiency

- Learning enables an organisation to balance the demands of its stakeholders and its environment
- Learning, when shared, reduces the likelihood of repeated mistakes.

Many people, both inside and outside organisations, frequently espouse the belief that investment in T&D makes little difference to either individuals or organisations. Some of the more common reasons why people fail to acknowledge the benefits of investing in learning include:

- A failure to see the hidden cost of learning by trial and error
- A belief that effective performance results from innate ability not learning
- A failure to demonstrate an explicit causal link between learning and effective job and or organisational performance
- An inability to distinguish between the effects of training and development and other factors
- A belief that trained staff will be poached and that other employers will reap the benefits of investment in T&D
- The view that, as long as an employee is performing competently in a current role, the organisation does not need to make any further investment
- A previous experience with T&D that did not work out.

Therefore, the goal of T&D activities in organisations should be to maintain and/or improve the performance of individuals and, in so doing, that of the organisation. We know from research that many organisations spend much time, effort and money on training and developing employees (including managers). They sometimes do not make the most effective use of these resources. The research findings inform us that some organisations implement highly-structured, strategic approaches to training, whereas other organisations implement more *ad hoc*, operational and reactive approaches. We contend that a major responsibility for any organisation is to invest in the training and development of its employees, by formulating and implementing best training practices. This includes programmes, objectives and systems for designing training activities and systematically evaluating them.

We know from the research that training is successful in developing new knowledge and skills. Fully-effective training practices are those that meet the needs of the organisation, while simultaneously responding to the needs of individual employees. We are also conscious of situations where learning is considered the easy answer to all problems and organisational challenges. It is often considered a panacea, even though a performance deficiency does not mean that a learning need exists. We emphasise throughout this book that a failure to perform may appear to be an individual skill gap but, in reality, it may be due to poor quality standards, unsuitable working conditions, ineffective equipment, lack of individual motivation, poorly designed work processes, or insufficient staff or resources. Therefore, learning may be one of the solutions an organisation should consider to redress this skill gap but it is unlikely to be the only solution.

ORGANISATION & STRUCTURE OF THIS BOOK

We have structured the book around a number of key decisions that you will have to make as a trainer:

- **Chapter One:** We begin with an explanation of the key concepts that are important for both novice and experienced trainers to understand. We define the terms that are important and explain the language of T&D. We provide an explanation of a number of T&D practices that you may use in your organisation and we present our training design model, which we use to shape the structure, and provide an overview, of the subsequent chapters

- **Chapter Two:** In this chapter, we consider some of the key issues concerned with establishing effective T&D in an organisation. We provide guidelines, outline a rationale for establishing best practice training processes and explain the types of decisions that need to be made and implemented, such as establishing budgets for training, formulating training and development policies and procedures, identifying roles and responsibilities for training and gaining support and financial commitments to T&D

- **Chapter Three:** In this chapter, we consider how people learn. We outline the factors that explain individual performance, including motivation, knowledge, skill and abilities. We focus on explaining individual learning theories and give examples of their application to T&D. We explain the main principles of adult learning and identify barriers to learning that are important for you to understand and to plan for

- **Chapter Four:** In this chapter, we focus on an issue that is central to your effectiveness as a trainer: Is T&D an appropriate response to the problem or opportunity that you face? We explain the types of questions you should ask when seeking to establish whether a formal or individual-based training solution is appropriate, or whether some other HR solution is more appropriate in the circumstances. We highlight some of the mistakes that can be made by training practitioners in using a training solution where it is not appropriate. In this chapter, we also explain the first key phase of the training design process – training needs analysis (TNA). We explain its purpose and outline its proactive and reactive uses. We discuss the steps involved in the needs analysis process and explain the main sources of information, internal and external to the organisation, from which you can gather data to set T&D priorities

- **Chapter Five:** We focus in this chapter on two important components of the training design process: writing learning objectives and developing the core content for the training programme you are designing. We explain the key principles that you should follow when writing learning objectives and indicate guidelines that you can use to generate the content of your training programme

- **Chapter Six:** In this chapter, we outline a number of instructional strategies that you can implement. We also consider the decisions involved in selecting training methods for your training event. We describe the options available to you and consider the strengths and limitations of each. We provide a summary of the appropriateness and potential effectiveness of each option in meeting knowledge, skill and attitude change objectives that you may set for your learning event

- **Chapter Seven:** In this chapter, we focus on the issues that you need to consider when preparing written training materials and designing effective visual aids to enhance the delivery of your training. It is most likely that you will be required from time to time to prepare handouts, training instructions, training aids and, at a more advanced level, write a training manual. Visual aids can significantly enhance the effectiveness of your training. We explain some of the issues that you need to consider when designing and using them

- **Chapter Eight:** In this chapter, we focus on the psychological dimensions of effective training delivery. These issues are less frequently covered in a T&D book, although they are fundamental to understanding your overall effectiveness as a trainer. We consider four important psychological and behavioural issues:
  - ° The psychology of effective communications
  - ° Interpersonal style and skills
  - ° Trainer and instructional style
  - ° The role of group dynamics of formal training situations

- **Chapter Nine:** In this chapter, we consider the skills you need to be effective in delivering formal course-based and one-to-one training activities. We explain some of the competencies and skills that the trainer must possess, or needs to develop, in order to deliver training. We provide guidelines to enable you to select the most appropriate delivery approach to meet the learning objectives that you set

- **Chapter Ten:** Managers are very important stakeholders in the T&D process. They can assist, or inhibit, your effectiveness as a trainer. In this chapter, we consider the role of the manager as a trainer and developer and outline strategies that managers use:
  - ° Corrective coaching
  - ° Mentoring
  - ° On-the-job training
  - ° Developmental performance reviews.

  We outline the types of skills that are common and unique to these strategies

- **Chapter Eleven:** In this chapter, we explain the factors that you need to consider when costing T&D activities. We explain the distinctions between learning costs, training costs and the opportunity costs associated with training and outline the steps that you should follow when calculating the costs of training. We conclude this chapter with a discussion of how you can calculate the return on your organisation's investment in training

- **Chapter Twelve:** In this final chapter, we consider how you should go about the evaluation of training. We emphasise that the training evaluation process begins early in the overall design process, even though it will not be possible to measure outcomes until after the training. We explain some of the practical issues that you should consider when designing and implementing an evaluation strategy. We provide advice on the types of methods that you can use to collect evaluation data and explain the types of questions that you should ask.

Figure 0.1 presents a summary of our model of the key elements of best practice T&D.

FIGURE 0.1: OUR TRAINING, DEVELOPMENT & LEARNING BEST PRACTICE MODEL

Linking Your T&D Explicitly to the Business Plan	Managing the T&D Function	Commitment to Learning	The Responsibilities of Individual Learners	Managing Resources for T&D	Measuring Your Performance as a Trainer
• What are the people and the training implications of your business objectives and plan?	• Does your T&D function have a clear and flexible strategy that achieves a coherent direction for itself?	• Does your organisation commit to, and proclaim, continual learning as one of the organisation's most valuable capabilities?	• Do learners take responsibility for learning by setting learning goals and seeking out experiences that will enable these learning goals to be achieved?	• Are the costs of the T&D function clearly identified? Are these budgets sufficiently flexible to enable speedy adjustment to contingencies?	• Have you clearly articulated the expected outcome or result of your T&D activities?
• Is training, development and learning an appropriate solution?	• Does your T&D strategy ensure that it is possible to articulate principles and guidelines that enable detailed and practical plans to be formulated?	• Does your organisation include the right to learn and develop continually in all contracts of employment?	• Do learners in your organisation make learning conscious, self-disciplined and as explicit as possible? Do they review learning progress?	• Is the T&D team appropriate in terms of the cost efficiency of the organisation?	• Where you cannot get direct financial measures, do you focus on other targets?
• How can you integrate T&D plans and activities with business strategies, objectives and plans?	• Is there an effective and efficient deployment and management of T&D resources?	• Does your organisation build into the agreed roles of all managers the need to focus on encouraging others to learn? Does it reinforce this through personal support and coaching?	• Do learners share learning with others as much as possible?	• Does your organisation monitor its training skills and resources against its performance?	• Do you validate the effectiveness of learning methods?

Linking Your T&D Explicitly to the Business Plan	Managing the T&D Function	Commitment to Learning	The Responsibilities of Individual Learners	Managing Resources for T&D	Measuring Your Performance as a Trainer
• Who should you network with in order to make an effective link between the priorities of the business and your training priorities?	• Does your T&D function contain staff who are expert in their roles and tasks and who are professional in what they do?	• Does your organisation have effective strategies to link individual learning with collective learning and learning across the internal and external boundaries of the organisation?	• Do learners identify the wide range of resources for learning and consciously exploit them?	• Does your organisation recruit and select T&D specialists according to professional criteria?	• Do you make direct links between the learning programme and the acquisition of new skills/knowledge?
• Is there clarity about the strategic goals that T&D plans at unit, team and individual level are expected to support?	• Is the T&D function capable of collaborating and continually striving to achieve excellence?	• Does your organisation encourage employees to challenge, innovate and experiment without fear of reprimand?	• Do your learners always seek and learn from feedback as well as enquiry?	• Is there a clear and well-communicated code of ethics governing the professionalism of T&D staff?	• Do you measure the impact of your training on individual performance?
• Do T&D plans identify the resources needed to implement them? Do these resources include personnel, time, finance and physical resources?	• Is the T&D function strategically capable?	• Does your organisation celebrate learning?	• Do learners have a strong motivation to learn?	• Is there an effective induction process for new staff? Are appropriate reward systems in place?	• Do you consider the return on your investment in T&D?

Linking Your T&D Explicitly to the Business Plan	Managing the T&D Function	Commitment to Learning	The Responsibilities of Individual Learners	Managing Resources for T&D	Measuring Your Performance as a Trainer
• Does your organisation identify the implications of resource problems or problems posed by wider HR policies and practices for the implementation of T&D plans?	• Do T&D staff build alliances with external and internal stakeholders and customers in order to provide a high-quality, business-focused service for the organisation?	• Does your organisation encourage and support learning from live problems and experience? Does it support reflection at crucial moments?	• Do learners intend to transfer the learning to the job?	• Are there clear career goals for T&D staff?	• Are you concerned with publishing your results of your return on investment studies?
• Does your organisation keep managers, teams and individuals regularly informed of all business policy, systems and practice changes relevant to their roles and work? Are the T&D implications of these changes quickly identified and responded to in the form of amended plans?	• Does your T&D function conduct regular environmental scanning, strategic reviews of its business and the T&D strategies of its competitors?	• Does your organisation encourage everyone to have learning goals and development plans?	• Do learners assess their self-efficacy to learn?	• Do you balance the specialist and generalist dimensions of your staff's job roles?	• Do you use methods that stand up to external audit and examinations?

Linking Your T&D Explicitly to the Business Plan	Managing the T&D Function	Commitment to Learning	The Responsibilities of Individual Learners	Managing Resources for T&D	Measuring Your Performance as a Trainer
• Does your organisation gather information to show that T&D plans are being implemented and that managers are fulfilling their T&D responsibilities?	• Is there a commitment to continuous improvement and to the enhancement of strategic capability within the T&D function?	• Does your organisation recognise the diversity of learners and the competencies of learning?	• Do learners have positive attitudes towards learning?	• Do training staff visit customers and suppliers to enhance their knowledge and experience?	• Are you concerned about the validity of your evaluation process?
• Is there a clear long-term vision that guides the work of the T&D function, which is expressed in a mission shared between managers and T&D specialists?	• Do T&D specialists conduct regular business performance reviews and collect data on how well the function is perceived?	• Does your organisation ensure that every employee has the opportunity to learn how to learn effectively and to exploit the full range of learning opportunities available?	• Do learners voluntarily participate in learning?	• Do you encourage the continuous development of training staff?	• Do you have your training regularly audited?
• Does your T&D function have a strategy that guides its operations? Is it shaped by the corporate T&D goals and the annual T&D plan?	• Do T&D staff conduct regular meetings with line management in order to identify the strategic and operational issues facing the business?	• Does your organisation support learners through the discomfort and uncertainty that is associated with learning?	• Do learners possess the trainability to learn?	• Do you have a systematic performance management process in place for T&D staff?	• Do you publicise the results of evaluation studies at the management board?

Linking Your T&D Explicitly to the Business Plan	Managing the T&D Function	Commitment to Learning	The Responsibilities of Individual Learners	Managing Resources for T&D	Measuring Your Performance as a Trainer
• Is your organisation's T&D strategy sufficiently flexible to be able to respond to change?	• Does your function continually seek to eliminate low-value work and to simplify T&D systems and procedures?	• Does your organisation invest time and effort in bringing people together to learn from each other?	• Do learners use external excuses to avoid participation in learning?	• Are training staff encouraged to take ownership of their careers?	• Do you consider the types of objections that are made to investment in training and address them?
• Does it provide a clear framework for practical plans that will facilitate its implementation?		• Does your organisation seek to empower others to take responsibility for, and manage, their own learning?			

SOME IMPORTANT LESSONS FOR PRACTICE

We have accumulated between us over 50 years of experience as T&D practitioners in varying roles as academics, practitioners and consultants. We set out here some of the key lessons we have learned and which are discussed in more detail in the chapters that follow.

T&D is Focused on Learning

This is a fundamental point and one that we continually emphasise throughout this book. How well you understand how individuals learn, and the way you incorporate these learning principles into your training programmes and activities, will determine your effectiveness. The strategies you use to analyse your training needs, to design your training and to select appropriate learning content are all concerned with creating the optimum conditions where learning can take place. Learning occurs when learners are motivated, mindful and focused on achieving mastery. You should never be diverted from your ultimate purpose, which is to ensure that learning is both the process and the outcome.

Training and the Organisational Context

All of the activities you undertake as a trainer occur within a specific context. We know from the research that the attitude of the organisation to learning will make a difference. Organisations that promote learning as part of their cultural make-up are helping you to perform your activities as a trainer.

Another element of context that is important is the level of support you achieve from managers and supervisors. The research tells us that the attitudes of managers to training as a process and towards learners will make a difference. Managers who take the time to understand the training content, to encourage learners to participate and to support post-learning transfer, will make your job as a trainer significantly easier.

Top Management Buy-In and Support

Top management commitment, or the lack of it, is one of the most frequently-identified factors explaining your level of success as a trainer. As a trainer, you can take steps to ensure that this support and buy-in is available. You need to ensure that your training activities are consistent with the strategic initiatives of the organisation. Your skill in networking with key organisational stakeholders is another dimension of your effectiveness.

Top management support potentially offers you a number of advantages. Where you have a champion at senior level, you are more likely to get financial and human resource support for your activities. You are also more likely to get greater involvement of managers in your activities and employees are more likely to participate on formal training activities.

Selling the Benefits of Training to Employees

The research strongly indicates that employees must be motivated to participate in learning. They must perceive that the training activities you design and deliver have both relevance and realism.

You can take a number of steps to ensure that the content of your training activities is relevant. Your skill in conducting training needs assessments is an important dimension of your effectiveness. However, it is also important that you involve the employee in this needs identification process. By doing so, you enhance significantly the possibility that he/she will see its relevance and see a relationship between the training content and the demands of their job.

Measuring What You Do

Measurement of your activities is a consistent theme emphasised throughout this book. We devote almost one and a half chapters to considering how you can undertake this task. We emphasise two aspects of measurement: evaluation of outcomes and measurement of the return on your organisation's investment. We emphasise the motto that "you cannot manage what you do not measure".

Effective measurement requires that you are conscious of both the costs and benefits of your activities, and that you ensure your training design incorporates measurement and evaluation. You can use the outcomes of your post-training evaluation to make decisions both concerning the content of your future training and the marketing of your training to key stakeholders within the organisation.

Chapter One

TRAINING & DEVELOPMENT: CORE CONCEPTS

LEARNING OBJECTIVES

On completion of this chapter, you should be able to:

- Define and differentiate a number of concepts relevant to understanding the discipline of training and development

- Describe the similarities and differences between training, development, education and learning as processes and outcomes

- Describe the similarities and differences between the various roles that trainers can perform in organisations

- Define the different learning processes that are practised in organisations and explain their uses in a T&D context

- Understand the main inputs to the training design process and describe their relevance.

- Understand the sequence of T&D design that the trainer should follow to achieve effective learning.

A Training & Development Scenario

You are presented with the following five learning situations. Based on your experience of training in organisations, describe the most appropriate process to achieve the task indicated in the description.

- You have just hired a new production operative. She is relatively inexperienced. She will need to achieve mastery of her job within a four-week period. The target for experienced operatives is to produce 120 units per day.

- John has just taken on the role of supervisor in a back office function within a large financial institution. It is John's first promotion to a position where he will be responsible for a team of 10 employees. He has a lot of uncertainty about how he should perform the role and he is very willing to accept whatever advice you can give him on an appropriate learning intervention.

- Patricia is an administrative assistant who is in her mid-30s. She has participated in relatively limited training and development in her career to date. She has now come to a crossroads in her career. She would like to take on a more responsible position, but finds that many doors are closed due to a lack of professional and educational qualifications. She is unsure about whether she should participate in some form of educational activity and what it will involve.

- Angelica has just joined the organisation as a new manager. She is a little unsure about what she will encounter. She has been with the organisation for less than a week but already is questioning whether she has made a mistake. She is a little stressed, because she wants to learn about the organisation quickly and understand how it ticks.

- Michael is concerned that his team of production supervisors are not sufficiently focused on quality issues. The organisation espouses a total quality management philosophy. All employees are expected to take responsibility for quality issues and be concerned with quality at all times. He wonders if sufficient measures have been taken to achieve this objective.

INTRODUCTION

We firmly advocate that T&D activities are important, because they enable organisations to adapt and manage to changing environmental conditions and to perform optimally in the competitive environment. The research reveals that training events are a major opportunity for learning. However, whether they are effective depends on the following factors:

- The design and implementation of the training itself
- The characteristics of the trainee
- The learning climate of the organisation.

Our experience indicates that the level of training practices in organisations varies considerably. At its worst, T&D is considered to be an isolated set of activities put together with little or no understanding of the needs of the business or the trainees and without determining the value of the training. We have also experienced and encountered many best practice training situations. Training, at its best, is a set of processes aimed at continuously improving employee performance, the performance of the organisation and the professionalism of the T&D function.

We are conscious that the ideal conditions may not always exist. There may be insufficient money, knowledge and expertise, time or training professionals. We recognise these limitations and, with this in mind, we outline both "ideal" and more practical approaches to implementing training activities in organisations.

UNDERSTANDING THE FUNDAMENTALS:
SOME TRAINING TERMINOLOGY

Before we explain the details of training design, it is important first to define a number of terms that you will encounter in the field of T&D. We have classified the definitions into three categories:

- Core T&D concepts
- T&D processes
- T&D roles.

Core T&D Concepts

We consider the following set of definitions to be core concepts because they are central to understanding the purposes and processes that underlie T&D activities.

Learning

The first and most important concept is learning. Learning implies that the individual has mastered new knowledge or skills and is able to apply them. It is, therefore, part of the process of successful T&D in organisations.

The concept of learning is also used in a more dynamic sense to describe employees who actively participate in expanding their skills and knowledge. Some commentators conclude that, to meet the continuous need to adapt and change, organisations will increasingly have to see themselves as "learning communities" or learning organisations. This is a very challenging idea. It requires:

- A free flow of ideas and knowledge within teams and with others inside and outside the organisation
- Employees to be highly motivated and encouraged to seek improvements and new ways of doing tasks
- Line management to be deeply involved in the training and development of their staff
- Appropriate structures and mechanisms to support continuous learning.

There are some characteristics of learning that are important for you to understand at this stage. We consider the following characteristics of learning to be of paramount importance:

- Learning is an active process, requiring active participation or involvement by the learner
- Immediate application or use of new skills and concepts improves learning
- Effective learning requires ongoing evaluation of progress and feedback. Reinforcing and acknowledging early successes improves learning
- Emotions impact learning and strong feelings have a powerful impact on the learning process.

Training

We define training as "a systematic process through which an employee is helped or facilitated to master defined tasks, or competencies for a definite purpose".

It specifies the correct way of doing the task and identifies specific behaviours that should be demonstrated. It should be an integral part of the work and development of an organisation.

As a concept, training has a number of distinctive characteristics:

- It tends to be for a shorter term and a more practical purpose than the other concepts described in this chapter

- Training focuses particularly on the skills, knowledge and attitudes required to carry out a job to the optimum level of performance
- Training is an activity applicable to all employees – senior management as well as junior employees.

Training can take place either "on-the-job" or "off-the-job". In fact, the two are often complementary. On-the-job training permits the trainee to learn in the actual working environment. This may take the form of guidance from a fellow employee or supervisor (peer learning), who demonstrates to the employee what is required to perform the task. This type of learning is sometimes described as "sitting by Nellie". However, not all sitting-by-Nellie-type training is effective, because "Nellie" may not have been trained to train others or may not implement best practices in his/her own job. Alternatively, organisations may have elaborate training programmes (off-the-job) to deal with areas such as induction, technical training, personal development and training for managerial or supervisory roles. This training may take the form of formal courses. The employee may participate in these courses on a day- or block-release basis or an external trainer may come into the workplace.

It is important to highlight that line managers have an important responsibility for training, in addition to the responsibility placed by the organisation on T&D specialists. Senior line managers have the responsibility for authorising overall policies and plans and approving the training budget. Middle and junior line managers need to be able to recognise learning problems and opportunities among their staff, to help create the appropriate learning response and to identify who should participate in training events.

Development
Development is a less tangible concept than training, but it is considered more systematic than education. We define it as a process or set of planned activities that will help an individual, over time, to develop to their full potential. Development focuses on enhancing a learner's self esteem and sense of identity. It involves elements of discovery, reflection and change. It may occur in an organisational setting or it may be a more personal set of activities.

When we refer to development in an organisation, we are primarily concerned with the growth, and advancement of employees. People are the most valued resource and, in line with this philosophy, the following principles are considered important in the context of development:

- Individuals have ownership of development
- Development is a flexible, and not always systematic, process

- Development requires an openness and willingness to learn from experience
- Experience is a central part of the development process.

For employees to develop, five conditions must exist:
- **Insight:** Employees must possess insight about what they need to develop
- **Motivation:** Employees must be willing to invest the time and energy it takes to develop themselves
- **Capabilities:** Employees must possess the skills and knowledge they need to develop effectively
- **Real world practice:** Employees must have opportunities to try their new skills at work in order to be effective
- **Accountability:** Employees must be accountable for internalising their new capabilities in order to improve performance and results.

Education

We consider education to be a major contributor to the learning process, both within and outside organisations. Though training and education are closely related and often occur at the same time, we consider education to be a broader concept, since it tends to have a stronger orientation towards the future. It focuses on learning that will help the employee to take on a new role, or to do a different job, at some future date. Education is also considered a broader intellectual process, because it involves activities that can change employees' attitudes and increase their knowledge and understanding. This enables employees to adjust more effectively to their working environment and allows them to cope with change.

Educational activities are more person-oriented than job-oriented and, when compared with training, educational objectives are less easy to define in behavioural terms. Some organisations spend heavily on educational programmes in the belief that investment in education will contribute to flexibility and ensure that employees are well prepared to meet future challenges.

Instruction and Teaching

Instruction and teaching are two related and important concepts. We define instruction as "the delivery of information and activities that facilitate the learner's attainment of learning goals". Instruction can also be defined as "the conduct of activities that are focused on helping learners' learn specific things".

The terms "teaching" and "instruction" are often used interchangeably. However, teaching can be defined as "those learning experiences in which the instructional message is delivered by a human being, not through the use of media such as videotape, textbooks or computer programmes". Instruction incorporates teaching and other learning experiences where the instructional message is conveyed by other forms of media.

We consider the following to be important features of teaching:

- The aim of teaching is to facilitate learning
- Teaching changes the ways in which learners can or will behave
- It involves implementing strategies that are designed to lead learners towards the attainment of specified goals
- It is a highly interpersonal and interactive activity, involving verbal and non-verbal communication
- In the ideal situation, it is a relatively systematic activity.

Orientation and Briefing
We define orientation as "a process whereby a learner is oriented to a place or position". It is concerned with helping a learner understand and function effectively in a new way. Briefing is a related activity, whose basic purpose is to provide the background of an organisation, a topic, place or situation in a concise and focused manner. Briefing sessions typically present cogent, highly organised, simplified and sequenced information and usually incorporate a Q&A session.

Figure 1.1 provides a summary of the main differences between the concepts that we have discussed so far.

Roles that Trainers Perform in Organisations

We now consider a number of roles that you may perform as part of your training brief in an organisation. You will most likely be required to perform instructor or facilitator type roles – however, between these ranges, there are many variations. We define six role concepts that are relevant to later chapters of this book.

Trainer Role
We define the term "trainer" as an organisationally-prescribed role that potentially involves some or all of the following activities:

- The delivery of training activities in formal settings. These settings can be course based or 1:1 situations. Many individuals who are called trainers perform this activity for the majority of their role performance
- The design of T&D activities, utilising knowledge of the organisational context, the specific problem or opportunity and knowledge of the learning process

	Overall Purpose	Major Application	Methodologies	Time Required	Delivered by	Strongest Features
Training	• To provide practical, results-oriented learning. This aim is applied to a professional, vocational or military context. It is aimed at achieving predetermined and clearly stated objectives, which are then measured to determine whether or not they have been achieved	• Focuses on processes and/or explicit behaviours such as performing specific skills, or meeting specified objectives in a cost-effective manner	• Experiential and participant-centred exercises, emphasising hands-on experience, practice and drills. Trainers have access to an extensive repertoire of highly developed methodologies to accomplish a variety of clearly defined outcomes	• Programmes vary greatly in duration, most commonly lasting one day to two weeks. However, a sequenced training programme with a number of separate training modules can last from three to six months	• Trainers or *Facilitators*. May use *Subject Matter Experts* in the development of the programme	• Most active and involving of the learner. Most cost-effective. Often has an evaluation component designed into it to determine whether learning objectives were met. Trainees contribute to their own learning, thus gaining content information, the skill for application and self-confidence
Development	• Focuses on the personal development and enhancement of employees and, in particular, on the development of self-esteem and confidence	• Prepares a person to take up a managerial position or take on a new role within an organisation	• Helps learners to enhance self-confidence utilising projects, self-managed learning and guided reading activities	• A long-term process of self-discovery and reflection by the learner	• The learner is the primary driver of development processes	• A reflective process that can pay back significant results to the individual and organisation, especially effective in management and professional development activities

	Overall Purpose	Major Application	Methodologies	Time Required	Delivered by	Strongest Features
Education	• The full development of the mind's capabilities, as well as imparting or acquiring knowledge – sometimes for no other purpose than for the sheer joy of learning	• Presents large amounts of content knowledge and is often used to develop in-depth mastery in one or more subjects	• Through the teacher, who often serves as a role model who passes on knowledge (or a particular specialisation or approach) to the student. Lectures or presentations are the most common approach used in education. May also include question and answer sessions, reading assignments, written assignments and periodic examinations	• Longest-term of all the modes discussed here. Now popularly considered a life-long activity (yet formal education is generally thought of as completed upon receipt of an undergraduate university degree). Frequently divided into segments (such as courses, class periods, semesters, grade levels or years)	• Educators, Teachers, Professors, Teaching Fellows	• Most thorough in its coverage (since time is often not a major factor). Generally used in delivering large bodies of content information. Especially effective in the theoretical realm and in focusing, in-depth, on a specialised field
Instruction	• Focuses on the means by which knowledge is transferred to a learner. It may use a person or technology to carry out the instruction task	• Focuses on providing (a) a large group of learners with a large amount of knowledge presented in a structured manner or (b) instructing in the performance of a skill	• Using technology or the trainer to present information in a didactic, logical and highly organised manner	• A short-term process of presenting knowledge in small and manageable chunks	• A trainer or some form of technology such as computer video or audio method	• Possible to instruct to large numbers in a cost-effective way. Can reach a large geographically-dispersed audience, if some form of E-learning technology is used

	Overall Purpose	Major Application	Methodologies	Time Required	Delivered by	Strongest Features
Teaching	• Focuses on the use of the human agent as the means of instruction and the set of associated skills required to teach a group or an individual	• Creating a learning experience for a group of individuals	• Utilising interpersonal skills to present information or ideas to trainees	• Usually short periods (up to 2 hours) where the trainer utilises skills to teach either groups or individual trainees	• Trainers, instructors, teachers and coaches	• Very effective where learners have lower levels of knowledge, skill and activity, lack of confidence in a training situation and where the trainees value a human contact
Orientation	• To orient a person to a place or position, especially to new situations, environments, ideas, values, or operating principles. Helps an individual understand how to operate comfortably in an unfamiliar setting	• Prepares a person to understand and function effectively in a new, or in a significantly different, environment and to achieve this preparation in the least traumatic manner	• Helps participants shift from their old orientation to a new one by starting where they are at the point of entry to an organisation or role. It introduces them to approaches and concepts, which are more appropriate to the new environment	• Usually from one-half day to one week in length	• Has not developed generic names to describe the person who delivers. Often uses a functional title such as *Programme Co-ordinator* or *Session Leader*	• Most supportive, since it does not remove participants from original orientation framework until a new one is firmly established. Transforms, while minimising the shock of the new environment

	Overall Purpose	Major Application	Methodologies	Time Required	Delivered by	Strongest Features
Briefing	• To provide the background on an organisation, topic, place or situation in a concise and focused manner	• Provides a broad overview or can focus on a particular part of a large programme in the most time-effective way	• Systematically presents cogent, highly organised, simplified and sequenced information. Usually followed by a question-and-answer session to clear up areas of ambiguity	• Shortest of all the modes discussed, this can be as short as 10 or 15 minutes and as long as 90 minutes	• Experts (who usually are incumbents in in-house positions)	• Most time-effective mode. Achieves a maximum amount of information transfer in shortest possible time. Spotlights most relevant and essential information, so recipient is not required to sort out the essential from the non-essential

- The management of training and development activities including budgeting, managing training resources and networking with other individuals within the organisation.

We wrote this book primarily for trainers who conduct these activities.

Instructor Role

We define an "instructor" as an individual who carries out highly-structured and scripted training activities. These activities are usually highly-controlled, where is a requirement to follow specific procedures and instructions and the learner may have limited involvement in the training design process. Examples of an instructor role may include the provision of production-type training, the delivery of induction training activities or other mandatory training activities, such as those concerned with health and safety training.

Facilitator Role

We define a "facilitator" as a trainer whose primary focus is on the process rather than the content of the training programme. This helps us to distinguish the facilitator from the instructor role. We consider the main characteristics of the facilitator role to be:

- The facilitator is concerned with managing the learning process and motivating the learner
- Learners take responsibility for learning; the facilitator's role is to shape, to encourage and to devise a structure within which the learning takes place
- The learning content is loosely defined; it may change significantly over the duration of the learning event and may be negotiated between the learner and trainer
- The facilitator is valued for his or her questioning, listening, probing, and motivational and summarising skills.

Many T&D activities in organisations require you to perform a facilitator role, such as team development and management development training.

Mentor Role

This role is frequently performed by a trainer in an organisation, but more usually by a line manager. The role of a mentor is to provide a more junior employee or peer with guidance and a clear understanding of how an organisation goes about its business. The mentor usually focuses on enhancing an employee's fit within an organisation. It is usually a 1:1 process, although team mentoring is more frequently practised in a training and development context. Generally a trainer will play a mentoring role in management level training activities, though it can be applied at lower levels. The mentor-mentee relationship may be highly formalised and structured, or it can occur in an informal way.

Coach Role

The role of a coach is to provide 1:1 guidance and instruction to improve knowledge, skills and work performance. The role of the coach is to enhance knowledge development such as facts and procedures, although this role is more likely to be used to develop skills. It differs from the mentor role in that the primary concern is with skill change rather than attitude change.

It requires the trainer to:

- Understand the trainee's job
- Meet with the trainee and mutually agree on the performance objectives to be achieved
- Mutually arrive at a plan/schedule for achieving the objectives
- Demonstrate to the trainee how to achieve the objectives
- Observe the trainee problem
- Provide feedback.

It is a similar role to that of instructor, although it places significantly more emphasis on the interpersonal relationships between the coach and the trainee.

Figure 1.2 provides a summary of the main differences between the different role dimensions that the trainer may perform in an organisation.

Concepts Relevant to Understanding the Learning Processes

The third group of definitions that we introduce in this chapter focus on learning processes that may be used by learners. We include in this section a number of important processes that form part of the methodology and tools of training and development.

Traditional Learning and Learning by Rote

Before the advent of books, the only method of learning was by repetition, or oral tradition. Learning by rote is still a useful method and is commonly used to achieve learning outcomes. Traditional learning started with rote learning when books were copied by hand. In time, teachers produced their own material, read out, or otherwise presented to students. Gradually, learners were invited to interpret the material they were given, orally at first, and later in essays and written examinations.

FIGURE 1.2: COMPARING INSTRUCTOR, FACILITATOR, MENTOR & COACH ROLES

	Overall Purpose	Nature of Relationship	Methodologies Used	Applications to T&D
Instructor	• To provide, in a highly didactic fashion, a closely-scripted training message in a sequential and cost-effective way to a large number of trainees	• A directed and high trainer-control-oriented relationship. Learners have very limited involvement in the instruction role	• Uses lectures, videos and other directive and highly-structured methods to delivery the training message	• Where there is a need to give a precise training message to a large number of trainees
Facilitator	• To encourage learning by using a range of techniques, including questioning, probing, summarising, reflecting, motivating and allowing learners to direct the context of the learning process	• A dynamic two-way relationship that is collaborative and where learners largely shape the content	• Uses a range of interpersonal skills and knowledge of group's processes to ensure that learning takes place	• Where there is a need to develop self-reliance, self-managed learning and team learning processes
Mentor	• A one-to-one, on-going relationship, designed to bring about attitude change and enhance the employee's fit within the organisation and within a particular role. This will vary depending on whether the mentoring is performed by a peer or someone more senior in the organisation	• An ongoing, one-to-one relationship that focuses on psychological as well as learning dimensions	• Uses interpersonal skills, one-to-one interactions and sometimes a mentoring agreement to shape the content of the relationship	• Where there is a need to develop management level employees, and prospective managers/supervisors and to communicate the culture of the organisation
Coach	• To provide one-to-one guidance and instruction to improve knowledge skill and work performance of learners. The coach may address deficiencies or opportunities	• Usually a one-to-one relationship that is short to medium term in duration	• Uses diagnostic skills, instruction, demonstration, practice and repetition to eliminate the performance deficiency	• Where there is a clear performance deficiency and/or a need to motivate the trainee to perform effectively

Socratic Teaching (Discovery)
Socrates, a philosopher, taught by asking questions. He believed that by leading the learner you could "show" the learner that he already knew what he was being taught. By asking a learner to discover or think out the answer to a question, the master ensures that the learner "owns" the learning, rather than learning by rote.

The Socratic method is considered effective for problem-solving-type learning situations and may be used by a manager both to enable an employee to discover an existing solution, or to work out how to deal with a real problem. Socratic teaching is considered similar to the "mentoring" approach practiced today in many organisations. It requires learners with strong ability and a range of work experience to draw upon previous experience.

Apprenticeship
Apprenticeship is a traditional method of learning practical skills. An apprentice usually starts by doing basic chores and gradually moves on to more skilled work until he/she achieves the same level as the master. Apprenticeship is valuable where skills are acquired through experience. Apprenticeship is now normally combined with formal learning – a combination of on- and off-the-job training and education.

Apprenticeship is most frequently used in the skilled trades, such as in engineering, electrical work, and carpentry. The apprentice must be able to demonstrate mastery of all the required skills and knowledge before being allowed to graduate to mastery level.

Apprenticeship has many strengths as a learning approach for the transmission, not only of complex skills and knowledge, but also the particular attitudes, values and beliefs of the "master". Some consider this dimension to be as much a disadvantage as an advantage.

Indoctrination and Orientation
In its present sense, indoctrination refers to a process whereby individuals are required to think in a particular way or within a particular framework of values. It commonly happens when new employees are recruited and they experience an intense socialisation process designed to ensure that they learn to conform to the demands of the organisation's culture. In its extreme form, it is described as "brainwashing" and may be forcefully carried out in some instances. In the context of training and development, it is generally accepted that many learning processes contain elements of indoctrination. Examples include total quality management and safety culture.

Learning by Experience
The research evidence highlights that learners only learn how to do a job by actually doing it. If learners are to succeed, they require space

to experiment – some of these experiments will inevitably fail. "Deep-ending", as it is commonly described in organisations, can be costly for the organisation as well as painful for the learner who makes the mistakes. A sensible compromise is to provide employees with knowledge that will enable them to perform, plus practice in a safe environment.

Trial and Error

This process is used when the learner tries to find the best way of doing something. In learning some tasks, trainers may find it an advantage to allow learners to discover for themselves the best way to do things.

Mental Organisation

This process is used when the learner attempts to put together a "mental picture" of what has to be learned and then uses this mental picture as a guide for future action. Once the trainee becomes familiar with a "drill", his/her actions become automatic or autonomous. Mental organisation forms the basis of any skilled task performance.

Behaviour-modelling

This learning process is central to all individuals. Children often observe intently the actions of their parents at work, or other children at play, and then try to imitate them. They are trying to model themselves or their behaviour on what they have observed in others. This method of learning is used extensively in all forms of training and is an important part of management development. Where interpersonal skills have to be learned, the trainee may "shadow" an experienced manager or trainer to observe how different situations are dealt with so that they can approach these situations in a similar way. This might include giving advice to a customer, dealing with a complaint, handling a disciplinary problem, etc.

Use of Language

A significant amount of learning takes place through the use of the written and the spoken word. Language is a powerful medium and it is important that the learner should ensure that it is used correctly and effectively. Trainers need to ensure that explanations they provide are clear and concise and that they are not jargon-ridden. This is not to say that jargon should never be used. Some organisational jargon has to be learned so that employees can communicate with one another. However, the key issue is that the jargon or technical language should be understood. Learning can be reinforced through the written word in the form of handouts, job guides, diagrams and training notes.

Reflection
This learning process is similar to mental organisation and follows on from learning by trial and error, behaviour modelling or the use of language. It is a process of thinking through, or mulling over, a particular learning experiences in order to draw out lessons that can be applied in the future. It is the basis of much managerial and professional learning. For example, a trainee who is learning to interview is observed by a trainer and given feedback on what went well and what areas need improvement. The trainee is then able to reflect on his/her performance and on the feedback, in order to improve or modify the way in which he/she conducts subsequent interviews.

Suggestion Learning
This learning process is one whereby the learner tends to accept statements as accurate without any real evaluation as to their correctness. Learners will not critically assess such statements or beliefs and may adopt attitudes in the absence of any logical justification. Suggestion learning can be a most powerful factor in conventionalising manners, customs and ideas. What learners learn through suggestion learning may not necessarily be what the course is explicitly designed to teach. Many induction programmes have major components of suggestion learning. The essential element of suggestion learning is acceptance with conviction in the absence of logical grounds, and should not be confused with suggestions that can be accepted or rejected – for example, "perhaps it would be better to do a job this way ...".

Mentoring
We have already talked about the mentor dimension of the trainer role. We concentrate on defining the mentoring process here. Mentoring represents a common informal practice in organisations, although organisations often implement formal mentoring programmes designed to enhance various aspects of an employee's learning process.

Central to mentoring is the mentor-mentee relationship. The mentor is usually someone other than the immediate supervisor (in formal mentorship programmes), who provides the protégé with support, advice, guidance, and comfort and may also perform a range of political functions.

Mentoring emphasises the notion of role-modelling, whereby the organisation selects individuals as mentors whom it considers have desirable attributes that should be copied by new employees. Mentoring is a common learning strategy in many graduate development programmes and on many high-flyer management development initiatives.

Coaching

Coaching is usually distinguished from mentoring in that the former focuses on the "job" and the competencies required to perform it effectively, whereas the latter has a wider remit and usually includes career, support and psychosocial issues.

Coaching is usually a one-to-one process but may be group-focused, and usually occurs in the context of the current job. Coaching is often reactive in that it is used to address performance deficiencies and is generally aimed at enhancing knowledge and/or skill.

Action Learning

Action learning processes focus on the use of projects to facilitate learning. They are commonly used for management development purposes and to develop advanced problem-solving and implementation skills. Action learning processes emphasise learning as part of a team, focusing on real organisational problems and emphasising both analysis and implementation as key components of the learning process.

Role-modelling

Role-modelling is an effective learning process and underpins many other learning processes, such as mentoring and coaching. Role-modelling involves a process of imitation or copying. One of the most important principles of this type of learning is the idea that the learner does not have to do anything except observe what is going on around him or her. No behaviour pattern is produced and no reinforcement is given. Therefore, individuals learn very effectively from observing the behaviour of others and the consequences that result.

Counselling

This is a process that contains learning and development dimensions. Counselling is defined as "a process that aims to help learners to help themselves". The skills that are required to enact a counselling process focus on forming an understanding relationship with the learner and helping the learner change specific aspects of their feelings, thinking and behaviours. Counselling, therefore, emphasises the goals of personal growth and development. These processes are facilitated by the trainer but are fundamentally determined by the individual learner.

Figure 1.3 provides a summary of the similarities and differences underpinning the different learning processes that we have explained so far in this section.

FIGURE 1.3: LEARNING PROCESSES: COMPARISONS & CONTRASTS

	Overall Focus	Key Characteristics of Each Process	Applications to Training
Learning by Rote	• Primary focus is on the capacity to recall facts and procedures	• Learning involves repetition; Simply acquiring knowledge, not necessarily understanding it; It is short-term, subject to great wastage; Confined to the cognitive domain / knowledge	• To learn rules and procedures in a range of areas, such as induction, health and safety, production training, manual handling and telephone technique
Discovery Learning	• Places an emphasis on self-discovery and the use of experimental learning activities to develop insights	• A process that focuses on the individual learner, who discovers through the use of experience; Learner is motivated to believe that he/she already knows; Learner does the thinking and feels empowered	• Management and graduate development; Continuing professional development activities
Apprenticeship	• A structured process of learning designed to turn a novice into a master using structured work experiences and instruction	• Learning through experience of doing; There is usually a master craftsperson involved or some expert; There is a specific timetable of activities, and may have formal knowledge inputs	• Learning of trades and professional areas
Indoctrination	• Designed to get employees to think in a particular way. It assumes a common values framework that employees are expected to buy into	• Designed to get people to think in a particular way; Assumes common value framework that it wants people to buy into (organisation culture); Derives from a powerful source; Can vary in intensity; It is regularly reinforced; May lead to brainwashing and blind compliance; In most organisations, it will only happen to a certain degree because of ethics; Manifests itself in socialisation, punishment, education, communication and reward systems	• Organisational induction, total quality management and customer service training
Learning by Experience	• A learning process built around specific experiences, reflection on these experiences and the development of principles that have application to other situations	• Experience provides the basis for effective learning; Learner encounters situations and reflects on them; From experience, the learner conceptualises and draws principles that can be applied in the future	• Learning of management skills in problem-solving and decision-making

	Overall Focus	Key Characteristics of Each Process	Applications to Training
Trial and Error	• A learning process that places emphasis on making mistakes and learning from those mistakes	• Learning is haphazard and unsystematic; Learning is dependent on learner doing things; Learning is based on learning from mistakes	• Learning of novel tasks usually in management and professional areas
Mental Organisation	• A process of learning that is largely internal and involves the learner making sense of experience and developing appropriate mental maps	• Learning is an internal cognitive process; Learner assembles experiences and formulates mental maps; Learner uses these mental maps to problem-solve and make sense of situations	• Applicable to many, if not all, learning processes
Behaviour-modelling / Role-modelling	• A process that uses the principles of social learning to facilitate learning in individuals through a process of observation and imitation of behaviour	• Social learning process involving imitation or copying; The person copied is well-respected and exhibits desirable behaviours; A process of observation and reading non-verbal behaviour as well as verbal, leading to the enhancement of self-esteem and self-efficacy; A natural process that happens in organisations	• Management development, organisational induction and graduate development
Reflection	• A process that emphasises reflection as part of experience. Learners may reflect while doing the action or reflect after they have completed it	• Reflection is an internal, and not very observable, process; Learner can reflect while doing things and when it is completed; Learner draws lessons from the reflection	• The development of professionals such as accountants, nurses and managers
Suggestion Learning	• This is a learning process that does not involve to any significant extent the critical engagement of the learner, who is more or less expected to accept the learning	• Learner is a largely passive and accepting agent; Learner accepts with conviction without any apparent logical arguments; The learning outcomes may not be those intended	• Usually has application to training areas that involve the acceptance of values

	Overall Focus	Key Characteristics of Each Process	Applications to Training
Mentoring	• A process designed to build the confidence of potential managers and to facilitate their buy-in to organisational culture and priorities	• Mentor / protégé or mentee relationship; Usually not one's boss but someone with seniority and experience; The mentor provides social support, networking advice, career advice or may act in a political sense; May be formal or informal; Time and/or duration may vary; Usually not about direct job-related issues	• Applicable to a range of areas, including management, leadership and graduate development
Coaching	• A process designed to develop specific knowledge and skills in a workplace setting, using the work itself as the content of the training activities	• Can be 1-1 or 1-many; Coach is usually one's boss; Focuses on task performance, motivation, improvement, and correction; Usually intermittent, triggered by the work itself, with a short cycle	• Applicable to management and non-management training, where there is a requirement for 1:1 training
Action Learning	• The use of complex projects or assignments in a workplace setting, to develop high-level problem-solving and strategic implementation skills	• The use of complex projects or assignments in a workplace setting to develop problem-solving and implementation skills; Concerned with enhancing Q learning – the ability to ask insightful questions about more situations (lateral thinking capacities); A management learning strategy; Group-based learning rather than solo learning	• Used primarily for middle and senior management development to develop advanced managerial skills and team-working
Counselling	• A process designed to develop personal awareness and problem-solving skills amongst learners	• A process of personal problem-solving; Can be directive or non-directive; Involves empathetic understanding; May be formal or informal; A process of self-discovery	• Used primarily for personal development and coping strategies

DESIGNING T&D: AN INTEGRATED MODEL

We proposed, in our introduction, that a model of the training design process informs the structure of this book. **Figure 1.4** outlines the model we propose to use. We briefly explain its main components in this chapter, however we will explore each component in more detail in later chapters.

FIGURE 1.4: OUR MODEL OF T&D DESIGN, DELIVERY & EVALUATION

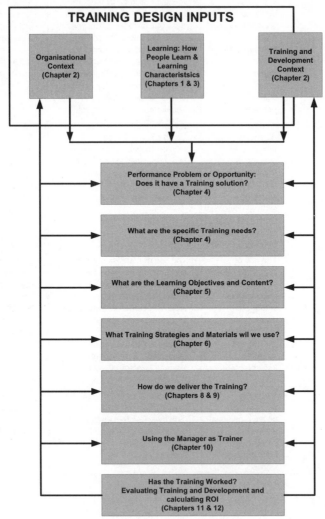

Training and development must be considered as an open system. The internal and external training system is open to influences from the organisational environment and it depends on its environment for inputs. The training design system takes inputs from the environment and transforms them into training outputs. The training system should therefore be responsive to the needs and demands of its environment. The environment provides the inputs for the system to replenish itself. We will briefly describe each component here.

Training's Organisational Environment

We suggest that there are three broad sets of factors that serve as inputs to training:

- **Organisational Context:** This set of factors consists of the organisation's mission, strategies, and resources, represent key inputs to the training process. We also consider the organisation's technology and characteristics of its work processes to be significant. T&D activities are interconnected with what happens in the organisation as a whole

- **Learner Characteristics:** The characteristics of the individual learner are also significant. Trainers need to be concerned and factor in a number of important characteristics. These include the learners, age, gender, learning preferences and styles, emotional maturity, level of trainability and motivation to learn

- **T&D Content:** We define this component as the characteristics of training structures and processes in organisations. We include in this group of factors resources for training, training specialists, policies and procedures, focus on training and the level of organisational support for T&D activities.

Training Design Processes

We include six components in the training design process. Each component has specific characteristics:

- **Performance Problem or Opportunity:** We premise this book on the idea that T&D represents one of several possible solutions to organisational or individual performance problems. Whether it represents an appropriate solution depends on the cause or source of the problem. It also depends on how costly other solutions are. A first essential step in the training design process focuses on finding out whether training is a potential solution to the problem identified and whether it is an effective solution

- **Needs Analysis Process:** The training design process begins with an identification of the learning needs. It is based on the assumption that a decision has already been made concerning the appropriateness and effectiveness of a T&D activity as a response to the problem or opportunity. The training needs identification process will focus on identifying those dimensions of the problem that are concerned with knowledge, skill or attitude. We will explain in more detail in **Chapter Five** the data-gathering process necessary to identify the learning issues

- **Design Processes:** The training needs that are identified serve as the input into the design process. We identify four key decisions that have to be made as part of the design process. Each area of training need is translated into a learning objective. As a trainer, you must make decisions concerning the type of content that is appropriate to meet these objectives. The trainer will also have to make decisions about the most appropriate learning strategy to use: Is it appropriate to use a course-based activity? A job instruction process? A 1:1 type interaction or some form of technological solution? You will then decide on particular learning methods and materials. We consider these issues in **Chapters Five** and **Six**

- **Delivery of Training:** Once you have all the design components in place, the next step involves delivery. You may deliver the programme using technology or you may personally deliver the training. You will use a range of interpersonal styles to make the learning effective. We consider how you can deliver training in **Chapters Seven, Eight** and **Nine**

- **Evaluation of Training:** Decisions about evaluation are made early in the training design process. Evaluation is a continuous process, which begins as training design is initiated. You will conduct both process and outcome evaluation. You will use process evaluation to determine how the training was delivered and the accuracy of the needs identification process. In outcome evaluation, you are concerned with the outcomes of the training conducted. We consider these issues in **Chapters Eleven** and **Twelve**.

BEST PRACTICE INDICATORS

Some of the best practice issues that you should consider related to the contents of this chapter are:

- A particular feature of an organisation that supports learning is the commitment of individuals to their own development and the support they are given by the organisation in that commitment. This support is often beyond the immediate or planned needs of the organisation, and is concerned with recognising the positive organisational impact of employees' motivation and ability to learn and develop themselves continuously

- Managers, mentors and any specialist T&D staff work together to create and maintain a workplace culture conducive to effective learning and the development of performance. This culture is one in which the learning achievements of individuals and teams are publicly communicated and recognised

- Coaching and counselling, appraisal and career planning are all recognised elements in every manager's role. Their consistent and equitable practice across the organisation is ensured by training and procedures, and by regular monitoring

- There is a flexible support system for T&D activity. It includes learning resource centre(s), self-directed learning packages, self-assessment guides, a staff development budget and the expertise to ensure tailored learning experiences
- All employees have equal access to sources of information and advice about T&D opportunities and resources
- Every employee has a personal development plan that is reviewed and updated annually and is generated through appraisal or work review
- Learning occurs in a multiplicity of ways, including the processes of training, education, development, orientation and indoctrination
- You will most likely perform different training roles, including trainer, facilitator, and coach and mentor roles
- The learning process is facilitated and occurs through activities such as role-modelling, suggestion learning, Socratic learning, experience, trial and error, coaching and counselling.

Reflections on the Training & Development Scenario

You could make these points about each of the five scenarios:

- The process you are concerned with in the first scenario is **training**. You have a relatively short time period in which to achieve your objectives and you are mandated to ensure that the production operative acquires the necessary job knowledge and skills to achieve experienced worker standard within a four-week period. You will be concerned to specify the requirements for the job and identify the core knowledge and skill elements. You are most likely to use 1: 1 instruction and carry out the task on-the-job.

- The most appropriate learning intervention to use here is **coaching** by an experienced supervisor. John is currently ambiguous about how the role should be performed. He has moved from a position where he directly performs the work to one where he has to work through others to achieve work objectives. You will need to be careful to select an experienced supervisor, who is an effective role model and who possesses effective coaching skills, to impart the skills of supervisor and develop John's confidence to perform the role effectively.

- The essential issue in the third scenario concerns participation in **education**. We emphasised in this chapter that educational activities are long-term learning activities.

They usually focus on the development of professional knowledge and expertise and usually involve the learner thinking differently about their role and developing critical skills to evaluate the professional context. Educational activities require a high level of motivation on the part of the learner. Patricia has a strong extrinsic or external motivation to participate in education, although she is likely to experience uncertainty about her capacity to be successful if she undertakes an educational programme.

- The primary process revealed in this scenario is concerned with socialisation, **orientation** and **induction**. Angelica has just joined the organisation. She is experiencing uncertainty and may eventually wish to leave the organisation. She has a large number of learning needs. She needs to learn about the organisation, its culture, its structure, her role and the expectations that the organisation has of her as a manager. You will most likely be able to facilitate her to make the transition to being a fully-effective employee by designing a systematic induction and orientation process, which will help accelerate her integration into the organisation.

- The process that scenario five reveals is **indoctrination**. Michael is concerned that all employees are committed to the concepts and philosophy of total quality management. He is concerned that supervisors are role models for high quality standards and that they consistently practice quality and implement high quality standards when they perform their work. It is likely that you will use some kind of learning intervention that seeks to reinforce the principles of TQM and secures complete buy-in to its concepts and philosophy.

Chapter Two

ESTABLISHING EFFECTIVE TRAINING IN YOUR ORGANISATION

LEARNING OBJECTIVES

On completion of this chapter, you should be able to:

- Understand the factors in your external and internal environment that will influence T&D in your organisation

- Understand the idea that T&D is an investment

- Understand the key components of the training management process, including mission, vision strategies, policies and plans

- Understand the different types of resources that you require to be an effective trainer

- Understand the competencies that you need to develop in order to be an effective trainer

- Understand a number of dimensions of your professional approach as a trainer and the factors that enhance your credibility within the organisation and within your profession.

A Training & Development Scenario

Read these two scenarios and provide your advice:

- Liam, 34, is your immediate direct report. You believe that in three or four years' time you will be moving out of your present position as area manager and you think that he is potentially the right person to succeed you. He is a quick-thinking, decisive, energetic sort of person, full of enthusiasm and prepared to steamroller his way through any obstacle. However, his management decisions are not always the wisest and, sometimes, they create more problems than they solve. While his colleagues and subordinates respect his energy, they resent his authoritarian style and his refusal to listen to advice. Since he joined the organisation 14 years ago, Liam has worked in the same department, except for his first six months when he moved around from area to area. You feel that, if you can give him the appropriate development over the next three or four years, he has the ability to be an excellent area manager.

- Ted is one of the longer serving members of your organisation, having joined when he was in his mid-20s. Before this, he worked in a number of different places, starting out originally as a messenger boy and gradually working his way up to Sales Representative. When he joined the organisation, he was viewed as a potential high-flyer and indeed, when he was in his early 30s, everyone predicted that he would reach senior management level, if not into the Board Room. Then, during the recession, promotional opportunities became fewer and fewer and now, 10 years later, Ted is still at middle management level at age 42. Up to about a year ago, this did not seem to bother him at all but, in the last couple of months, he has become very withdrawn, irritable and dissatisfied with his job. His performance has declined and he appears to have little interest in his work, arriving late and frequently not well presented. Apparently, there are no problems at home and you guess that Ted's career has "plateaued". Ted has a long time to go before retirement and you think that he still has a lot to contribute to the organisation.

What issues would you consider when preparing an individual development plan for each employee?

INTRODUCTION

We focus in this book on providing you with the knowledge that you require to make T&D work in your organisation. A significant proportion of this book focuses on your role in designing, delivering and evaluating T&D activities. This chapter focuses on a more macro issue: What factors do you need to consider when establishing T&D in your organisation? It is possible that the T&D function may be in an embryonic stage in your company. Alternatively, your organisation may undertake some T&D activity already or it may have a well-established T&D function. Even if the last is the case, you can still get ideas from this chapter on how to improve your overall approach.

We examine a number of internal and external factors that influence how T&D will operate in your organisation. External factors include competition, the regulatory and legal environment and external stakeholders. Internal factors include your organisation's culture and structure, its strategic objectives and its product and service characteristics.

It is important to establish a strong foundation for an effective training function. This will involve support and buy-in from senior management, the formulation of a training vision and mission statements, training policies, plans and the acquisition of resources for training.

In the final sections, we focus on what you as a trainer need to do in order to enhance your credibility and professionalism. We explain the competencies that you should possess as well as some of the ethical dilemmas that you may encounter in performing your role.

T&D: AN INVESTMENT, NOT SIMPLY A COST

When you start to think about T&D in your organisation, you should think of all learning activities as an investment in capability. It is, however, sometimes problematic to calculate precisely the contribution that T&D can make to an organisation. Many variables combine to explain the long-term contribution of training to individual and organisational performance. Nonetheless, you can make the following points when asked to justify investment in training and development:

- Induction and basic skills training assist employees to attain the required standard more quickly, thus reducing the learning cost of the new job
- Employees who have undertaken a T&D programme, or who are involved in continuous development, provide better quality goods and services

- Staff who have been properly inducted and trained tend to remain longer with the organisation and achieve greater job satisfaction
- Training employees in safe working practices reduces the number of accidents
- Organisations that publicise their T&D policies attract higher calibre applicants to job vacancies and improve customer relations
- Opportunities for T&D and career progression reduce staff turnover and sickness rates
- T&D opens the opportunity for a more flexible use of human resources
- General morale is raised when organisations offer development opportunities, leading to improved attitudes and perceptions
- Individuals increase their market value by acquiring specific skills or knowledge required by other employees
- Employees also enjoy enhanced self-esteem and job satisfaction.

The benefits of training often occur some time after the initial financial outlay. This list of benefits may well convince an employer that investment in T&D is a worthwhile consideration.

If you are to make the argument that training is an investment, then you must be prepared to evaluate it. We will consider this topic in **Chapter Ten**. In this chapter, we will concentrate on the benefits of training. For example, the CIPD makes a distinction between "pay-back" and "pay-forward" in explaining the benefits of training. Pay-back is defined as "the financial return on an investment in training". Did the monetary value of the results exceed the cost of training? Pay-forward describes benefits from investment in training that cannot easily be expressed in monetary terms, such as improved customer service levels, raised morale and greater workforce flexibility. **Figure 2.1** presents a summary of the pay-back and pay-forward elements of investing in T&D.

These two lists provide evidence that training can make a difference. However, getting this message across is not easy. You are likely to encounter difficulties in persuading managers to invest in T&D. Typical barriers include the excuses that:

- There are other priorities for spending
- They cannot spare the time of experienced staff to train the inexperienced
- They cannot see that there is a return on investment.

These reasons illustrate that many people are still not convinced. Therefore, the task you face is to identify benefits more robustly.

FIGURE 2.1: EXAMPLES OF PAY-BACK & PAY-FORWARD FOR T&D

Pay-back	Pay-forward
• Increased profitability, reduced time inputs • Improved performance against budget • Reduced staff turnover • Improved output or productivity • Reduced absenteeism • Improved quality • Shorter processing times • Reduced error rates and scrap • Reduced re-work • More new customers / markets • Reduced overtime • Fewer accidents and lower compensation bills • Less need to use agency staff • Less stoppage time / down-time	• New ideas • Improved responses to crises • Improved customer satisfaction • Greater flexibility of workforce • Improved morale • Delegation of decision making • Fewer grievances • Enhanced skill levels • Increased confidence to deal with change • More positive attitudes amongst staff

STRUCTURING T&D: SOME FACTORS TO CONSIDER

Training activities are influenced by factors outside of the organisation and by the characteristics of the organisation itself.

Factors in the external environment will impact directly or indirectly on your organisation's strategies and policies and on how T&D responds to strategic changes.

External Factors

Some of the more important external factors that may directly or indirectly impact T&D include location, demography, political and legislative influences, the economic and social characteristics, all of which influence organisational actions and the influence of technology. Let's look at each in turn:

- **Location:** This refers both to the location of industry, and the location within the industry of individual organisations. For instance, companies that are located in heavily populated areas have less problems in recruiting labour. On the other hand, those not in this situation must aim their T&D strategy to provide an internal source of employees suitable for promotion. This has implications for T&D policies

- **Demographic Trends:** The main issues here are birth rates, death rates and migration trends, which influence the working population size and age profile – as a result, they impact recruitment and training policies. Ambitious individuals are attracted by employment in other countries offering higher status and rewards. Ages, marriages, households, migration, the size of the labour force, and an increase in the population because of rising birth-rates impact schools and universities. They also result in a tendency for corporate T&D programmes to concentrate more on the early training of young recruits. The recent decline in birth rates has resulted in a decreasing number of young people entering the workforce, forcing employers to demand greater flexibility from their current workforce, as trained young people are not available. It has also caused employers to consider attracting individuals not currently in the workforce to join or rejoin. Another impact is the level of immigration, particularly relevant in recent years, which gives rise to the need to develop training for various ethnic groups

- **Political and Legislative Issues:** These refer to the main systems of law and justice and the influence of government policy. They cover a wide range of controls, ranging from establishing the minimum age at which full-time work can be done, to the enactment of the Equal Opportunities legislation. Such control can determine the nature of T&D – for example, there can be no exclusion of women or ethnic group members from T&D simply on sexist or racist grounds. The implications, however, go beyond this. In order to comply with the legislation, many organisations have reviewed their recruitment and selection training to change both behaviour and attitudes. Managers responsible for interviewing may need to be trained not to ask questions that could be viewed as discriminatory and to approach selection decisions in a more objective manner. Changing attitudes is clearly a long-term process, requiring more support and reinforcement following any training event. Legislative demands on training and development are also clear in areas such as employee participation and industrial/employee relations issues, including legislation relating to unfair dismissal, which has implications for the way that managers operate disciplinary procedures. Training is required to explain those procedures: why they are necessary; the implications of not implementing them and the behavioural skills required to implement them effectively. The national training framework will also influence training and development activities. National training initiatives such as "Excellence Through People" and training grant support for new company start-ups have had an impact in encouraging a planned approach to T&D, particularly in small organisations

- **Economic Factors:** A range of macro-economic factors will affect the organisation, including: inflation/deflation/stability; recession/growth/stability; exchange rates; interest rates; taxation and spending power. These factors, together with the activities and behaviours of competitors, will have an impact on the profitability of the organisation. In turn, this will affect the money available, and priority areas, for T&D in the organisation. The availability of government or other grant money may also be an influence. Large customers and suppliers (including government) of an organisation may also impact an organisation's T&D by making conditions relating to T&D activities and policies that must be complied with in order for economic dealings to take place

- **Social Factors:** A range of social pressures will have an impact on T&D. These will include employees' expectations for greater T&D opportunities and a focus on careers rather than just jobs, as well as:
  - ° Increases in the numbers of dual-career families
  - ° Increases in the numbers of mothers returning to work immediately after child-bearing
  - ° Expectations of equal opportunity and positive action
  - ° The return to work of women who have been long-term home based carers
  - ° Pressures for early retirement, home-based working, flexible hours
  - ° Increases in part-time working and in contract working.

  Large organisations are now likely to respond to these changes/pressures more quickly and to reflect them in their T&D policies and activities

- **Technological Developments:** Changing technology – whether industrial or information technology – will impact T&D. Technology change impacts the organisation in a number of ways including:
  - ° Understanding the kind of impact the system has on the role with the organisation
  - ° Acknowledging the importance of the nature of new working practices needed for the system and the timing involved
  - ° Understanding the reaction of employees to the system
  - ° Accepting that they themselves need training
  - ° Being aware of the role of the "computer department" and its interaction with staff
  - ° Accept complete commitment to the system's adoption and usage and its complete efficiency and effectiveness
  - ° Taking part in the planning of training activities aimed at producing maximum attainment of objectives.
  - ° These new demands on employees need to be addressed by appropriate T&D.

The introduction of new technology has some very direct implications for T&D activities, including consideration of:

- ° What category of employee will be required in future?
- ° What additional skills are needed?
- ° Who will require what sort of training?
- ° Is it possible to maximise organisational efficiency by retraining, or by redeploying?
- ° What sort of training is needed now?
- ° What training can be obtained, and from where?
- ° Will new patterns of supervision require new training?
- ° Are there individuals not suited to the new system, due to physical disability or inappropriate mental ability?
- ° Are career paths identifiable, and what will be the impact of IT on promotion opportunities and career structures?

Internal Factors

There are a number of internal factors that you need to be aware of when managing T&D activities. The most important factors are the organisation's strategy, culture, structure, product and service characteristics, characteristics of its internal labour market and the influence of internal stakeholders. Let's look at each in turn:

- **Business Strategy:** The strategies that the organisation implements in order to be competitive will have an influence on T&D. Organisations that pursue cost leadership, for example, will require their core employees to be highly skilled in order to produce products and services at the lowest cost relative to competitors. Organisations that pursue differentiation-type strategies are concerned that human resources add value and help to differentiate its products/services from those of competitors. Some organisations serve a niche market, providing a very specialised product or service that requires a unique set of skills – T&D can contribute these skills and ensure that they are updated on a regular basis

- **Organisation Culture:** An organisation's culture represents its core values and beliefs and the things that it considers important. Organisations can use T&D to develop and reinforce elements of the culture and help to ensure that employees put into use the core values that the culture espouses. Cultures that value openness, sharing of knowledge and continuous learning are more likely to facilitate T&D. Culture will also impact the practices of the T&D specialist: For example, role-oriented cultures may reinforce an instructor-type approach, while cultures that are more open and empowerment-focused may encourage a more facilitative approach to training

- **Organisation Structure:** The organisation's structure refers to the way in which it divides its activities, its patterns of communication, the nature and definition of its job roles and the nature of authority within the organisation. Organisations that have a more hierarchical or functional-type structure are also likely to have a centralised training function, in which trainers emphasise their specialist expertise. Organisations that operate a more business unit or divisionalised or matrix-type structure are more likely to encourage training to be decentralised and more in touch with the needs of the business unit. Therefore, the structure of your organisation has implications for the type of competencies that you require to perform your role effectively and may explain how your role is defined

- **Product and Service Characteristics:** Whether your organisation produces a product or service will impact the types of T&D activities that you undertake. Product-type companies tend to require production, manual skills and supervisory training. The knowledge and skill requirements are very precise – for example, operators are expected to be skilled to experienced worker standard and to internalise and take ownership of product quality. Service-type companies tend to be more concerned about customer satisfaction and the skills to customise service provision to meet the specific needs of customers. Service-type organisations are likely to invest more in the softer, less tangible skills and to invest significantly in developing their managers and front line employees

- **Internal Labour Market:** The internal labour market consists of the definitions of jobs, the nature of job categories, career and promotion paths and policies on issues such as promotion from within. It also covers the extent of lateral moves and the promotion of multi-skilling and flexibility within the organisation. Some organisations have highly structured labour markets, with very clearly defined job categories that require very specialist training and the continuous updating of skills. Other internal labour markets advocate promotion from within rather than going to the external labour market. Organisations that encourage promotion from within are more likely to invest in T&D and pay attention to career issues. Multi-skilling strategies are also an important influence on training activity and usually make a significant demand on you as a trainer to develop skill profiles and prepare individual development plans

- **Organisation Stakeholders:** There are a number of stakeholders that you should be concerned to engage with and take their priorities into account when making decisions. The active support of top management is important for the T&D function. If you can achieve this, then all other types of internal support will be easier to secure. You will need to develop a good working relationship with line managers. If line managers are committed, they will be of major assistance and help your T&D activities. Training specialists are usually part of the human resource team. This will give you the opportunity to exchange some helpful ideas and information, since some of your activities will have implications for other human resource activities such as recruitment and selection, performance management and equal opportunities.

HOW TO ESTABLISH EFFECTIVE T&D IN YOUR ORGANISATION

The process of establishing an effective T&D function in your organisation – acquiring resources, enhancing your credibility and developing training systems and processes – takes time and expertise. Therefore, it will be worthwhile to start small and gradually justify your activities through demonstrating success and tangible outcomes. Here, we outline a number of issues that you will need to consider. We focus on some of the training processes that you should put in place, the type of resources you require and the different role approaches that you can adopt. We first consider the importance of gaining the support of top management.

Securing Top Management Support for T&D

One of the most important challenges you will face is securing top management support for T&D. It is very valuable where it is secured, since the most senior person in an organisation usually sets its agenda. Thus, the values and priorities of the chief executive or managing director need to be carefully observed. Where the chief executive has a personal belief in the value of T&D and is committed to supporting it, then this will represent an important asset. **Table 2.2** outlines levels of top management support that may be available to you. You should however ensure that the support you receive is real support rather than that which is "politically correct".

Some chief executives may actually sponsor specific learning events. This can give a training initiative a level of credibility that it would not otherwise have. Sometimes senior management or the CEO may be interventionist. The CEO may prescribe some of the training activities that you should carry out.

You can enhance the level of support you secure from senior management in a number of ways, including:

- Finding out, first and foremost, what interests and preoccupies the "target" – showing a prime concern for supporting the manager's objectives and agenda
- Demonstrating an understanding of the business or operations, what the key measures are and what challenges/problems are being experienced
- Making formal connections into business decisions through membership of project teams, review bodies and steering groups
- Demonstrating real bottom-line and organisational effectiveness gains from well-managed training interventions
- Publicising success stories internally, especially those that affect business results
- Gaining good publicity for the organisation through the media and public platforms
- Creating strong links with people who influence the organisation as a whole and creating added value for them
- Sound benchmarking with competitors or leading organisations, and questioning the positioning of your own organisation against them
- Briefing managers in the purposes of your training activities and their relationship to business objectives and strategies
- Developing a schedule of training activities for a specified time period and checklists of managers' responsibilities for training and development
- When you conduct training activities, encouraging trainees to meet with their managers before training to identify opportunities to apply the training
- Continuously communicating information on the benefits of your training activities and, at intervals, conducting a training audit
- Holding managers accountable for ensuring that employees attend training by ensuring that the organisation should incorporate a development dimension in the performance appraisal process
- Encouraging managers to develop their skills to coach, to mentor, to instruct and to provide developmental feedback
- Demonstrating accountability by showing managers how their training budget is spent and how the training activities you have completed relate to individual, team and organisational performance.

FIGURE 2.2: LEVELS OF SENIOR MANAGEMENT SUPPORT FOR T&D

	Type of Support	Characteristics	T&D Response
High Support	• CEO drives T&D agenda personally	• T&D involved in major strategic decision • Priorities set by CEO • Constant review by CEO	• Close contact with business issues • Flexibility of resources • Strong influencing skills by specialist
	• Top team full commitment	• Regular briefings / dialogues take place • Priorities debated and agreed • Focus on return on investment	• Uses top team commitment as backer of messages • Involves director in appropriate programmes
	• Individual director sponsorship	• Driving force behind sponsored programmes	• Exploits business advantages of sponsorship and seeks to extend influence
	• Subcommittee of board as "steering group"	• Likely that T&D specialist is secretary • Reviews programmes and suggests advice on priorities	• 'Manages' the committee • Uses decisions effectively gain influence
	• Passive CEO support	• Signs documents relating to HRD on request • Shows support when asked	• Utilises willingness to give desired messages • Seeks greater interest
	• T&D director as champion	• Director HR represents views of T&D and board	• Thorough briefing • Close familiarity with HRD
Low Support	• No representation	• Control by budgets	• Seeks better representation

Adapted from Mayo (1998).

THE CONTRIBUTION OF T&D TO THE CORPORATE PLAN

You should be aware of some elements of your organisation's "strategic" process, especially its organisational mission, its strategic objectives and its business plan.

The Organisational Mission

The organisational mission is a statement that covers the purpose of an organisation and expresses the aspirations and ambitions of its members. It gives the overall "reason for being" of the organisation, and describes what the organisation wants to become.

The most effective mission statements are short, clear, and identify how the organisation is unique. Mission statements provide a vision that employees can identify with.

Examples of mission statements include:

- To provide an hotel service that bring the guests back
- To provide travel advice and booking where the customer always comes first
- To contribute to human health by developing drugs, ensuring that our business and our people grow
- To write the news that people want to read.

Mission statements have a range of purposes. They are helpful in explaining to customers, investors or stakeholders what the organisation is all about. They can be used to motivate employees. The strategic objectives of the organisation can be formulated from the mission to guide organisational activity.

Strategic Objectives

Strategic objectives are longer-term goals for the organisation, which result from a strategic planning process and which help to translate the mission statement into action. They need to be carefully worded to be as specific as possible, and indicating some relevant measure of performance. These objectives need to reflect the balance of priorities in an organisation and should focus on a limited number of critical issues. If too many objectives are written, covering too many issues, then the focus and direction of action becomes lost under pages of "nice to have's". Examples of strategic business objectives include:

- To shorten the development time for new products so that the stage from research to the market is less than three years
- To become an organisation that is much more clearly focused on business objectives – where all individuals are continuously updated on business issues and each has a set of clear personal and departmental objectives to work to.
- To launch two new products each year
- To improve customer service so that complaints are reduced to less than one customer
- To respond to all queries from the public within 24 hours
- To have 97% of all Council-owned properties occupied
- To employ more women in senior positions – to increase the percentage from 5% now to 25% over the next five years
- To acquire a similar-sized management consultancy organisation
- To move from the production of manual to electronic controls
- To reduce the number of house repossessions due to mortgage arrears.

A key feature of effective training is its capacity to align its activities with the strategic imperatives of the organisation. You will need to give this issue very particular consideration. There are a number of things that you can do to support the strategic imperatives of your organisation. We suggest that the following are worthy of consideration:

- You should examine the portfolio of training activities that you offer. How do they reflect current best practice and what type of offerings do you make by type of training and by audience?
- You should assess employee perceptions of growth and learning opportunities within the organisation
- You need to be continually focused on environmental and organisational changes and how they impact the knowledge and skill requirements of your organisation's employees
- You need to address how the work environment supports your learning activities.

Figure 2.3 provides a summary of the questions that you should ask when analysing the strategic alignment of your T&D function with the strategic priorities of the organisation.

Business Plans

Business plans focus on specific activities that the organisation intends to achieve within a specific time period. Although business plans can be short- or long-term and may take many different forms, they are designed to show how the organisation's strategic objectives will be achieved.

Integrating T&D with the Organisation Mission

In some organisations, mission statements or objectives do not exist in written form. Where T&D activities are not driven by the organisational mission and objectives, then they will probably be determined by factors such as:

- Demands from line managers
- Requests from individuals
- Good ideas seen elsewhere
- The interests and ideas of training and development professionals
- *Ad hoc* demands from senior management, usually in response to an organisational problem
- Problems identified elsewhere
- Repetition of previous years' actions.

FIGURE 2.3: EVALUATING THE STRATEGIC ALIGNMENT OF YOUR T&D FUNCTION: KEY QUESTIONS

Characteristics of Training Function	Alignment with Overall T&D Strategy	Alignment with Specific Training Programmes
Scope of Learning Solutions	• What is the ratio of classroom activity to other learning strategies? • What is the ratio of expenditure on different learning activities • Does the organisation place too much emphasis on formal training? • Does training demonstrate flexibility in its use of learning solutions?	• Does classroom or formal training represent the most appropriate solution? • Are one-to-one learning strategies an equally effective solution? • Have managers faith in the value of formal or classroom-based training?
Target Audience for Training	• Who receives the majority of training in the organisation? • Do you focus primarily on operational or management employees or both? • Do you invest resources in training your suppliers, customers or business partners? • Are there groups within your organisation that are significantly undertrained?	• What do your employees need to know to contribute to organisational performance? • What are the T&D needs of your suppliers and customers? • What types of training interactions will encourage the participation of your suppliers and customers?
Priority of T&D Needs	• What are the key groups that need to be trained, given your strategic priorities? • How long does it typically take to respond to priority employees? • How appropriate are the solutions you provide? • How can you gather information to identify priority groups from a training perspective? • What is the shelf life of particular training and development needs? • Do you distinguish between important and urgent training needs?	• Do you timetable your training activities? • Do you know when particular groups need to receive training? • Do you show a concern for speed *versus* quality in the training solutions you provide? • How do you gain access to target audiences when designing specific training solutions? • Can you be more efficient in designing and delivering specific training solutions?
Employee Perceptions of Learning and Development Opportunities	• Does the organisation seek to be an employer of choice? • Do you encourage your employees to enhance their employability? • Do you experience a retention problem and how are you using training to address it? • Are there core groups of employees who are essential to your competences? • What are the learning preferences of your employees? • What is the motivation level of your employees to participate in learning and development?	• How do employees perceive opportunities for development? • Are employees aware of specific learning and development opportunities? • Do you advertise your learning solutions to appeal to the motivations of your learners? • Do you involve employees in design and delivery decisions? • Do you evaluate the perceptions of your employees to specific learning events?

Characteristics of Training Function	Alignment with Overall T&D Strategy	Alignment with Specific Training Programmes
Support for Learning	• Does your environment support employee learning? • Do you have a positive learning climate? • Do your managers believe in continuous learning? • Are your managers role models in emphasising the importance of learning? • How do your training policies, practices and actions contribute to a positive learning environment?	• Do you indicate to employees the particular support you will make available to them? • Do you explain what you expect employees to do differently as a result of training? • Are there specific work environment factors that are obstacles to effective transfer? • Have you systems to use supervisors before and after training to support transfer? • Do you ensure that there are sponsors for specific learning events?
Training and Strategic Direction	• Do you understand the strategic needs of the business? • How are external environmental changes impacting skills and capability requirements? • Do you need to reallocate your resources to ensure better strategic alignment? • Is your training mission statement appropriate given your business objectives? • Do you continually seek to clarify the strategic needs of the business?	• Who do you interview when conducting organisational needs analysis? • Do you regularly talk to senior managers to understand the business needs? • How do specific core training programmes align with strategic priorities? • Are there current training programmes that are not worth the investment of organisational resources?

Created from Truelove (1997); Ford *et al.* (1997); Lynton and Pareck (2000).

On the surface, your T&D may seem sensible, logical, problem-oriented and meeting real needs but, if T&D is not carried out in the context of a long-term organisational direction, it may cause the following problems:

• T&D actions may conflict with the mission/objectives
• T&D actions may fail to provide necessary support for the mission/objectives
• There will be lost opportunities, where T&D could have contributed to organisational success

As a result, T&D will not be seen as key to corporate success in the future. The bottom line for the organisation is that strategic initiatives and changes may fail because the necessary contribution from T&D was not identified and did not happen.

T&D activities can contribute to the organisation's mission in one or more of four areas:

- **Skills:** New skills to be learned, different skills to be emphasised, skills not needed any more. The skills may be manual skills (those now relevant to electronic rather than manual components); personal skills (self-development); interpersonal skills (influencing others); management skills (coaching, leadership); business skills deriving the financial implications from different courses of action)

- **Knowledge:** New knowledge about the external environment (new legislation and its implications for the organisation); new knowledge about the internal workings of the organisation (knowing strategic objective's priorities, new systems, organisation, and roles)

- **Attitudes:** Examples here include adaptability to change; being flexible; management style; training and development philosophy; increasing business focus

- **Culture:** Culture change involves changes in all three of the other components, and a shift in the underlying view of "the way we do things round here" and "what it's like here". It is therefore the most difficult of all the changes to accomplish, is inevitably longer term, and requires enormous organisational effort to maintain and re-energise in the early years. However, it has the potential to offer the greatest impact on the organisation, the greatest improvements and the greatest shift towards achievement of the mission.

The critical question is how can the T&D contribution be linked with the mission and strategic objectives? This is easier in those organisations where the mission and objectives are clearly articulated, written and communicated to all employees.

Figure 2.4 provides a summary of the different levels of contribution that the T&D function can make.

FIGURE 2.4: USING T&D TO ACHIEVE STRATEGIC OBJECTIVES

Level	Who is Making the Link?	Using What Information?	Resulting in What Action?
Senior Management Level	• Senior managemen t and T&D Department	• Their strategic objective which declares the need for some form of performance management system in order to link more effectively business objectives and individual performance behaviour	• T&D joins working party to define the system and its operation, and T&D is involved in the identification of alternative methods, design, timescale, costs, methods/timescale of development, organisation support, and implementation over next 3 years
HR Department level	• T&D Department	• Know that one strategic objective is to reorganise four major departments in order to speed the development of new products	• T&D Department identify a need for introduction of change management workshops, and a portion of trainer's time to be specially allocated to change management consultancy
Middle Management Level	• Manager of IT Department	• Knows that one strategic objective is to become a technology-based organisation and to increase dramatically the use of internal IT systems	• Decides with his senior group that the IT department must become more customer- and user-centred to achieve this objective. Instigates (with help from T&D Department) a training programme aimed at improving interpersonal skills of IT staff over next year
Supervisory Level	• Team leader of Plastic Bottle Department	• Knows that the plastic bottles development is key to the organisation's success and must get to market next year	• Asks T&D Department to do some team-building development with the team so that they can operate as effectively as possible. T&D Department says they will help at the expense of some other areas not critical to organisation success
Individual Level	• Individual	• Knows that a merger is on the agenda	• Wants to understand more. T&D Department offers an article on the human implications of mergers to them

Created from Mayo (1998) and Megginson *et al.* (1993).

A number of different plans within the organisation are likely to require an input from T&D, including are human resource and equal opportunity plans:

- **Human Resource Plan:** Human resource plans focus on analysing an organisation's HR needs arising out of its business plans, and developing the appropriate personnel policies. The T&D specialist is well-placed to make a contribution to the HR plan – for example, they should be able to provide the planner with useful information on the current state of skills and knowledge amongst existing employees. This can be very valuable in making decisions, such as the extent to which an organisation embarks on a recruitment campaign to bring in "new blood" or follows a policy of internal promotion. The HR plan can provide the T&D function with helpful information on the training and development needs of employees – for example, the plan may highlight that retirement among supervisors is going to be very high over the next few years, and there is an urgent need to develop more junior staff to fill supervisory positions.

- **Equal Opportunity Plans:** Equal opportunity plans and programmes are adopted by many organisations to combat discrimination at work. T&D often feature large in these plans, especially in the following areas:

  ° Equipping women and ethnic minorities to progress into areas of work where they have been traditionally under-represented. The T&D specialist can advise on the appropriate training, or other developmental activities such as planned experience or coaching, that should go into the equal opportunity plan

  ° Raising awareness amongst managers in the organisation of equal opportunity issues. Again, training is often seen as the key to this, especially by off-the-job courses designed to encourage members to reflect on their own prejudices as well as those found more widely elsewhere.

  ° Making sure that employees involved in the recruitment and appraisal processes have a good knowledge of the relevant provision of the law. Staff also must be made aware of the possible misunderstandings that can arise between people of different cultural backgrounds.

FORMULATING T&D POLICY STATEMENTS

Skill in formulating T&D policy statements is an important building block necessary in order to establish an effective T&D function. We define a T&D policy as a written statement of intent, a set of guidelines that says something meaningful about how the organisation views T&D.

Reasons for Formulating T&D Policy Statements

The most fundamental reason for formulating a T&D policy statement is to demonstrate how T&D contributes to the goals of the organisation. Written policies on training and development perform a number of important functions:

- **Guidelines for Managers:** A written policy can provide guidelines for managers when making T&D decisions:
    - ○ It can help managers to identify organisational priorities and support (financial and otherwise) when advising/agreeing appropriate T&D for their staff. It can help managers make decisions and judgements without having to contact someone in the training department to find out what official policy is – for example, when someone requests funding for an evening class in a job-related subject
    - ○ The policy can help the organisation explain to employees why they will be supported for some forms of T&D, but not for others. It can help explain why different groups of employees might receive different treatment
    - ○ The policy can give managers an indication of their expected role in T&D. Managers may be tempted to leave the responsibility of T&D to the training department, but a policy spelling out the importance of on-the-job learning and manager coaching will point managers in a different direction. It will certainly help the training department to use this in fending off inappropriate requests
    - ○ The need for consistency in decision-making is important. Policy statements provide a framework for managers to work within. They help to ensure that the decisions they make are in line with the expressed intentions of the organisation
- **Guidelines for Employees:** A written policy can be used to inform employees only if it is widely circulated, if it is up-to-date and if it is used as intended to guide management decisions and actions. If these conditions are not met, then the policy will misinform employees

    The communication of the T&D policy is frequently neglected. The argument that employees will ask for it if they need it does not hold, because many employees will not even be aware that it could exist. Expecting managers to use the policy with employees and show it to them is similarly inadequate. This route does reinforce the role of the manager in the individual's development, but provides no failsafe mechanism for those employees whose managers have yet to take their responsibility for T&D fully on board. There is no substitute for making sure that each employee receives a copy of the policy on joining the organisation, or at induction, and that policy amendments are circulated to all. Managers are frequently reluctant to share T&D policy content, unless an employee forces the issue by requesting development/financial support and not accepting a negative answer. The policy is then brought out as a backup. Much of this reluctance is caused by the desire not to be put in the position of defending the policy. This negative approach can only be dispelled by the involvement of both line managers and employees in training policy formation process

Where the policy is well communicated, it can be helpful in shaping employee's expectations in respect of T&D. It should provide employees with clear ideas about the development they are likely to receive, the external development that is likely to be supported and how it links into career opportunities in the organisation. It should also make employees aware of development priorities and how development is an essential contributor to the future success of the organisation. This information should generate commitment to the organisation, and to developing within it

- **Response to Legislative Demands:** The environment, in the form of legislation covering health and safety, racial and sexual discrimination, employee involvement and industrial relations issues, has an impact on the provision and direction of T&D policies in organisations. A T&D policy can be used to reflect the organisation's approach to training and commitment in these areas. For example, the policy might contain a statement that T&D opportunities will be offered to all irrespective of race, creed, sex or age. On some occasions, the policy is a requirement to meet statutory demands, as in the area of health and safety

- **A Means of Changing the Direction of T&D:** Writing a new T&D policy can be used to clarify a change in the direction of T&D. If a written policy did not exist in the past, then development decisions would be made on the basis of custom and practice – looking backwards and repeating the past rather than looking forward to creating a new future. A written training policy articulates what will happen in the future and is therefore a visible sign that things are changing, and it is a useful tool to help others understand the nature of the change

- **Putting T&D on the Organisation Strategic Agenda:** The review and rewriting of T&D policy can be used as an opportunity to involve senior management in discussions about the T&D contribution to the organisation's objectives; the role of the T&D department, and the role of the others in T&D. It provides a forum for debate on changes that the T&D function identifies as vital to the future of the organisation, but which line managers have not yet recognised. An example might be to include a statement on the importance of self-development, with development being the individual's own ultimate responsibility and the reasonable support to be expected from line managers. By including this in the written policy, the issue is raised for discussion. Involving a representative group of line managers as well as senior managers in the debate is a way of encouraging their commitment to the policy that is ultimately agreed

- **A Vehicle for Employee Involvement:** Policy preparation can provide an opportunity for employees, employee representatives and trade union representatives to be involved in understanding the direction of the organisation and contributing to the T&D response. This does not mean, of course, that employees are allowed to determine policy, but that they are given sufficient information about the organisation and its situation to offer well-grounded proposals. These proposals would then be given consideration when drawing up the policy. Involving employees in policy-making allows managers to take into account employee needs that they might not have been aware of, and it helps in communicating and gaining commitment to the policy

- **Creating a Positive Public Image:** A further purpose of a T&D policy is to present a positive external image to potential employees and customers, and one of the major benefits seen to arise from this is in recruitment. The possibility of planned T&D and career progress can be used to attract better quality candidates, and a demonstration of senior management support for these promises is reflected in the T&D policy. The policy can be used to encourage the selected candidate to accept the offer made

  A commitment to T&D as described in the policy statement can also be important evidence for customer/suppliers of the quality of the organisation's products and services. Large purchasers and suppliers, including the government, are in a position to make demands on the organisation in terms of their approach to T&D – and the policy statement can be used to demonstrate compliance

  In more general terms, a publicised T&D policy can project the organisation as an employee-centred and caring employer. This positive image is particularly good for the employer where the general public buys their products/services.

How to Write a T&D Policy Statement

Writing a policy takes skill and a degree of understanding of the organisation, its future direction and the contribution that people can make to its success. You should be clear about the reasons for the introduction of such a policy and what objectives it is designed to achieve. The policy should state which categories of people will be affected – the overall presentation style should be positive and unambiguous.

A T&D policy should specify the organisation's intentions or expectations in the areas listed below.

- **Aims:** The specific aims of the policy should be set out in relation to the overall aims and objectives of the organisation

- **Commitment:** The policy should include a statement of intent to the effect that the policy will be fully supported by senior management and backed up with appropriate action. Senior management should also indicate what action will be taken if the policy does not receive appropriate support

- **Responsibility:** The specific responsibilities of individual jobholders in the implementation and development of the policy should be detailed. Often these postholders will be required to report to senior management on a regular basis regarding the overall policy implementation

- **Resources:** For any policy to be successful, it must be properly resourced. This frequently means more than simply identifying the finances available. The policy should also outline, for example, the time commitments the organisation is willing to make for individuals to pursue personal development. It may also specify the need for new, or additional, training support staff

- **Assessment of Workforce Needs:** The methods intended to analyse training needs in the workforce should be specified. Effective assessment of workforce needs will also require the definition of standards against which performance can be measured

- **Methods of T&D:** The policy document should also set out the emphasis that is to be given to the various different methods used in T&D – for example, on-the-job/off-the-job training, development opportunities, coaching, mentoring, and distance learning. Often organisations will use a mix of such methods, depending upon their specific needs

- **Methods of Evaluation:** If training is to be economic and effective, it will be necessary to undertake periodic external evaluation to assess to what extent organisational objectives are being met. Both the specific T&D programmes and the overall effectiveness of the T&D policy should be monitored

- **Career Opportunities:** It is important for employees to understand that their efforts towards personal development may be rewarded by career progression opportunities. The policy should outline the possible career outlets of different programmes

- **Benefits:** Benefits other than individual career progression – for example, incremental rewards – should also be indicated. The benefits accruing to the organisation as a whole as a result of the effective implementation of the policy should also be outlined

- **Identification and Communication of Results:** Once evaluation has been completed, the result should be communicated to the senior management team and, as soon as possible thereafter, to the workforce. It is the employees, through their own efforts, who are ultimately responsible for making the T&D policy a success. Letting them know the results is common courtesy and may stimulate others into pursuing personal development initiatives.

Gaining Commitment to the T&D Policy

Realistically, the development of a T&D policy statement will require input and involvement from several levels of management, each taking on a different level of responsibility:

- **Senior Management:** Senior management is responsible for determining the aims and objectives of the organisation and for formulating the strategic plan, and have the following specific responsibilities in relation to the organisation's T&D policy:
  - ○ They must create and maintain a positive attitude towards training and development and give it its rightful priority as a means of fulfilling organisational aims and objectives
  - ○ They must specify the content of the T&D policy and identify the resources necessary to meet the policy aims and objectives
  - ○ They must maintain a consistently high level of interest in T&D in order to ensure its continued evolution

- **Line Managers:** Larger organisations may have a specialised personnel or training officer who is responsible for the production and communication of the T&D policy. In smaller organisations, the responsibility for T&D from conception to implementation may lie with one person, the owner/general manager. However, line managers and supervisors should understand their individual responsibility for the personal development of each staff member. This will require frequent, formal assessments of individual performances, as well as informal input designed to extend and develop each employee. It will also require line manages to be fully conversant with the content of the T&D policy and its relationship to the organisational aims and objectives. However, this level and intensity of line manager involvement and responsibility for T&D may be difficult to obtain in day-to-day organisational practice, as line managers will generally prioritise what they perceive senior managers to value – for example, meeting targets and keeping control. Ideally, then, line managers will be responsible for maintaining the impetus for policy initiatives and ensuring their implementation. In practice, however, T&D policy may meet with some resistance at this level.

FIGURE 2.5: EXAMPLES OF T&D POLICY STATEMENTS

Resources
We will strive to spend 5% of salary and wages on formal and on-the-job T&D for the forthcoming year.
Responsibilities for Training
It will be the responsibility of the general manager and a designated assistant manager to ensure the T&D needs of our employees are constantly reviewed. The designated manager will formally oversee an assessment of the T&D needs of operational employees on a quarterly basis. It will be the duty of the general manger to review and assess the development of managerial employees on a quarterly basis.
Diversity / Equality
We will strive to provide an environment in which equality and diversity are not only encouraged, but also embedded in our culture and ethos. We will introduce a diversity-training workshop to be conducted annually in order to communicate a heightened awareness of the challenges and benefits of working in a diverse environment. We are an equal opportunities employer and will not discriminate on any of the nine grounds outlined in the Employment Equality Act 1998 in relation to the provision of T&D.
Induction Training
Our commitment to our newest team members is that they will receive induction training within the first month of joining the company. They will receive an introduction to their roles, our policies and procedure, training on health and safety, information on our employee support structures and an understanding of our culture. The goal of this training is to facilitate an easy integration to the company and develop and promote a high performance organisation.
Managers and Leaders
We will provide developmental direction on leadership and supervisory skills on an on-going basis to our team leaders to ensure that we utilise and develop their skills in a fast-changing and competitive environment. The training provided will be driven by the feedback we receive from supervisors and subordinates. The goal is to develop managers who understand and take responsibility for the development of each staff member and to foster positive attitudes towards a progressive training policy.
Craft and Apprenticeship
All craft employees will be given time and financial support to pursue courses and training that are job-related and that will enhance their skills within the organisation. The extent of the support will be determined on a case-by-case basis and will be influenced by the relevance to their roles. We will also endeavour to facilitate non-crafted employees to take craft and apprenticeship positions within the company when they become available. Our goal is to have our craft employees perceive our organisation as one where their skills and crafts are respected and utilised, and that they have the opportunity and support to keep their skills updated.

- **Employees:** Management should seek the views, ideas and concerns of the workforce before the final T&D policy document is ratified by senior management. Consultation will improve the quality of the document, as it will provide the means to incorporate the knowledge and experience of all those who may be affected. This can stimulate improved co-operation within the organisation, and unpopular decisions may be accepted if it is perceived that all viewpoints have been considered. Consultation can also reduce the potential for misunderstanding.

The policy must be communicated widely throughout the organisation, so that all employees have the opportunity to understand:

- Senior management's intentions
- The organisation's responsibility for providing individuals with T&D opportunities
- The guidelines regarding levels of responsibility and accountability for those implementing T&D initiatives (including line managers and training specialists)
- How employee relations can be enhanced.

Note that, once an organisation has committed itself to a course of action and has ensured the commitment of its employees through a process of consultation, failure to meet employee expectations of the policy can lead to resentment, disillusionment and lack of motivation and organisational aims and objectives will not be achieved.

Reviewing T&D Policy Statements

Once a T&D policy is formalised and implementation has commenced, it will be necessary to monitor the results, content and relevance of the policy on an ongoing basis.

External factors that may influence the achievement of objectives include the health of the economy, new technologies and legislation. The organisation may have to review its T&D policy to deal with the effects of these factors.

You may need to review your training and development policy for any one or more of the following reasons:

- The availability of new training methods and delivery mechanisms
- A change of emphasis of T&D – for example, from induction and basic skills acquisition to personal development and continuing change
- Changes in employee expectations, leading to a change in demand for development

- A need for retraining as a result of economic and business fluctuations – for example, during periods of recession and boom
- Changes in the nature of the work process and the role of the individual – for example, as a result of new technology
- Changes in customer requirements
- A need for reallocation of resources. During times of recession, T&D is often one of the first areas to be cut back, even though this usually transpires to be a false economy
- A need to assess the achievements and results of present development policy. It is logical that reviews of policy should be undertaken on a regular basis. Monitoring should thus be an ongoing process, constantly evaluating the outcomes against the stated aims.

The following are some of the issues that you will need to consider when reviewing your organisation's T&D policy statement:

- **Is the Commitment Ongoing?:** The policy review should explore attitudes to T&D at all levels. The policy may be failing in its intent because senior management are not fully committed. They may have "signed up" for the initial policy implementation, but become less keen when it came to delivery, perhaps because of the drain on financial resources. Having a policy that is not fully supported by senior management is an unacceptable situation, since it renders the policy (and the T&D function) ineffective. Attitudes to T&D can also be problematic where line managers and supervisors are not fulfilling their responsibilities. Attitudes of employees below management level may be negative because of a lack of information, resulting in failure to see the benefits of T&D and its relationship to organisational success, or because the rewards are perceived to be inadequate. Explaining more fully the individual benefits of personal development may be sufficient to change these negative perceptions. This function is an ongoing requirement, incumbent upon line managers
- **Are Your Resources Adequate?:** Insufficient funding for T&D programmes may be a result of misguided attitudes. Equally, it may be because the policy was incorrectly articulated and financed initially. Economic factors may lead to financial resources, earmarked for T&D, being redistributed. Whatever the reason for such cutbacks in resources, they should be acknowledged, so that the policy review is based on reality. Resource factors may be an identifiable blockage. Managers may not have the time to undertake individual needs analysis, or pressures of production deadlines may mean that staff may not be free to undergo training. Freeing these types of blockage necessitates a reaffirmation of

senior management commitment to giving people permission to alter deadlines and reschedule priorities in an appropriate and responsible manner

- **Is the Style of Delivery Consistent?:** Even where the T&D policy has total support from all stakeholders in organisations, a blockage may result from the type or style of training and development process used. For example, a greater emphasis on on-the-job training as opposed to off-the-job training may produce the desired results. Distance learning materials rather than attendance at courses may be more appropriate. All methods of delivering T&D programmes should be subjected to scrutiny and alternatives considered

- **Is the Consultation On-Going?:** The analysis of information and identification of blockages will determine a future course of action. Where policy and the development programmes are reviewed, all parties in the organisation should be consulted prior to any final revisions to the policy.

A T&D policy should be not just modified to meet the demands of change but, in addition, to correct any underlying inadequacies. Those who initiate policy, however, are sometimes reluctant to change it, since this may imply shortcomings in their original formulation. Modifying and reviewing policy also requires even more consultation than the original policy development. Expectations raised by the original intent of the policy may now have changed, so everyone affected by the potential effects of review must be consulted. Negotiating such a review of policy is often harder than introducing it initially.

FORMULATING T&D PLANS

The next issue you must consider is the formulation of T&D plans. You need to consider three levels of planning:

- **Strategic** or organisational plans that set out the general direction of T&D within the organisation
- **Operational** plans that focus on the more immediate issues and may address a six months to one-year period
- **Individual** plans that address the specific learning needs of individual employees.

We will spend the remainder of this section considering the components of these three planning outputs.

Strategic Organisational T&D Plan

The aim of the strategic T&D plan is to set out the general direction that T&D will take within the organisation over the foreseeable future, which in most cases is a time span of three to five years. It is a process, therefore, that deliberately takes a long-term view to create a vision of the future.

Strategic training plans are most likely to be linked to the mission and strategic objectives of the organisation, and will primarily address organisational and functional/departmental training needs, and, occasionally, occupational needs. They may be drawn up as an integral part of the corporate planning process but, more usually, they follow on from corporate planning processes, and are a response to the T&D issues arising from the overall plan. If the plan is developed by the T&D function, it will often represent many days of work analysing the direction of the organisation, and the role that T&D needs to play in supporting that. It will contain such items as:

- A mission statement for T&D and for the T&D function
- Key changes in the direction of T&D to meet the organisational requirements for the future, summarised in terms of strategic objectives
- An exposition of the role of the T&D function in the future, and how this could/should be marketed
- Identification of the role of T&D actions
- Resource considerations and return on investment.

Strategic T&D plans serve four main purposes:

- They allow management to set down clearly what it intends to achieve from its T&D philosophy and policies and how these will support the organisation's overall business objectives – for example, a key objective over the next three years may be to raise the general level of competence among first-line management through a policy of continuous self-development
- The strategy should indicate how the T&D function is expected to realise its longer-term objectives
- The strategy should identify what resources will need to be committed. No organisation has unlimited resources. The strategic training plan should constitute the driving force in determining the allocation of training resources.

Figure 2.6 gives an example of a strategic or organisational T&D plan, while **Figure 2.7** recommends a process to follow.

FIGURE 2.6: EXAMPLE OF A STRATEGIC T&D PLAN

Training & Development Strategic Plan

1. Vision / Mission

Business Mission

- To create an integrated bank that is pre-eminent in personal banking in Europe.

Training Mission

- To create a learning organisation
- To support managers and individuals by providing T&D advice and resources in order to promote a high performance organisation

2. Strategic Business Issues

- Improve profitability in short term (one to three years)
- Introduction of new technology to remove administration from branches
- Integration and rationalisation of high street banks with saving banks
- Shift of orientation towards sales and service
- Attraction and retention of new entrants and returners
- Improvement in the quality and succession cover for management at all levels

3. Training & Development Strategic Issues

- Identify the skills needed to perform all new roles and produce resourcing plans
- Improve the quality of the top 500 managers and identify credible successors for all jobs designed as key by the end of next year
- Identify a strategy for improving sales skills
- Identify the development needs for each stage of the integration of retail and savings bank branches
- Identify the new roles and skills necessary to introduce new technology

4. Training Objectives

- Junior branch staff: to ensure that all new and junior branch staff are able to meet service and sales performance within specified time scales
- Supervisory branch staff: to provide basic supervisory skills on appointment and to ensure competence in sales
- Branch managers: to prepare newly appointed managers for their role on appointment and to improve the competence of existing managers
- To expand the provision of computer-based training, distance and open learning and learner-centred approaches
- To run training events that are fewer in number and more closely linked to organisational objectives, and which are identified by senior management as key to organisational success
- To support the organisation's major culture change initiative
- To encourage / persuade line managers to take the primary responsibility for the T&D of their staff (and not leave it to the T&D Department) so that they spend at least 5% of their time on staff development activities.

5. Resource and Volume Implications

- Volume: off-the job training should be increased by 80% to 100% in the next three years
- Budget: an increase in budget from £15m to £18m will be necessary next year, together with an additional 40 staff that will be recruited in the current year
- Organisation: it will be essential to improve the co-ordination from head office; to create a T&D Research and Development facility and to introduce learning resource centres at HO.

Adapted from Moorby (1991).

FIGURE 2.7: RECOMMENDED PROCESS FOR DEVELOPING A STRATEGIC/ORGANISATIONAL T&D PLAN

	Target Date
Step 1: Initiating the Process The Business Unit Trainer/T&D representative briefs the Head of Business Unit on the recommended approach for compiling the Business Unit Strategic T&D Plan	End January

⬇

Step 2: Head of Business Unit Sets the Process in Motion Head of Business Unit emails his/her management team the following request: • To formalise the T&D requirements of their business • To complete the Strategic T&D Needs Questionnaire (sent as an attachment with the email) by the next Management Team Meeting	Within 5 working days of Step 1

⬇

Step 3: Filling in the Strategic T&D Needs Questionnaire All members of the Management Team complete this questionnaire. They may or may not include members of their teams in this task	By next Management Meeting

⬇

Step 4: The Management Meeting The objective from this meeting is to devise a Business Unit Strategic T&D Plan. The Business Unit Trainer and/or the T&D representative facilitate this meeting.	End February

⬇

Step 5: Finalising and Arranging the Business Unit Strategic T&D Plan Using the outcomes from the Management Team Meeting, the Business Unit Trainer formally writes up the Business Unit Strategic T&D Plan. This document is reviewed and signed by the Head of Business Unit	Within 5 working days of the meeting

⬇ **End February**

Step 6: Validation of the Individual T&D Plans The agreed Business Unit Strategic T&D Plan is communicated to all staff members. Line managers are encouraged to validate individual T&D plans against the Business Unit Strategic T&D Plan.	End March

⬇ End March

Step 7: Finalising Course Participation for all Staff Members All managers pass on the individual/team T&D plans to the Business Unit Trainer who fills in the Business Unit T&D Schedule. Each employee registers for their programmes via the Business Unit Trainer and/or T&D representative	**End April**

Note: This document is an example of a planning process used by the Learning and Development Team in AIB Capital Markets.

Operational T&D Plans

A T&D operational plan (often referred to as the training plan) is concerned with existing operations and the immediate issues and problems surrounding them. It is short-term, often coinciding with the organisation's annual budgeting cycle. In general, T&D operational planning assumes a fairly constant environment and can be specific about the sorts of activity that will be carried out in support of business operations – for example, programmes of on- and off-the-job training, timetables, reviews, activities, etc.

Operational plans are normally intended to specify T&D activity over the coming year, and need to be written in such a way that performance over the year can be assessed against the plan. The annual operational plan is a step towards achieving the strategic plan and therefore also needs to be constructed with the strategic objectives clearly in mind. Where the organisation does not construct a strategic T&D plan, an operational plan is still useful to clarify T&D activity over the year, and to share this across the organisation. The resulting plan, however, will lack a long-term perspective and direction.

The operational plan is likely to contain the following:

- Statement of T&D policy
- Strategic T&D objectives
- Operational objectives covering:
  - ° T&D courses, numbers, dates and trainer days
  - ° Other T&D interventions
  - ° Direct support for other T&D processes and systems
- Individuals responsible for which activities and when
- Budgets and other resources.

Examples of operational objectives include:

- To set up a learning resource centre to be functioning by the end of the year
- To provide *Management of Change and Innovation* workshops over the year, sufficient for every manager over a certain grade to have a place
- To redesign the procedures, and the shape, of induction training so that it becomes a two-day event with a waiting list of less than six weeks.

Operational T&D plans may have a range of purposes. As a result, and given the wide diversity of organisations using them, we can expect to find a considerable variety of plans. Some will be large and comprehensive, others will be highly focused, perhaps on the needs of a particular key group of employees, or in relation to a specific project.

It is likely that you will have to produce one of three types of operational plan:

- **Fully Comprehensive:** This type of plan will cover all employees from top management downwards and will draw together many different areas of activity. It considers all of the organisation's human resources, so that senior management can see the overall position.

  One problem with this type of plan is to find a meaningful way of analysing all the employees within an organisation, especially within larger organisations. For example, you could use the following broad distinctions:

  ° Newly recruited employees

  ° Newly promoted employees

  ° Existing employees

  ° Employees subject to particular change or development.

  Another approach may be to use an occupational differentiation, where you have a large organisation with a diverse labour force. For example, a large manufacturing company could employ the following classification:

  ° Production employees

  ° Technical employees

  ° Clerical staff

  ° Specialist staff

  ° Junior managers

  ° Middle managers

  ° Senior managers.

  It is possible that not all of these groups of employees will actually require formal T&D activity during the planning period.

- **Sectional or Group of Employees:** In this approach, you do not attempt to draw together all T&D activities into one overall document, but you adopt a more selective approach and develop a number of separate, but related, plans. This approach is relevant to the larger organisation and has the merit of specificity and of tying ownership of the plan to a particular department or group of employees.

  The drawbacks of this type of approach are that:

  ° T&D activities overall in the organisation may lose their cohesiveness

  ° There can be unnecessary duplication of effort

  ° Senior management may have difficulty in agreeing priorities or seeing the bigger picture.

- **Problem-Centred:** This type of plan will focus on a particular problem or development required of the T&D function. For example, the plan could be built specifically around T&D policies and activities to be followed over the planning period to encourage more innovative management. Another example would be a T&D plan designed to meet the needs of a new governmental regulatory order, say in the area of health and safety.

  This approach does have the advantage of being highly focused on business interests, but it can be narrow in scope, and in the context of an operational plan it may ignore wider developmental needs.

Individual T&D Plans / Personal Development Plans

Personal development plans are a statement of the intended development of that individual over a specified period. They rest on an assessment of development needs, usually identified jointly by the individual and his/her manager. In circumstances where the needs and plan are imposed by the manager, the plans are unlikely to be effective or to have commitment from the individual. Although managers may have responsibility for making sure development planning takes place with each member of their staff, the plan needs to be owned by the individuals, as does their individual development.

Some development planning will result from the output of assessment and development centres and, in these cases, a variety of people may be helping the individual to achieve their development goals.

In many organisations, there is no formal process of individual development planning, and plans will only exist for individuals with identified potential or for the staff of "development-minded" managers. Some individuals may have an agreed development plan with their manager, but nothing is even written down. Other individuals may find themselves in a position where there is no managerial support for their development, and their only chance of a development plan is to write their own and to solicit support from any likely sources. Although this can be effective and says a lot for the individuals involved, it is not usually as powerful as manager-supported development.

The key items to be included in a development plan are:

- Development goal
- Development activities
- Timescales
- Review of progress.

Figure 2.8 presents an example of a personal development plan. We will provide more detail on the personal development planning process in **Chapter 10**.

FIGURE 2.8: EXAMPLE OF A PERSONAL DEVELOPMENT PLAN

Personal Development Plan				
Name:		**Employee Number:**		
Priority Areas for Development:				
Details:				
Needs	**Activity**	**Relating to which Competency(s)**	**Resource**	**Time Scale**
Intellectual Capacity – showed strong intellect, and critical analytical skills; articulates and highlights the key sales trends that support the proposed direction	Develop broader strategic awareness – become involved in strategic project	Intellectual Capacity – showed strong intellect, and critical analytical skills; articulates and highlights the key sales trends that support the proposed direction	Line Manager	Success of Project X after 6 months
Needs	**Activity**	**Relating to which Competency(s)**	**Resource**	**Time Scale**
Personal Qualities – displays a positive, enthusiastic and "can do" approach	Develop skills to challenge the actions of others who behave in a manner inconsistent with the organisation; Agree to coach 2 identified individuals	Personal Qualities – displays a positive, enthusiastic and "can do" approach	Training Specialist	Report on outcome coaching sessions in 4 months
Statement of Outcome: Formal Leadership Development Programme, external Business School followed by external coaching.				
Employee:		Date:		
Line Manager:		Date:		
Facilitator:		Date:		

Summary

These three components of the T&D planning process have a number of common features, which it is important for you to understand:

- First and foremost, the three plans – strategic, operational, and personal – should be firmly rooted in the organisation's wider business planning. Unless this occurs, the training planning process will be ineffectual and will never command the confidence and commitment of managers outside the T&D function

- The planning process in each case needs to be carried out professionally: the relevant information should be gathered and analysed carefully; each element of the plan should be worked through systematically; and the planning process should be carried out at set times

- Each plan must recognise the need for flexibility. Change can be very rapid – a re-organisation, a new business opportunity, a change in regulatory regulations – and plans may have to be modified, perhaps fairly drastically. Planning systems should have provision for regular reviews – say, quarterly for operational plans and annual for strategic plans

- Plans should be written in a way to be readily understood, not only by T&D practitioners, but also by line managers. Readable and interesting plans can be powerful vehicles for promoting T&D within the organisation. Indeed, plans co-written with managers are more effective and are more likely to be implemented.

SECURING RESOURCES FOR T&D

Financial Resources

Securing a training budget is an important issue. Exactly how the budget is prepared will depend upon the following key factors:

- The organisational structure, which affects the way in which the T&D department relates to the rest of the organisation. Some departments are designated as profit centres, supplying services to line managers on request and charging accordingly, and sometimes contracting their services and resources (premises, equipment) to external clients for a fee. Such departments are expected to pay their way, costing their services and overheads to determine the prices charged and operating a profit and loss account. In other organisations, the training department is regarded as an overhead, and allocated a budget

- The financial systems and controls that operate throughout the organisation. Zero-based budgeting assumes starting with a blank sheet and receiving an allocation justified by the estimated cost of carrying out the training plan, possibly limited to agreed priorities. More usual is the annual budget allocation, the content and size of which depends on many factors. Of particular significance are the importance accorded to the T&D function, the level of its activity, and the T&D manager's tenacity and skill in "fighting his/her corner" when the budgets are being finalised

- The size of the budget is likely to vary from year to year depending upon the profitability of the company, or in a public sector organisation, upon government policy. This is an added challenge because training or retraining needs can be greatest when financial resources are at a premium. It is always necessary to plan well ahead and to assess the probable future requirements carefully so that whatever finance is available goes to the real, and acceptable, priorities. Regular monitoring of expenditure is essential, so that any discrepancies are noticed at an early stage, and corrective action taken before the situation gets out of hand.

Whether the budget consists only of amounts earmarked for special purposes is likely to depend on the organisation's accounting norms: most "active" training budgets now contain contingency sums that are not so earmarked and which can therefore fund unanticipated costs. Where such contingency sums are included, there may be a temptation to create or "find" ways of spending them; in some organisational cultures, unspent budgets may be thought to promote future budget reductions.

Although budgets very from one organisation to another, you will need appropriate systems for forecasting the financial resources required and for controlling those allocated. In order to implement a budgetary system for training, you will need to have the following in place:

- An adequate T&D plan
- The expenses to be incurred in achieving the plan must have been identified and estimated
- The responsibility for items of expenditure must have been allocated between training specialists and other managers
- Account classification must have been made so that expenditure can be allocated to specific cost areas
- Cost information must be recorded accurately and a mechanism for feeding back the collated information must exist, so that individuals can take corrective action when required.

Securing Financial Resources for Training

Securing financial resources for training is often very political and is usually subject to your organisation's accounting rules. There are basically four options available to you, as outlined in **Figure 2.9**

- Centrally funded as an overhead cost
- Funded through negotiated annual contributions from units
- Combination of 2 above with "central subsidy"
- Free market approach.

The latter approaches are perhaps more problematic and require considerable negotiation skills. Whatever model you decide on, it is important that you have freedom to buy-in external resources.

FIGURE 2.9: FUNDING MECHANISMS FOR T&D IN ORGANISATIONS

Mode of Funding	Advantages	Disadvantages
1. Centrally funded as an overhead cost; resources cut to that budget and events provided free to users	• Stability, clarity, ease of planning • Reinforces importance of training and development • Not subject to 'client' unit budget difficulties	• No ownership by units, so use of events may not be taken seriously • Central focus may not meet the real needs • Risk of complacency by T&D
2. Funded through negotiated annual contributions from units	• Relatively stable for planning purposes • Units have ownership of their budget • Opportunity to create internal client relationships	• Assumes the nature of demand does not change through the year • Risk of renegotiation especially when reorganisation takes place
3. Combination of 2 above with a "central subsidy" (for strategic programmes and/or making the use of internal resources attractive financially)	• Combines the advantages of 1) and 2) • Judicious application of central subsidies enables priorities to be given to strategic change and cross-organisational issues	• Has some of the disadvantages of 1) and 2) but to a lesser extent
4. Free market approach – departments contract events by event and pay the advertised price	• Able to be really responsive to the needs of unit • No scope for T&D to "peddle its own agenda"	• A lot of time is spent in selling and negotiating • No ability to plan resources – so will keep in-house resources to a minimum • "Numbers" overtake quality • Difficulty in giving any cohesive messages across the organisation • Becomes a supplier rather than a support for the strategies

Adapted from Mayo (1998).

Pricing T&D Activities

This is a very relevant issue if your T&D function is expected to make an internal profit. The general consensus is that this approach is not effective, because it imposes a major burden on the training function. However, there is evidence that training functions are increasingly required to cost out their training activities. **Figure 2.10** outlines a number of pricing options that you can use.

FIGURE 2.10: PRICING OPTIONS FOR T&D IN ORGANISATIONS

Pricing Approach	Objective	Comments
Standard training day rate	• Simplicity, volume, "bums on seat"	• Focus is on cost rather than value; training as a commodity
Activity-based cost price	• To reflect true costs of development and delivery	• This is better, but problem of forecasting product life for development recovery; also more work involved
Consultancy-based price, at cost	• Straight, no-frills internal price	• Value of offering may not be appreciated
Consultancy-based price at market rate less discount(s)	• To demonstrate both true value and benefit of internal customer	• Gives flexibility to control messages
Consultancy-based price, at market rate	• To demonstrate value of solution offered and awareness of market	• Places T&D firmly in competitive market

Adapted from Mayo (1998).

You should view training resources as the input required to enable a training plan to be implemented. The range of resources that can be drawn upon includes people (the trainer him/herself), and facilities (the self-learning package, a walk-in open access resource centre, a training room) and money (the training budget). However, it is often not so much the resources themselves that achieve results but the skill with which they are managed.

Credibility and influence are enhanced when the training specialist is accepted as the focal point in the organisation for advice and information about training activities (both internal and external):

• As the source of specialist knowledge and experience about learning in a work context

• As the co-ordinator and monitor of the organisation's training policy, plans and budgets

• As a competent trainer

• As a successful (line) manager of the training department, its staff, the training centre and learning aids.

It is through contacts with top managers that you benefit from key resources of political support for your activities.

The recognition that successful training does not have to take place in a training centre is powerfully reinforced by the application to T&D of new technologies, which have three main effects:

- Computers, videotape-recorders, compact disc, interactive video systems, access to computerised databases, intranets and the Internet have greatly increased the choice of flexibility of learning systems available. Wherever there is a computer terminal, there is a potential training resource

- Application of the new technologies are changing the perceptions of training. Effective training is no longer so widely perceived to be primarily a classroom-based activity. However, in the right circumstances, the "course strategy" remains a very important method of achieving training objectives

- New opportunities are being opened up for employees who have in the past been "disenfranchised" from training and educational programmes because they worked shifts (and so could not attend "normal" courses on a regular basis), or worked in dispersed units or in small organisations, or could not be released for training, or lived in an area without a local college. The new technologies have enabled sophisticated "open learning" systems that make it possible for employees to study at home, at work (even in the car on the way to and from work) or wherever they wish, to embark on their studies when it is suitable for them (as opposed to the fixed enrolment date of an educational institution), to have access to a very wide range of courses, irrespective of where the learner happens to live, and to construct their own learning environment.

All training resources ultimately cost money, and you are responsible for advising on the best use of the available resources to facilitate learning. To do this, requires up-to-date knowledge of the resources on which to draw and how they can best be employed.

Physical Resources

You may be fortunate to have customised internal training facilities, and/or you may be able to avail of external training facilities:

- **Internal Training Facilities:** These can range from residential management centres, off-the-job training rooms (room equipped with simulators), to learning resource centres containing hardware and software of many kinds. Some organisations derive an income from hiring out such facilities to other less-well-equipped organisations, thus adding to the training budget. The availability of general organisation resources such as desktop PCs, video conferencing systems, a corporate intranet and/or access to the Internet facilitates a wide choice of delivery. Records, such as job descriptions, training undertaken, competences achieved, can also be a useful internal resource, as they can save much time searching through information.

- **External Training Facilities:** External facilities consist of private-sector courses and consultants; professional associations, public sector education and training services and courses run by agencies such as FÁS. Numerous organisations offer a wide variety of courses on almost every aspect of training. Reductions in the number and size of T&D departments and the sophistication of new methods of delivery have resulted in an increased demand for outsourcing and for external courses. Selecting the right course is a difficult, but important, task if the company is to benefit from what can be a very considerable financial outlay.

People Resources

You have a number of options here:

- **Line Managers:** Many organisational training policies emphasise that the training of their staff is ultimately a line management responsibility, and indeed most learning takes place in the day-to-day work situation. Managers can act as coaches, mentors, appraisers and role models for subordinates, as well as helping them to identify and use the many learning opportunities that occur in the course of normal work and, in the "learning organisation", increasing emphasis is being placed upon these aspects. In addition, successful off-the-job training relies heavily upon the trainees' receiving suitable briefing by their managers prior to the training and being given support to transfer their learning to their work. Line managers' commitment to training is crucial not only to maximising the benefits of formal course training, but also a powerful factor in creating and developing a climate that expects and supports training interventions as a normal part of organisational life. At an operational level, line managers, especially if they are good trainers, are an important source of lectures for induction and other in-house training programmes

- **Training Specialists:** An experienced T&D specialist is potentially one of the major contributors to an organisation's training operation. The extent to which his/her role and skill are put to profitable use depends in practice upon many variables, in particular upon his/her credibility, technical competence and the degree of co-operation received from fellow managers

- **Trainers:** Trainers act as the essential link between the learner and the training plan and include managers (when coaching their own staff), tutors overseeing trainee technologists, craft trainee supervisors and operator instructors

- **Former trainees:** Satisfied "customers" are very important in helping to create informed opinion about the T&D function. They can be of major assistance in getting a new form of training accepted. Past trainees can make helpful contributions as speakers or syndicate leaders

- **Consultants:** Consultants are a valuable source of expertise, and organisations considering employing them should apply similar criteria to those used in selecting courses. An external consultant can often achieve results that would not be possible by using internal staff. It is not only the wider expertise that a consultant is likely to bring, but also the advantage of being unaffected by internal policies and value systems

- **Professional Bodies:** The growth in professionalism in many fields of employment in recent years has led to new professional bodies being formed. The T&D specialist needs to be familiar with those professional associations relevant to his or her organisation. They can supply detailed information on training courses and programmes that lead to membership qualifications, and of post-qualification short courses to assist their members to keep up to date in specialist fields – courses an organisation could not normally afford to run internally.

Outsourcing T&D Activities / Using Consultants

A major issue is whether you should contract or outsource training and development activities. There is strong evidence that T&D departments outsource some or all of their activities. However, there is evidence that this approach can produce mixed results. There are a number of arguments for, and against, it as a strategy.

For	Against
• Reduced direct overhead cost • Reduced management attention • Ability to control against strict performance criteria • Availability of wider range of skills	• Lack of commitment to organisational goals • Lack of long-term ownership • Degrees of freedom in controlling performance • Risks in lack of continuity of key skills

Whether you decide to outsource depends on the general philosophy of the organisation. Some organisations take the view that all T&D activities should be conducted in-house; others consider it a more cost-effective option to outsource.

There is evidence that organisations use consultants and there is a move towards more long-term relationships in their use. Consultants can help in a number of areas such as:

- Assistance with determining the strategic T&D framework; sometimes consultants can see an overview or can collate views given to them from different sources
- Working with top management to establish their considered approach to people development
- Researching learning needs and client perceptions
- Setting up learning partnerships
- Designing, running and evaluating specific programmes
- Designing and implementing systems and processes
- The evaluation of resourcing choices
- Programme / event evaluation
- Benchmarking with other organisations
- Facilitating "political" workshops or meetings
- Presenting particular messages at corporate events.

Choosing consultants is often a difficult task. Trying out new consultants is a risk, therefore it is prudent to opt for a piloting arrangement.

YOUR PROFESSIONAL APPROACH AS A TRAINING SPECIALIST

We conclude this chapter with some discussion and advice on how you can enhance your credibility as a trainer within your organisation and profession. We consider four issues that you should take proactive steps to enhance:

- Your personal credibility
- Your professional ethics
- Your networking activities
- The continual development of your T&D competencies.

Your Personal Credibility

Your personal credibility is an important asset that opens doors to opportunities and will give you an important source of influence within the organisation. Your personal credibility is very much dependent on your perceived expertise and track record within and outside of the organisation. **Figure 2.11** presents a list of tasks that influence your credibility.

We will discuss some of the factors that enhance some of these elements of your credibility.

FIGURE 2.11: THE BALANCE SHEET OF CREDIBILITY FOR AN EFFECTIVE TRAINER

Assets	Liabilities
• Business knowledge and expertise	• No experience other than T&D
• Business understanding	• Expert knowledge in guru-speak
• Listening to business problems with interest	• Talking psycho-babble and seeing every problem as having a soft-centred solution
• Logical argument	• Emotional argument
• Accepting reality	• Refusing to accept the shadow side of organisations
• Working with reality	• Working with dreams and idealism, living in hope of Utopia
• Respect for all	• Respect only for perceived role models
• Personal charisma	• Skewed personality
• Caring passionately about people development, rejoicing in their success	• T&D is just a job to be done
• Self-aware; conscious of others' perceptions	• Unaware of impact of own behaviour
• Social skills	• Unwilling to socialise
• Persuasive skills	• Dogmatic style
• Problem-centred consultancy	• Solution-centred prescription
• Helping people learn from each other	• Wanting to control learning
• Natural sharer and collaborator	• Internally focused, jealous of personal knowledge
• Taking time to network internally / externally	• Lost in a personal world
• Understanding the need for short-term gains	• Expecting people to buy into the long term naturally
• Looking for opportunities to help and support	• Looking for opportunities to push own agenda
• Looking for allies and working with them	• Coming in tangentially
• Able to manage the "shadow side"	• Regarding politics as irrelevant
• Money-conscious	• Regarding money as a nuisance factor
• Data-oriented	• Dealing in immeasurable
• Taking time to get to know people personally	• Working through paper and email
• Brave in standing up for values and beliefs	• Blowing with the wind
• Doing what he or she promises	• Enjoying talking rather than doing
• Talking about success in manager's language	• Talking about success in HRD language
• Flexibility and adaptability	• Perfection

Devised from Kraiger (2001) and Mayo (1998).

Your Professionalism

The professionalism with which you carry out your T&D will considerably impact your credibility as a trainer. Training involves situations where you may encounter potential conflicts of interest. You may also be asked to undertake activities that are considered unethical and against good professional practice as a trainer. You are expected to show respect for your learners, to be open in the purposes of your training activities and be objective and impartial in the assessments you make of learners. **Figure 2.12** provides a summary of the ethical issues you need to consider.

FIGURE 2.12: ETHICAL ISSUES FACING A TRAINING SPECIALIST

Ethical Issue	Key Questions for T&D Specialists
Objectivity	• Does the T&D specialist make T&D decisions consistent with objective principles? • Does the T&D specialist use objective principles to decide the right and wrong of particular actions? • Does the T&D specialist take account of the individual's level of moral development?
Openness and Criticism	• Does the T&D specialist accept different opinions and perspectives? • Does the T&D specialist give balanced criticism to trainees?
Outcomes of Training	• Does T&D lead to positive or negative outcomes? • Does T&D lead to the optimum positive outcome? • What is the balance between individual and organisational outcomes? • Which category of outcome is more important?
Equality and Justice	• Does the T&D specialist promote equality of opportunity? • Do T&D activities respect privacy and confidentiality of participants? • Does the T&D specialist make appropriate assessments of trainees? • Does the T&D specialist ensure informed consent? • Does the T&D specialist promote freedom of thought and action in T&D activities?
Motives as a Trainer	• What are the motives of the trainer? • Does the trainer have the appropriate professional expertise? • Does the trainer's activities conform to the training specialists code of ethics? • Does the T&D specialist operate within a specific area of expertise? • Would the T&D specialist let personal preferences over-ride accepted training practices?
Personal Moral Standards	• Would the T&D specialist resign if he/she has to compromise personal moral standards? • Would the T&D specialist refuse to carry out unethical activities?

Your Competencies as a Trainer

Throughout this book, we emphasise the importance of your competencies and capabilities. You need to be an expert in understanding learning and the training design process, but you also need to have a good knowledge of the business. You are expected to be familiar with the core business values. There are, however, specific competencies and capabilities that you should also posses. **Figure 2.13** provides a summary of these.

FIGURE 2.13: COMPETENCIES & CAPABILITIES OF TRAINING SPECIALISTS

Consultancy skills	Personal skills	Project management
Facilitation skills	• Teamwork	• Bid management
Change management	• Business / commercial awareness	• Programme management
Integrity	• Learning needs analysis	• Credibility
Judgement	• Diagnostics	• Self-managing expertise
	• Developing and delivering learning solutions	• Project management
	• Subject expertise	

These competencies you will develop through specific learning activities, formal courses and the experience of designing and delivering training in organisations. We consider some of these competencies in more detail in **Chapter Eight**.

Enhancing your Networking Skills

Networking is an important dimension of your work as a training specialist. There is strong evidence indicating that effective training specialists are skilled in networking with key stakeholders, internal to and external to the organisation.

You can enhance your networking ("building social capital") in a number of ways:

- In order to build social capital, you must evaluate your networks. We know from research that people have a distorted, incomplete "mental map" of their personal or organisational networks. We also know that people who have good mental maps are more influential and effective as networkers

- The network must have variety. The research tells us that similarity is the enemy of networking. Similar people tend to have similar networks. If you have diversity in your network, then you will have greater network reach

- Focus on the work and non-work elements of your network. The research tells us that many people have networks that focus only on work or make a very clear distinction between personal and work life. The most effective social capital accumulators have the capacity to spread the focus of their network. This may include involvement in professional groups, cultural or sporting organisations, community groups, etc

- Large diverse networks are effective for getting lots of new information, learning about new opportunities and finding necessary resources. Large networks are not that effective, if your purpose is to build consensus or develop a sense of mission. Small networks are better if your concern is building group loyalty, identity and a sense of common purpose.

We know from the research that the way in which you behave during your networking activities is as important as the extent of your network. We can identify a number of rules that you should follow:

- **Be Open and Prepared:** It is important that you are open to ideas, people and opportunities, but you must also be prepared. This requires you to learn the skills to network effectively. Your level of preparation must match the opportunities available

- **Be Ethical:** The best advice here is that you should treat everyone as equals. Do not be concerned with title, status or prestige. We know that the true value of a network is in the information and support that you derive from it. It is best to understand a network as a level and fair playing field. Do not get involved in the network simply just to get something back. It is recommended that you give for the sake of giving

- **Be Proactive:** If you require help, the advice is that you should be proactive. In order to get help, you must ask for it. Acknowledge the people who help you. It is also recommended that you listen attentively to those who speak to you. Networking is not effective when you monopolise the conversation

- **Be Committed and Circulate:** Your level of commitment to the network is very important. The research tells us that networking requires patience, takes time and most important of all, means that use the help you get. You should talk to as many people as possible and establish their identities, your needs and the resources you can contribute. Everyone in your life is part of your network. This includes your family, friends, neighbours, professionals, suppliers, clients, co-workers, clubs, associations and voluntary groups.

Your networking skills do not develop by accident. They demand you to be focused and systematic in your skills development. Some of the skills you can develop are:

- **Research and Planning:** You should research networks to identify the ones best suited to you. This requires that you pay attention to news, current events and local developments. Ask questions where necessary and then devise objectives and appropriate strategies

- **Communication and Promotion:** Your communication skills will determine your overall network effectiveness. Your use of language should be appropriate, concise, open, honest and articulate – and most important of all, you must listen. Understand your strengths and how to use them. You must also learn how to express your strengths and to promote yourself and your organisation

- **Keeping Records:** You should keep thorough and accurate notes. This requires that you keep lists, that you write reminder notes about people you meet and, if you have a business card, that you use it. You will be more effective when you are organised. Be clear what you want to say and how you want to use your time

- **Follow-Through:** This is a most important behaviour. If you make commitments to yourself or others, make sure that you follow-through. If you are given a piece of advice, act on it or where you are given a contact, follow-through on it.

BEST PRACTICE INDICATORS

Some of the best practice issues that you should consider related to the contents of this chapter are:

- T&D is treated as a significant value-adding process by top management. It is intended to make a major contribution to the achievement of performance targets at corporate, unit, team and individual levels

- There is a public commitment from top management to value all staff by providing T&D opportunities that will enable them to achieve targets related to business objectives, and to use their skills and experience in ways that encourage personal initiative and progress

- A director at Board level with expert T&D knowledge carries specific responsibility for T&D as all or part of their role

- Clear corporate T&D goals, an annual T&D plan and consistent HR policies provide the framework for all T&D activity in the organisation

- At corporate and unit level, there is regular review of T&D needs against business goals and targets
- T&D is held by top management to be a primary responsibility of all managers
- Managers' job descriptions explicitly identify their responsibility for ensuring the training and continuous development of their staff. They are appraised regularly in relation to that responsibility
- Training programmes, company policy and procedures, and development, guidance and monitoring all measure the effective performance of those with T&D responsibilities
- T&D resources are structured rationally to support business objectives. T&D resources deployed at unit level are intended to respond to local, as well as to corporate, needs
- Any T&D resources retained functionally at centre are geared to add value by strategic planning, by co-ordinating T&D strategies and integrating them within wider HR policies, and by resourcing organisation-wide needs or other strategic initiatives.

Reflections on the Training & Development Scenario

These two scenarios reveal some of the issues that you should consider when preparing individual development plans.

Scenario one is concerned with preparing an employee for promotion and advancement within the organisation. Liam has many positive personality characteristics and, in particular, he possesses strong emotional resilience. He has skill development needs in two key areas: decision-making and managerial style. He also has a relatively limited range of experience. The planning time frame is three years. Your target is to develop Liam to be an effective area manager. You could incorporate a number of elements into his individual plan.

- He will need to get a broader base of experience, with some planned periods of experience in each department/area
- He will benefit from specific coaching on his management style. He may also benefit from some formal development, in order to enhance his self-awareness of his current style and how best to change it
- He needs to be given situations where he can enhance his decision-making. There may be specific project experiences
- You will need to link his development to clear performance objectives and structured feedback. You may consider the use of 360-degree feedback.

Scenario two is concerned with an employee whose career has plateaued. Ted reveals many of the characteristics of an employee who is dissatisfied and demotivated. Nonetheless, you have a strong belief in the potential contribution that Ted can make. Therefore, you need to approach this planning process with sensitivity.

One of the first issues that you need to establish is the reason for the decline in performance and behaviour. This may involve some form of counselling intervention designed to explore collaboratively key issues inhibiting motivation. You will also need to explore Ted's expectations and how he views his career with the organisation.

You may need to discuss the possibility of a job transfer, a new project or some form of secondment outside of the organisation to give a new impetus and enhance his motivation. It is more likely that you will be concerned to have a shorter planning period with clearly defined review periods. These are necessary to monitor progress and take further corrective action if necessary.

Chapter Three

HOW DO ADULTS LEARN?

LEARNING OBJECTIVES

On completion of this chapter, you should be able to:

- Distinguish between pedagogy and andragogy and explain the implications of this categorisation for your style and practice as a trainer

- Explain the different metaphors you can use to describe your role in the training process

- Explain how thinking has changed about how adults learn and its implications for your practice as a trainer

- List the characteristics of the learner and the needs of the adult learner

- Describe the laws of learning and their application for the training programmes you design

- Explain the concept of learning styles and their relevance for the training methods and practices you use

- Explain some of the misconceptions about the adult learning process

- List the main conditions that facilitate effective adult learning.

A Training & Development Scenario

The training manager at Abbeydex, a Computer Call Centre, was asked to train 500 newly-recruited staff in a two-month period in induction, customer care skills, sales skills, trouble-shooting skills, and the basic computer training skills. This was a request from the parent company in the US and they expected almost instant results.

The HR Director was also involved in the project and wanted to expedite the process as quickly as possible. He took a somewhat Machiavellian approach to the project. Abbeydex's financial resources were limited because it had invested most of its training budget into an in-depth management development programme. He decided to use their in-house trainers to execute the programme.

The project was fraught with difficulties on a number of fronts:
- At least 30% of the new employees were people returning to paid employment after long periods of between 10-20 years out of the workforce. These people had little or no computer experience and suffered from acute technophobia.
- The remaining 70% were school leavers who, while computer literate, had limited job experience and were quite nervous and apprehensive about their new jobs.

To speed up the training project, it was decided to train 50 people together at a time. The burden on the training department was tremendous, with trainers having to resort to lecturing large groups using a microphone and a podium.

Although the training was carried out in the prescribed period, it was an unmitigated disaster. Sixty percent of the mature returners left the company and the employees who got through the two-month programme developed a very poor skill set. They kept making mistakes with customers and contributed to a downturn in sales.

The net result was that the HR director was forced to resign and the training manager was relocated. The company lost €2.2 million in this episode.

INTRODUCTION

Learning lies at the heart of training and development. Whether you adopt a formal and systematic learning process or a more informal and *ad hoc* approach, learning is a necessary pre-condition for anything that you wish to achieve.

To learn is to gain knowledge or skill in a particular area. You will find that many trainers use the terms "competence" and "capability" to express the objective of learning. They often say things like "I want to be competent in a job role" or "to possess the capability to carry out certain activities to the highest standards". This type of discussion places an emphasis on the results rather than on the change process of learning.

We are concerned in this chapter with the process of learning. We focus on the philosophical aspects of learning, in addition to the characteristics of adult learners, and the more important learning "laws" that you should be aware of as a trainer. We believe that it is important that you have a basic conceptual grasp of what learning is and why it is central to your effectiveness as a trainer.

PHILOSOPHIES & METAPHORS OF LEARNING

We first consider some of the philosophies of learning. We explain three metaphors that are commonly used to describe the learning process. If you fully understand the learning process, it will help you design more effective T&D activities.

Understanding Learning Philosophy

The two primary learning philosophies are: Pedagogy and Andragogy.

Pedagogy
Pedagogy is derived from the Greek words "ped", meaning "child", and "agogus", meaning "leader of". Therefore, pedagogy literally means the science of leading (teaching) children. Historically, from the Middle Ages to the early 20th century, the pedagogical model was primarily used to teach.

Pedagogy represents the traditional, most frequently implemented and trainer-centred approach to learning. It is based on a number of important assumptions:

- You make all the decisions about the learning process and the learner is a submissive receptacle
- The learning is standardised and progressive because it is aimed at a group of learners uniform in terms of age and experience

- The training activities you implement are subject-oriented. There is a strong emphasis on subject matter content
- The learner brings little experience to the learning situation. The learner is essentially dependent and inert
- Lectures and formal inputs are the backbone of the pedagogical approach. The pedagogical approach is now considered less appropriate in the adult learning context, although it may have relevance depending on the subject matter.

Andragogy

Andragogy is described as "the art and science of helping adults learn" and can be viewed as the antithesis of the pedagogical approach. Knowles's model is the backbone of this philosophy and is based on the premise that, as an individual matures, the need to be self-directed, to have opportunities to use experience in the learning process, to be active and to participate in organising and structuring the learning process all develop.

If you wish to implement an andragogical philosophy in your training, you need to be concerned with the following androgogical assumptions:

- **The Desire to Know:** Adults need to know why they need to learn. Adults have a keen desire to establish "What is in it for me?", before they invest in the process. You need to emphasise the importance of the training event in terms of improving the effectiveness of the learner's performance to their jobs and lives
- **The Need to be Self-Directed:** Adults like to be responsible for themselves and may resist situations where they are being forced to learn. Trainers need to empower learners to enhance their skills and abilities and nurture this self-directed need
- **The Need to Build on their Experience:** Adults have developed experience over many years, which needs to be tapped using appropriate learning methods. These methods include:
  ° Group discussion
  ° Role-plays
  ° Case studies
  ° Problem-solving activities
  ° Action learning.

A group of adults will learn much more from each other than they would from listening solely to a trainer. On the other hand, adult experience can be viewed as negative, as we can develop biases that can inhibit our ability both to change and to develop new ideas. This can sometimes manifest itself in the training room.

If you are to successfully implement the androgogical model, you need to be concerned with clearly diagnosing the needs of your learner, and involving them in the formulation of the learning objectives and the design process.

Figure 3.1 presents a comparison of pedagogy and andragogy.

FIGURE 3.1: COMPARING PEDAGOGY & ANDRAGOGY

	Pedagogy	**Andragogy**
Elements	**BASIC PRINCIPLES**	
Climate	• Formal • Authority-oriented • Competitive • Judgmental • Controlled didactic	• Informal • Mutually respectful • Consensual • Collaborative • Supportive
Planning	• Primarily by trainer	• By participative decision-making
Diagnosis of needs	• Primarily by trainer	• By mutual agreement
Setting of goals	• Primarily by trainer	• By mutual negotiation
Designing a learning plan	• Content units • Course Syllabus • Logical sequence	• Learning projects • Learning content sequenced in terms of readiness
Learning activities	• Transmit techniques • Assigned readings	• Inquiry projects • Action learning • Independent study • Experimental techniques
Evaluation	• Primarily by trainer	• By mutual assessment of self-collected evidence
About	**ASSUMPTIONS**	
Concept of the learner	• Dependent receptacle	• Increasingly self-directing
Role of learner's experience	• Role of trainer's experience	• A rich source for learning by self and from others
Role of trainer	• To instruct and be knowledgeable	• To facilitate and shape the learning
Readiness to learn	• Uniform by age level and curriculum	• Develops from life tasks and problems
Orientation to learning	• Subject-centred	• Task or problem-centred
Motivation	• By external rewards and punishment	• By internal motivation • Curiosity

Adapted from Knowles *et al.* (1998).

We do not present these two categories of philosophy as representing good/poor training practice. They are best viewed as approaches to training to be considered in terms of their appropriateness for particular learners in particular situations. If pedagogical assumptions are realistic in a particular situation, then pedagogical strategies are appropriate. For example, if a learner is entering into a totally new content area, there will be a strong dependency on a trainer, until enough content has been acquired to enable self-directed inquiry to begin.

A significant amount of current training practice is based to a certain degree on the philosophy of andragogy. If you wish to implement an effective andragogical approach to training, you need to be aware of the following implications for your style and approach as a trainer:

- Motivation of the learner is an intrinsic process. Your role as a trainer is to create a learning environment that captures these intrinsic drives

- Self-directed learners might need your support. Your role is to recognise when this need exists and to provide the appropriate support

- Whenever possible, you should tap into the experience of each learner. Knowles would argue that "to deny a learner's experience is to deny the learner"

- Participative learning methods are more appropriate because they use the learners' experience to the benefit of others; they also ensure that the learner's span of attention is widened and that more learning takes place

- The content of the training programme should be a contract between you and the learner. This helps to meet the learner's needs for relevance

- Where you decide to impart knowledge to learners in a passive manner, you should provide ample opportunities to reinforce the learning by varying the methods that you use.

Some Metaphors to Explain the Learning Process

We suggest that there are three metaphors of learning that may be of value to you in seeking to understand your role in the learning process. Knowledge of these metaphors should enable you to clarify the purpose of the learning activity, your role within the learning process and the role that the learner is expected to perform.

- **Jug and Mug:** The "jug and mug" approach to training is essentially a pedagogical approach. You, the trainer, are viewed as the fountain of knowledge, the subject matter expert. Your task is to transfer your knowledge and experience to the trainee, like a jug (the expert) filling the mug (the trainee). Rogers described this approach as the traditional trainer-centred approach. If you adopt this metaphor, you will be expected to develop a detailed programme of learning and follow it strictly. Your trainees will have limited involvement and are generally not expected to question the content. Your learners are required to digest information and memorise it. It is a good idea to use this approach when you engage in training activities related to explaining policies and practices of the organisation – for example, it can be used in induction training and elements of operator training, training on health and safety and quality

- **Potter and Clay:** A "potter and clay" metaphor is concerned with shaping the behaviour and attitudes of your learners. It is a metaphor that you are likely to use in many modern training activities. For example, if you are training in safe working practices, total quality management or customer service, your role as trainer is to shape the learner's behaviour and ensure that their attitudes are in line with the values espoused by the organisation. This metaphor is linked to the Jesuit maxim: "Give me a child before seven years and I will train him for life". It is possible to consider this metaphor as a form of brainwashing, in that you know what is best for the trainee and you set out to achieve it. Part of this *modus operandi* requires you to use methods that reinforce the message you seek trainees to take on board and to demonstrate behaviours consistent with the behaviour you wish trainees to demonstrate

- **Gardener and Plant:** The "gardener and plant" metaphor is learner-centred, where you take on the role of facilitator. Your task here is to assist, realise, enable and promote the natural potential for learning that the trainee possesses. You empower the learner, develop their growth potential and allow them to reach their potential. You share responsibility for learning with the learner and your task is to encourage a climate of continuous development through experiential learning. This type of learner-centred learning will lead to significant, lasting and pervasive learning because the learner is involved. In this way, the learner will learn the process of learning, as well as the content of learning.

Figure 3.2 presents a summary of the main features of each metaphor.

FIGURE 3.2: CHARACTERISTICS OF THREE TRAINING METAPHORS

Element	Jug & Mug	Potter & Clay	Gardener & Plant
Conception of the Learner	• Learner is passive and dependent • Learner is directed	• Learner is relatively passive and open to behaviour and attitude change • Learner behaviour is shaped	• Learner is active and independent • Learner is self-directing
Role of Trainer	• Trainer is a subject matter expert • Trainer dictates the content and process of learning • Trainer more likely to devise tests to monitor progress • Trainer focuses on the evaluation of learning • Trainer maintains a distant relationship with the learners • The trainer controls the learning event	• Trainer is a role model for the behaviour and attitudes desired • Trainer uses methods of learning that reinforce the behaviours and attitudes • Trainer uses intensive training processes • Trainer evaluates the learning in terms of the alignment of behaviour and attitudes to the ideal required	• Trainer is concerned with designing an effective learning process • Trainer focuses on creating a climate for learning • Trainer focuses on identifying the needs of the learner • Trainer will negotiate the outcomes of the learning • Trainer provides resources for the learner • Trainer uses a facilitative approach
Characteristics and Outcomes of the Learning Process	• Memorisation of information • Rote learning of knowledge • Structured and clearly timed learning methods • Learning is content- centred	• Learning is about change in behaviour and attitudes • Learner accepts the behaviour as appropriate • Learning agenda is set by the organisation	• Self-managed learning methods. • Focus on discovery learning • Learning is a long term, accumulative and continuous process

CHANGES IN THINKING ABOUT THE LEARNING PROCESS

It is clear from what we have discussed so far in this chapter that our thinking about the learning process has changed in the last 20 years. When we think about the learning process, we usually focus now on both the processes and outcomes of learning.

Processes

We define the process by which people learn as the way learning takes place. We can use the terms "approaches to learning" or "methods of learning" to describe the types of decisions that you will be required to make when you design training activities.

However, the term "process" has another meaning. It can refer to the internal process that a learner experiences during learning. We have a lot yet to learn about this internal process, although we do know that experience leads to learning. We will say more about this a little later.

Traditionally, we considered that learning took place in a structured manner and that people could only be instructed or taught. Our more holistic and comprehensive view of the learning process shows that people can learn in six different ways:

- Learners can be **taught**: This is a typical "jug and mug" approach and is associated with the use of a narrow range of methods under the control of the trainer. It involves rigid roles for both the trainer and the learner and usually involves the learning of knowledge and the imparting of information. This approach is potentially problematic where the trainer does not have effective training skills

- Learners can be **instructed**: This is similar to the first approach, although it is associated with psychomotor rather than cognitive skills. It generally involves a learner being shown what to do, with supporting explanations about how to do it. There is significantly less uncertainty about the learning outcomes. Again, success depends on the skills of the instructor/trainer

- Learners can **experience**: Learners can learn through new experiences and challenges. The key challenge for organisations is to provide a variety of experience that is relevant to the job and to structure the processes so that learning is predictable and effective for both parties

- Learners learn from **trial and error**, failure and success: This learning process is not subject to control or structure. The learner experiments and may make mistakes, which are regarded as learning opportunities. The learner may also have successes from which they learn

- Learning can be based on **observation** and **perception**: This is a natural and important part of the learning process. It is an incremental learning process and involves the learner making sense of the world through "seeing" things in a particular way and giving meanings to what is "seen".

Learning Outcomes

Knowledge of what learners are supposed to learn, and ensuring that it is known and understood, are vital components of the learning process. Two types of learning outcomes are relevant:

- **Vertical:** Learning how to do what the learner can already do, better, differently or to a higher standard. We can label this as vertical learning because the learner is simply increasing or building on a current level of competence

- **Horizontal:** Learning to do something new or different from a learner's existing capabilities. We describe this as horizontal learning because the learner's view of the world is being extended.

Many learning situations are a combination of both types of learning and the relative emphasis given to each one will vary depending on the objectives of the learning process.

We now have a more integrated notion of the learning process. Research points to significant changes in our thinking about learning. These changes in assumptions about the learning process are summarised in **Figure 3.3**.

UNDERSTANDING LEARNING THEORIES

We now focus on some of the main laws and theories of learning that are relevant to you, as a trainer, and which will inform your training style and activities.

Laws of Learning

Psychologists have identified certain influences, commonly referred to as the "Laws of Learning", which can either help or hinder the learning process:

- The **Law of Intensity** states that the rate of learning is more rapid when material is organised into meaningful relationships. This has important implications for the way you sequence training content

- **The Law of Contiguity** in a learning situation refers to nearness in time. For learning to take place, for example, the associated learning event must fall within a certain time limit

- **The Law of Exercise** means that the trainee is exercising what has been learnt. For example, performing a skill in conditions favourable to learning tends to improve subsequent performance. In simplistic terms, the learner is practising what has been learnt; this is termed an "exercise" by psychologists

FIGURE 3.3: HOW RESEARCH HAS CHANGED OUR ASSUMPTIONS ABOUT THE ADULT LEARNING PROCESS

Variable	The OLD Thinking	The NEW Thinking
Physical Movement	• We are normally discouraged from moving while we are learning	• Now we know that some people need to get up and move in order to learn. They are the more physical learners
Learning through Experience	• We are often given the theory first, but not allowed enough opportunity to try it out through "hands on experience"	• Most people learn well when they can act first, then theorise or reflect afterwards. Learn through experience - and that includes mistakes!
Talking out Loud	• We are usually told not to talk out loud while we are learning	• Researchers have found that talking a problem out loud and summarising what you are learning out loud in your own words is not a sign of madness! It is an important learning skill, hence the benefits of group discussion
Collaboration	• We are normally told not to "cheat" or discuss the subject with other people	• We now know that "co-operative" learning where learners pair up to teach and test each other, is a huge advantage • When you see how someone else tackles the subject, it not only gives you a new view, it is also more enjoyable!
Big Picture	• Most topics are presented bit-by-bit, thereby building up the detail towards a final conclusion	• Many people need the "big picture" first and often find a tedious build-up of information confusing • It's difficult to do a jigsaw without seeing the picture on the box. When you get a quick "feel" of the subject first, you can see how it all fits together
Level of Participation	• The old assumption was that the trainer was the instructor • His or her job was to fill the empty heads of the students with knowledge! • The trainer took the central, active role, the students the passive role - waiting to be "filled up'"	• We now know that learning with understanding cannot happen with input alone • Learning must be an entirely active experience • The trainer can only provide the conditions in which students want or need to learn

Created from Knowles *et al.* (1998).

• **The Law of Effect** states that a response leading to a satisfying result is likely to be learned, whilst a response leading to an unsatisfying result is likely to be extinguished. The idea of satisfaction goes beyond mere pleasure. For example, to be satisfying, the result must fulfil some need or motive of the individual in the learning situation. In this sense, some psychologists refer to this learning as reinforcement rather than the law of effect. It is important to note that some unsatisfactory consequences of learning can be as effective as satisfactory consequences if they are vivid, novel, or striking

- **The Law of Facilitation and Interference** occurs where one act of learning assists another act of learning – for example, if some stimulus in the new situation needs a response already associated with it in the old situation. However, it will hinder the new act of learning if some stimulus, which needed one response in the old situation, needs a different response in the new situation.

The application of laws are referred to as **conditioned** learning.

Silverman's Nine Principles of Learning Theory

Silverman (1970) formulated nine core principles of learning. He summarised them in this way:

- Learners learn from what they **actively do**
- Learning proceeds most effectively when the learner's correct **responses** are immediately reinforced – effective feedback
- The **frequency** with which a response is reinforced will determine how well the response will be learned
- **Practice** in a variety of settings will increase the range of situations in which learning can be applied
- **Motivational** conditions influence the effectiveness of rewards and play a key role in determining the performance of learned behaviour
- Meaningful learning (learning with **understanding**) is more permanent and more transferable than rote learning, or learning by some memorised formula
- People learn more effectively when they learn at their **own pace**
- There are **different kinds** of learning and these may require different training processes.

Kingsland's Approach to Learning

A further approach to learning was developed by Kingsland, based on his theory that learning is a combination of **cognitive** (thinking), **affective** (feeling) and **behavioural** (doing) components:

- **Cognitive** learning is related to aspects of behaviour, which we might call "insight". So cognitive learning is concerned with various aspects of knowing, such as perception, memory, imagination, judgement, reasoning and problem-solving. There is a close relationship between cognitive theories and "discovery" learning, whereby trainees are set tasks that involve searching for and selecting stimuli on how to proceed

- **Affective** learning concerns the involvement and response of individuals within the learning process so that they perceive the interaction as being conducive to their commitment. In organisational terms, this type of learner becomes involved in an ongoing informal exchange of feelings between all other individuals involved in the learning process, such as the learner's supervisors, as well as external customers

- In characterising human **behaviour**, it is conventional to refer to it in terms of stimulus and response. The stimuli are very often external to the individuals, but they may also be internal. For example, the external stimuli could be very definite, such as the changing of a traffic light. Subtle stimuli might only be discerned or picked up by those especially attuned to them – for example, a manager's tone of voice. An example of internal stimuli could be where the completion of one operation or a particular job or task triggers another. For example, an accountant's duties might involve a sequence of tasks, one automatically following the other.

In terms of conditioned learning, these three faculties correspond with associating new experience and data primarily with ideas, patterns and structures (cognitive); with human contexts (feeling); or with physical responses and actions (behaviour). Individuals will have all three patterns of association, but in varying degrees.

ADULT LEARNING STYLES

Kingsland's Personality Spectrum

Kingsland developed a personality spectrum that illustrates the learning styles of individuals with the overlapping of feeling, doing and thinking. He refers to these areas simply as A, B or C. In the case of a particular individual, a small amount of one of these attributes would be represented by lower case a, b, c.

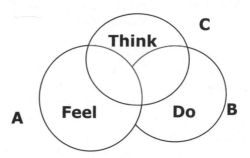

Source: Kingsland (1986).

This spectrum is further developed to produce seven combinations or different styles of learning: **reactive, proactive, holographic, adaptive, communal, functional** and **molecular**.

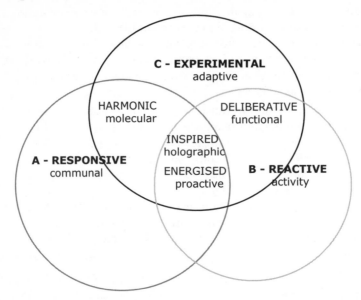

- **Reactive:** The stimulus for the reactive or activity style is typified by action-based learning, with perhaps numerous trials. Reactive learning can also take place where there is a need in an organisation for immediate action to be taken and the individual learns as the task is carried out. This style of learning can also be supported by practical instruction of some kind. The more formal development of the employees within this context must involve training activities that stimulate the learners both physically and mentally, in every respect.

- **Proactive:** The learners thrive on tough business games that are perceived as a challenge. They are highly "energised" to learn and seek challenging projects that lead to the successful identification of opportunities. In an organisation, this identification would be of opportunities for the business as a whole. The learning event must, therefore, be highly "charged" and be behaviourally and emotionally challenging, because learning for this type of learner must be highly demanding in every way.

- **Holographic:** These learners are inspired by their need for self-actualisation and may be regarded by others as visionaries. They may project a powerful image, because they strive to change or transform an organisation and to adopt an innovative approach to all work-based activities. A T&D event would have to be inspirationally demanding and relevant, otherwise it would not be regarded as necessary by this learner and, consequently, the transfer of learning would not occur

- **Adaptive**: This is learning by experiment and is different from reactive learning. Employees should be actively encouraged to learn by experiment on an on-going basis. The learner's style consists of experimentation with new ideas and methods for procedures, assessing how they work and, therefore, learning from the results of the experiments. These learners very often assist an organisation in adapting to rapid changes, as they need the changing circumstances to allow them to experiment. This, in turn, helps the organisation to implement change. A learning event must be varied and provide opportunities to experiment with an appropriate work-related problem so that the learner can present, and relate to, tangible outcomes

- **Communal**: Responsive learners within communal learning are those who become actively involved not only in their own development, but also that of other learners, managers and the organisation itself. Such learners are motivated by small group activities where the learning can be shared and where myths and stories about the organisation can be recited. The purpose of these myths is to retain the "identity" and external perceptions of the organisation's standing and value to the general public. Communal learners need to have a "sense of belonging" and they are caring and sympathetic if difficulties arise in the learning of their peers. These learners appreciate coaching and mentoring from other "like" individuals who have a caring or people-oriented approach to human resources, rather than a market-led or market-oriented approach

- **Functional**: This style of learner acquires knowledge or skill in a methodical or deliberate manner, where the learning event is pre-determined or prescribed on a formal basis. The learner is content to be trained systematically, where the learning event is regarded as a short sharp injection of training rather than being developed on an on-going basis. This shorter event provides an opportunity for the learners to acquire specialised expertise, but on a de-personalised basis. An organisation with a bureaucratic structure, functional delineation areas, changes occurring infrequently and which is formal and predictable would be suitable for this type of learner

- **Molecular:** The learner here flourishes as an interventionist who is interested in focusing on areas that will be of mutual benefit to individuals, groups, departments and to the organisation as a complete holistic entity. These learners must be provided with learning events that lead to positive outcomes, because they like to create synergy both within and outside the organisation – for example, by developing and learning from productive experiences with the organisation's direct suppliers and customers for the benefit of everyone involved. This can help to protect the organisation's survival and ensure its growth.

Kolb's Learning Style Theory

Kolb formulated a theory of learning by identifying four learning styles and arranging them into a model. His contribution to researching learning styles did not end with this model; he also analysed the different types of learners. Kolb postulated that a learner's dominant learning styles is the result of "our hereditary equipment, our particular past experiences and the demands of our present environment".

He identified four learning styles, defined as:

- The **diverger** combines concrete experience and reflective observation and can consider situations from many perspectives. This style characterises many human resource managers

- The **converger** combines abstract conceptualisation and active experimentation and favours the practical application of ideas. This style is often found amongst engineers

- The **assimilator** combines abstract conceptualisation and reflective observation and has strength in inductive reasoning and creating theoretical models. This type of learner can be found in research and planning departments

- The **accommodator** combines concrete experience and experimentation and is a risk-taker who excels in carrying out plans and experiments. This type of learner characterises many of those who work in marketing or sales departments.

An important development of Kolb's (1979) work is the Learning Style Inventory (LSI), which he describes as "a simple self-description test, based on experiential learning theory". It is designed to measure the learner's strengths and weaknesses as a learner in each of the four stages of the learning processes:

- Concrete experience
- Reflective observation
- Abstract conceptualisation
- Active experimentation.

The objective of the questionnaire is to help individuals to identify their dominant "learning style" – the way that they go about solving problems.

According to Kolb, the four stages can be combined to form two major dimensions of learning: first, a concrete/abstract dimension, and second, a reflective/active dimension. Results can be logged on a chart incorporating these two dimensions, and a dominant learning style is allocated to each quadrant, as shown in **Figure 3.4.**

FIGURE 3.4: KOLB'S LEARNING STYLES CLASSIFICATION

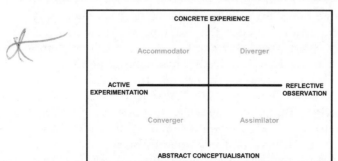

Source: Kolb (1974).

Honey and Mumford's Learning Styles

Honey and Mumford (1995) also researched learning styles, basing much of their work on Kolb's ideas. They refined Kolb's categories and used them to profile the type of trainee (identified by learning style) most likely to benefit from certain types of learning situations. Honey and Mumford propose the following learning styles:

- **Activists:** Enjoy the here and now; dominated by immediate experiences, they tend to revel in short-term crisis and fire fighting activities. They thrive on the challenge of experiences but are relatively bored with implementation or longer-term consolidation. Activists are the life and soul of the party

- **Reflectors:** Like to stand back and ponder on experiences and observe them from different perspectives. They collect data and analyse situations before coming to any conclusions. They like to consider all possible angles and implications before making a move, so they tend to be cautious. Reflectors enjoy observing other people in action and often take a back seat

- **Theorists:** Are keen on basic assumptions, principles, theories, models and systems thinking. They prize rationality and logic ability, and tend to be detached and analytical and are unhappy with subjective or ambiguous experiences. Theorists like to arrange disparate facts into coherent theories, and tidy and fit them into rational schemes

- **Pragmatists:** They positively search out new ideas and take the opportunity to experiment with applications. They are the people who return from courses brimming with new ideas that they want to try out. Pragmatists respond to problems and opportunities "as a challenge" (activists probably would not recognise them as problems and opportunities).

The learner's preferred style has important implications for the kind of learning methods and approaches that you adopt. This is particularly important because for example we know that activists and reflectors learn best in one-to-one instructional situations whereas pragmatists learn best from coaching programmes.

Activists learn more easily when they can get involved immediately in short "here and now" practical activities and when there is a variety of things to cope with; they are not put off by being "thrown in at the deep end". Activists do not learn well when they are required simply to observe and not to be involved or when they are required to listen to theoretical explanations. Highly-structured massed practice sessions, such as where an activity is practised over and over again, would also not be liked by the activist.

On the other hand, **reflectors** learn best when they are allowed to watch, observe or listen and then think over or review what has taken place. They certainly need to "look before they leap" and to be given plenty of time for preparation. Being "thrown" into situations without warning would lead to an adverse reaction from reflectors.

In coaching situations, pragmatists need to work with activities or techniques that have an obvious practical "pay off"; they must concentrate on practical job-related issues. For the pragmatist, the content of the coaching session must not be theoretical but clearly related to their own reality.

An individual's learning style preference can be assessed in a reasonably objective way by means of a questionnaire, preferably administered prior to the beginning of any training interaction coaching sessions. The benefits of this data for you as a trainer are that:

- It will help you to design training events that fit in with the predominant style of the trainees
- If the results of the questionnaire are "fed back" to learners, it can help them to appreciate the difficulties they might experience with particular training methods that, out of necessity, may have to be used during the training
- It enables you to identify learners who may need special attention because their learning style contrasts significantly with the methods that you propose to use
- It allows you to put into perspective the learners' observations and comments about the training content and approach.

Left-Brain/Right-Brain – Brain Dominance Theory

A fourth perspective on learning styles comes from left-brain/right-brain theory or Brain Dominance Theory, which argues that right-brained and left-brained people think and acquire information in different ways.

Other versions of the theory split the brain into four quadrants:

- The upper quadrant A typifies cerebral processing
- The lower left B quadrant is structured and organised
- The lower right C quadrant is emotional, feeling and concerned with interpersonal orientation
- The upper right D quadrant is concerned with imaginative qualities.

FIGURE 3.5: LEFT BRAIN / RIGHT BRAIN THINKING

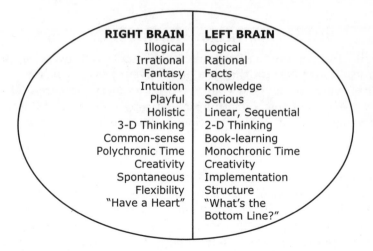

RIGHT BRAIN	LEFT BRAIN
Illogical	Logical
Irrational	Rational
Fantasy	Facts
Intuition	Knowledge
Playful	Serious
Holistic	Linear, Sequential
3-D Thinking	2-D Thinking
Common-sense	Book-learning
Polychronic Time	Monochronic Time
Creativity	Creativity
Spontaneous	Implementation
Flexibility	Structure
"Have a Heart"	"What's the Bottom Line?"

We know from research that how a person learns is highly dependent on the way they receive and apply information. People perceive and learn through different systems tied to their basic senses and learning can be described as a "filtration" system, directly related to a person's senses. Due to this, communication and learning are linked closely together. The average person has one primary system as their method of learning but can use a blend of systems.

This theory identifies three categories of learning styles:

- **Visual:** People who are "visual", learn best by seeing or watching how something is done. The written word is their favourite communication process. Examples of how these type of people learn best are through graphics, process flows, checklists, video and demonstration. Example: "I see what you mean"

- **Auditory:** People who are "auditory" learners prefer to hear how something is done. Trainers need to talk them through skills, discuss them and use verbal instructions. Examples of what works best for learners with this communication style are lectures, being coached verbally through a process, meetings and audiotapes. Example: "I hear what you mean"

- **Kinaesthetic:** This style of learning describes people who communicate primarily with their senses of touch and emotions. They learn by doing things in a "hands on" environment, by either physically touching something, "getting into it" or "getting a feel for it". Kinaesthetic learners deal with their feelings about a subject in order to learn. When they feel comfortable with a subject, they retain the information better. Example: "I think I have a feel for that now".

CHARACTERISTICS OF THE ADULT LEARNER

As well as understanding learning styles, when you design training activities, it is important that you have in your possession some other pieces of information about your potential learners. Research tells us that you should know something about four individual differences: age, intelligence and ability, emotional state and learning maturity.

Age

There are a number of important differences between young and adult learners. Generally speaking, adult learners learn more slowly and may have more difficulty "grasping" new material than younger learners. Furthermore, if the adult makes a mistake early in training, then the error is likely to persist and correcting it becomes more difficult. You can employ a number of strategies to manage group training or 1:1 training sessions to compensate for some of the difficulties that adult learners experience. You should:

- Avoid, where possible, instruction that relies on the need for memorising large amounts of information. This is a very ineffective strategy to use

- Ensure that the learner has had a chance to demonstrate that one task has been mastered before moving on to the next

- Make sure that errors are corrected as soon as possible because they tend to persist with the adult learner; ideally, you should try to ensure that errors do not occur at all

- Where possible, you should try to instruct the task in meaningful "whole" parts rather than smaller stages that do not seem connected to each other

- Provide variety by changing or modifying your methods of instruction; repetition of the same method can tire adult learners, who like variety

- Longer uninterrupted learning periods are appropriate for adult learners, whereas they are not as effective with younger learners. On the other hand, interrupted or short sessions may cause forgetfulness in the adult learner

- Let the adult learner proceed at his/her own pace and let them compete against themselves rather than against targets achieved by others in the training session

- The "discovery" method can be useful, provided that the tasks are carefully graded into tasks of different levels of difficulty

- With complex tasks, get the adult learner to learn in stages that gradually increase in complexity or difficulty

- Avoid formal time limits for the completion of different phases of the task and do not use formal tests of progress to assess achievement. This is counter-productive

- If a task has to be learned in parts because of its complexity or breadth, use the cumulative parts method – a, a+b, a+b+c, etc.

Levels of Intelligence and Ability

You should not assume that there is a standard or "clone-like" adult learner. Research tells us that there will be greater disparity in intelligence and intellectual ability amongst adult learners than younger learners. Therefore, some of the suggestions we make may need to be modified. You should customise your approach to suit the profile of your learning group.

The learning principles and tactics that you employ should be modified, depending on the ability or intelligence level of the learner. Higher-ability learners are more likely to be able to work from general principles to concrete situations and, depending on the complexity of the task, to cope with learning a task as a whole, rather than breaking it into parts. It may be more appropriate to teach the principle and theoretical aspects to learners with more academic experience before demonstrating and practising. In the case of learners with less academic experience, it may be better to tackle the practical aspects first, before dealing with the theory.

For learners who have less effective learning abilities:

- Use small learning steps and employ the cumulative part method that we explain later

- Proceed from concrete examples to general principles;
- Avoid unstructured learning situations, because lower ability learners are more easily distracted by irrelevant information
- Keep explanations brief, because the learner may have difficulty understanding long, expansive instruction
- Employ short learning sessions that will prevent possible boredom and discouragement
- Make sure that there are plenty of opportunities for practice.

The modern view on intelligence is that learners have multiple intelligences. Howard Gardner has carried out extensive research on the concept of intelligence and has exploded the theory that we are born with an intelligence that is immutable and can be definitively measured. Gardner defined intelligence as "an ability to solve a problem, or make a product that is valuable in at least one culture or community". He went on to say that "an IQ test won't show you whether you can cook a dinner, or conduct a meeting". Gardner identified a number of different intelligences:

- **Bodily-Kinaesthetic:** Such people enjoy touching, feeling and tapping (surgeons)
- **Interpersonal:** Good personal knowledge of one's strengths and weaknesses, "without good self-knowledge, people make mistakes in their personal lives" (Gardner)
- **Intrapersonal:** People with high levels of intrapersonal intelligence are good at understanding other people and what motivates them. Nowadays, employers prize this intelligence. People who have high levels of this intelligence also have self-knowledge and understand their own feelings, strengths and weaknesses
- **Logical-Mathematical:** Associated with deductive reasoning, patterns, abstract symbols and geometric shapes (statisticians)
- **Musical-Rhythmic:** Having a musical ear being able to carry a tune and having a sense of rhythm (musicians)
- **Naturalist:** Enjoys the outdoors and feels stifled by confined places. They enjoy learning from nature and have a natural affinity with animals and plants (gardeners, botanists, zoologists).
- **Verbal-Linguistic:** High verbal communication intelligence in both spoken and written language (teachers and broadcasters)
- **Visual-Spatial:** Involves the ability to think in pictures (artists, architects or navigators, hairdressers)

You should be aware of the varied potential and intelligence of your learning group. You can use this information to shape the learning process. **Figure 3.6** presents the eight intelligences and explains what the learner and trainer can do in the case of each one.

Physical Readiness

The learner's physical readiness is an important consideration, especially for certain types of training situations. The training situation may demand certain requirements such as physical fitness, visual acuity, hearing, etc.

Emotional State of Learner

A learner's emotional state may influence how and what is learned. Anxiety, fear or failure and lack of confidence are the sorts of feelings experienced by some learners that can negatively impact motivation and willingness to learn.

You can use a number of strategies to deal with the emotional characteristics of the learner:

- Allow the learner to control the pace of the session. Nudge them forward in a gentle manner – for example, "Do you feel confident now to move on to the next step?"
- Structure the session tightly and avoid the discovery method
- Set more easily attainable goals and do not make comparisons between the learner and other learners
- Give plenty of guidance and emotional support and continuous or frequent feedback on progress. This will bolster the learner's motivation and self-confidence
- Reassure the learner when there are periods of little or no progress, which are fairly natural in learning situations
- Divide up the instruction into short, easily managed stages
- Ensure that the learner is not left to practise for long periods on their own because, if they get into difficulty, they will need to be given assistance quite promptly.

FIGURE 3.6: MULTIPLE INTELLIGENCES & LEARNING

Intelligence	What is it?	Learners Like To	Trainers Can
Intrapersonal	• Sensitive to one's own feelings and moods • Knows own strength and weaknesses • Uses self-knowledge to guide decision making and setting goals	• Control own feelings and moods • Pursue personal interests and set individual agendas • Learn through observing and listening • Use metacognitive skills	• Allow students to work at own pace • Assign individual, self-directed projects • Help students set goals • Provide opportunities for students to get feedback from one another • Involve the students in journal writing and other forms of reflection
Interpersonal	• Sensitive to the feelings and moods of others • Understands and interacts effectively with others.	• Enjoy many friends • Lead, share, mediate • Build consensus and empathise with others • Work as effective team members	• Use co-operative learning • Assign group projects • Give students opportunities for peer teaching • Brainstorm solutions to problems • Create situations in which students are given feedback from others
Bodily – Kinaesthetic	• Uses one's body to communicate and solve problems • Is adept with objects and activities involving fine or gross motor skills	• Play sports and be physically active • Use body language • Do crafts and mechanical projects • Dance, act, or mime	• Provide tactile and movement activities • Offer role playing and acting opportunities • Involve the students with physical activity • Allow the students to move while working • Use sewing, model making, and other activities that use fine motor skills
Verbal – Linguistic	• Thinks in words • Uses language and words in many different forms to express complex meanings	• Tell jokes, riddles or puns • Read, write or tell stories • Use an expanded vocabulary • Play word games • Create poems and stories using the sounds and imagery of words	• Create reading and writing projects • Help students prepare speeches • Interest students in debates • Make word games/searches, crosswords, puzzles • Encourage the use of puns, palindromes, and outrageous words

Intelligence	What is it?	Learners Like To	Trainers Can
Logical – Mathematical	• Approaches problems logically • Understands number and abstract patterns • Recognises and solves problems using reasoning skills	• Work with numbers, figure things out and analyse situations • Know how things work; Ask questions • Exhibit precision in problem-solving • Work in situations in which there are clear black-and-white solutions	• Construct Venn diagrams • Use games of strategy • Have students demonstrate understanding using concrete objects • Record information on graphs • Establish time lines and draw maps
Musical – Rhythmic	• Sensitive to sounds in the environment, including melody and tone • Aware of patterns in rhythm, pitch and timbre	• Listen to and play music • Match feelings to music and rhythms • Sing, hum and move to music • Remember and work with various musical forms • Create and replicate tunes	• Rewrite song lyrics to teach a concept • Encourage students to add music to plays • Create musical mnemonics • Teach history through music of the period • Use music and folk dancing from other countries
Naturalist	• Sensitive to the natural world • Sees connection and patterns within the plant and animal kingdoms	• Spend time outdoors • Observe plants, collect rocks, and catch animals • Listen to the sounds created in the natural world • Notice relationships in nature • Categorise and classify flora and fauna	• Use the outdoors as a classroom • In the classroom, have plants and animals for which students are responsible • Conduct hands-on science experiments • Create a nature area on the playground
Visual – Spatial	• Perceives the visual world accurately • Creates mental images • Thinks three-dimensionally • Is aware of relationship between objects in space	• Doodle, paint, draw or create three-dimensional representations • Look at maps • Work puzzles or complete mazes • Take things apart and put them back together	• Draw maps and mazes • Lead visualisation activities • Provide opportunities to show understanding through drawing or painting • Have students design clothing, buildings, play areas, and scenery

Adapted from Gardner (1999).

The attitudes and enthusiasm of the trainer are important influences on how well the learner learns a particular skill. However, trainers must guard against being over-exuberant. "Hyping up", or stimulating high motivation before and during training, may create anxiety and apprehension in some learners. This is particularly the case if the trainer, at the same time, minimises and is unrealistic about the difficulties of learning complex tasks. These emotions may be felt by the learners because of doubts and fears aroused by the memory of previous failures in their earlier experiences of educational or occupational learning environments. Your sensitivity, style and approach throughout the training event, but especially in the early stages, can help in eliminating, or at least lessening, the emotional blockages and barriers that might interfere with subsequent learning.

Learners who are over-confident or arrogant may need to be managed in a way that challenges and utilises their capabilities –f or example, give them an opportunity to lead the session or give a presentation on their views to the group, followed by a Q&A session.

Learner Maturity

Another individual difference that you should take into account is the "maturity of the learner". Maturity in a training context is not referring to the learner's chronological age, but rather the learner's:

- Capacity to set high, but attainable, learning goals
- Willingness and ability to take responsibility for learning
- Education and previous experiences.

If you have a relatively immature group of learners, you should try to ensure that they "walk before they run". If you push learners too fast, it is likely to have a negative impact on learning time and their motivation. With such learners, you may need to be persuasive, be in control and be more direct. As the learner matures, you can then become less structured in your approach and concentrate on guiding, advising and supporting. A mature learner will respond more effectively to a participative, challenging and collaborative learning situation.

MISCONCEPTIONS ABOUT ADULT LEARNING

Many misconceptions exist about learning and the adult learning process, in particular the following.

Learners over a Certain Age Cannot Learn

This is a common misconception. There is little evidence to support such a myth; anyone at any age can learn. It may, however, take longer for an older learner to learn, because their rate of learning and retention may become slower with age. But, if an individual wants to learn, then he/she can.

It is the learner's personal approach to life that influences learning. The major positive factor that adults bring to learning is their motivation: they already have an idea of the relevance of what they learn. This is something younger learners sometimes lack. Adults have the capacity to learn a vast number of new skills and apply them effectively to a range of situations. Information may be absorbed at a slower rate and is therefore less likely to evaporate.

Technophobia

Many organisations that have experienced staff shortages have recruited more mature employees. This more mature employee may not have been exposed to new technology prior to this experience and can suffer from a fear or a block to using it. This creates problems for trainers whose task may be to run induction training or teach basic technological skills. Training strategies can be employed effectively to overcome technophobia. The core issues are creating a safe environment where learners can discuss their lack of confidence. Reassurance from the trainer is vital.

The Person who Learns Fast is Best Suited to the Job

In some ways, this statement could be accurate, in so far as some learners experience a high level of achievement if they are continually learning new things, rather than coping with routine work, which is relatively easy to learn.

It is important to get the balance between the different aspects of a job, which the learner can master with time, and the more mundane work, which is done routinely. If there is an imbalance, the person who learns quickly and is seeking new or more difficult tasks will become demotivated because their interest in the learning process is not sustained. This is one of the essential reasons why you should know the ability level of your learners.

It is important to recognise that learners will not be motivated, if they are considered to be less effective learners and labelled as such. Learners at all levels must be encouraged. Less effective learners are more suited to routine tasks of a less complex nature. It should be noted too that there are learners who learn some of the more routine tasks very fast, but soon become very bored if there is nothing new to learn. A trainer needs to use some tricks here – they can get the fast learner to work with the other learners as a coach or guide, or give the fast learner more complicated problems to work on and to present their findings to the group.

There is a Strong Correlation between Academic Success and Performance on the Job

It is not correct that only high academic achievers will succeed. On the contrary, an individual may have a long list of academic qualifications but possess very little business acumen or practical intelligence. It is not possible to specify that a degree, in whatever subject, will ensure that the person becomes an entrepreneur. However, possession of a degree does suggest that a person will have a level of analytical skill that will help in a position when a situation needs to be analysed, the problem identified and problem-solving skills applied, as most degrees include this essential element.

It is necessary, however, to consider the late developer – not only those in the early to late teens, but also the older developer, those who did not recognise their own abilities until quite late in their lives. There are also those learners who did not have the opportunity, for a whole host of reasons, to study for a formal qualification. This type of learner can be very successful in the workplace

People Learn all they Need to Know on the Job

This is generally not a correct statement. It is true that employees do learn on the job; indeed, they are continually learning on the job every day – for example, by exploring and experimenting how a task can be done more efficiently or more effectively to save time, energy or cost. Through experimenting, the learner can learn to do the job in many different ways.

Learning is a continual process, but it would be most undesirable for an employee to attempt to perform a job on a production line for example, without first acquiring the basic knowledge and skills needed. A good example of this misconception relates to management and supervisory skills. The fundamental skills of management are often overlooked or regarded as capable of being learnt on-the-job. The preferred approach is that potential supervisors or managers should learn the essential skills and acquire the knowledge needed for these positions, through structured learning activities.

People Learn Nothing from Mistakes

Some learners do not learn from their mistakes, as they hold the misguided attitudes that "... oh well, everyone makes mistakes" and that mistakes are best forgotten. This negative reaction will not lead to performance standards being achieved and is sometimes indicative of learners who perceive themselves to be inferior or incapable in some way. This attitude may be a result of a previous mistake that was poorly handled by a trainer or manager. A trainer or manager should be supportive and encourage an employee by coaching or counselling where appropriate. Some learners make mistakes merely because they lack self-confidence, rather than because of any lack of ability. Encouragement is imperative, if employees are to learn from the mistakes they make. A mistake needs to be regarded positively as a learning opportunity.

It is natural that employees will make mistakes from time to time, but those employees who view it as an opportunity for learning and self-development will become valuable employees. Employees should be encouraged to communicate their experiences of mistakes, as others may make the same mistakes. This is particularly important where there is a health and safety aspect that requires corrective action.

People Learn All They Need to Know at the Beginning of their Careers

Internal and external environments are constantly changing; many organisations now view the culture of their organisation as a "change culture". As a result, many employees have at least one career change. The reasons are varied, but one is that many individuals perceive a change as a career development strategy. Thus it is not true that one learns everything one needs to know at the beginning of a career.

Telling and Exhortation by an Instructor is the same as Learning by Listening

This is false because fatigue leads to lack of interest and boredom, irrespective of the topic. However, there are a few exceptions, such as an outdoor activity to develop individuals in decision-making and personal effectiveness, including team-building. The activity itself increases and retains the level of interest of the learner. The feedback discussions are generally lively and highly participative, indicating the level of response to the activities, and reinforcing what has been learnt.

Effective instruction consists of question and answer sessions, demonstrations that are seen clearly, and accompanying supporting material. Learners should be constantly stimulated to retain their interest. This is not an exclusive list, but emphasises the importance of varied learning methods to heighten retention by learners.

Consideration of the length of periods of instruction is fundamental to the success of a learning event. Appropriate breaks of relevant durations are essential and should be designed into the programme schedule. It is a good idea to build in shorter breaks of approximately five minutes every hour. Adults are not used to sitting in one place for long periods.

Psychologists consider that it is impossible for learners to retain everything they are taught, and generally agree that retention is approximately 25% of what is learnt; the reinforcement of learning is therefore extremely important.

UNDERSTANDING CONDITIONS OF LEARNING

We made a brief reference to the laws of learning earlier in this chapter; here, we go into more detail. We will address the practical implications of these well-established principles when we consider training design and delivery.

Sequencing the Training Material

Training content should follow some logical order that makes sense to the learner. If this is achieved, it will make learning, as well as subsequent recall and application, much easier.

There are a number of "laws" that will help you to arrange material in the best order:

- **Proceed from the easy or simple to the difficult or complex:**
  This represents a fundamental principle. In some tasks, learners must acquire basic knowledge or skill before progressing to more complex material or situations. Moving to the latter too quickly, before the fundamentals are in place, will result in learning gaps

- **Proceed from what the learner knows to new or unknown material:** The trainer/instructor must try to build on what the learner already knows or can already do. Forging a link between the known and the unknown will usually make new learning much easier, not just because learners may feel less anxious handling or dealing with new material, but because they start from a pre-established base of knowledge

- **Proceed from the practical or concrete to the more abstract and theoretical:** Learners will eventually learn general principles or rules if, initially, those principles or rules have been demonstrated or illustrated by way of concrete example. Asking them to acquire abstract principles in isolation, without first clearly showing the specific and relevant situations to which the principles apply, will hinder the build-up of their knowledge and understanding.

Whole *versus* Part Learning

Another important consideration is whether or not to cover what has to be learned in one complete session, or whether to break it up into smaller sessions. For instance, if the skill to be learned is made up of several elements, should it be learned all at once or should the learner be taught the elements separately, before combining them into the whole? The answer to this question seems to be "it depends".

The "whole" method is more advantageous than the "part" method when:

- The learner is intelligent (making a very able person learn a series of easy parts may have an adverse effect on motivation)
- The learning of, and practice on, the task or skill is spread out over time rather than massed into a short time frame
- The task or skill is not particularly complex and the elements that make it up seem to "fit" together naturally.

Setting Objectives and Sub-Objectives

In order to stimulate and sustain a learner's motivation, you should outline the learning objectives to be achieved at the beginning of the programme. This will give the learner a clear idea of what has to be accomplished as a result of the one-to-one training or coaching experience. Furthermore, it will allow learners to judge their own performance against the objectives set.

If objectives are to be valuable in a learning context, the following conditions must be met:

- Objectives must be within the learner's ability to achieve them
- Feedback on how well the objective is being met must be given to the learner at appropriate intervals
- Learners are given specific challenging objectives rather than modest objectives or no objectives at all, or simply encouraged to "do your best".

Apart from telling the learner about the overall learning objectives at the outset, you can influence the learner's ongoing attitudes and motivation towards the learning programme by setting or agreeing a series of shorter term or interim objectives with him/her. Having progressive learning objectives will allow you to monitor the learner's achievement more closely and also, to a certain extent, to alert the organisation to workplace activities required to reinforce the learning following the training.

This link is vital to consolidate learning. Training is not a stand-alone activity. Learning can evaporate, if the trainee is not given the opportunity to use the skills in the workplace – for example, a presentation skills course needs to build in on-the-job opportunities to complete at least four presentations in the workplace soon after the course is completed. Coaches need to be identified to give structured feedback to the trainee so that they can develop their skills to a high level on-the-job.

Providing a Meaningful Context for Learning

Apart from stimulating the learner's motivation by setting learning objectives, you need to structure the learning environment in a way that maintains alertness throughout the training sessions. Sessions that are run as on-the-job training sessions are already placed in the context of the work environment and little can be done to make the learning more stimulating. However, some aspects of training may have to be taught as separate items and may not be directly related to what has gone before or what follows. Giving an overview of the task and showing its relationship to other tasks and activities provides a more meaningful context in which the learning can take place. Another way in which a meaningful context can be provided is by simulating an environment that resembles, as closely as possible, the real working conditions – for example, using models of the workplace.

Directing Attention

There will be occasions when you have to draw the learner's attention to particular elements of the material to be learned. These features may be associated with any of the six senses: Vision, Hearing, Touch, Smell, Taste, and the Proprioceptive sense (this sense relates to the position and movement of the body – for example, balance).

Guidance, Prompting and Cueing

These terms are very similar in that they are all used to direct learners at times when they are physically involved in doing something and you feel that there is a need to provide some help. Although they are explained separately for reasons of clarity, their function is the same.

Guidance

Guidance can be given in two ways:

- It can be a form of demonstration in which you show the learner the "right way to do something", such as how to hold a tool properly before they actually use it.
- It can be used when mistakes can occur and the learner is alerted to the need to take care or to work more slowly.

It is particularly important to provide guidance in the early phase of the learning of complex tasks. Errors that are made at this time are likely to be repeated and subsequently, learning resources will have to be devoted to unlearning those early mistakes. It is also important to prevent errors occurring in training where serious safety problems or damage to equipment might result.

However, there are circumstances in which allowing errors to be committed might be more beneficial to learning, than making correct responses. This needs to be monitored carefully.

You will need to consider the amount of guidance you provide. Observing a learner's reaction to guidance will give some indication of how much is welcomed and needed and how far the trainer can go before there is a danger of boredom and demotivation. The learner may perceive that he/she does not have sufficient independence and control over the learning situation, if the trainer is too controlling and thus he/she may not learn as effectively as possible.

Prompting
Prompting as a skill is most applicable to learning verbal material and not to procedural tasks. After some initial learning of information, the learner may be required to recall it and is helped accomplish this task by being "prompted" by the trainer. Skilful questioning of the learner may also act as a form of prompting, leading to the correct response or action. As with guidance, prompting appears to be particularly effective in the initial phase of the learning process. We will say more about it in **Chapter Eight**.

Cues
You can speed up the learning process by providing or highlighting easily identifiable and easily remembered cues that trigger the correct response or sequence of actions. For example, in some forms of social skills training such as selling, you can direct the learner's attention towards cues such as a customer's facial or oral expressions, tone of voice, etc. This will help the learner to interpret particular social situations and helps them to behave appropriately.

Practice and Rehearsal

It is the learner who learns. Therefore it is necessary to ensure the learner's participation and active involvement if learning is to be effective. Practice and rehearsal are two of the most important activities that learners must engage in, under your influence and direction, in order to acquire new knowledge and skills.

There are two initial conditions that you should be aware of, if "practice is going to make perfect":

• The learner must be motivated to improve performance
• You must provide feedback on an on-going basis, both during and at the end of the practice session.

Similarly, for **rehearsal** to be an effective method of ensuring that verbal or procedural material is remembered, you must involve the learner in active retrieval and recall of the material, during the training or coaching session. This form of activity is important because:

- It requires active participation by the learner, which helps to maintain attention and interest
- Active recall gives the learner an opportunity to practise the material
- Giving constructive feedback about accuracy will indicate to the learner what he/she does or does not know and should also help them to direct and allocate subsequent effort and time to perfecting the knowledge/skill.

Distribution of Practice

You will need to consider whether practice should be completed all at once (massed) or spread over several sessions (distributed). It is difficult to provide conclusive guidelines, although the following should be considered:

- **Distributed Practice:** In learning manual skills, distributed practice is usually more effective than massed practice, both in terms of the phases of learning and of retention of learning
- **Series of Sessions:** When the material to be learned does not make immediate sense to learners, or cannot be associated with what they already know or are skilled in, it will be more difficult to learn in a single session as opposed to a series of sessions
- **Timing is Crucial:** The ideal time interval between practice sessions and the timing of the session itself will depend on the nature of the task to be learned and on the learner's personality, previous experience, etc. If the interval is too long, then forgetfulness may become a problem and a relearning or a "warm-up" period may be necessary. On the other hand, if the interval is too short, then learners may become bored or suffer from mental or physical fatigue.

Feedback, Knowledge of Results and Reinforcement

Learners need to know how well they are doing at all stages in the learning process. This will ensure that they learn effectively and improve performance. Feedback may focus on how well a learner performs a particular task. Alternatively, you can direct the learner to look out for cues and information that allows the learner themselves to judge how effectively the learning is progressing.

You should be concerned with two important features of feedback:

- How much to give
- How specific to make it.

We know from research that too much specific feedback in the early stages may not necessarily lead to improvements in performance. If you overload the learner with too much detailed information about performance, it may only serve to confuse and may also have a depressing effect on their motivation.

The general recommendation on feedback seems to be to give the learner a small amount early on, increase the amount and specific detail as the learner improves, withdraw it gradually as the skills to be learned become more established, and finally exclude it altogether.

When giving feedback, you should not ignore your learner's emotional needs. Some form of emotional reward – for example, saying "well done" – should follow effective performance of parts, or the whole, of the task. However, the learner should not become overly dependent on your emotional support as their confidence and performance may be adversely affected when support is withdrawn. On the other hand, praise or reassurance is necessary and important when progress is slow or non-existent and the learner needs to be motivated to achieve a higher level of performance.

Retention and Forgetfulness

Forgetting what was originally learned is a common enough experience. It is important to ensure that skills and knowledge learned in training situations are retained and transferred to the work context. This may be difficult to achieve if there is little or no opportunity to use the knowledge and skills immediately or on a relatively frequent basis in the work context. You can employ a number of strategies in the training context that can facilitate retention and prevent or minimise forgetfulness:

- Introduce a job aid – any form of printed document containing verbal or pictorial material kept in the place of work that can be used as a memory-jogger or as a procedural guide for a difficult, complex or infrequently performed tasks
- Use distributed, rather than massed, practice sessions
- Train to produce over-learning in the learner – train to a level of performance above that strictly needed to achieve the training objectives
- Introduce further supplementary practice sessions after the learner has achieved the required level of mastery
- Encourage the learners to engage in mental practice or rehearsal when they return to their work locations
- Make the training as meaningful as possible by linking it with the learners' previous knowledge and experience and by organising and sequencing it to make initial learning easier

- Ensure that the way the training and coaching sessions are run motivates the learners stimulates their interest and is not an experience they would rather forget
- Ensure that the learner is an active participant in the session rather than merely a passive recipient of the material.

Retention of learning is facilitated when the learner is allowed to watch and perform a task in addition to being told how to perform it. Incorporating hands-on training into a lesson plan significantly improves learners' learning retention.

Figure 3.7 shows retention percentages after 60 days for three types of training.

FIGURE 3.7: LEARNING RETENTION LEVELS FOR DIFFERENT INSTRUCTIONAL APPROACHES

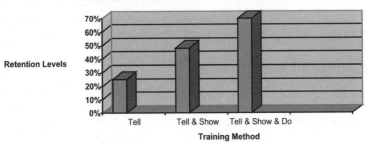

Criticism and Punishment in Training

We know from research that constructive criticism has both advantages and disadvantages in a learning context. You should be concerned that criticism does not destroy employees' confidence or self-esteem. The way in which you communicate criticism is important.

If learners have been previously continuously criticised in the workplace, it may take a long time, extreme patience and understanding to re-establish the self-value of those individuals before any forward steps can be assumed or indeed measured in any way. The re-building of a learner's self-esteem is a lengthy process and as a trainer you need to be patient.

We believe that punishment and fear of any kind are not conducive to the learning process. Research indicates that these activities inhibit individualism, stifle creativity, induce a sense of failure and produce neuroses, all of which deprive learners of their dignity.

FIGURE 3.8: PRINCIPLES AND CONDITIONS OF LEARNING

	Principles
1:	Learning is an experience that occurs inside the learner and is activated by the learner. No one directly teaches anyone anything of significance.
2:	Learning is the discovery of the personal meaning and relevance of ideas.
3:	Learning (behavioural change) is a consequence of experience.
4:	Learning is a co-operative and collaborative process.
5:	Learning is an evolutionary process; it evolves over time.
6:	Learning is sometimes a painful process.
7:	One of the richest resources for learning is the learner him/herself.
8:	The process of learning is emotional as well as intellectual.
9:	The processes of problem-solving and learning are highly unique and individual.
	Conditions
1:	Learning is facilitated in an atmosphere that encourages learners to be active.
2:	Learning is facilitated in an atmosphere that promotes and facilitates the individual's discovery of the personal meaning of ideas.
3:	Learning is facilitated in an atmosphere that emphasises the uniquely personal and subjective nature of learning.
4:	Learning is facilitated in an atmosphere in which difference is good and desirable.
5:	Learning is facilitated in an atmosphere that consistently recognises learners' right to make mistakes.
6:	Learning is facilitated in an atmosphere that tolerates ambiguity.
7:	Learning is facilitated in an atmosphere that encourages openness of self rather than concealment of self.
8:	Learning is facilitated in an atmosphere that encourages openness to others' ideas.
9:	Learning is facilitated in an atmosphere in which learners are encouraged to trust in themselves as well as in external sources.
10:	Learning is facilitated in an atmosphere in which learners feel they are respected by their peers and the trainer / instructor / facilitator.
11:	Learning is facilitated in an atmosphere in which learners feel they are accepted.
12:	Learning is facilitated in an atmosphere that permits constructive confrontation.

Devised from Gagné and Medsker (1996) and Smith and Ragan (1993).

The Learning Environment

There is a strong body of research evidence indicating that effective learning will be transferred to the workplace, if it takes place in an environment that is conducive to learning. The comfort and relaxation of learners can help learning. The external environment may also be significant. If, for example, day release or evening classes have to take place several miles away from a trainee's work or home, this is not likely to enhance the motivation to learn.

Some of the issues that you need to consider in this respect are:

- Every learner has worth as a person. An individual is entitled to maintain his self-respect and dignity. The learner's feelings are important and should be respected. Criticising learner behaviour is differentiated from rejecting him/her as a person

- Human beings have a capacity to learn and grow. Generally, people do what they have learned to do and usually follow the habits that have guided them in the past. Thus, they tend to be consistent in their actions. However, they also change their attitudes and beliefs and develop new ways of doing things as a result of new emotional-intellectual experiences

- The most effective type of learning – that which is most likely to influence attitudes and behaviour – comes through having emotionally-involving experiences and reflecting upon them. Individuals learn as they are stimulated and challenged to learn. They develop ways of behaving as they get responses (feedback) from other persons about, or to, their behaviour

- A permissive atmosphere – a group climate conducive to free discussion and experimentation with different ways of behaving – is a necessary condition for learning. Only when an individual feels safe enough to behave normally is it possible to detect the behaviours that are unproductive – those that are not effective with other persons. In a non-judgemental atmosphere, a trainee is more likely to be receptive to feedback from others and willing to try different ways of expressing her/himself

- The training role carries responsibility for helping the learner learn from their experiences. This involves facilitating the development of conditions within the group that will be conducive to learning and guiding the learning experience. It implies that the trainer, as a person, influences events within the group and that his/her behaviour is also a legitimate subject for examination. In fact, the trainer's willingness to encourage scrutiny of their own role behaviour is a crucial factor in furthering the growth of a climate that permits examination of the role behaviour of members of the group

- The most productive way to work is to share the diagnosis of problems and, collaboratively, to plan and evaluate activities. This approach leads to greater emotional involvement on the part of participants. It results in greater member commitment to decisions

- The study of group process – how work is done and the characteristics of the interaction among persons as they work – helps to improve group efficiency and productivity. The crucial factors that interfere with co-operative effort more often lie in the manner in which people work together than in the mastery of technical skills. Problems of involvement, co-operative effort, relationships between individuals, and of relations between individuals and the group are all of universal nature. The best place to study such problems is in the immediate present. Hence, examination of what is going on in the group, the here-and-now, provides the richest material for learning. Every member can participate meaningfully to the examination because they have witnessed and experienced the data being discussed.

Intellectual Readiness

Learners bring something with them to any new learning situation. This will include previous experience, a level of existing knowledge, specific skills, special aptitudes, general potential and capacity of learning, etc. This will have an influence on how ready learners are to undertake the training that is being planned for them.

In some cases, it may be necessary to introduce basic or remedial training before proper training can begin. In other cases, it may be possible to speed up the training, or even omit some of it, if learners have already mastered some of the skills or have sufficient knowledge.

Motivational Readiness

One of the strongest findings from the research is that learning is negatively affected if the learner has no desire or is not motivated to learn. Most positively, it can be a rewarding experience for both the learner and the trainer when the level of motivation to learn is high.

There are a number of factors that potentially might influence trainee's motivation. These include meeting their needs, rewards and incentives, the perceptions, expectations and attitudes that they hold.

There are four categories of needs that can be met in a training situation:

- **Safety Needs:** These needs relate to the security that can be achieved through training. This is when the learners know that they can undertake potentially dangerous tasks safely and without danger to themselves

- **Emotional Needs:** These needs are satisfied when trainees are able to see that learning new skills and acquiring additional knowledge will affect their performance by giving them more control and independence in what they do and by giving them a feeling of achievement, confidence-confidence, autonomy, approval, acceptance and recognition in the eyes of other workers, and a feeling of belonging

- **Intellectual Needs:** Being able to master new skills and new knowledge is stimulating for many trainees. They need variety in what they do and the opportunity to exercise curiosity in finding out about the what, why and how of the learning that they are undertaking

- **Self-fulfilment Needs:** Most people like to feel that they have "got somewhere" and in this respect training or learning helps to provide a meaning and sense of purpose.

Which of the above needs are important for any particular learner will depend on their personality, background and experience.

Broadly speaking, there are two main forms of reward or incentive that are linked with learning events. There are those that are closely associated with the task itself, called "intrinsic", and those that are more in the way of being an outcome of performing the task, called "extrinsic" outcomes:

- **Intrinsic Rewards** come from the satisfaction that derives from being able to perform the job properly – for example, preparing a column of figures that balance, receiving the thanks of satisfied customers, building a house, etc, are all activities that provide intrinsic rewards

- **Extrinsic Rewards** are independent of the task and include such rewards as money, promotion, enhancement career prospects, receiving a certificate. Therefore, the task itself could be boring and not intrinsically rewarding but the incentives that go with it provide the motivation.

We conclude this chapter with an outline in **Figure 3.9** of the main findings that research indicates will help you design high quality T&D activities.

FIGURE 3.9: SUMMARISING WHAT WE KNOW ABOUT THE ADULT LEARNING PROCESS

Motivation to Learn

- Adults seek out learning experiences to cope with specific life-changing events.
- The more life-changing events an adult encounters, the more likely he/she is to seek out learning opportunities. Just as stress increases as life-changing events accumulate, the motivation to cope with change through engagement in a learning experience increases. Since the people who most frequently seek out learning opportunities are those who have the most years of education, it is reasonable to guess that for many of us learning is a coping response to significant change.
- The learning experiences adults seek out on their own are directly related – in their own perceptions – to the life-changing events that triggered the seeking.
- Adults are generally willing to engage in learning experiences before, after or even during the actual life-changing event. Once convinced that the change is a certainty, adults will engage in any learning that promises to help them cope with the transition.
- Although adults have been found to engage in learning for a variety of reasons – job advancement, pleasure, love of learning and so on – it is equally true that for most adults learning is not its own reward. Adults who are motivated to seek out learning experience do so primarily (80-90% of the time) because they have a use for the knowledge or skill being sought. Learning is a means to an end, not an end in itself.
- Increasing or maintaining one's sense of self-esteem and pleasure are strong secondary motivates for engaging in learning experiences. Having a new skill or extending and enriching current knowledge can be both, depending on the individual's personal perceptions.

Learning Design

- Adult learners tend to be less interested in, and enthralled by, general courses. They tend to prefer single-concept, single-theory courses that focus heavily on the application of the concept to relevant problems. This tendency increases with age.
- Adults need to be able to integrate new ideas with what they already know if they are going to keep, and use, the new information.
- Information that conflicts sharply with what is already held to be true, and thus forces a re-evaluation of the old material, is integrated more slowly.
- Information that has little conceptual overlap with what is already known is acquired slowly.
- Fast-paced, complex or unusual learning tasks interfere with the learning of the concepts that they are intended to teach or illustrate.
- Adults tend to compensate for being slower in some psychomotor learning tasks by being more accurate and making fewer trial-and-error ventures.
- Adults tend to take errors personally and are more likely to let them affect self-esteem. Therefore, they tend to apply tried-and-true solutions and take fewer risks. There is even evidence that adults will misinterpret feedback and "mistake" errors for positive confirmation.
- The curriculum designer must know whether the concepts and ideas will be in concert or in conflict with the learner and his/her values. Moving from a service to a sales philosophy requires more than a change in words and titles. It requires a change in the way people think and value.
- Programmes need to be designed to accept viewpoints from people in different life stages and with different value "sets".
- A concept needs to be "anchored" or explained from more than one value set and appeal to more than one developmental life stage.

Learning Preferences

- Adults prefer (by a factor of seven) self-directed and self-designed learning projects to group-learning experiences led by a professional. The adult learner often selects more than one medium for the design. Reading and talking to the qualified peer are frequently cited as good resources. The desire to control pace and start/stop time strongly affects the self-directed preference.
- Non-human media such as books, programmed instruction and television have become popular in recent years. One piece of research found these media very influential in the way adults plan self-directed learning projects.
- Regardless of media, straightforward "how-to" is the preferred content orientation.
- Self-direction does not mean isolation. Self-directed projects involve an average of 10 other people as resources, guides, encouragers and the like. The incompetence or inadequacy of these same people is often rated as a primary frustration. But even for the self-professed, self-directed learner, lectures and short seminars get positive ratings, especially when these events give the learner face-to-face, one-to-one access to an expert.

The Learning Environment

- The learning environment must be physically and psychologically comfortable. Adults report that long lectures, periods of interminable sitting and the absence of practice opportunities are high on the irritation scale.
- Adults have something real to lose in a classroom situation. Self-esteem and ego are on the line when they are asked to risk trying the new behaviour in front of peers and cohorts. Bad experiences in traditional education, feelings about authority and the preoccupation with events outside the classroom all affect the in-class experience.
- Adults have expectations and it is critical to take time up-front to clarify and articulate all expectations before getting into content. Both trainees and the instructor/facilitator need to state their expectations. When they are at variance, it should be acknowledged and a resolution negotiated. In any case, the instructor can assume responsibility only for his/her own expectations, not for those of trainees.
- Adults bring a great deal of life experience into the classroom, an invaluable asset to be acknowledged, tapped and used. Adults can learn well from dialogue with respected peers.
- Instructors/facilitators who have a tendency to hold forth rather than facilitate can hold that tendency in check, or compensate for it, by concentrating on the use of open-ended questions to draw out relevant trainee knowledge and experience.
- New knowledge has to be integrated with previous knowledge; that means active learner participation. Since only the learners can tell us how the new fits or fails to fit with the old, we have to ask them. Just as the learner is dependent on us for confirming feedback on skill practice, we are dependent on the learner for feedback about our curriculum and in-class performance.
- The key to the instructor/facilitator role is control. The instructor must balance the presentation of new material, debate and discussion, sharing of relevant trainee experiences and the clock. Ironically, we seem best able to establish control when we risk giving it up. When we shelve our egos and stifle the tendency to be threatened by challenge to our plans and methods, we gain the kind of facultative control we seem to need to effect adult learning.
- The instructor/facilitator has to protect minority opinion, keep disagreements civil and unheated, make connections between various opinions and ideas, and keep reminding the group of the variety of potential solutions to the problem. Just as in a good problem-solving meeting, the instructor/facilitator is does less advocating than orchestrating.
- Integration of new knowledge and skill requires transition time and focused effort. Working on applications to specific back-on-the job problems helps with the transfer and follow-up after training and increases the likelihood of that transfer. Involving the trainees' supervisors in pre- and post-course activities helps with both in-class focus and transfer.
- Learning and teaching theories function better as a resource than as a "one best way" or directive.

Created from Smith and Ragan (1993), Gagné and Medsker (1996) and Gilley *et al.* (2002).

BEST PRACTICE INDICATORS

Some of the best practice issues that you should consider related to the contents of this chapter are:

- Learning is an active process and adults prefer to participate actively. Therefore, those techniques that make provision for active participation will achieve faster learning than those that do not

- Learning is goal-directed and adults are trying to achieve a goal or satisfy a need. Therefore, the clearer, the more realistic and relevant the statement of the desired outcomes, the more learning that will take place

- Group learning, insofar as it creates a learning atmosphere of mutual support, may be more effective than individual learning. Therefore, those techniques based on group participation are often more effective than those that handle individuals as isolated units

- Learning that is applied immediately is retained longer and is more subject to immediate use than that which is not. Therefore, techniques must be employed that encourage the immediate application of any material in a practical way

- Learning must be reinforced. Therefore, techniques must be used that ensure prompt, reinforcing feedback

- Learning new material is facilitated when it is related to what is already known. Therefore, the techniques used should help the adult establish this relationship and the integration of material

- The existence of periodic plateaus in the rate of learning requires frequent changes in the nature of the learning task to insure continuous progress. Therefore, techniques should be changed frequently in any given session

- Learning is facilitated when the learner is aware of progress. Therefore, techniques should be used that provide opportunities for self-appraisal. Learning is facilitated when there is logic to the subject matter and the logic makes sense in relation to the learner's repertoire of experience. Therefore, learning must be organised for sequence and cumulative effects.

Reflections on the Training & Development Scenario

This scenario reveals a common mistake made by many trainers, who fail to consider the fears and expectations of adult learners.

First, senior management had unrealistic expectations about the training period and the time necessary to learn. Key issues that should have been investigated were as follows:

- The training department did not conduct an analysis of the characteristics of the training population and identify their implications for the design of learning events

- The age and experience of the learning population appeared to be very relevant factors. They had relatively less trainability, due to long periods away from structured training situations

- The training objectives tended to focus on sales and customer care issues. These objectives required that learners achieve important behavioural and attitude change. These types of learning objectives are less likely to be achieved in large group learning situations

- Adult learners may experience a fear of technology. This was the case in this scenario. Where learners have fears about technology, it needs to be managed more sensitively that happened in this situation. Where fear exists, it should be addressed with an appropriate learning intervention.

- Time is an important issue in this scenario. Learning is a gradual or incremental process. It needs to be appropriately scheduled in order to maximise learning transfer.

We know from the research that small group learning is more effective when the learners are mature. Small group learning (maximum of 10) provides learners with an opportunity to build trust and become familiar with a training environment. Small group learning situations are useful in that they provide opportunities to practice skill development. Learning methods that are useful in achieving opportunities for practice include role-plays and group discussion.

Chapter Four

IDENTIFYING & ANALYSING TRAINING & DEVELOPMENT NEEDS

LEARNING OBJECTIVES

On completion of this chapter, you should be able to:

- Define the nature of a training need and explain the purpose of training needs analysis

- Identify the possible triggers for learning in organisations and ask appropriate questions to identify whether they have a T&D solution

- Discuss the different issues that need to be considered at different levels of analysis

- Identify a range of methods that can be used in needs assessment and identify the advantages and disadvantages of each method

- Identify and evaluate a number of approaches that you can use to identify training needs at a work or job level

- Identify and understand the value of a number of different methods to identify training needs at the person or individual level

- Identify and understand the role of different organisational stakeholders in the training needs identification process

- Identify some of the issues involved in analysing training needs data and the issues to be considered in prioritising training needs

- Identify and define some of the outputs that you may derive from the training needs analysis process.

A Training & Development Scenario

The following situations involve a number of different kinds of performance problems. For each situation:
- Indicate whether the general source of the performance problem is managerial and organisational shortcomings, individual employee shortcomings, or external influences
- State the specific source (family problems, etc.)
- Indicate what action should be taken to resolve the problem.

CASE 1: John, a 22-year assembly line worker, falls victim to a serious drinking problem after his wife suddenly dies. Because of his drinking, his on-the-job performance falls significantly and his absenteeism – particularly on Mondays – rises dramatically.

CASE 2+ Denise, a newly-appointed office manager, fares poorly as a supervisor. She cares little about planning and organising, refuses to delegate, and runs the office like (in the words of a subordinate) a "little Hitler". Denise was promoted because of her expert skills as a claims analyst and because she was the senior employee in the work group.

CASE 3: Ruby, a clerk-typist in her fourth day on the job, is really not sure what her job duties and responsibilities are. Her supervisor has little time to discuss job details with her and has not informed her specifically of what he expects. As a result, she gets involved in jobs that her boss disapproves of, and he chews her out.

CASE 4: In an effort to improve the morale of its work force and the quality of its small electronic calculators, Proactive Instruments enriched the jobs of several assembly-line workers. Workers now assemble components in teams rather than individually, and team members make many decisions formerly made by supervisors and the quality control staff. Many workers like their new job roles and have improved their quality. Some, however, dislike the teamwork and get into frequent conflicts with other team-members. For many of these workers, job dissatisfaction and quality problems have actually increased over previous levels.

CASE 5: Mark was recently promoted from telephone-line repairman to crew supervisor and wants desperately to do what a good supervisor should do. But, in his desire to make sure none of the subordinates make mistakes, he often gets directly involved in their work. He is often seen doing the work of a subordinate, while he or she stands by. Questioned about his practice by another supervisor, Mark said, "If you want something done right, you've got to do it yourself". Mark spends so much time doing his subordinates' work, that his supervisory duties are largely neglected.

INTRODUCTION

As a trainer, you are likely to play an active role in the training needs identification process. If you are a training manager, you will likely be involved in higher-level analysis of training needs and focus on macro or organisational issues. If you are an on-the-job trainer, you will likely have a direct role in analysing jobs and tasks. In all of these roles, a key issue you will be concerned with is ensuring that the methods you use gather the appropriate data so that you can make a sensible assessment of whether the problem or opportunity has a training solution.

If you identify training needs systematically, it will provide you with valuable information on who needs training and what trainees need to learn. It will give you a good indication of the tasks in which employees should be trained and the types of knowledge, skill and attitude that the training will be expected to develop. Identification and analysis of training needs will also provide you with information to determine whether to purchase training from an external supplier or to develop training using internal resources. The training needs process is a direct feed-in to the learning design process, specifying learning outcomes and objectives and developing content. We consider these issues in later chapters.

In this chapter, we focus on the process of identifying and analysing training needs. We consider some of the questions you should ask and the issues you need to consider in putting the process into practice. We outline the different types of data collection methods you can use and the advantages and limitations of each. Finally, we deal with how you can analyse these needs and make decisions on priorities.

DEFINING THE TRAINING NEEDS IDENTIFICATION & ANALYSIS PROCESS

Needs identification and analysis is the first component of the training design process. Effective training needs identification is a task that you will be expected to carry out on many occasions or, at a minimum, be able to provide advice to managers on how it should be conducted. We define a training need as a "need for human performance improvement arising from a deficit or an opportunity that can be met by an appropriate training intervention."

Training needs identification is the process by which you measure the nature of the need. It tells you how much training is needed, and whether a training solution is an appropriate response to address the problem or opportunity.

You should view the training needs identification and analysis as both a reactive and proactive process. A reactive training needs scenario is the more common scenario for a trainer. You may be required to address a performance deficiency, such as when employee's performance does not match the standard for the job. A proactive training needs analysis is opportunity-focused. It seeks to identify what training needs may arise in the future.

Training needs analysis usually involves organisational analysis, analysis of work and tasks and person analysis.

Organisational analysis will focus on both the external and internal context. We give each of these dimensions specific emphasis in this book. A primary focus of organisational analysis is with determining the appropriateness of training, given the organisation's business strategy. It also considers the resources available for the training and the levels of support available. It is important to specifically isolate the team level as an important dimension. The dramatic increase in the use of teams as an organisational strategy, combined with the realisation that teams sometimes fail, makes team-training issues an important component of the needs analysis process.

Work and task analysis focuses on identifying the key tasks, knowledge, skill and attitudes that need to be emphasised in training for employees to complete their tasks to experienced standard.

Person level analysis involves determining whether performance deficiencies result specifically from a lack of knowledge, skill, ability or whether they arise from motivational issues. The analysis at this level may also focus on the readiness of the employee for training.

We will say a lot more about each level and the types of questions that you should ask later in this chapter. **Figure 4.1** presents the basic components of training identification and analysis process.

LEARNING TRIGGERS IN ORGANISATIONS, TEAMS, JOBS & INDIVIDUALS

There are many learning triggers that exist in organisations. We believe that learning triggers exist at four levels:

- The organisation
- The team
- The work
- The characteristics of individuals.

Typical business/organisational issues that are likely to emerge include a reduction in turnover, declining profit margins and increased competition. It is likely that these three problems for example, will have both training and non-training solutions.

FIGURE 4.1: THE TRAINING NEEDS ANALYSIS & IDENTIFICATION PROCESS

Levels of Analysis							
ORGANISATIONAL				JOB			INDIVIDUAL
↑	↑	↑	↑	↑	↖	↗	↑
Analysis of strategic plans	Analysis of HR plans	Team functioning	Training surveys	Job analysis	Performance and development plans		Role analysis

Process of Identification

Step 1
- Specification of the objectives
- Identification of the data sources
- Identification of the data collection methods

Step 2
- Collection of data and initial interpretation
- Identification of problems with "non-training" solutions

Step 3
- Detailed interpretation of data
- Identification of key areas where training is an appropriate solution
- Development of recommendations

Step 4
- Identification of training priorities
- Preparation and implementation of recommendations

A reduction in revenue/profits, for example, may require a change in sales or marketing strategies, head-count reduction, reorganisation and/or increased market penetration. It is also likely that some form of training solution may be appropriate. This could include leadership training, performance management, change management and training for the managerial team, or T&D initiatives in areas such as finance training. Strategy and communication may also be appropriate.

Business organisation level issues have important implications for the role of the training specialist, the types of training solutions generated and the realisation that formal training may not be the primary source of learning. The following five organisational level activities reveal particular training and development needs:

Acquisition of companies	• Leadership skills in managing the acquisition • Skills in managing the integration of cultures • Skills in managing conflict issues that emerge
Organisational Restructuring	• Changes in professional knowledge • Training in team cohesiveness • Training in communications and conflict management
Increased Innovativeness	• Training in idea generation techniques • Training in skills to evaluate new product or innovative ideas • Training skills in brainstorming/other idea generation techniques
Implementation of New Technology	• Training for older employees to deal with fears of new technology and technophobia • New skill sets may be required • Changing role expectations and knowledge requirements
Implementation of Total Quality Management initiatives	• Employees will need to understand the philosophy of TQM • Development of skills to identify quality defects • Skills to develop and implement processes and procedures related to quality

These five examples illustrate that organisation level changes and initiatives can have a direct impact on T&D needs.

Team level issues are likely to have implications for training and development needs. The research indicates that teams require two types of skills to be effective:

- Task skills are the skills needed by team-members to master the team task
- Team-members also require teamwork skills that focus on attitudinal, behavioural and knowledge dimensions of teamwork. These teamwork skills include skills in communicating, interacting, co-ordinating, monitoring and leading.

Some of the skill needs issues that emerge from a focus on the team level of analysis include:

- Knowledge and understanding of team roles and task roles
- Team working skills, including team awareness, team communication, team leadership, team adaptability and team cohesiveness
- Team motivational skills, to reinforce the value of team-working and why individuals should be team-focused
- The relationship between he individual and the team
- The role of team conflict and differences and how to manage them.

The job level focuses on expertise. Most of this expertise comes from experience on the job. Formal training can help, by focusing on the facts, concepts and procedures of a job, although expertise is usually gained through experience. This experience may be achieved through observing and modelling others performing tasks repeatedly, seeing the consequences of mistakes.

The requirements at the job level include:

- Achievement of proficiency in fundamental skills for the job
- Skills to adapt procedures and standards to suit a situation
- Skills to make good decisions quickly and see the big picture
- Skills to notice details and understand system effects
- Skills to be situationally-aware when performing the job and to maintain job efficiency.

Individual or personal level issues will focus on characteristics of the individual such as self-awareness, self-esteem and career development. Individual level learning needs may be addressed through customised T&D solutions such as coaching, development planning, and mentoring and external education initiatives.

DEFINING THE PROBLEM/OPPORTUNITY: IS TRAINING THE ANSWER?

Training is frequently wasted in organisations. It is often prescribed as a solution to an organisational problem or opportunity when, in fact, it is not appropriate at all. Many management practitioners and training specialists agree that a significant number of performance problems or opportunities do not stem from a lack of T&D.

A key issue you will face as a training specialist is to decided whether the problem or opportunity has a training solution. We call these factors learning triggers. **Figure 4.2** presents a set of triggers, two of which are internal and one external. We define a learning trigger as something that needs to be changed.

We suggest that learning triggers occur at different levels in an organisation:

- **The Organisational Environment:** This refers to the organisation at a macro level and refers primarily to the external context. It may relate to how well the organisation is competing, its relationship with suppliers, customers or other external bodies. These factors may trigger potential opportunities for learning or pose problems that may have a training and/or development solution. This level is increasingly important but less likely to be considered, as part of the training needs process

FIGURE 4.2: EXAMPLES OF LEARNING TRIGGERS INTERNAL & EXTERNAL TO THE ORGANISATION

Level of Analysis	Source of Trigger		
	Internal		External
	Positive Trigger	Negative Trigger	
Organisational Environment	• New customers • New products/services	• Poor competitive position • Change in suppliers and distributors • Loss of customers • Customer complaints	• Changes in competitive structures • New legislation • Changes in current legislation • Changing customer expectations • New/changed supplier requirements
The Work Environment	• Changes in organisational morale • Restructuring and change initiatives • Outputs from performance management process • Requests from managers	• Decrease in productivity • Increase in accident levels • Down sizing • Skill shortages and succession management issues	• Professional body requirements • Demands from quality creditors and regulatory bodies
Team Environment	• New team formation • Demands for innovation	• Team conflict • Poor team performance • Poor team leadership • Lack of team working	• New merger or acquisition
The Nature of the Work	• Changes in technology/introduction of new equipment • Changes in work processes and methods • Multi-skilling and cross-skilling	• Resistance to changing processes • Unwillingness to adopt new work processes	• Impact of working time legislation • Equality and diversity legislation • Changing notions of production
Characteristics of Employees	• Demands for employability • Demands for educational activities • Changing psychological contract	• High turnover of staff • Low commitment and job satisfaction • Low employee motivation	• Characteristics of the labour market

- **The Work Environment:** This level refers to changes occurring within the organisation, in relation to its culture, structures, strategy or size. It could therefore refer to issues such as the overall morale of the organisation, skill shortages and difficulties with succession planning
- **The Team Environment:** This level refers to the dynamic of a team, its functioning, team conflict issues and leadership
- **The Nature of the Work:** This level refers to characteristics of the work itself. It addresses questions such as what skills are required? What work methods and processes are currently used? How well does the organisation respond to customer needs and expectations? What changes in production are proposed? How can services be delivered more efficiently? These are issues that may give rise to or trigger training requirements
- **Characteristics of Employees:** This level focuses on the employee. It considers the impact of issues such as employee demands for training, changing employee expectations, demands to enhance the employability of employees in the event of down-sizing and negative issues related to levels of motivation and job satisfaction.

Defining the Problem/Opportunity

Learning activities should respond to, and be designed to meet, a need, which may be defined in terms of a problem (high error rate, customer complaints) or a new situation (a new employee, the introduction of a new IT system). In a new situation, there is always a learning need. The learning will take place regardless, so the aim should be to focus the learning process to make it as positive, effective and speedy as possible.

In the face of a problem, however, learning is not always the answer. For example, a production line supervisor may note an increasing number of sub-standard goods being passed as perfect, and ask for a training programme in identifying defects. However, a more in-depth analysis of the problem may reveal that it is caused by poor lighting conditions. Staff are fully aware of what constitutes a defect, but are unable to see them in the poor lighting. Examples of the sort of factor that could impair performance include:

- Poor quality materials
- Unsuitable working conditions
- Inefficient equipment
- Lack of motivation
- Badly designed working methods
- Insufficient staff

- Insufficient resources.

The flowchart in **Figure 4.3** sets out the "performance technologist" approach to identifying the reasons for low performance. It will help to identify correctly:

- The problem
- Whether learning is the answer or part of the answer.

A new situation automatically brings a learning need. Many new situations arrive unexpectedly, leaving insufficient time to plan and prepare a learning response. There are a number of organisational indicators that can help predict when a new learning need may arise. Because these are organisational indicators, they also help to ensure that the learning need and its solution are linked to organisational requirements. These include:

- **Strategic business plans:** Plans for expansion and/or diversification will give rise to learning needs
- **Re-structuring:** Reductions in numbers of staff or de-layering will lead to changes in job specifications and performance requirements
- **Legislation:** Changes in employment law may mean managers must become familiar with new procedures and learn new behaviours
- **Sectoral developments and competitors' changes:** Where one organisation leads, others often follow. This also provides the opportunity to learn lessons from how other organisations handled the change (a process often referred to as benchmarking)
- **New technology and systems:** The introduction of new IT systems will give rise to learning needs, not just for those who operate the IT systems themselves, but possibly also for those who provide the input or use the output, who may have to provide and manage information differently
- **Management and performance information:** This information may also highlight differences in performance between different areas of the organisation. The causes or the solutions may involve learning needs.

In order to make a judgement about the extent to which the problem or opportunity can be addressed using a training and/or development solution, you need to ask a number of questions. We identify some general questions that you may ask. **Figure 4.4** provides a summary.

FIGURE 4.3: MAGER & PIPE'S PERFORMANCE ANALYSIS MODEL

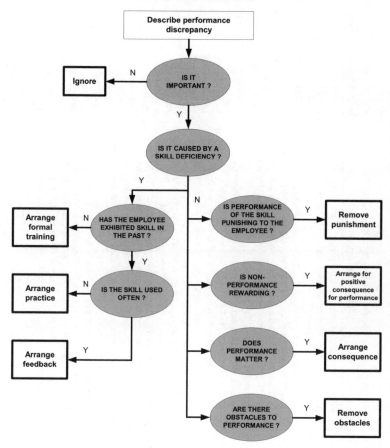

Source: Mager and Pipe (1999).

WHO SHOULD BE INVOLVED IN THE NEEDS ASSESSMENT PROCESS?

Your goal in conducting a training needs analysis is to determine whether a training need exists. It is very important to include key stakeholders within the organisation in the process.

Figure 4.5 shows the questions that you should ask. Four sets of stakeholders will have information and perspectives about training needs at the four levels of analysis that we have identified. These stakeholders are: senior level management; middle level management; trainers and subject matter experts.

FIGURE 4.4: QUESTIONS TO ASK ABOUT PROBLEMS & OPPORTUNITIES

Problems	Opportunities	Whether Problems/Opportunities are Worth Addressing	Possible Responses	Training Decisions
• Who is involved with the problem? • What is happening now? • What events led up to the current situation? Can you think of anything that may have contributed to its development? • What consequences have stemmed from the problem? • When did the problem first appear? How did you first notice it? • Where did the problem first appear? Can you track it to one source or location? • Why did you think it is happening? • How did you notice it? What specific situations can you pinpoint in which the problem was evident? Could you describe them? • How much is the situation costing the organisation in tangible (hard) and intangible (soft) measures of performance?	• What is the opportunity, and why do you think it exists? • Who will be affected by it? • What events led to discovering the opportunity? Can you think of anything that may affect its realisation? • What consequences are likely to stem from efforts to pursue the opportunity? • When and how did evidence of the opportunity first appear? How was that evidence recognised? • From what trends, business issues, customer needs or expectations, or other external issues did the opportunity arise?	• Whose performance is at issue? Which person, which group? • What is the actual performance discrepancy? Describe the actual and the desired performance • Is the problem worth solving? Is it a big enough problem to bother about? How much does the problem cost? What happens if you ignore the problem? Estimate the cost in some way so that a solution can be found that costs less than the consequences of living with the problem • Is it possible to apply a fast fix? • Are expectations clear and are resources adequate, is performance quality visible, and is feedback on performance being given? • Are the "consequences" properly balanced? Or are people in some way rewarded for doing things wrong? (for example, if someone does not complete their work properly will someone else do it for them?) List all the negative and positive "consequences" of poor performance that are evident, from the point of view of the people involved • Do the people involved already know how to perform effectively? Could they perform in the past? Are the tasks performed often? Perhaps better feedback is needed, or some refresher practice or job aids • Consider task changes as solutions; simplify the task, remove obstacles to performance • Do the poor performers have the potential to change? • If it seems after all this that the performance gap is worth closing, and T&D is appropriate, then describe the T&D solutions and calculate the costs. Select the most practical and cost effective T&D solution and implement it.	• Will the problem or opportunity be addressed with the implementation of systems, procedures or processes? • Can the problem or opportunity be addressed with new/ revised job roles and responsibilities? • Does the organisation need to hire new human resources? • Is there a requirement for new or revised knowledge skill and attitude?	• What do trainees need to learn? • Who will receive the training and in what order? • What types of training will be delivered? • What will the frequency of training be? • What methods of learning will best bring about learning? • What will the training cost? • Will we use a buy *versus* design training option?

FIGURE 4.5: STAKEHOLDER PERCEPTIONS OF ORGANISATIONAL PROBLEMS: LEVELS OF ANALYSIS

	Senior Managers	Middle/Line Managers	Learners	Training/HR Specialists
Organisational Environmental Level	• Can we use training to respond to competitors? • How can we use training to meet regulatory requirements?	• Will we meet the demands of customers and suppliers better through training?	• Will training make one more employable in the external environment?	• Do I have the budget to buy training services externally? • Can training contribute to competitive advantage?
The Work Environment Level	• How does training support our business strategy? • Is training important to achieve our business objectives?	• Do I want to spend money on training? • Am I willing to allow my employees to participate in training? • What are my values in respect of learning?	• Will promotion and advancement options exist? • Will my skills be utilised in the organisation? • What career support will I get?	• Do managers support training? • Are they willing to release employees for training? • Is there a culture of learning? • Will the training be transferred to the job?
The Work Level	• Does the organisation have clearly defined jobs and skill requirements? • Are those skills necessary to complete in the marketplace? • What functions need training?	• Will training make a difference to the quality of service or product? • Will we be able to respond to customer needs quickly?	• Will training contribute to achieving successful completion of tasks? • Will it enable me to work better within a team? • Will I achieve my immediate objectives?	• How will I identify training needs? • What priority tasks should be trained? • What knowledge skills and other characteristics are necessary?
The Person Level	• How motivated are employees to work to achieve the strategic requirements of the organisation? • Can training be used to secure commitment and manage expectations?	• Who should be trained as a priority within my department? • Will training bring added benefits to the morale of our employees?	• Should I participate in training? • Am I admitting failure if I take up training? • What rewards will follow from participation in training?	• Will I get the co-operation of employees? • Are employees motivated to attend training? • Will I be able to identify those employees who particularly need training?

Created from Rothwell (1996) and Gibbs (2002).

Senior level management generally view the needs assessment process from the broader organisational perspective. Instead of focusing specific jobs, they are involved in determining whether training is related to the organisation's business strategy; and, if so, what type of training is appropriate.

Senior level management are also involved in identifying what business functions or units need training (person analysis) and in determining whether the company has the knowledge, skills and abilities in the workforce that are necessary to meet its strategy and be competitive in the marketplace.

Middle management is more concerned with understanding how training may affect the attainment of financial goals for the units they supervise. As a result, for mid-level managers, organisational analysis focuses on identifying:

* How much of their budgets they want to devote to training
* The types of employees who should receive training (engineers, or core employees who are directly involved in producing goods or providing services)
* Identifying jobs where training can make a difference in terms of improving products or customer service.

Trainers need to consider whether training is aligned with the business strategy. However, trainers are primarily interested in needs assessment to provide them with information to administer, develop, and support training programmes, including determining whether training should be purchased or developed in-house; identifying the tasks that need to be trained; and determining top and mid-level managers' interest and support for training.

While senior management are usually involved to determine whether training meets the organisation's strategy and then to provide appropriate financial resources, they are not usually involved in identifying which employees need training, the tasks for which training is needed, and the knowledge, skills and abilities and other characteristics needed to complete those tasks. This is the role of subject matter experts, who are commonly found in large organisations.

Subject matter experts are employees, managers, technical experts, trainers, and even customers or suppliers, who are knowledgeable in relation to:

* Training issues including tasks to be performed
* Knowledge, skills and abilities required for successful task performance
* Necessary equipment
* Conditions under which the tasks have to be performed.

There is no rule regarding how many types of employees should be represented in the group conducting the needs assessment. Still, it is important to get a sample of job incumbents involved in the process, because they tend to be most knowledgeable about the job and can be a great hindrance to the training process if they do not feel they have had input into the needs assessment.

You should have a number of options available to you in order to gather information from these different stakeholders – see **Figure 4.6**.

IDENTIFYING T&D NEEDS AT THE ORGANISATIONAL LEVEL

An organisational-wide review of training needs is both time-consuming and expensive, although it is potentially a very important exercise. The primary reason for conducting an organisation-wide review of training needs is to gather objective data about the training investment required, in the short and longer term, to meet organisational goals. Analysis of training needs at this level provides top management and training specialists with good quality data on T&D. It will also enable key stakeholders to make decisions about the nature and extent of the role of training in achieving strategic objectives and it will inform T&D policies and plans.

An organisational level analysis takes place within the context of the organisation's strategic goals and priorities and the current configuration of the T&D function. Organisational level analysis requires the systematic identification at all levels in the organisation of the current and future training needs. It requires a systematic review of this information and the development of recommendations. We now outline in more detail some of the issues you should consider when conducting an organisational level analysis of training needs.

Step 1: Preparation of the Review

The importance of preparation is key to the success of an organisation level training needs analysis and involves obtaining a clear brief, specifying the precise objectives of the exercise. The brief should cover the scope, objectives and the time horizon of the review, the degree to which it is confidential, the authority that the reviewer is given for access to relevant information, when the results are required and the person to whom the final report is to be sent.

When the objectives of the review have been clarified, your next step is to ensure that all employees who are likely to contribute to it are informed.

FIGURE 4.6: STRATEGIES FOR INVOLVING KEY STAKEHOLDERS IN TRAINING NEEDS IDENTIFICATION

	Formation of Project Team	Questionnaire to Managers	Manager with Own Team	Interview with Managers	Interviews with Learners	Group Discussions with Managers
	Bring together a variety of people from different areas of the organisation	Produce a set of questions to send to managers	Bring together managers/teams for discussion of issues	Arrange interviews with individual managers	Gives guidance to individuals to quantify changes/ solicit views	Bring groups of managers together, from within/across functions
Pros	• Encourages the sharing of ideas • Devolves responsibility • Developmental in itself for project team members • Increase potential for acceptance • Efficient use of time • More likely to be innovative	• Saves time on gathering information, particularly if managers are situated at different sites • Can be completed when it is convenient for managers	• Continues the development of relationships • Uses existing relationships to save time	• Opportunity to check understanding • Opportunity for in-depth discussion • Convenient for managers • High response • Rich source of information • All views heard	• Leads to commitment to learning • Develops learning skills as part of process	• Synergy from shared ideas • Speedier ways of gathering information • More of a strategic view
Cons	• Not all views heard • Time needed to develop the team • Depends on getting the right mix in the team	• Might not ask the right questions • No feedback process for checking understanding • Time taken to analyse responses • Response limited by questions • Impersonal • Potential poor response rate • Functional emphasis	• Insular • Falls back on previously held assumptions	• Time consuming • Relies on trainer's understanding of new product • Functional emphasis	• Time consuming • Large amount of data to be assimilated	• Getting people together (logistics) • Dominant views take over • Relies on trainer's facilitation skills

This is necessary for three reasons:

- You rely on the co-operation of senior manages and others. It is, therefore, important that the purpose of the investigation, and how and when he or she proposes to carry it out, are fully discussed in advance with the appropriate staff – for example, it should be made clearer that the review is not part of an organisation and methods or work-study exercise. This initial activity has an important part to play in the formation of attitudes and will help determine the acceptability or any resultant training activities

- The investigations may involve asking searching questions, which may cause adverse reactions from some employees who might adopt a less than co-operative attitude if, as can easily happen, they misconstrue the intention. This is particularly likely if the organisation climate is unsettled. A review that takes place soon after a company has been taken over may well run into difficulties. Even if the organisational climate is favourable, the reviewer should nonetheless explain the purpose of the review to the staff concerned and obtain their co-operation. The review should be regarded as an opportunity to nurture positive attitudes to training, but training needs are often weak spots in an organisation and those concerned tend to be sensitive when questioned about them, especially if they regard the investigation as an implied criticism

- A third reason for advising those involved of the impending review is that, given advance notice, they can collect the information that will be required, for example, by updating organisational charts or job specifications, where available, and by preparing labour turnover statistics. This can save every one a great deal of time and is particularly important where line managers responsible for drawing up job descriptions and standard specifications for their subordinates.

Finally, the most appropriate starting-point must be determined. This will depend upon many variables, such as urgency of action in particular areas, staff availability, the purpose of the investigation, the personal choice of the assessor and the degree to which line management is prepared to co-operate.

An organisation chart showing the relationships of different departments and the formal lines of responsibility is a useful document, but it is important to remember that these charts often show much less information than may be needed. To be of value, they must be up-to-date and indicate the real areas of responsibility and lines of communication, not just those of the formal organisation. If, as is often the case, no chart exists, it may be necessary to draw up new-style "maps" as the review progresses. The data shown on such "maps" must be continually cross-checked against the perceptions of other managers to reflect management's view on future operational priorities.

Step 2: Collection of Data and its Initial Interpretation

Although, in theory, information has first to be collected before it is interpreted, in practice it is artificial to separate these two processes, as they tend to take place simultaneously. The reviewer interprets and records facts and opinions, at times seeking more detail and at other times deciding that more information is not required. During this process, comments on current and former training policies and interventions will be received. This feedback must be taken into consideration when formulating the organisation's training plan.

The level of support that employees and line mangers are prepared to give will certainly influence top management's decision as to the resources that will be made available. Organisations are always faced with the problem of competing claims for limited resources and it is helpful to be able to argue a case that has organisation-wide approval. The case must be based on acknowledged training priorities, the rationale for these priorities must be explicitly expressed, and alternative strategies (for example, job redesign ort he recruitment of ready-trained employees) shown to be less cost-effective than training interventions.

Methods of Collecting Information

Depending on the focus of the investigation, information might be obtained by:

- Reference to strategic planning documents relating to marketing, production, staffing, etc.
- Analysing minutes of management meetings
- Selecting data from operational records such as personnel statistics, job descriptions, accident records, training reports and staff appraisal forms. Accounting records can often also be very revealing – for example, costs/returns of waste board or metal can yield dramatic evidence on precision in manufacturing, which in turn may reflect on operator competency
- Formal and informal interviewing, especially with people in charge of key departments. Senior managers often have operational aims not found in the published forward plans
- Questionnaire surveys
- Discussions with the training and development committee, which can provide information on training requirements and the priority areas.

FIGURE 4.7: EXAMPLE OF A STRATEGIC T&D NEEDS QUESTIONNAIRE

Introduction

This document is to be used in the initial stages of the T&D Department Plan for the coming year. It is expected that this form will trigger your thinking while you prepare for the upcoming Management Meeting at which the departmental T&D needs will be defined and agreed. Ideally you should focus on integrating the following four levels of T&D needs that will need to be filled over the coming year:

- Organisation-wide T&D needs, to fulfil the strategic goals of the business
- Business Area T&D needs, to fulfil the business area's objectives
- Business Unit T&D needs, to fulfil the business unit's objectives
- Individual employee T&D needs, to maximise the potential of each staff member.

This document is structured into three sections. Each section aims at focusing your attention in different areas. This document must be completed by you, as a Business Unit Manager, and brought before to the next Management Meeting.

Section 1: The Strategic Business Needs

In thinking about your strategic business needs over the coming 12 months, what are the top three challenges facing you and your team? Taking into account these main challenges, what learning and development should take place? (Prioritise in order of importance).

Key Challenges	Key Learning and Development
1.	1.
2.	2.
3.	3.

In thinking about your business unit, what key legislation/regulation/policy changes will come into force over the coming 12 months? Taking into account these changes, what learning and development should take place? (Prioritise in order of importance).

Key Challenges	Key Learning and Development
4.	4.
5.	5.
6.	6.

In thinking about your business unit, what key technological changes will take place over the coming 12 months? Taking into account these changes, what learning and development should take place? (Prioritise in order of importance).

Key Challenges	Key Learning and Development
7.	7.
8.	8.
9.	9.

Section 2: Your Own Team Development Needs

Using the results from the Management Development Centre (MDC) for your Business Area/Business Unit, identify (using the competency clusters below) the three main development areas for your team for the next 12 months.

• Managing Work • Time and Task Management • Problem Solving • Decision-Making • Business Writing	• Managing and Developing Self • Initiative and Innovation • Continuous Learning • Understanding Others • Communication and Impact • Commitment and Co-operation
• Managing and Developing People • Coaching and Developing Others • People Management • Influencing • Building Relationships • Team Player	• Strategic Focus and Leadership • Leadership • Change Management • Customer Service • Strategic Awareness

Key Learning and Development
1.
2.
3.

Section 3: Miscellaneous Issues, Particular to Your Business Unit's Needs

Are there any upcoming events that will impact on the Training and Development needs in your department over the next 12 months (for example, maternity leave, career break, staff turnover staff promotion, etc)? Taking into account these changes, what learning and development should take place?

Key Events	Key Learning and Development
1.	1.
2.	2.
3.	3.

In thinking about the timing of training for your department over the next 12 months, what times of the year are particularly *inconvenient* for participating in training and development programmes?

Start of the month in general (please tick) ____   Any month in particular (name) _____
End of the month in general (please tick) ____   Any season in particular (name) _____

Our Team's Training and Development Budget is _____ Euro
(The target for the division being 6% of the total payroll)

In thinking about your team's Training and Development needs for next year, please note that XYZ's policy is to allocate a minimum number of 6 days Training and Development per team member over the coming 12-month period.

The date for the next Management Meeting is _____

Note: This document is an example of a questionnaire used by the Learning and Development Team in AIB Capital Markets.

You have a number of generic methods to select from when conducting a training needs assessment at the organisational level. Because no one method is superior to the others, multiple methods are usually used. The methods we suggest vary in the type of information as well as the level of detail of the information they potentially provide. We provide a detailed summary of the advantages and disadvantages of a range of data collection methods in **Figure 4.8**.

FIGURE 4.8: ADVANTAGES & DISADVANTAGES OF ALTERNATIVE NEEDS ASSESSMENT DATA COLLECTION METHODS

Method	Advantages	Disadvantages
Questionnaire	• Assess information from a large population • Produces quantitative data which is easy to analyse • Suitable for jobs involving intellectual tasks or knowledge employees • An economical way of surveying many people • Individuals can complete questionnaires at their own pace • All respondents are asked same questions in same format • Material gathered can be easily analysed • Comparatively inexpensive to produce and administer • Can be used with jobholders spread over a wide area • Provide a cost-effective and reliable means for gathering both qualitative and quantitative feedback • It is a non-obtrusive means of gathering feedback • Relatively simple and straight forward and does not require an excessive amount of time • Structure on the questions helps with the analysis of data	• Does not provide highly specific or targeted data • Requires careful construction to be objective and statistically viable • May get back many inappropriate responses • Heavy dependence placed on recall and respondents may not answer honestly • Result depends on the quality of the questions asked • Response rate to questionnaires is not high (<30%) • Questions can be ambiguous or misunderstood by respondent • There is no opportunity to check understanding • Respondents may look to give the "right answer"

Method	Advantages	Disadvantages
Interviews	• May collect initial data for idea generation or validate findings from other data collection methods • Yields most detailed information • It is an opportunity to share ideas • Allows probing when descriptions are unclear or inconsistent • Interviewer can check for understanding • Useful for long and short-cycle jobs • Flexible in terms of time • Records views, opinions, attitudes, perceptions and observations • Appropriate instrument to use at occupational and individual level for both reactive and proactive studies	• Most time-consuming and expensive method of collecting data for a needs analysis • Requires experienced interviewer to direct the conversation effectively • Over-dependence on the interviewer's contribution and ability to mention all tasks • Interviewee can distort facts, by not answering honestly or not being able to verbalise what he or she feels • Sometimes difficult to analyse results • It can be difficult to get access to people to conduct an interview
Observation	• Allows first-hand understanding of work systems • Most effective in manufacturing environment • Illustrates what the job holder actually does rather than what they say they do • Few people are needed to conduct the analysis and recording is done by the observer • Minimal, if any, disturbance caused to the operations process • Helpful when analysing tasks which the holder had difficulty in describing • Clear picture gained of total job conditions and content • Flexible in use of time • Opportunity to ask questions and test knowledge • Empirical data produced and can be proved or disproved	• Observations may alter an individual's behaviour, skewing data • Requires observer knowledge of the work being performed • Observer needs refined observation skills • Expensive and time-consuming to observe activities and prepare the job analysis schedule • Inappropriate for jobs consisting of intellectual rather than manual tasks • May require the trainee to give feedback during observation • Not all of the jobs may be observed depending on the frequency of the tasks • Difficult to record in useful format • Data provided are not generally significant enough to draw conclusions with a relative degree of certainty

Method	Advantages	Disadvantages
360 Degree Feedback Performance Reviews	• Inexpensive data source – information already collected • Correlates training with performance and competency expectations • Ideal for top-level managers to receive feedback, as they may not get any on a day-to-day basis • The 360-degree method encourages peer feedback	• Not a good guide for targeted training programmes, particularly at department and company-wide levels • Requires extensive analysis to aggregate data to departmental or organisational levels • Tends to be reactive rather than proactive, focuses on areas in which employees demonstrated developmental needs, rather than the direction that the organisation is moving in • Staff and line managers sometimes reject this process
Group Discussions	• An individual's input can help others to recall more relevant material • Results are gathered and verified in a short time period • Misunderstandings can be clarified immediately	• It may be time-consuming and expensive • Needs skilful control of the group • People may be inhibited by higher-ranking staff and analysis may be costly and difficult to structure
Diaries	• Useful for long-cycle jobs • Comparability inexpensive • Can be used with jobholders over widely-dispersed geographical area	• May take a long time to collect data • Jobholders need instructions on how to complete the diary • Can be time-consuming • Can be a nuisance for jobholder to carry around • Could be an interruption to the working activities of the jobholder
Read Technical Manuals and Records	• Good source of information on procedure and process • Relatively objective • Good source of task information for new jobs and jobs in the process of being created	• May experience difficulty in understanding technical knowledge • The material used may be obsolete • Can be time-consuming • Depends on the quality of the manual

IDENTIFYING T&D NEEDS AT THE JOB LEVEL

You have a wide range of options available to you here. The most common methods include common skills analysis, competency analysis, problem analysis, critical incident analysis, repertory grid analysis, interpersonal skills analysis, role analysis, stages and key points analysis, manual skills analysis, faults analysis and activity sampling analysis. We will give a brief description of each and indicate where it is appropriate. The methods we discuss here are applicable to a wide range of situations.

Common Skills Analysis

A description of the skills required to ensure competence in a specified range of jobs and tasks. These jobs, tasks and required skills are not organisation-specific and therefore need to be expressed in a way that can be understood by a variety of organisations. This analysis is often described as core analysis, as it involves determining the core transferable skills.

This method is often carried out at a national level, rather than an organisational level, *via* committees and working papers with comments from employers. It is an appropriate method where skills need to be transferable to a wide range of tasks and differing organisational settings. This method is appropriate for professional skills, such as computer programming, legal, accountancy and even managerial skills.

Common skills analysis has a number of advantages. Specifically, it is transferable between organisations and gives managers and individuals clear expectations about development. It has disadvantages in that it is time-consuming and it is difficult to produce good quality usable results. Organisations sometimes overlook certain categories of employees because of preconceived ideas about those particular groups – for example, where employees are expected to have the skills before joining the organisation and, therefore, it is deemed to be inappropriate in carrying out any analyses, especially in relation to core skills.

Competency Analysis

This method is defined as preparing behavioural data describing effective performance in a given range of jobs. Senior managers select jobholders so that there is a mix of outstanding and adequate performers. A highly-trained analyst, using a form of behavioural event interview, interviews these jobholders.

Individuals are asked to describe a situation in which they played a key role. The interviewer will probe the issue or problem: What the individual did and why? What their thought processes were? And the outcome? The interviews are usually taped and the transcripts are analysed to identify use of the different competencies, in both breadth and depth.

A competency profile is produced for each individual role and matched against the separate performance ranking of each individual by a group of senior managers. Thus, the competencies that define outstanding performance are identified. The competencies are described using a selection of behaviour indicators.

It is considered more useful for senior jobs, which are difficult to analyse. Once a desired competency profile has been identified for a given group of jobs, it can be used to identify training and experience required for jobholders. A current critical debate centres on whether all competencies are equally trainable. Although it may be possible to train individuals in all, it may require so much effort in some areas that a better way forward may be to ensure that those particular competencies are always selected at the recruitment stage.

Competency analysis is very valuable in that it expresses needs in behavioural terms. It also has generic application. It is, however, very time-consuming and quite complex to undertake.

Problem Analysis

This is a reactive approach. Once a problem has been identified, this approach involves collecting data about where it occurs, when it occurs, how frequently it occurs, who is involved, what the consequences are, and most importantly why it occurs.

The data needs to be collected from all parties involved in the problem, or those directly affected by the problem. A third party – for example, the trainer – usually collects the data. Informal interviews and meetings are the most effective way of collecting the data. It will provide a clear definition of the problem, an assessment of whether training has a contribution to make to its solution; and if so, an identification of the knowledge, skills and attitudes (if relevant) that need to be developed to aid problem solution, together with suggestions on how these needs can be met.

This method is appropriate in a wide range of circumstances, as long as there is sufficient goodwill to discuss problems openly.

Critical Incident Technique

Similar to problem analysis, this technique concentrates on certain parts of the job, and is therefore not comprehensive. In this case, the analyst needs to know of critical incidents that are related to successful performance of the job and those related to failure in the job.

The chief sources are the jobholder(s) and their supervisor or manager. If group activity were part of the working patterns within the organisation, a key source of information would be the incidents that have proved to decrease or enhance the effectiveness of that team or group.

The data is usually collected by asking the jobholders and supervisors to build up a diary of the incidents, writing them down as they happen. An alternative could be for the analyst to interview the jobholders and their supervisors and ask them to reflect back on the incidents and their consequences.

It is appropriate where some aspects of the job are clearly more fundamental than others and a comprehensive analysis is not required as job performance is generally satisfactory.

Repertory Grid Analysis

This type of analysis collects data about the constructs that people use to describe successful performance in a given job. Data is collected about performance in the whole job, and does not require the job to be broken down into parts. It is important, though, that all those contributing data have a good understanding of the job, and are in agreement over the job description. The analysis is also frequently used to identify needs related to "changing one's mental map" by applying the analysis both before and after a training event.

The constructs are elicited by means of a structured process. "Judges" are asked, either individually or as a group, to compare the skills of a set of people all doing the same job. The name of each member of the set is written on a separate card. Three of the cards are pulled out to start with and the judges are asked to describe a way in which one of the three performs better than the other two, and to label the skill that is being used. All the cards in the set are used in every combination possible, and are gone through as many times as required. The results of this process are a list of skills that differentiate performance, and are thus potential training needs. A grid is drawn up with the names of the individuals across the top and the skills down the side. Each individual is scored on a scale of 0 to 10 against each skill.

The grid can be used to identify general and individual training needs in that particular job. This method is particularly appropriate for management and supervisory development.

Interpersonal Skills Analysis

Interpersonal skills analysis concentrates on the interpersonal skills needed to carry out a job to the required performance standards. The skills are broken down into much greater detail than for other analysis.

These skills may relate to the management and supervision of staff, ability to co-operate with colleagues, response to being managed, team member's skills, team leader skills, and client and customer relationships – in fact any "people" aspect of the job being analysed. The emphasis is on identifying which skills exist and to what extent in the people involved rather than identifying what skills are needed (this stage of the process would already have been completed).

The main sources are the jobholders themselves. Their managers, clients, customers and colleagues may also be used to provide support data. The data is often collected during group exercises in which trained observers analyse all face-to-face behaviours and locate them in pre-defined detailed categories.

The main outputs are profiles of behaviours. The extent to which they are displayed can be produced for each person, and these can be used to identify both group and individual training needs.

Job / Role Analysis

Job/role analysis involves collecting information on the business role of the jobholder(s), including the duties and behaviours necessary for effective performance of the role – see **Figure 4.9**.

The main data sources are the jobholder(s), their manager and other members of the role set (the people with whom they regularly interact in order to do the job). All the individuals involved produce lists of duties and behaviours independently, and then discuss them collectively with help from the analyst. The differing perceptions of the different parties will be the focus point in these discussions.

The main outputs are an agreed list of duties and behaviours, and an understanding, through the discussion, of an agreed role. Development needs can then be identified, ensuring that any areas that caused problems in the discussion are given special attention. Any differences in perception and expectation that are not resolved are not training needs but require senior management action to resolve.

This method is particularly useful for management and supervisory roles where shared perceptions are important to successful performance. The technique might be particularly useful for the dedicated trainer role, as there is often misunderstanding in this area and the role is constantly changing.

FIGURE 4.9: STEPS IN CONDUCTING A JOB ANALYSIS FOR TRAINING PURPOSES

Many training activities are built around the actual duties and responsibilities that a job requires. Some of these include recruiting, testing, orientation, training, promotion, career development, equal employment, compensation, and so on. For example, effective recruiting, training, or compensating of an employee would be impossible unless you knew precisely what the employee was supposed to do. Job analysis is the process of determining the duties, tasks, and responsibilities of a job and provides a great deal of critical information to use in making personnel decisions. It is important that personnel administrators ensure that this activity is performed accurately.

Two general methods may be used to conduct a job analysis. One method is to use a "generic" or standardised system found in many organisations. Standardised methods generally employ lengthy checklists whereby employees check the job duties and responsibilities that apply to their jobs. Some organisations develop their own non-standardised system. An organisation may choose to develop and use its own system so that it may gather the specific kind of information it desires. Both systems have advantages and disadvantages; the method a particular organisation chooses depends on the purposes of the job analysis, the time available to develop a system, and the specificity of the information required.

Job analysis itself is actually an information-gathering process; the data collected is used to prepare documents that are commonly used to make personnel decisions. Perhaps the most common document is the job description, a one- or two-page summary containing important information about the job - major duties and responsibilities, working conditions, and so on.

Job Description Questionnaire

1. Employees Name:
    Title:
2. List the names and job titles of persons that you supervise and the percentage of time spent in supervision.
3. What is the lowest grade of grammar school, high school, or college that should be required of a person starting in your position?
4. What special type of training, skill, or experience is necessary for a person before starting in your position?
5. What training or experience is necessary for a person after assuming your position, and how long before the average person could be assumed to perform his or her own work satisfactorily without close supervision?
6. What machines or equipment do you operate in your work and for what percentage of your time?
7. What do you consider to be the most important decisions that you make in the course of your work, and what percentage of your time is devoted to making such decisions?
8. What responsibility do you have for handling money, securities, or other such valuables, and what is your estimate of the daily amounts of such?
9. What responsibility do you have in dealing with customers or other persons outside the company?
10. What things about your work surroundings (working conditions, hours, out-of-town travel, physical requirements, etc.) should be included in a description of your job?
11. What activities do you perform only at stated periods (weekly or monthly) or at irregular intervals?
12. What specific duties do you perform in the usual course of your daily work, and approximately what percentage of your workday is spent in each activity? (Please try to use active verbs such as type, file, interview, etc.)

Strategic Key Points Analysis

With this method, the job is described in terms of stages of activity – that is, the major steps that must be accomplished in order to complete the job. The instructions that must be followed in order to complete each stage are noted together with any key points that are seen as critical to ensure success.

The main sources of data are the jobholder(s) and supervisors or trained job instructors. The supervisor normally observes the jobholders in action and makes the appropriate notes on a pre-structured form.

The main outputs are a three-column form showing the stage, the instructions on how to achieve it, and key points. The skills are critical to successful performance begins to merge in the key points column. This method is most appropriate for semi-skilled jobs. The jobs need to be relatively simple, with a maximum learning time of a few days.

Stage	Instruction to Perform Stage	Key Points
1. Turn on system	• Switch on plug • Switch on machine at the back • Insert system disc • Remove system disc • Insert data disc	• Do not insert discs and then turn on • If nothing happens, remove disc before trying again
2. Select file and input mode	• Press RETURN for file menu • Select customer sales data file using cursor – press ENTER • Next menu, select action – "INPUT CUSTOMER DATA" using cursor • Press ENTER	• If press ENTER, nothing happens • If press RETURN, it will go back to main menu
3. To input	• Put on SHIFT LOCK and key in data	• Only capitals are accepted • If SHIFT LOCK not pressed then error message "Bad data" • Press CANCEL and start again pressing SHIFT LOCK first

Manual Skills Analysis

This method collects information about the hand, finger and body movements required to perform a job successfully. The analyst observes experienced workers and records hand, finger and body movements on a pre-structured sheet. This method is appropriate for short-cycle repetitive operations, for example, assembly work and other factory work, but can be applied to any jobs for which manual dexterity is important, such as potters or picture framers. It is a highly specialised and detailed technique and should only be used for difficult and unusual parts of a job, where stages and key points analysis, for example, would be insufficient.

Element of Job	Prepare for assembly
Left hand	Reach bin for No 1 circuit board, grasp between T & 1 at corner. Pick up and bring forward to bench
Right Hand	Loosen and rotate jig on bench with T & 1
Vision	Check colour of bin to ensure correct board and check position of jig to accept board
Other senses	Feel for position guide mark on jig
Comments	As jig is 360° rotating jig, it is vital that correct position is selected to accept board

T – thumb, 1 – first or index finger

Faults Analysis

This method concerns itself with faults that commonly occur in performing a job, especially those that are costly. Information about these faults is described in terms of how to recognise them, what causes them, what effect they have and how to prevent them. The main method used is observation and interview of experienced workers. Fault details are presented in the form of a table or a "decision tree". New employees can then use these as a training tool.

IDENTIFYING T&D NEEDS AT AN INDIVIDUAL LEVEL

You have a number of options available to examine training needs at the individual or person level. These methods include assessment and development centre data, customer and client data, data from subordinates and colleagues, self-assessment data, data from discussions career development plans.

Assessment and Development Centre Data

Assessment centre data may be available from the selection procedures that a new recruit has just experienced. It is available in organisations where assessment centres are held for particular employees at key organisational levels with a view to identifying capacity for promotion. Development centre data is often very similar, but the emphasis here is on agreeing an appropriate development plan for each individual to give them the best chances of promotion in the future.

Those who are being assessed will take part in a variety of different activities (team and individual) related to their potential work-roles. Trained observers, including HR and training professionals and sometimes senior managers of the organisation, will observe them throughout. Detailed ratings of behaviour can be produced, especially in the area of interpersonal skills. The quality of the data is dependent on the skill and training of the assessors. The data is described in behavioural terms and this helps in clearly identifying training needs.

Informal Feedback

This can consist of *ad hoc* comments from one manager to another about the performance of an individual member of staff. Where you decide to collect the data deliberately, it may be collected by telephone, or *via* a written request for general comments, or by using a checklist or questionnaire. The method you use will depend on the type of job and organisation. A training manager might collect performance data about training specialists by contacting the heads of the departments, which they liaise with, and service. Telephone contact or a letter asking for broadly-structured information may be appropriate for this purpose.

Subordinate and Colleague Data

This data is most likely to be unsolicited, although some organisations do collect this sort of information in a structured way. This data is most likely to be in the form of complaint rather than praise, and is often presented in an emotional climate, depending on culture of feedback within the organisation. It is vital therefore that the receiver of the data receives full and precise accounts of what has happened, and also collects the viewpoint of the subject of the data. The quality of the data is only adequate in so far as specific examples are fully checked from all viewpoints.

Self-Assessment Data

This consists of comments by the individual to the effect that they are experiencing difficulty with a part of their job and see the solution as some form of training. Sometimes self-assessment questionnaires are used by organisations.

The data may be vaguely presented, for example, "I need to go on an assertiveness course". On the other hand, it may be clearly thought through with examples of situations where the individual has experienced difficulty and their perceptions of the causes of the difficulty, for example, "I find it difficult to remind others about information they have promised me without being aggressive with them. I want to be able to remind them firmly and assertively without being aggressive". This data is sometimes hard to collect in organisations where pay is directly linked to performance, and where individuals do not feel secure enough to admit that they have a problem.

The quality of this data will depend on the ability of individuals to assess themselves. The request to attend a training event, in itself, is not good quality data – it may not indicate a training need, but rather that the individual sees it as a perk, or enjoys attending courses, relevant or not. Good quality data will be backed by situational examples.

Data from Work Discussions

Any comments from an individual during work discussions that indicate that they do not understand a part of their role or objectives, or are having difficulty putting their understanding into practice due to lack of the appropriate skills. A manager should be constantly receptive to this type of data, and any discussion is a potential opportunity to collect it. Once the manager has identified a potential problem, the best way to introduce it is to give individuals every opportunity to raise it themselves.

The manager is likely to get the best quality data provided he/she encourages the individual to raise the issue and offers full background information.

Career Development Plans / Performance Reviews

This data consists of the title and description of a job that the individual may be promoted to in a specified time span. There may be an analysis of the knowledge, skills and attributes required in the new job. The difference between the new requirements and current requirements will indicate potential training needs. Data in the career planning system needs to be made available to the individual's current manager, as does data from any assessment or development centre that the individual has attended. The current manager and perhaps the individual's potential manager will each need to work with the individual to identify the needs from the data available and determine how to satisfy them. The quality of this data is dependent on the full involvement of all parties.

ISSUES AT DIFFERENT LEVELS OF ANALYSIS

We will now address some of the issues you should consider at different levels of analysis.

Organisation Environment Level

You will more than likely focus on this level if you are a training manager. If you are a direct trainer, you are more likely to focus on the work and individual employee level.

At the organisation environment level, you will direct your attention to assessing how well the organization is interacting with its external environment. The following are some of the issues that should be addressed:

- Who are the key stakeholders outside the organisation considered critical for the organisation success?

- How does the organisation interact with its external environment?

- What demands do customers, suppliers, distributors, stockholders and regulators make in terms of training requirements?

- How effective is the organisation's strategic plan in helping it to manage its external environment?

The Work Environment

The focus of investigation here is with what is happening inside the organisation. A host of factors may be relevant here, although we suggest that the following are important issues:

- What are the current priorities within the organisation?

- How well does the organisation meet the requirements of a high performance work organisation?

- What are current perceptions about how well the organisation operates?

- How well is the organisation equipped to meet customer requirements, supplier requirements, etc?

- What factors currently contribute to high performance?

The Work Level

This level focuses on characteristics of the work, including the workflow across departments, team functioning and jobs. We have already highlighted some of the methods you can use, including interviews, focus groups, questionnaires, etc. When you are examining performance issues at this level, you will need to address these issues:

- Have job performance standards been formulated and expressed to employees so that they know exactly what results are expected of them?

- How well do performers understand, and agree with, the job performance standards?

- How attainable and realistic are the job performance standards, in the opinions of the employees?
- How well are the employees able to recognise when they should take action?
- How free are employees to perform without interference from other tasks, distractions from the work environment, or safety hazards?
- How efficient and effective are existing work policies and procedures?
- How adequate are the resources supplied to do the work? Have employees been given appropriate time, tools, staff, information, and equipment?
- How clear are the consequences of performance? Do performers receive timely, specific feedback on how useful their labours are to customers, suppliers, distributors, and other stakeholders?
- How meaningful are work consequences from the employees' standpoint?
- What value do employees associate with the results of their efforts? How and when are they rewarded for achieving exemplary results? Do they perceive the rewards to be fair and equitable?

Characteristics of the Employee

This is generally called person level analysis. Your focus will be to investigate issues that impact the performance of employees and the extent to which their competencies match the work requirements.

As a direct trainer, your work will likely focus to a large degree on this level. You should consider the following issues:

- What kinds of people are doing the work?
- How were people chosen for the work they do?
- How are people hired, terminated, transferred or promoted?
- What competencies do the people possess?
- How well has the organisation achieved an effective match between individual competencies and work requirements?
- How long have the performers been doing their work?
- How often have performers had occasion to practice all aspects of their work?
- How do the performers feel about the work they do? Their work environment? The organisational environment?
- How motivated are the performers?

ANALYSING YOUR DATA

When implementing the identification of training needs process you need to "achieve a balance between time spent on analysis and yielding timely beneficial training opportunities". Companies often spend too much time on data collection and use sources that take much longer and consequently may not be a useful source of information in the attempt to identify the training needs. Choose a few different sources. Balancing quantitative and qualitative data is essential. You need to focus on short and long term needs of the company. This will allow the organisation to prepare for future demands and address current training deficiencies.

Analysis of Interview Data

Due to the quantity of data in interviews, a considerable amount of time is required to analyse the data. Due to the volume of data, it may be difficult to extract the precise information required, so it is important to constantly refer to the original goals of the training needs analysis to keep focus on original information being sought.

Once the analysis has been completed, a formal report with recommendations should be prepared and used in conjunction with other sources of data to prepare an overall picture of the training needs of the organisation.

Analysis of Survey Questionnaires

Because of the importance of the data, it is very important to set out guidelines when analysing survey questionnaire results:

- Consideration must be given how to treat incomplete or partly incomplete questionnaires
- Where more than one person is analysing the data, great care must be taken to make sure each person is using the same methods of analysis
- When using computers, constant checks must be completed for data errors
- Decisions on how to treat "questionable" answers should be made *before* analysis.

Once the data has been extracted, it must be analysed and will then be used along with other sources of data in order to get a clear picture of the training needs of the organisation.

Analysis of Focus Groups

Information gathered from a focus group may not be very specific and will most likely be qualitative in nature. When attempting to analyse feedback from a focus group, care must be taken to minimise bias, which can be systematically introduced into the focus group process in a number of ways:

- Moderator phrasing questions that leads the participants to only one conclusion
- The group being dominated by one or two participants, thereby getting an unbalanced view from the group as a whole
- By the facilitator not guiding or structuring group sessions properly
- Not having well defined goals from the outset.

When analysing data from focus groups, you must constantly refer back to the group's original goals and objectives in order for it to be an effective process. Again, focus groups should not be used as a stand-alone approach, but should be used in conjunction with other data-gathering methods.

Analysis of Observations

Observation is a valuable method to use in conjunction with other data-gathering methods as part of a systematic approach to determining individual, as well as organisational, training needs. It is an effective way of gathering qualitative and quantitative data.

The analysis should be carried out by an experienced and knowledgeable individual/s, who have knowledge of work processes, procedures, methods and practices. Usually a previous employee is used, as great knowledge is known within.

When the analysis of the data gathered is completed, a clear picture should be generated of what the training needs of the organisation are. However, the analysis may uncover various non-training needs. Any training and non-training recommendations must reflect genuine needs at organisational group and individual levels – for example, training may not be the answer to some of the needs uncovered in the analysis, which may be solved through a different method. Before proposing non-training or training solutions, the facts, figures and feelings collected need to be validated.

IDENTIFYING YOUR T&D PRIORITIES

When training needs are identified, it may not be possible to meet all of them, so it may be necessary to prioritise training. Issues to be taken into consideration when prioritising training needs are:

- Where do the major training "gaps" exist?
- How urgent is the training?
- Does the training fit in with the organisational goals?

- What are the resources available and the costs involved?
- Does it require a buy or design decision?
- At what level do the training needs exist?
- Does the training need address an operational or organisational issue?

It is important that any training needs are needs and not wishes. There are three questions you should ask to make a judgement here:

- **Question 1:** Will meeting the need improve current performance in the individual's present job? Priority training has to be targeted at improving individual and organisational performance. The job in question must be the job defined by the organisation – not the individual

- **Question 2:** Will meeting the need enhance performance in an expended or changing job? Where an expanded or changing job is planned for the individual, training to help them meet the new requirements of that job is a priority

- **Question 3:** Will meeting the need enhance or enable appropriate performance in another job (promotion or development move)? Backing up career and succession planning with appropriate training and development is a priority for organisations.

Any training and non-training recommendations must reflect genuine needs at organisational, group and individual level. These needs are not merely present deficiencies but responses and initiatives required to confront future change. Once this has been done, you need to clarify the type of intervention required (coaching, classroom training, computer-based training, etc) and then prioritise them according to level of urgency.

Whatever means of gathering data, once gathered, it must be analysed in great detail to determine what action to take. Data only becomes meaningful information once it has been organised and interpreted.

When all of these are taken into consideration, a training plan should be drawn up and presented. The end result of the training needs identification process is the production of a T&D plan. You should produce the plan, and should use it to strategically plan what kind of training will be conducted in the future.

OUTPUTS FROM THE T&D NEEDS PROCESS

There are a number of important outputs that you can derive from a training needs process. These include an individual development plan, job descriptions, person specifications and competency profiles and job training specifications.

Individual T&D Plans

The output of development needs identification at the individual level is an individual T&D plan. This is similar in form to job level analyses, job descriptions, person specifications and any job training specification – but is tailored to the needs of an individual. There are three main parts to this plan:

- Identification of the skills and/or knowledge area to be developed – for example, planning, coaching, interviewing or report-writing skills

- Description of the development goal. This describes in more detail where and how the skills needs to be applied, and any factors crucial to success – for example, "to write reports based on scientific data, in summary form, so that they are understandable to non-scientists"

- Description of development activities, which may include course attendance, but more importantly other activities such as meetings/discussions with others, coaching from the line manager, short periods of job rotation, acting as a representative on a committee and so on. These activities need to be timed and reviewed.

The following example of an individual development plan is based on a senior secretary/personal assistant who has been nominated to attend and present progress reports to a committee, which includes senior department managers.

Development Goal	Development Activities	Progress	Date
To present factual material in a confident and structured way to senior audiences	Agree purpose / length / style of presentations to the committees with manager	Completed No problems	10 Nov
	Attend presentations skills event and use the committee presentations in practice sessions	Date agreed for Jan	10 Jan
	Give short presentation to the secretaries' group on current secretarial training; Get feedback from them	Done in Dec. Time planning identified as a problem	2 Dec
	Coaching meeting with manager – learning from the event and the secretarial presentation – any problem areas to resolve	Discuss time planning with manager and agree to meet again after course	9 Dec
	Run through presentation with manager and ask for feedback		
	Presentation to the committee – manager to get some feedback from members		

It is crucial that the plan be agreed between the individual and their manager through a process of discussion. Although the plan will be the individual's own, the manager has a key role in coaching and in reviewing progress towards the goal and application of the new skills.

Job Description

All the forms of needs analysis described in this chapter result in, or require, initial agreement on some form of job description. The type of job description that is produced will vary depending on the method used. Some techniques will result in a thorough description, such as the comprehensive task, knowledge, skill and attitudes analysis, or stages and key points analysis. Others will be confined to describing a part of the job, as in problem analysis. Others will require that analysis and their data sources agree on a broadly-defined description, concentrating perhaps on six or seven key result areas or output areas, as for repertory grid analysis and competency analysis.

On many occasions, an up-to-date job description will be in existence, such as one that has just been written for recruitment or job evaluation purposes. As long as it is not biased in any way, this data can be used in its current form for the analysis of training needs, or can be used as the basis of a more detailed description.

Person Specification and Competency Profiles

The person specification is derived from the job description, either directly, as in key task, knowledge, skills and attitudes analysis, and manual skills analysis, or less directly, as in interpersonal skills analysis or repertory grid analysis.

Competencies are job skills defined in behavioural terms and can be used alone or in conjunction with the traditional person specification. Both describe necessary attributes to perform the job. Both the specification and the profile describe the essential knowledge, skills and attributes or competencies that any individual needs to possess in order to carry out the job as described to the performance level required (adequate or competent performance). There may well be a person specification or competency profile in existence which is appropriate and adequate, or which can be developed.

FIGURE 4.10: CONDUCTING A TRAINING NEEDS ANALYSIS: GUIDELINES FOR GOOD PRACTICE

Dimension	Key Issues to Consider
Context and Aims	• Are you concerned with defining the gap between what is happening and what should happen? • Are you also concerned with positive issues such as satisfying a learning and development need, such as multi-skilling or preparing employees for higher levels of responsibility? • Is there a clear justification for the needs analysis? • Have the cost dimensions been examined and justified? • Is there senior management support and buy-in for the analysis?
Levels of Analysis and Data Sources	• What level of analysis do you intend to focus on? Is it organisational, team, work or individual or all levels? • What is the time-scale to conduct the analysis? • Do you possess the skills to conduct the analysis? • What data sources can you access to conduct the analysis? • Does the organisation have written sources such as employee files, requests for training, requests for job transfers, exit interview results, accident reports, employee complaints, performance appraisals, job descriptions and productivity reports? • Who are the key informants in the organisation? • Do you have access to customers, employees, suppliers, management and external consultants?
Methods of Data Collection	• What data collection methods have you considered? • Do you possess the expertise to use individual and group interviews, questionnaires, focus groups, observance, job analysis, psychometric testing? • What are the cost implications associated with the use of each method? • What implications does the use of a particular method have for confidentiality? • Do you possess the skills to analyse the data outputs of different methods? • Are there cultural sensitivities associated with the use of particular data collection methods?

Analysis of Data Collected	• What time-scales are available in order to conduct the analysis?
	• Do you have the internal expertise to conduct the analysis?
	• Who will you involve in the analysis?
	• How do you intend to protect the confidentiality of the data?
	• How will you identify training *versus* non-training type problems?
	• Have you considered non-training reasons for performance gaps such as employees forgetting to perform, lack of clarity about expectations, poor feedback, lack of physical resources and/or time, poor job documentation, an inappropriate organisational culture and/or lack of clarity about performance expectations?
	• How do you intend to categorise T&D needs:
	  • At what level does the need exist?
	  • Is the need concerned with doing things well, better or with doing new and better things?
	  • What type of report outputs do you intend to produce?
	  • Who will you involve in the data analysis process?
	  • What criteria will you use to prioritise your training needs?

Publicising Findings and Securing Resources	• How will you disseminate your findings? • Who will you formally present your findings to? • How will you make a case for training resources? • What time-scale will you plan T&D activities for?

BEST PRACTICE INDICATORS

Some of the best practice issues that you should consider related to the contents of this chapter are:

- A collaborative TNA process leads to review at corporate level of outcomes of past T&D activity, and agreement on needs to be met by the forthcoming annual training plan. The training manager/HR director is a full partner in this process and has the responsibility for the preparation of that plan and its submission to top management

- At business-unit level, the TNA process involves managers working with T&D specialist personnel to identify the skills and attitudes needed to achieve unit business targets, to assess the current work-force profile, to identify any gaps representing T&D needs and to plan how to meet those needs

- At organisational level, the TNA process emerges from that individual appraisal and from team reviews that form part of the performance management process

- Prioritisation of T&D needs at all levels is determined by reference to clear criteria that are well communicated to all employees

- At all organisational levels, the TNA process is supported by a set of simple procedures to ensure its consistency, regularity and fairness of use across the organisation

- Be sure to include key stakeholders in the needs assessment process. Their involvement at this phase will help solidify support for training

- Conduct an organisational needs assessment to evaluate the current climate for learning. This should help policies and practices for training as well as other HR practices

- Conduct person or individual analysis to determine employee readiness for training. A successful training intervention requires that you should gather data to determine the best approach to training as well as how to promote the training intervention.

Reflections on the Training & Development Scenario

The purpose of these scenarios is to illustrate the types of situations that are appropriate for a T&D solution.

Scenario one reveals a problem unsuitable for a training solution. The performance problem arises from an external influence – a personal problem. The most likely solution to address the problem is some form of counselling intervention or participation on an employee assistance programme.

Scenario two reveals a problem that may be solved with an appropriate training intervention. The key dimensions of the problem concern the employee's attitude towards the task of supervision and the style of supervision used. Denise needs to be given feedback on her managerial style. This should enhance her self-awareness. Some form of coaching solution would be appropriate to help develop her skills to delegate, plan and organise effectively.

Scenario three reveals an induction problem. The employee, Reilly, is a new employee. She has knowledge deficiencies concerning the job. She also experiences problems concerning the expectations of her boss. This problem can be solved using a training solution. The most appropriate training solution is a structured, induction programme, which should be delivered by the supervisor. There are relationship issues that need to be addressed in order for the induction to be effective.

Scenario four reveals a team problem. It is likely that some form of team training solution may be appropriate. The focus here will be on team-working skills. Four dimensions of team-working skills are particularly relevant:
- Team-building skills to enhance the cohesiveness of the team and integrate less effective team-workers into the team
- Team conflict management skills to address the dysfunctional aspects of the current team
- Skills to cope with team decision-making and develop the confidence of team-members in making these decisions
- Skills in effective team leadership.

The scenario also reveals elements of a selection problem.

Scenario five reveals a problem that can be easily solved using a T&D solution. Mark currently does not have an understanding of the supervisory role and of the need to work through his subordinate to achieve task completion. He would benefit considerably from a formal supervisory development programme and some form of job coaching.

Chapter Five

TRAINING DESIGN: OBJECTIVES & CONTENT

LEARNING OBJECTIVES

On completion of this chapter, you should be able to:

- Describe the main components of the training design process
- List the types of questions you should ask when designing a learning event
- Describe the reasons for setting smart learning objectives and identify the characteristics and benefits of well-written learning objectives
- Describe the different types of learning objectives that are appropriate
- Describe some of the "rules" that you should follow when developing training course content
- List the rules that should be followed when sequencing training content.

A Training & Development Scenario

The company is an engineering contractor. Your managing director states that the company really must do something about its estimating. After some research you discover three things:

- The "model" the MD wants replicated is an employee named Jack, who has been kept on beyond retiring age, because there are no satisfactory replacements

- There is a shortage of estimators who can price any of the company's projects

- Before you can bring any of the existing estimators up to Jack's standard, someone must train replacements.

You set up a working party of chief estimators, who decide that the only people who can train the replacements are the six people who will eventually be trained as senior estimators.

Estimators are rarely instructors: the last people who would willingly face an audience. However, the six chosen are all competent performers in different aspects of their occupation. They learned their skills on the job, with some coaching from senior colleagues. None of them have been on a formal training course with the company.

The estimating managers tell you they can spare all six estimators together for just one week.

Your task is to devise the outline of a week-long event that will turn the existing estimators into competent instructors.

INTRODUCTION

We considered the training needs analysis process in **Chapter Four**. In this chapter, we move on from the needs analysis process to consider how these needs translate into learning objectives and learning content. We focus on two elements of the training design process in this chapter:

- The formulation of learning objectives
- How these learning objectives translate into content.

We also integrate key principles about how people learn as part of the design process. You can refer back to **Chapter Three** to refresh your memory on adult learning principles and theories.

The training design phase is concerned with preparing the blueprint for a training programme or intervention. In your real work experience, you will be asked to plan and design training activities that range from straightforward to highly complex – for example, the task could involve anything from the design of an on-the-job training activity to the design of a complex management development programme. The key decisions are essentially the same irrespective of the complexity involved. It is critical that you are clear about the key learning objectives, the content and structure of the training event that you propose to run.

COMPONENTS OF THE TRAINING DESIGN PROCESS

We suggest that the overall training design process can be represented in the following sequence of activities:

- Specifying learning objectives
- Specifying learning content
- Selecting learning methods
- Structuring and sequencing the training programme.

These activities fall within the systematic training model. Systematic training can be defined as "training specifically designed to meet defined needs". It is planned and provided by people who know how to train and the impact of the training is carefully evaluated. A systematic model, however, is based on the premise that training and development is the appropriate course of action. **Figure 5.1** presents an outline of the components of a systematic approach to training design.

FIGURE 5.1: COMPONENTS OF T&D PROCESS

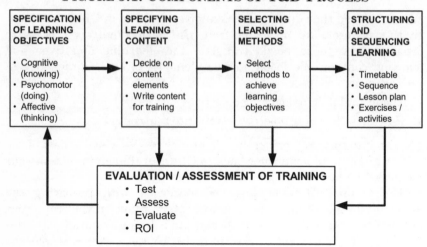

You should remember that the design of training activities is not an exact science, but involves judgement and intuition and a certain amount of "trial and error". **Figure 5.2** presents a checklist of questions that you should consider when designing a training event.

LEARNING OBJECTIVES: PURPOSES & CHARACTERISTICS

We have already emphasised that the process of setting learning objectives is an important part of training design.

Learning objectives serve three main purposes:

- Define the desired learning outcomes that you can expect to achieve your training event
- Provide guidelines for the design of the training programme and help you with the selection of learning methods and activities
- Provide you with criteria to enable you to evaluate the training activity.

Learning objectives provide a critical link between the identification of learning needs and the actual design and delivery of learning. Well-written learning objectives should possess the following characteristics:

- They should be as clear as possible, ideally indicating the specific behaviours to be achieved
- They should be as quantifiable as possible
- They should be achievable within the time scale specified for the training.

FIGURE 5.2: CHECKLIST FOR DESIGNING A TRAINING EVENT

Contextual Issues

TRAINER CHARACTERISTICS

- What are your characteristics as a person? Your values?
- What is your perspective on adult learning and self-development?
- What do the words "learning" and "development" mean to you?
- Do you accept and treat adult learners as individuals, with individual learning needs? Are you sure? Do you accept the full implications of the question?
- Do you adopt a "helping" rather than a "teaching" stance?
- Do you positively discourage adult learners from dependence on you?
- Do you positively discourage yourself from believing that you know best what is good for them?
- Do you see yourself as a co-learner?
- To what extent might there be a gap between what you think your approach to learning is (your "espoused" view) and what it is in practice (your "in-use" approach)?
- What are your own learning/development needs in terms of this particular event?
- What are you hoping to achieve personally?
- What are you hoping to achieve personally?
- What are you hoping to help the learners to achieve for themselves?

LEARNER CHARACTERISTICS

- Who are they?
- What are their characteristics as people? Their values? How different are they from one another?
- What are their perspectives on learning and self-development?
- How do they view the words "learning" and "self development"?
- How do they prefer to learn?
- Do they prefer to develop themselves, or be 'developed'?
- How might they be helped to develop their individual approaches to learning?
- What are their learning/development needs?
- How have these needs been identified?
- Have the learners themselves been involved in the identification of these needs?
- If not, how will you/they ensure the success of the event?
- What do they want to get out of the event?
- How do you know?
- Could it change as the event progresses?

The Organisation
- What are the organisation's values? Its views on what should be achieved?
- What specifically does the organisation want? How will success be measured?
- What would be the political implications of such "success" or "failure"?
- How does the answer fit with your own personal values?

The Psychological Contract
- Do all the stakeholders know where they stand in relation to the event? Do they appreciate the implications of what adult learning involves?
- Has an appropriate psychological contract for the event been achieved?

LEARNING EVENT CHARACTERISTICS

The Purpose

- In view of the above answers, what should be the purpose of the learning event? Who should decide it?
- Is it appropriate that the purpose should be clarified before the event? Or should it be left until the event is under way? Again, who decides? If not the learners, why not?
- Are all concerned fully aware of the implications arising from such an approach?
- What mix of learning aims (informing/skilling/developing) and levels of learning (memory, understanding, application, transfer) is appropriate to this particular learning event?
- Is the truism that "adults learn by doing, not by being told" reflected in the purpose?
- Is the purpose Justifiable? Realistic? Practicable? Within the constraints which apply ... from everybody's point of view?
- Will the purpose be "owned" by the learners? Are you sure?

The Design

- In view of the purpose, what learning design is appropriate?
- Will the learners themselves be involved in deciding the design? If not, why not?
- What methods/approaches would be most effective in meeting the purpose? In what mix?
- If the learners are not involved in this decision, why not? Can the approach be justified? From whose point of view?
- What is the environment within which the design will be implemented?
- What abilities are assumed in those participating in the event? Are these assumptions realistic?
- Is the design creative? Is it capable of being implemented a number of times? Does it need to be?

Implementation / Delivery

- What factors should be considered in implementing the design?
- What should be your role?
- What should be the role of the learner?
- Do you possess the necessary mix of interpersonal skills to implement the design? Do you have the ability to: Ask the right questions to help self-discovery? Listen actively without prejudging what is said? Allow learners to make mistakes and take responsibility for their own learning? Withstand the emotional pressure from those who may wish to be "taught the right way"? Help learners "own" their own learning?
- Have you the necessary conviction to persist in this approach even when feelings are running high? Are you sure you can be "comfortable" in your resistance?

Evaluation / Validation

- What evaluation of the learning event should there be? Who should take the decision? If the learners themselves are not to be involved, why not?
- When should the broad decision be taken?
- What methods should be used? What alternatives are available? Who should review them?
- How should the different perceptions and needs of those involved be accommodated?
- What should be evaluated? The purpose of the event? The design? The implementation? The evaluation process chosen? The totality? Or something else?
- Who should decide? When?
- What should be the order of priority?
- How quick must the evaluation be? Why that quick?
- What are the longer-term implications of the event?
- When should the evaluation be carried out? Continuously throughout the event? At the conclusion? At some other time?
- Who should be involved in the evaluation? If the learners themselves are not involved, why not? Who else must be considered?
- What other follow-up should there be?

Most trainers agree on the value of setting learning objectives, although there are dissenting views. Some trainers find that rigorous objective setting makes the learning activity "too cold and clinical", whereas others point to difficulties in composing objectives, especially those reflecting attitudinal learning outcomes.

Turning needs statements into learning objectives is not always an easy task. It is relatively simple to write tangible objectives from statements in the psychomotor (skills) areas, but much more difficult when you are focusing on knowledge, attitudes and longer-term training needs.

We summarise some of the benefits and difficulties associated with setting learning objectives in **Figure 5.3**.

COMPONENTS OF A LEARNING OBJECTIVE

There are three main components to a learning objective, which can be summarised as:

- The required **performance** or action that the learners are expected to display at the end of the programme
- The **standards** that the learners are expected to reach
- The **conditions** under which they are to perform.

FIGURE 5.3: ADVANTAGES & DISADVANTAGES OF SETTING LEARNING OBJECTIVES

Advantages	Disadvantages
• They give a sense of direction • They help focus the attention of the learner • Their achievement helps the motivation of the learner • They provide a measure of performance to both the learner and trainer • Learning outcomes can be measured more objectively • They may increase the trainer's pride and job satisfaction • Learners are clearer about what is expected of them on completion of the training • They provide the opportunity to sit down with the manager to discuss progress	• They tend to be imposed by the trainer rather than negotiated • There is sometimes little or no involvement of the individual learner • Achievement is largely dependent on the performance of others, over whom they have no control • It often becomes a one-off paperwork exercise; once set, they may never see the light of day again • Difficult learning objectives may be set for which there is no chance of achievement • There may be little or no feedback on how well an individual is performing • Difficult to measure what the learner has achieved • They are a mechanism to impose order; however, they may impose too much order

The following are examples of learning objectives that reflect the three components:

Knowledge Objectives	Skill Objectives	Affective Objectives
• At the end of this two-day induction programme, you will be able to recall the main features of the organisation. You will be able to define the primary business objectives of the organisation	• At the end of this one-day programme on employee selection, participants will be able to prepare a job description to a required format specified by the HR function	• At the end of this week-long programme of customer service training, participants will recognise the importance of consistently delivering high quality customer service when interacting with customers
• At the end of the two-day induction programme, participants will be able to recall / list the rules related to the use of email within this company and ensure their consistent application	• At the end of this year-long diploma programme, you will be able to write a training policy statement that reflects the needs of the business and conforms with good practice, external training benchmarks and current laws	• Participants, on completion of the two-day programme, will be continually conscious that they have ownership of quality issues when performing their duties on the assembly line
• Participants, at the end of this two-day programme, will understand the rules to be followed when performing work in order to comply with the requirements of the FDA	• At the end of this three-day job skills course, you will be able to conduct independently a change over on the screen-printer machine, following manufacturing instructions from one product to another during a production cycle	• Participants will, on completion of this one-day programme on customer care, take full ownership of customer complaints and respond to them
	• At the end of this two-day team-building programme, participants will be able to make proposals during regular team meetings for change in a positive and non-threatening way.	• At the end of this weeklong induction programme, participants will accept responsibility for safe working within the plant and implement safe working practices when performing their duties

Figure 5.4 identifies a number of questions that you should consider to guide your analysis of a learning objective to determine its level of acceptability. A *No* answer to any question will pinpoint a characteristic that is missing or ambiguously stated. Clarity is judged by whether or not another person's restatement of the objectives is consistent with your intent.

FIGURE 5.4: QUESTIONS TO CONSIDER WHEN SETTING LEARNING OBJECTIVES

1. Is it clear WHO will be performing the action?
   It is not always necessary to state the "who" explicitly (the learner, the student, the trainee), unless there is potential for confusion about who is performing the action. Objectives should be written in terms of the performance outcomes you expect of the learner.

2. Is it clear WHAT the learner will be doing? Is the behaviour observable and/or measurable?

3. Is it clear UNDER WHAT CONDITIONS the learner will be performing?
   There are two dimensions to this characteristic:
   a) it may be appropriate to specify what the learner will be provided with during the learning event
   b) it may be appropriate to describe the situation in which you expect the behaviour to occur (when conducting a CAA board meeting ...; when confronted by an irate customer ...; when preparing to submit a proposal).

4. Is it clear WHAT LEVEL OF PROFICIENCY OR COMPETENCY is expected?
   This may be stated in such terms as a number of percentage of correct test items, a change in score on an attitude inventory, execution of a process according to a prescribed sequence or other criteria. If time is a factor in successful performance, that may be specified as well.

5. Is it clear WHEN this behaviour is expected to be demonstrated?
   This characteristic is usually stated in terms of the length of the instructional experience (at the end of a session, at the end of a week, after a certain number of practice sessions).

LEARNING OBJECTIVES: CLASSIFICATIONS & TYPOLOGIES

We will consider three models or frameworks that you can use when preparing training objectives. These hypotheses are theoretical, although they have useful application to the training area.

Bloom's Typology of Learning

Bloom (1976) developed a categorisation of cognitive or knowledge capacities that is of considerable value to a trainer. This model has a number of benefits; in particular, it suggests a hierarchy that can be relatively easily applied to a range of training situations that you are likely to encounter.

Bloom makes three major divisions of learning objective, each called a "domain":

- The cognitive – information and knowledge
- The affective – attitudes, emotions and values.
- The psychomotor – muscular and motor skills, but not interpersonal skills.

The Cognitive Domain (Knowledge)

This domain is based on a hierarchy ranging from mere knowledge of facts to the intellectual process of evaluation. Each category within the domain is assumed to include behaviour at the lower levels:

- **Knowledge:** This is based on recall and on the means of dealing with recalled information. It comprises:
  - ° Knowledge of specifics (terminology and specific facts)
  - ° Knowledge of ways and means of dealing with specifics (conventions, trends and sequences, classifications and categories, criteria and methodology)
  - ° Knowledge of the universals and abstractions in a field (principles and generalisations, theories and structures)
- **Comprehension:** This is the ability to grasp and utilise the meaning of material. It embraces "translation" from one form to another (words to numbers), interpretation (explaining, summarising), and extrapolation (predicting effects, consequences)
- **Application:** This involves the ability to use learned material in new situations. It necessitates the application of principles, theories, rules etc.
- **Analysis:** This involves the ability to break down learned material into component parts so that the internal structure is made clear. The analysis of relationships and the identification of the parts of a whole are vital
- **Synthesis:** This refers to the ability to combine separate elements so as to form "a new whole". Deduction and other aspects of logical thought are involved
- **Evaluation:** This concerns the ability to judge the value of material, with such judgements based on definite criteria or standards.

The Affective Domain (Attitudes and Values)

This domain is "attitudinal" in focus and ranges very widely, from heeding the simple reception of stimuli to the complex ability to characterise or value concepts. Many training activities that you will be asked to design focus on changing attitudes. Examples include developing positive attitudes to customer service, quality and health and safety. Bloom suggests that there are five major categories of attitude objectives:

- **Receiving:** This involves the trainer "attending" to, or heeding, messages or other stimuli. Awareness, willingness to attend and controlled attention are included here
- **Responding:** This involves the arousal of curiosity and the acceptance of responsibility in relation to a response

- **Valuing:** This involves recognition of the intrinsic worth of a situation so that motivation is heightened and beliefs emerge
- **Organising and Conceptualising:** This involves the patterning of responses on the basis of investigation of attitudes and values, and also the beginning of the building of an internally-consistent value system
- **Characterising by value or value concept:** This involves the ability to see, as a coherent whole matters involving ideas, attitudes and beliefs.

The Psychomotor Domain (Skills)
Bloom also indicated a skill category, although it is very narrowly-focused on the development of motor skills:

- **Reflex Movements:** He defined these as involuntary motor responses to stimuli. They are the basis for all types of behaviour involving bodily movement
- **Basic Fundamental Movements:** These are inherent movement patterns, built upon simple reflex movements
- **Perceptual Abilities:** These assist learners to interpret stimuli so that they can adjust to their environment and are the essential foundation for skilled movement. Visual and auditory discrimination are examples
- **Physical Abilities:** These are the essential foundation for skilled performance. Speed, exertion and flexibility are examples that are of relevance in operator skills and computer skills
- **Skilled Movements:** These are the components of any efficiently performed, complex movement. They cannot be acquired without learning and require lots of practice
- **Non-Discursive Communication:** This comprises the advanced behaviours involved in the type of communication relating to movement, such as ballet. Movement becomes aesthetic and creative at this level of the domain. This is rarely relevant in the training context.

Some researchers have built on Bloom's ideas and put forward more development-type categorisation – for example, Simpson proposes an alternative classification of psychomotor objectives. He suggests that there are seven categories of psychomotor objective:

- **Perception:** This involves the use of the learner's sense organs in order to obtain those cues essential for the guidance of motor activity – sensory stimulation, cue selection and translation (of sensory cases into a motor activity)

- **Set:** The state of readiness for the performance of a certain action – mental, physical and emotional states
- **Guided Response:** This necessitates performance under the general guidance of an optimal performance model and involves imitation, trial and error
- **Mechanism:** The ability to perform a task repeatedly with an acceptable degree of proficiency
- **Complex, Overt Response:** The performance of a task with a high degree of proficiency
- **Adaptation:** The use of previously-acquired skills so as to perform novel tasks
- **Origination:** The creation of a new style of performing a task after the development of skills.

Rackham and Morgan (1997) provide a very useful classification of interpersonal skills that can be used by the trainer to write interpersonal skill learning objectives:

- **Seeking/Giving Information:** Asking for/offering facts, opinions, or clarification from/to another individual or individuals (you ask your supervisor about the meaning of a new work rule)
- **Proposing:** Putting forward a new concept, suggestion, or course of action (you make a job enrichment suggestion to your supervisor)
- **Building and Supporting:** Extending, developing, enhancing another person's proposal or concept (in a departmental meeting, you suggest an amendment to someone's motion)
- **Shutting Out/Bringing In:** Excluding/involving another group member from/into a conversation or discussion (in a departmental meeting, you ask a quiet member to give his/her ideas)
- **Disagreeing:** Providing a conscious, direct declaration of a difference of opinion, or a criticism of another person's concepts
- **Summarising:** Restating in a compact form the content of previous discussions or considerations (before giving your comments in a departmental meeting, you summarise the arguments that have been presented).

THE CRAMP MODEL

Stammers and Patrick (1995) suggest a model of learning objectives, which they call the CRAMP model. They identify five components to the model:

- **Comprehension:** The development of general understanding (Bloom's cognitive domain)

- **Reflex Development:** The production of fast, reliable patterns of response or manipulation (Bloom's psychomotor domain)
- **Attitudes:** The changing or development of new attitudes (Bloom's affective domain)
- **Memory:** The recall of specific facts and figures (Level 1 of Bloom's cognitive domain)
- **Procedural Learning:** Acquainting the learner with procedures that are easy to follow (Level 2 of Bloom's cognitive domain).

CRAMP is a very useful model, because it specifies the methods that are most appropriate for each type of objective. For example, if the objective is comprehension, then it is appropriate to use projects, written materials, talks, manuals, discussion and argument. If the objective relates to attitudes, then the trainer should use role-plays, psychological simulations, group exercises, case incidents, scenarios and role models. **Figure 5.5** provides an illustration of this matching process.

FIGURE 5.5: THE CRAMP MODEL & LEARNING METHODS

C	R	A	M	P
Comprehension	**Reflex Development**	**Attitudes**	**Memory**	**Procedural Learning**
Is the objective to develop general understanding?	Is the objective to produce fast, reliable patterns of response or manipulation?	Is the objective to change or develop new attitudes?	Is the objective to remember specific facts and figures?	Is the objective to acquaint the learner with a wide range of procedures that are easy to follow but nonetheless important?
If **Yes**	If **Yes**	If **Yes**	If **Yes**	If **Yes**
↓	↓	↓	↓	↓
WHAT ARE THE LEARNING METHODS AVAILABLE?				
↓	↓	↓	↓	↓
Written Material Talks Discovery method Discussions and Argument Projects	Simulations Practical Demonstration Supervised practice Stamina Development	Example or Role Models Case Studies Group Exercises Role Playing Psychological Simulations	Mnemonics Jingles Repetition Active use of the information to be remembered	Algorithms (Flow Chart) Checklists Practical Demonstration

Adapted from Stammers and Patrick (1975).

BOYDELL'S MODEL OF LEARNING OBJECTIVES

Boydell (1997) takes an alternative approach, suggesting that the trainer needs to consider both the type of learning and the level of learning.

Types of Learning

Learning About Things

Learning about things is broadly speaking about "knowing". This covers a broad spectrum of knowledge and understanding, including memorising or being aware of basic information, data, facts, existing explanations, rules and standard procedures. At a deeper level of learning about things, it encompasses the following:

* The ability to think for yourself
* To create new ideas
* To create possible new solutions to "problems"
* To use questioning and insight to create new solutions where none currently exist
* Thinking things through, collecting and analysing data, drawing conclusions, are all part of this level of knowing about things.

Deeper still is the ability to understand whole fields of ideas and the way these are interrelated, by having a holistic overview of the way different sets of information or ideas are connected together. A specific example here is the ability to see how the various functions and departments of your organisation are part of a larger whole, and how are they all interdependent.

Learning to Do Things

"Learning to do things" is concerned with skills and techniques that can be used to facilitate management, control processes, enhance productivity and quality and thus improve customer satisfaction and increase profitability or value for money when using public funds.

This type of learning involves dealing with relatively standard, routine "programmed" tasks, by selecting and applying the appropriate technique. All organisations have many standard processes that are often written down in various procedure manuals.

However, "doing things" gets more complex when tackling "problems". Faced with a variety of techniques, you have to know which are appropriate for your particular situation, and to what extent it or they will need modifying to suit your own unique circumstances. This involves, for example, decision-making, processing information, evaluating alternatives, choosing solutions and allocating responsibility for implementation. Doing these sorts of things requires initiative and the courage to step into the unknown and to take risks when the outcomes are uncertain. This is very different from simply following standard procedures.

A further level of complexity arises when you need to weave whole sets of techniques together, so that they become interconnected and co-ordinated, thus creating new processes, products and services. Doing this requires competencies such as organising, co-ordinating, mental resilience and the ability to cope with uncertainty, to balance the requirements of competing alternatives, to see things in terms of "*both* this and that", rather than the relatively simple terms of "*either* this or that*". For example, a successful manager has to be able to learn both to lead and to hold themselves in the background, both to be dynamic and be reflective, both to be confident and to be humble, both to be able to keep a close relationship with their staff and to keep a suitable distance.

Learning to Become Yourself
As well as "learning to do things", managing requires us to "learn to be". It can be described as becoming yourself, to develop your own unique style of managing and to achieve your full potential. It is therefore important to develop the ability to assess yourself, so that you can identify your strengths and under-utilised opportunities, as well as aspects that need to be strengthened and developed further. A basic requirement is to learn to accept feedback from others and to see how this can form the basis of a personal development plan.

As you develop further, you don't just wait for feedback but seek it actively and consciously, both from others and by reflecting on your own behaviour, thoughts, feelings and your intentions. From this, you can prepare your own development plan.

Gradually, this will increase your self-confidence, your awareness and your realistic appreciation of your own abilities. This will also enable you to re-examine critically your value system and draw conclusion(s) for yourself, to judge critically your own motivation, work habits and ethical values. Once we become conscious of our own deep values, beliefs and assumptions, we can also become aware of what we really want to achieve in life. We get a feeling for what our sense of purpose is and do something worthwhile not only for ourselves but also for our organisation, profession, community or society.

Learning to Achieve Things with Others
The fourth type of learning is "learning to achieve things with others", which is where outcomes cannot be fully measured in terms of what individuals "take away", but rather by what is created together. Team-working is a good example here, as carrying out your excepted role within a team requires teamwork and co-operation with

other team members. It also requires using your best abilities in meetings, workshops and so on.

As well as team-working, another example is managers who, with increasing experience, need to be able to help other members perform to the best of their ability, thus showing leadership by inspiring and leading others. This way of working calls for the ability to work with diversity – working with people whose backgrounds, values, beliefs, skills, attitudes, language, customs, norms are different from ours. Therefore, learners need tolerance and respect for different personalities, cultures and opinions, and the ability to cohabit and co-operate in heterogeneous national, ethnic and cultural environments.

In fact this can be quite difficult – for example, engineers see personnel specialists as soft and out of touch with "real" issues. Personnel specialists on the other hand, see engineers as narrow-minded and mechanistic. Whether we are in finance, marketing, sales, public relations, research and development, we tend to see ourselves as "normal" and to have negative stereotypes about others.

Levels of Learning

Each of the four types of learning progresses through three levels, starting from being relatively simple and gradually deepening and becoming more complex. We call these Level 1, Level 2 and Level 3 learning, or simply Levels L_1, L_2 and L_3.

Level 1 (L_1) is about getting things "right", according to currently accepted ideas, procedures, norms, etc. At its best, this level enables you to perform, to do things well, and to meet current accepted standards. These standards usually come from outside, from someone else other than yourself, such as your boss or an expert, or already accepted procedures.

At Level 2 (L_2), you are now thinking and acting for yourself. This requires a much more independent form of learning than L_1. Being taught (the essence of L_1 learning) is not appropriate here. We need to use processes that involve you, the learner, in thinking for yourself, making your own meaning from your own experiences, of the situations you find yourself in, or the puzzles with which you are grappling. Therefore, learning is less off-the-job and more on-the-job, using the very issues that you are concerned with as the vehicles for learning.

Level L_2 moves us on from implementing into improving and pushing out the frontiers of what we do already. It is an incremental approach, involving a wide range of gradual, partial and incremental changes. Where more radical changes are involved, we need a third type of learning: (Level 3 – L_3).

FIGURE 5.6: LEVELS OF LEARNING

Learning about Things	**From L₁**	Knowing basic information, data, facts, standard products
	to L₂	Thinking for oneself, creating new ideas, trying out new solutions
	then to L₃	Understanding complex ideas or whole fields of ideas and the way these are interrelated
Learning to Do Things	**From L₁**	Using standard tools and techniques
	to L₂	Choosing what to do and finding ways of doing them better
	then to L₃	Weaving whole sets of techniques together, balancing opposites, creating new processes, products and services
Learning to Become Yourself	**From L₁**	Accepting personal feedback and development plans from others
	to L₂	Actively and consciously seeking feedback from others; personal reflection; devising your own personal development plan
	then to L₃	Becoming aware of your basic perspectives and assumptions; working with a sense of purpose - doing something worthwhile for your organisation, profession, community or society
Learning to Achieve Things With Others	**From L₁**	Fitting in well and being accepted by others; carrying out expected roles and tasks within a team
	to L₂	Influencing others; helping team members and teams to work effectively
	then to L₃	Working with diversity; recognising, accepting and valuing a wide range of stakeholders

Source: Boydell (1997).

Large-scale change, by its very nature, involves large numbers of people such as a wide range of stakeholders who, as the word indicates, have a "stake" or interest in the organisation and its changes. Levels L_1 and L_2 learning cannot on their own handle this type of situation. It is not possible to manage large-scale change through using a standard formula or recipe (L_1). Such situations are far too complex for simplistic approaches. Neither will the continuous improvement approaches of L_2 be adequate here. The essence of this level of learning is to make incremental improvements to what already exists, rather than creating something new, which is what L_3 is about. We therefore sometimes refer to this third level as *innovating*. In this way, we go from learning to do things better (L_2) to learning to do better things (L_3).

Level L_3 is often also called *integrating*, because you need to be able to connect together different sets of ideas, perspectives, processes and people. You are moving from the somewhat individualistic stance of independence in L_2 to one of interdependence and of being mutually connected and supportive. This level of learning therefore needs to go beyond "thinking for myself" to ways of working together and "thinking with each other".

Figure 5.7 provides a summary of the types and levels of learning.

WRITING LEARNING OBJECTIVES

In order for learning objectives to be effective, they must satisfy certain criteria. In particular, they should be:

- **Realistic**: The objectives that are set must be attainable. They must not be so straightforward that there is no element of challenge nor so overwhelming that their achievement seems hopeless to the learner

- **Relevant**: If the objectives are to have any meaning, they must be seen to have direct relevance to the job or personal situation. This can mean either that they will have an impact on work performance now or in the future, or that they will have some influence on the learner's personal development

- **Positive**: If objectives are to have direct relevance, they must also be of benefit to the individual. Consequently, objectives are drafted to provide a positive outcome rather than stipulating what a learner will no longer do as the consequence of attending a programme

- **Certain**: Vague objectives are not objectives. Objectives should clearly specify who will achieve what, by when and under what circumstances. They should also state how success will be measured and any cost or time constraints involved

- **Justifiable**: No matter how laudable the learning objectives of a programme are, the true measure of their success is seen by organisations in financial terms. Unless it can be demonstrated that the organisation will receive some return on its investment in the training, the programme may be considered as an unnecessary drain on resources

- **Learning focus**: Objectives relate to the knowledge, skills and attitudes that the organisation wants to enhance

- **Brevity**: Minimise the objective to a single sentence that is precise and limited

- **Action Verbs**: Use action verbs that allow for easy measurement and observation

- **Evaluation**: Objectives should provide a method of measuring success by building in a standard of expected performance

- **Guide Content**: Objectives should help the trainer concentrate on most relevant themes when preparing content.

FIGURE 5.7: DOMAINS & LEVELS OF LEARNING

About Things	To Do Things	To Become Yourself	To Achieve Things with Others
L₁: Learning Level 1: Learning to Implement; Dependent Learning; Conforming			
• Recall and explain correctly facts, concepts, theories, procedures	• Do things well by carrying out existing procedures and processes correctly, to the desired standards as specified or laid down by others	• Accept feedback, for example during appraisal • Accept and implement a personal development plan drawn up for you by someone else in order to meet gaps between your desired and actual performance	• Recognise and respect existing norms of behaviour and standards of performance; "fit in"/accepted by others • Understand and carry out specified roles and tasks within a team
L₂: Learning Level 2: Learning to Improve; Independent Learning; Competing			
• Reflect on experiences and make your own meaning from them • Think for yourself, devise your own concepts, theories and hypotheses	• Do things better by carrying out systematic improvements to existing procedures, processes, products and services • Handle a wide variety of tasks and decide your own priorities	• Actively seek, obtain and evaluate feedback on the way you manage yourself • Reflect on the way you manage yourself - your thoughts, feelings and intentions • Set your own personal career/life objectives • Draw up and implement your own personal development plans in order to manage yourself better in a wide variety of situations and/or to meet your life and career objectives	• Influence others by challenging existing norms, standards and ways of doing things when you think that these need to be changed or improved • Enable colleagues, teams and individual team members to delight their internal and external customers
L₃: Learning Level 3: Learning to innovate; Learning to Integrate; Inter-dependent learning; Co-operating			
• See overviews, large-scale patterns and inter-connections • Think holistically across whole fields of knowledge • Think creatively by suspending judgements and considering alternative perspectives/ assumptions	• Do better things by working together with a range of stakeholders and hence creating whole new ways of working, new processes, products and services	• Understand and manage your basic perspectives and assumptions • Review and achieve career and life objectives in terms of doing something worthwhile for your organisation, profession, community or society	• Identify a wide range of stakeholders in any situation, initiative or project • Recognise, accept, respect and empathise with the feelings, positions, perspectives and "world views" or mental models of these stakeholders

Source: Boydell (1997).

DEVELOPING TRAINING CONTENT

The learning objectives you set determine the content you will include in your training programme. The trainer can often identify content that is related to the learning objective but not essential to it. Content should be assessed in terms of what must be learned to achieve the objective. The trainer needs to prioritise and determine what *should* be included and what *could* be included.

Working Out Content

In the absence of a job analysis and information on training needs, there are two techniques that can help the trainer to work out course content. Both are equally useful and it is usually a question of using the technique that feels most comfortable. However, we point out that a proper and systematic training needs analysis is a core component of the systematic training process.

Learning Maps

Learning maps (sometimes referred to as "mind-maps") are an effective and easy way to assemble information about a subject. The difficulty in trying to collect information is that we tend to try and put it all down in a logical step-by-step format but continually have to revise it as new elements and ideas spring to mind. Learning maps recognise that learners do not think in logical steps, that there is often a constant stream of unconnected bits of information flowing from learners' minds and that the trainer should capture it in that format. This can be facilitated in the following way:

- Start by drawing a picture, word or phrase at the centre of a page to stand for the topic
- Take the main ideas associated with the subject as they occur to you and let them branch out from the central idea. Express these branches as key words, pictures or symbols. Build up the overall "map" as thoughts occur with sub-branches coming out of main branches. This process more accurately reflects how we think and does not seek to funnel ideas into a logical, step-by-step sequence
- Draw connections between areas with lines or arrows. Use colour, if possible, to create a visual impact.

You may want to re-draw the map later; this is okay and helps it lodge in your memory. The map should represent the sum of knowledge, thoughts and ideas about the subject and can be added to or developed at a later stage without any difficulty. Because of the visual nature of the map, it is much easier to see connections between ideas or spot areas that are in need of development.

Horizontal Plan

As the name suggests, this process seeks to lay out the content of the training in a highly visual manner but with a potential flow built-in. The idea is to identify the headings and sub-headings of the subject and build the content around this plan. This process again makes use of the random thought patterns that occur when developing training material. One very simple and practical way of doing this is:

- Use "Post-it" notes to capture the key words or phrases that describe a section of content and stick them to the wall. Continue this process, until you have identified a large number of items
- Start to move them around, grouping them into related subject areas. Lay the groups together left to right in a line
- Identify subject headings for each group of notes and write that on a note above the group
- Start to shape the flow of the material by moving groups/subject areas around.

Again, this is quite a visual way of representing the sum total of information on a subject. It is also flexible and adaptable.

Sequence and Timing of Training Content

Once you have decided on the content that is appropriate to achieving your learning objectives, the next decisions you have to make are:

- What is the sequence of the content?
- What time should be allocated to each component of content?

Training content is usually sequenced in a logical order to reflect the training needs. Learning order is an important issue. Learning one task may be impossible or difficult until another is learned. Learning one task before another, even though not required, may facilitate learning the second task. Learning two tasks or content areas together may be feasible.

Sequencing is a necessary activity. Some tasks may have to be scheduled in a particular order. Others may prove helpful if scheduled in a particular order. Other areas of content may be scheduled in any order without consequence to themselves or to remaining tasks/content areas. You will be guided in making sequencing decisions from the results of your training needs and task analysis outputs.

You may find a number of patterns:

- Some areas of content/tasks may be subordinate to others. Some tasks may be subordinate to several others. Some may be neither but simply follow one another in performance

- In some situations, it may be appropriate to schedule subordinate content or tasks first because they are considered prerequisites. In other situations, subordinate tasks are scheduled first because that sequence will facilitate the learning process
- Tasks performed early are scheduled to be learned early, whereas the alternative is that tasks performed late are scheduled to be learned early
- The performance sequence and learning sequence may differ. Sequencing is more likely to be effective, the more accurately you have identified prerequisite issues and content/task relationships.

Figure 5.8 summarises a number of guidelines and principles that you should follow when sequencing training content.

The second issue you need to consider when sequencing content is the time you should allocate to each component of content. This activity can be undertaken in the form of a daily session plan. **Figure 5.8** provides an example of such a plan.

We identify four key components that you should consider.

- **Focus on the Session:** You should specify the primary purpose of the session, which will be determined by the learning objectives you set
- **Training Aids / Materials:** You should specify what materials and/or training aids you require in order to deliver the training programme
- **Critical Learning Points:** This is a very important component that helps you to focus on the priority content areas that you wish to include
- **Schedule of Training:** We will say more about this issue in the next chapter. For now, you should sequence the training content along the lines we have indicated earlier. You should also pay attention to the following issues:
  ○ Make sure that you allow sufficient time to introduce the programme, identify the objectives and include an icebreaker, in order to create a positive learning environment
  ○ Alternate theory/information sessions with skill/practice sessions. The former should be 20-30 minutes in duration; the latter can be longer, depending on the number of participants
  ○ Be aware of the session immediately after lunch. This should, where possible, be a practice session or involve an activity that allows the trainees to participate in the learning process
  ○ Allow sufficient time to review the learning and provide a summary of key learning points.

FIGURE 5.8: GUIDELINES FOR SEQUENCING THE CONTENT OF YOUR TRAINING PROGRAMME

- Consider the need to get the attention of the trainees. Trainees learn only when they pay attention to training. Their motivation stems from some benefit or value on the training. This has implications for initial training content.
- Trainees only believe, listen to and learn from materials that they consider being influential or credible. Materials are influential/credible if they are based on expertise and are attractive to trainees.
- Trainees learn most easily when the training content is put in a context of something they already know and is taught using familiar concepts and terminology.
- Trainees learn best, when, in addition to having 'hooks' for the training content, they have a mental set or posture of the overall content before they go into details. Trainees receive a mental picture when provided with an overall structure of the new information at the beginning of the training.
- Trainees can perceive only limited amounts of information at one time. Research generally reveals this capacity to be seven meaningful pieces of information, plus or minus two pieces.
- Trainees can perceive and remember longer amounts of information if the information is grouped or chunked.
- It is prudent to start from existing knowledge, skill and attitude.
- If trainers have limited experience of training, then it is appropriate to place easily learned tasks early in the learning event.
- Trainees learn better from training materials that combine text and illustrations. Word messages can be enhanced or made more understandable by the use of illustration.
- Trainees learn ideas better when they are presented with examples of those ideas.
- Content sequence can be organised in the following ways; known-unknown, concrete -abstract, general, particular observation – theory - reasoning, simple – complex, overview – detailed.
- Introduce broad concepts and technical terms that have relevance throughout the training, early on in a programme.
- Continuity of content is generally more effective to a series of unconnected activities.
- If trainees are to learn, it is not sufficient for the materials to merely explain the information well. Trainees must have opportunities to respond to the information, or practice the skills being taught.
- The sequence of content should include opportunities for learners to ask questions about the information or provide exercises, which require trainees to practice the skills.
- Ensure that you mix sessions to ensure that there is a balance of passive and active components.

FIGURE 5.9: A DAILY SESSION PLAN

Focus of the Session:	
Training Aids / Materials Required:	
Critical Learning Points:	

SCHEDULE OF TRAINING

Time:	Content and Activities	Methods of Learning	Trainer

COMMON ERRORS IN TRAINING PROGRAMME DESIGN

We conclude this chapter with some pointers on the main errors that are made when designing training programmes. It is a frequent, but not advisable, situation that you may not what your learners need to achieve. As a result, you may design a "know what" learning event when he should be designing a "know how" event. At worst, the learning event may achieve nothing. Equally, you may not make the objectives clear to the participants at the outset.

Training not Aimed at the Target Audience

Because you have not clearly analysed your training needs and considered the characteristics of your learners, the training you design may be inappropriate. It may be:

- Too easy, so that the learner's time is completely wasted: they knew it all already. It may be difficult to persuade them to attend future events in the same programme
- Too difficult, so that the participants do not learn. The difficulty may be that the trainer does not explain jargon or other long words, or that he/she assumes that they know more than they do
- Irrelevant, such as giving a history of the company to an audience waiting to learn about the use they can make of a new product.

Wrong Medium of Presentation

Inexperience may lead you to rely too much on one method or make an inappropriate selection given you learning objective. For example, you may use:

- A lecture instead of an illustrated presentation. Immediately after the event, participants remember only about 20% of what they hear. This may treble, if participants can both see and hear, but not if the trainer talks to, and about, his visual aids while participants are trying to read them
- A presentation instead of a demonstration and practice
- Most trainers love the sound of their voices, but participants learn skills only when they are given an opportunity to perform and practice them
- Still pictures where a cutaway model, video or film would be more effective. If the trainer wants to explain the working of a car engine, then a cutaway model is ideal.

Poor Organisation and Presentation

A whole host of problems may arise here. The main errors include:

- Material presented in an order that is illogical to the audience. If the trainer wants to demonstrate how a car is assembled, it will probably be clearer to learners if the instruction begins at final inspection and they are talked through the process backwards. They will then see how the parts contribute to the whole
- Visual aids not in the right order when needed, or even upside down. Nothing puts an audience off faster than to see a trainer searching through a pile of overhead projector transparencies for the one he/she wants next
- Visual aids illegible to all accept the front row.
- Reading a learned paper intended for publication. Trainers cannot read and address the audience simultaneously. If you have to give a paper, then present it, and use the written version to check that the argument is followed.

Insufficient Preparation

An experienced trainer may get away with a few notes. A person making a presentation, however, needs to be word perfect. A trainer whose audience can see that he is improvising loses credibility. Here are some of the more common problems:

- Poor logistics: Learners have all suffered from poor logistics at one time or another when attending learning events.
- Poor instructions on how to reach the venue: Half the group arrives late
- Room too large or too small: The audience is too scattered to form a group or so crowded that it is uncomfortable
- Room too hot or too cold for comfort
- Too much noise outside the room: The audience is distracted
- Poor acoustics: The speaker cannot be heard at the back
- Seats too hard or too soft
- Too early a start for learners to reach the venue on time
- Sessions too long: The learners' attention wavers or they become too tired to learn
- A late finish: Learners leave early or cease to pay attention
- Coffee and tea late or cold
- Coffee and tea noisily prepared in an adjoining room, so that learners stop paying attention
- Breaks too short for people to finish their discussions and/or eat their meals
- Visual aids not available when needed
- Unsuitable accommodation for the final test
- Instructor assumes that "teacher teaching = learners learning".

Poor Pacing

A very common fault is that trainers insist on presenting too much material for learners to absorb. Learners learn at their own pace, which can be fairly slow. Pressing on regardless will leave the audience reflecting on the last two points made, and eventually opting out altogether. Trainers may then have the choice of reaching some of their objectives fully or all of their objectives incompletely.

Bad Timing of the Learning Event

People will not appreciate an earlier start to the day than they would normally have. Likewise, if a trainer organises a training event on Friday afternoon, participants will be thinking of their weekend instead of the subject.

The Belief that Telling or Exhortation Alone Will Change Behaviour

It is very difficult to persuade employees to adopt safe practices. For example, it requires a law, or at least an enforceable rule, to make them wear hard hats or safety glasses. Managing directors who tell staff that they must all work harder if the company is to survive will have little effect, but presented with the hard facts of impending closure, the employees are likely to respond to the threat to their jobs.

BEST PRACTICE INDICATORS

Some of the best practice issues that you should consider related to the contents of this chapter are as:

- Base your learning objectives on a thorough training needs analysis process
- Involve the learner in the process of formulating learning objectives. This will ensure better buy-in to the learning intervention
- Be clear on the type of learning that is involved. Are you concerned with emphasising the learner's knowledge, developing skills or changing attitudes?
- Be sure to specify the target behaviours that you wish to develop and use an appropriate action verb. Specify a statement of the content using a noun to describe the task and provide a statement of the conditions and the standards
- Decide on the best sequence in which to present your training content. You should be aware of the need to orient the learner, to present, to demonstrate and explain, to ensure that the learner observes and practices application of content and to get the learner to apply the content
- Be aware of the limitations of your learners when you sequence your content and when you make decisions about the amount of content
- Use your course time effectively. Decide what activities can be completed as part of pre-course work
- Each session of training should have a clear focus and a set of critical learning points associated with it
- Objectives have three key components – the learning or performance, the standard and the conditions of learning – that you should continuously keep in mind
- Your training content should reflect the learning objectives you set
- You should divide your course into clearly identifiable sessions.

Reflections on the Training & Development Scenario

The following represents a possible solution to the training design problem.

Objectives: At the end of the programme, learners will be able to instruct newcomers to the company to reach their own level of competence in estimating.

Criteria: The participants will have prepared and presented two lessons, the second of which will be clearly understood by their colleagues and they will have designed the practical exercises that will enable their learners to consolidate their knowledge.

Timetable
Day 1
- Introductions
- Ice Breaker, Objectives and Overview
- Encouragement; you know your subject and can learn to teach it. The aim is learners 'learning by doing'; get them started and coach them when necessary.
- Learning about objectives, criterion tests and lesson design.
- Learners start to prepare their first lessons.

Day 2
- Half day; learners finish preparing their own lessons
- Half day; half the learner's present lessons, which are recorded on CCTV and then appraised by both the other learners and the tutor.

Day 3
- Half day; the remainder of the learners present their lessons.
- Discussion on the results to date. Note that each student learned from his predecessor.
- Half-day presentation on visual aids. Test the visual aids presentation: even the best of lectures is only moderately effective.
- Review the lessons of the presentation on visual aids.
- Discuss the implications for future lessons.

Day 4
- Learners prepare their second lesson and practical work.

Day 5
- Learners present their second lessons in reverse order, ideally with at least one of the estimating managers present.
- Final summing up and review.

Chapter Six

TRAINING DESIGN: STRATEGIES & METHODS

LEARNING OBJECTIVES

On completion of this chapter, you should be able to:

- Describe the main elements of the instructional sequence
- Explain the alternative instructional strategies that you can use to deliver your training
- Understand the types of learning objectives that are appropriate for each learning strategy
- List the different types of training methods that you can use
- Explain the advantages and disadvantages of different learning methods
- Understand when particular learning methods are appropriate
- Understand the guidelines to follow when using ice-breakers or buzz-groups.

A Training & Development Scenario

Consider the following training situations and indicate the strategies and methods you might adopt:

- You recruit four or five secretaries and typists a year. Each is fully trained. However, your management is very particular about the layout of letters, reports, memos and other documents.

- Your managing director is to be interviewed on TV for the first time tomorrow.

- Your company is going to launch a complex new product next week. Details about this have been kept very confidential. Now all the internal and external sales force, the receptionists and telephonists, managers of all functions and some accounts staff need to know about it.

- Your company is facing severe competition, which requires that it cut production costs by at least 10%. Your managing director does not want to call in consultants.

- Several members of your workforce have recently suffered from back injuries by lifting 25 kilo (55lb) sacks.

INTRODUCTION

In **Chapter Five**, we discussed two elements of the training design process: formulating learning objectives and developing training content. In this chapter, we explain the overall instructional strategy that you can select, and the types of training methods that are appropriate.

The training or instructional strategy refers to decisions you make on your overall approach. For example, do you need to deliver a theory session, a skill session, or some session concerned with knowledge, results and procedures? We define learning methods as the specific means you intend to use to deliver the training. For example, if you are required to plan a session where you need to present specific information to a large group of trainees, or where the training involves a 1:1 situation, you may use a lecture for the former and mentoring or coaching for the latter.

We provide you with specific advice and guidelines on these two components of the training design process.

THE ELEMENTS OF INSTRUCTION

We discuss a number of instructional strategies later in this chapter. In this section, we explain the main elements of the instructional sequence. These key elements are concerned with:

- Gaining the attention of your learners
- Informing your learners of the objectives
- Structuring the recall of previous learning
- Presenting your training content
- Providing guidance to the learner
- Eliciting performance from the learner
- Providing feedback
- Assessing learner performance
- Ensuring retention of the learning and its transfer.

These instructional events are the same irrespective of the learning outcome. If your training fails, it is likely that you omitted one or more of the steps – for example, in training for skills, a common error is to include no practice or insufficient practice.

Step 1: Gaining the Attention of the Learner

Your first task during training is to gain the attention of your learners. You can do this in a number of ways: by introducing an icebreaker, by gesturing or by the tone of your voice. You could also relate an experience or situation to your learners to gain their attention and emphasise the importance of the content that you intend to cover. You can use some form of ice-breaker, energiser or session-shaker. **Figure 6.1** provides some guidelines for their use.

Step 2: Inform your Learners of the Training Objectives

The reason for ensuring that this step is completed is simply this: when your learners understand the learning objectives, they create expectations and these are likely to persist over the duration of your session or programme. It is very important that you seek to connect the learning objective to the motivation of your learners. You can also enhance the motivation of your learners through the recall of a relevant experience.

We know from learning theory that your learners are more likely to understand the objective, if you make the performance component clear. You can state the objective verbally as well as including it in the written materials.

There are different strategies that you can use for different types of objectives:

Learning Objective	Trainer Strategy to Inform Learners of Objective
Knowledge Objectives	• Use of verbal communication • Demonstration of the concept
Verbal Information	• Inform your learners what they are required to state, describe or explain • Explain the level of detail that is required
Motor Skills	• Use a demonstration so that the learner has a picture of the required behaviour
Intellectual Skills	• Provide an example in order to convey the objective • Present a problem and a framework in order to solve the problem
Attitudes	• It may not be appropriate to state the desired attitude up-front • Let your learners experience an event and learn the attitude objective when reflecting on the experience • You will need to judge when it is appropriate to state the objective; this will depend on the subject matter

Step 3: Integrating Previously Learned Material

You will facilitate and enhance the learning of new material, if you take steps to integrate material that your learners have learned previously. For example, if you are focusing on knowledge objectives, then it is useful to refer to previously learned concepts or rules. The same rule applies to verbal information. You could, for example, provide an outline or summary or ask your learners to recall an experience that is relevant to the new information. You could also use questioning techniques or some form of handout to achieve this task.

If your learning objectives focus on motor skills, you could use a mental procedure that explains the execution of the task. In the case of intellectual skills, you will need to summarise previously learned rules or principles. The recall of previously learned attitudes is more complicated, so you may need to provide an appropriate example to illustrate your attitude. The example needs to be brief and focused.

Step 4: Presenting Your Content to the Learners

At this point, you will present the new content to your learners. If you are focusing on intellectual skills, for example, then you should explain the dimensions of the skill and use examples to illustrate the key components or dimensions. You will need to show how the skill differs from other related skills. You should organise verbal information in a sequence that is most meaningful to your learners. If you are training in motor skills, then they need to be demonstrated, pointing out the important dimensions.

We provide you with more guidance on presentation and direct instruction in **Chapter Nine**.

FIGURE 6.1: USING ICE-BREAKERS, ENERGISERS/SESSION-SHAKERS & BUZZ GROUPS

	Definition	Objectives	Membership	Timing	Planning & Design
Ice-Breakers	• An introductory activity intended to start a learning event in an interesting informative and enjoyable manner	• To introduce the learner(s) to the trainer, the training programme, the format and methods of the programme • To introduce the learners to each other and start the process of relationship-building • Enable the learner to make an initial verbal contribution	• Everyone should be involved, including the trainer who encourages openness by also being open	• The size of the group will largely determine the time involved • Usually takes 15-25 minutes to complete • Do not impose too much of a burden initially on learners	• You could use an ice-breaker that linked closely to the content of the programme • You could use a fun exercise that is simply an introduction • Ice-breakers are readily available, however you can design your own activity

	Definition	Objectives	Membership	Timing	Planning & Design
Energisers / Session-Shakers	• Energisers are essentially session-shakers. They are short sharp, impactive activities that are unrelated to the content of the programme	• To enhance the motivation of the learners where there is evidence that it is dipping • To enhance the energy level of the group where you observe it is flagging • To encourage the relationship-building process within the learning group	• All members should be included. Do not use an activity that isolates some members of the learning group	• There is no set time. You need to observe the energy level of your team • Do not over-use: it may be perceived as an excuse for avoiding serious learning	• They need to be short, so not as to eat into learning time • They are not included in the programme plan • Consider using them immediately after a heavy midday lunch break • You can also use them where the previous session was theoretical and involved high levels of communication • Use them at the start and subsequent days of an extended training programme • Many party games can be used as energisers. You should not be concerned about the levels of your learners in terms of experience and ability

	Definition	Objectives	Membership	Timing	Planning & Design
Buzz Groups	• Informal and less structured activities, introduced at any time during a T&D programme. They consist of an impromptu division of the learning group into smaller groups to discuss an issue that has emerged during the learning event	• To add variety to the training programme • To encourage the learners to discuss issues that emerge during the training programme • To give quieter members a chance to speak in a small group • To enable a variety of views to emerge during the training • To obtain a range of views on a complex issue • To enable learners to learn from each other	• Involve all participants on the training programme • It usually involves a team of three or four participants • Ensure that the groups are sufficiently small to encourage discussion and contributions • Need careful facilitation if they are used with a large group	• Usually used for quick discussion and consideration of issues • Typically, they take between 10-15 minutes • They can be used at any point if you consider them to be beneficial	• They may be spontaneous, but it is possible to plan them as part of the formal training programme • They can be used as a preliminary to a question and answer session • The buzz group should be asked to consider a narrow question or topic • They can be used to give learners a voice in a process and discuss complex issues

Justification for Using Ice-breakers, Energisers and Session-Shakers	
• To break the ice and reduce the tension in the training room. • To assess the knowledge and skill level of the learners at this stage in the learning process. • To encourage participation in the form of questioning and discussion.	• To enable participants to consider particular items that might arise during an input or discussion. • To develop learning points and enable the development of a summary of key learning points.

Adapted from Rea (1996) and Beard and Wilson (2002).

Step 5: Providing Guidance to Your Learners

The purpose of this step is to ensure that your learners encode the content. You want to ensure that the new content is made as meaningful as possible. You can achieve this step in a number of ways:

- Provide your learners with concrete and relevant examples that illustrate more abstract ideas
- Provide further elaboration on each idea that you presented in Step Four
- Provide some examples and get your learners to analyse each example
- If you are teaching rules, then you could provide a set of problems and get your learners to identify which rules apply.

We provide more guidance when we focus in more detail on specific instructional approaches.

Step 6: Getting your Learners to Perform

You have now come to the point where you require your learners to demonstrate what they have learned. This step is often called practice. You have a number of options depending on the particular learning objective that you have in mind:

- If your objective is concerned with verbal information, you could ask them to state the verbal information in the correct sequence
- If the focus is on intellectual skills, you could give your learners a problem and ask them to apply or demonstrate the skill
- If your objectives are more cognitive in nature, the most appropriate strategy is to give your learners an unfamiliar or complex problem and have them derive an appropriate solution
- For motor skills, the best strategy is to get your learners to execute the performance
- If your skill is particularly complex, it may not make sense to get the learners to practice the total skill or complete task.

Step 7: Provide Feedback to Your Learners

When your learners have participated in practice, your next task is to communicate to your learners the extent to which the performance were satisfactory.

It will often be the case that the feedback is built-in and immediate. Corrective or formative feedback is important, because it concerns the manner of performance and it provides advice to the learner about how to improve.

Step 8: Assessing the Learning

Your end result in any training situation is to ensure that a particular standard is achieved. You will help to ensure that the standard is achieved through guidance, corrective action, and shaping, and repeated practice to ensure that the learning is reinforced.

At some point, you will find it appropriate to conduct an assessment or administer a test, whose purpose is to ensure that the learner can perform the task consistently. The learner should complete this task without assistance and to a preset standard of quality. You should select a test that matches your learning objective and is not overly difficult.

Step 9: Enhancing Retention and Learning Transfer

We define retention as "the ability to reproduce a learned behaviour or component of knowledge after a period of time has elapsed". Transfer of learning is the ability to use the learned skill in a different context. We consider the issue of transfer in **Chapter Twelve**.

We will now consider six different instructional strategies that focus on different types of learning objectives. **Figure 6.2** provides a summary of the strategies.

MAKING DECISIONS ON YOUR TRAINING OR INSTRUCTIONAL STRATEGY

Your instructional strategy refers to the overall approach you intend to use to achieve your learning objectives and deliver your training content. Your training or instructional strategy provides your overall framework. It will have a major influence on the training methods you will use, the types of training materials you will need to support your strategy and the amount and types of visual aids.

You can adopt one or more of seven generic training or instructional strategies. You may use a combination of strategies within one training course, depending on the nature of your learning objectives. **Figure 6.3** provides a summary of each of these instructional strategies.

FIGURE 6.2: INSTRUCTIONAL ACTIVITIES, ASSOCIATED ACTIONS & LEARNING METHODS

Instructional Activity	Key Internal Learning Policy	Key Trainer Action	Appropriate Training Methods
Gaining the attention of your learners	• Enhancing internal motivation • Heightened awareness • Ensuring reception of your learning message • Create an expectation concerning the learning outcomes	• Get the attention of your learners • Use of voice to attract attention	• Ice-breakers • Visual presentations • Presentation
Inform your learners of the learning objectives	• Reinforce the expectation • Help learners to make a link between objectives and their expectations • Reduce any ambiguity that may exist in respect of the purpose of learning	• Inform your learners about the purpose of the session • Identify what learners will be able to do on completion of the session	• Lecture or presentation • Video or slide presentation
Integrating previously learned material	• Developing learner comfort with the learning • Facilitating retrieval of previous learning • Getting the working memory operational	• Ask questions to facilitate recall • Present a problem which facilitates recall • Provide an example which brings to mind previous learning	• Handout or outline summary • Brief presentation on prior learning • Case scenario or problem-solving exercise
Present your content to your learners	• Perception and recall process • Selective perception and attention • Potential for information overload	• Structuring the presentation appropriately • Ensuring that the presentation is at the correct pace • Breaking the material into appropriate segments • Using your voice to make the content interesting	• Lecture or didactic presentation • Handout for technical elements • Video, if the material is procedural or technical • Flow-charts and other sequencing devices
Providing guidance to your learners	• Reinforcing the learning • Semantic encoding • Enhancing learner motivation	• Getting your learners to visualise the skill • Suggesting a framework to structure the material • Identifying key learning points	• Summary of the key learning points • Video summarising the key points • Practice or problem scenario

Instructional Activity	Key Internal Learning Policy	Key Trainer Action	Appropriate Training Methods
Getting your learners to perform	• Active involvement of your learners • Getting your learners to respond to materials • Developing self-confidence and self-efficacy	• Ask learners to perform • Provide space to perform unaided • Observe and listen to performance • Do individual or team performance	• Case study or problem-solving task • Complex unrelated problem • Practice of a skill or application of a rule • Role-play performance • Business game or simulation
Provide feedback to your Learners	• Reinforcement of key learning points • Enhance the internal motivation of learners • Achieve higher quality of learning	• Listen and observer performance • Give informative feedback • Correct where necessary • Relearn elements that were incorrect	• Use feedback on an individual or team basis • Summarise the positives and negatives of performance • Restate the key learning points
Assessing the learning	• Retrieval of learned information • Reinforcement of learning • Identification of learning gaps • Enhance motivation and intention to transfer learning	• Require learner to work independently and unaided • Select a test that reflects the learning objective • Administer assessment in a positive and constructive way • Emphasise the learning dimension rather than the testing/assessment component	• Structured assessment • Tests or examinations • Group task, which is rated • Complex problem or case study • Business game task, which is assessed
Enhanced retention and learning transfer	• Retrieval of learning • Generation of learning to different situations • Ensuring motivation and intention to transfer • Enhancement of task self-efficacy	• Provide varied practice • Ensure that practice elements build on each other and are cumulative • Provide tips to enable learning transfer • Ensure that there are spaced reviews to reinforce key learning points	• Written summary of key learning points • Brief supervisors to ensure that learning is reinforced in the workplace • Technical manual or flow-chart • Follow-up session to review transfer

Created from Gagné and Medsker (1996).

FIGURE 6.3: SUMMARY OF INSTRUCTIONAL STRATEGIES

Session Type	Purposes of Session
General Theory	• To deliver a technical course • To explain a theory or new developments • To operate in a didactic mode
Declarative Knowledge	• The focus is on knowing that something is the case • To enable learners describe, summarise and list • To enable learners learn a thread of meaning that runs through large amounts of information
Concept Learning	• The focus is on specific sets of objects, symbols and events that are grouped together • These concepts may be abstract or contract • A focus on presenting a concept, using an exploratory or discovery approach
Rule-Learning	• Present trainees with a set of rules and procedures • The rules can be procedural or relational • The focus is on developing adherence to these rules and procedures
Problem-Solving	• The focus is on combining rules and concepts • Application of rules to unique problems in order to solve problems • Development of high-level problem-solving skills
Skill-Based	• Focus on skills that involve gathering information • Development of skills that involve procedures or psychomotor activities • Development of skills to diagnose

A General Theory Session

If you wish to deliver a theory session, then your instructional strategy will be a general theory session. You might typically be expected to deliver such a session as a technical training course or as part of a management development programme. Theory sessions should be short, because the didactic nature of the session may reduce learner interest and motivation. An effectively-designed theory session will comprise:

- Introduction
- General body
- Conclusion.

The Introduction

The introduction will perform the following functions:

- **Gain interest:** This is where you grab the trainees' attention, by using a joke, a cartoon, a graph on the overhead projector, a controversial statement, a story of common interest, or a startling question, relevant to the training subject
- **Check current knowledge:** You should know the quantity and the quality of the trainees' knowledge, so that you can pitch the presentation at the right level. To find out the level of current

knowledge, you can ask a few questions or try a written test. You should have made basic inquiries about the trainees before the session. If you had contact with the trainees recently, you will already know what they know. If you have access to training needs analysis data that will also help

- **Orient:** This is where you set the scene: Explain the session title and relate it to the trainees' current relevant knowledge and experience. If there has been a previous relevant session, go over the information presented in that session, preferably by using questioning techniques

- **Preview the session:** You might lose the element of surprise here, although best practice recommends that you should preview the session

- **Motivate:** Why should the trainees sit and listen to you? They will not, unless you motivate them and create the need to learn. To satisfy that need, they will then listen to you.

In the introduction, you should show the trainees that the subject matter of the session is important. The message is: If they acquire this knowledge, they can make a contribution to themselves and to the organisation. You should show the learners how this particular learning fits into the total picture, since they will want a general idea of where they are going. In addition, telling the trainees what ground they will cover in the session provides a target, establishes appropriate expectations about the content of the session, and allows trainees to check the programme for themselves. The simplest and most direct way of achieving this is for you to tell the trainees the learning objective(s) of the session.

The Body of the Session
In this portion of the session, you transfer the bulk of the information to the trainees. You should plan to break this into logical segments, and a time or priority order may provide the pattern. For example, one fact may have to be learned before the second fact can be understood. The most effective method is to develop each segment around an objective.

Once you define the number and sequence of segments in the body of your session, you can build them into the three logical steps of explanation, activity and summary (EAS):

- **The E (Explanation) Step:** In this step, you give trainees new facts or allow them to discover new facts. The easiest and most common method is to "tell" the information, although it is often the least efficient method. We know from research that trainees use only about 11% of their learning capacity if a trainer relies entirely on hearing to get the message across. In addition, you will find it difficult to keep their interest long enough. The most satisfactory method is to make use of the trainee's sense of sight through visual aids, along with telling. A more challenging method, and one that requires more skill, is to use questioning techniques to elicit the information from the trainees

- **The A (Activity) Step:** Learning by doing describes the A step. Within one session, the E and the A cover the same content, with the E completed from a trainees-receiving-new-information point of view, while the A is completed from the trainees-doing-it point of view. It may be difficult to achieve this component, if your material is very theoretical.

  The A step should closely resemble the on-the-job behaviours you require. This resemblance will increase the meaningfulness of the activity and thus reinforce the message in the E step.

  The A step provides four important advantages for you as a trainer:
  - First, it indicates to the trainee how much of the information he or she has retained and thus highlights weaknesses
  - Second, the quality of the activity tells you whether the E step was satisfactory. It makes no sense to go on to the next explanation, if the preceding explanation has not been understood or cannot be applied by the trainees
  - Third, the A step separates one explanation from the next explanation and thus stresses structure within continuity
  - Finally, if you have made each EAS segment equivalent to one objective, then this will provide you with a good structuring device.

- **The S (Summary) Step:** In this step, you bring all the key pieces together and tie up loose ends. It provides you with an opportunity to ask for questions from the trainees before going into the next EAS segment.

Conclusion

This is a difficult component to complete. Your conclusion should incorporate five basic items:

- **Review or Recap:** Briefly, go over the main themes in the session. Emphasise important or key points
- **Test** to ensure that learning has taken place. Make the test either oral or written, or require some performance activity that will demonstrate the level of learning achieved
- **Link** to subsequent sessions on the programme
- **Clarify** and allow time for questions to clear up any problems or misunderstandings

- **Finish,** leaving the trainees in no doubt that it is complete – for example, ask the question, "Before I finish, do you have any final questions?".

We now set out in **Figure 6.4** some guidelines that you can follow when completing a general theory session.

FIGURE 6.4: GUIDELINES FOR CONDUCTING A THEORY SESSION

INTRODUCTION
• Did you grab the interest of the trainees?
• Did you orient the trainees to the subject in general?
• Did you test the current level of the trainees' knowledge?
• Did you use past experience of the trainees to introduce the session?
• Did you give a preview of what was to come?
• Did you activate the trainees?
• Did you state the session objective(s) correctly?
• Did you display prominently the session objective(s) throughout the session?

BODY
Explanation Step
• Did you help the trainees to discover information?
• Did your visual aids have sufficient impact and imagination?
• Did your visual aids have sufficient variety?
• Did you use visual aids correctly?
• Did you use questions effectively?
Activity Step
• Were the activities of sufficient duration?
• Did the activity steps reinforce the explanation steps?
• Were the activities sufficiently imaginative to maintain interest?
• Was there sufficient variety in the activities?
• Did the trainer use the activity steps to test the session objective(s) progressively?
Summary Step
• Were summaries presented at appropriate places in the session?

CONCLUSION
• Did you summarise the main points of the session?
• Did you ensure that the session objective(s) had been achieved?

Adapted from Delahaye (2000).

A Declarative Knowledge Session

Many training activities, especially in the technical or scientific area, involve declarative knowledge, which involves "knowing that" something is the case. When you set an objective such as "'to understand a particular component of content", you are talking about declarative knowledge. Words that are used to describe declarative knowledge include: "explain", "describe", "summarise" and "list".

A declarative knowledge session may consist of three categories:

- Labels and names, which involves the pairing of information; making a connection between two elements
- Facts and lists, which may describe a relationship or which may be learned as individual facts, seemingly apart from other information
- Learning a thread of meaning that runs through an extensive body of information.

Declarative knowledge sessions can prove difficult to design. You need to be an experienced trainer to design and use this type of instructional strategy. This type of session will usually be conducted with trainees who have moderate to high cognitive ability levels. **Figure 6.5** sets out the components of a declarative knowledge session.

A Concept Learning Session

Many management development and technical training programmes require participants to understand concepts. Concept learning focuses on sets of specific objects, symbols or events that are grouped together on the basis of shared characteristics and which can be referred by a particular name or symbol. Concrete concepts are known by their physical characteristics, whereas abstract concepts are not perceivable by their appearance. Many management concepts such as the "learning organisation" and "total quality management" are concepts of an abstract nature.

You have two general approaches available to instruct on concepts:

- An inquiry, exploratory or **discovery** strategy, where you present the learner with examples and non-examples of the concept, and use these to prompt the learner to discover the concept underlying the examples
- An **expository** strategy, where you present the concept, its label and its critical aspects early in a session. An expository strategy does not present many examples and non-examples; however, it follows a discussion of a best example and how it embodies the characteristics of the concept. You then encourage learners to develop their own examples, but not until you have examined critical attributes of the concept.

FIGURE 6.5: STRUCTURE FOR A DECLARATIVE KNOWLEDGE SESSION

INTRODUCTION	
Gain attention; Arouse interest & motivation	• Use of novel, contrasting, and paradoxical events, the interjection of personal / emotional elements, and making clear how the present learning relates to other learning tasks
Establish your instructional purpose	• Relate instructional goals to personal life goals or job requirements; make instructional goals personally relevant; present the goal in an interesting, dynamic format; remind learners of requirements for successful attainment of the objective; and let learners know the form in which they need to remember the material
Preview session	• Some structure can be a useful form of preview; also outlines or maps
BODY	
Recall prior knowledge	• Organisers, use of metaphoric devices, and reviews of prerequisite concepts
Process information	• **Labels/ names** Organisation: clustering and chunking Elaboration: elaboration into sentences • **Facts / Lists** Association: use of images Organisation: expository and narrative structures, recognising patterns, clustering, chunking and elaboration • **Organised Discourse** Association: imagery, metaphoric devices Organisation: analysis of expository and narrative structures, use of graphic organisers such as frames and concept maps Elaboration: Elaboration model
Focus attention	• Underlining, listing, and reflecting; pre-, post-, embedded questions
Employee learning strategies	• Previously noted strategies (all but advance organiser) • Mnemonic techniques such as single-use coding, peg-words, the method of loci, keywords, and the use of rhymes, stories, or jingles • Rehearsal
Practice	• The role of practice; consider differential needs for practice for recall versus recognition learning tasks and for verbatim versus paraphrased recall; consider needs for spaced practice
Evaluate feedback	• Consider feedback needed for labels, facts, and lists (evaluate correctness of associations of elements) as contrasted with the feedback needed for organised discourse ("understanding")
CONCLUSION	
Summary/review	• Cognitive structures, learner-generated summaries, interim summaries
Transfer knowledge	• Increase the number of possible connections in the learner's mental map, the role of application in a variety of settings, learners making inferences
Remotivate & close	• Show how learning can help the learner
ASSESSMENT	
Assess performance	• Use a test or other method
Feedback and Reinforcement	• Review components where learners did not achieve the required standard

Adapted from Smith and Ragan (1992).

You can use the instructional strategy set out in **Figure 6.6** for concept sessions.

A Rule Learning Session

Many training events focus on rules, which constitute a major part of operator training, manual handling, health and safety, employment law, codes of behaviour as part of an induction course. You will most likely have to conduct this type of session on numerous occasions.

In a training context, rules may be of two types:

* Relational rules set out the relationship among two or more concepts
* Procedural rules are a generalised series of steps initiated in response to a particular circumstances to reach a specified goal.

You can use an inquiry approach to train learners on rules.
You might follow this sequence:

* Present learners with a puzzling situation that shows the relationship among the variables in question. You may demonstrate or describe the situation
* You can ask the learners questions about the situation that they answer in the form of "Yes" or "No". Questions should eventually move on from questions verifying the nature of the situation to questions gathering data about the situation
* At the conclusion of the session, learners should be able to state a formal principle or rule about the relationships of the concepts involved
* Learners should be encouraged to discuss the inquiry process itself, including those approaches that were more beneficial.

Typically, you would typically use this approach when training managers on the application of, say, employment laws. You should be aware that this strategy is time-consuming and requires considerable expertise. Before you start training on a procedure, the steps of the procedure must be clear. You should verbally describe the procedure following these guidelines:

* The procedure steps should be described in clear, unambiguous sentences
* Each operation step should represent a single elementary action
* When possible, each step should be dichotomous, resulting in the selection of one of two possible paths
* Decision steps should be stated in the form of a question
* Operation steps should be stated as imperative sentences.

Use the approach in **Figure 6.7** for a rule-based session.

FIGURE 6.6: STRUCTURE FOR A CONCEPT LEARNING SESSION

INTRODUCTION	
Engage learner attention **Arouse interest and motivation**	• Highlight concept label, use unusual picture or humorous story regarding concept, and provide interesting information on origin or history of concept, and present first matched example and non-example. Use inquiry approach
Establish instructional purpose	• State concept explicitly in expository session. Delay statement in an inquiry lesson
Preview Lesson	• Overview process of inquiry approach. Point out importance of examples and non-examples and practice in session
BODY	
Recall prior knowledge	• Review concepts constituting critical attributes of concept. Use techniques such as informal questioning, formal pretext, advance organiser, or analogy
Process information	• Expose learners to best example and/or definition. Emphasise critical attributes. Consider matched examples and non-examples. Present concept in range of settings with diversity of non-relevant attributes
Focus attention	• Isolate critical attributes in examples with high-lighting such as boldface type, colour, or a simplified drawing
Employee learning strategies	• Generate concept maps, analogies, mnemonics or images
Practice	• Identify examples from previously unencountered instances that range in difficulty and setting • Explain categorisations. Generate examples
Evaluate feedback	• Feedback contains attribute isolation
CONCLUSION	
Summarise and review	• Restate critical attributes • Repeat or paraphrase key information
Transfer knowledge	• Apply outside classroom • Provide further examples
Remotivate and close	• Show how learning can help student
ASSESSMENT	
Assess performance	• Test ability to isolate critical attributes in examples and to point out their absence in non-examples • Test including range of common and non-relevant attributes
Feedback and reinforcement	• Provide score or other performance summary • Identify problems of over- and under-generalisation

Adapted from Delahaye (2000).

FIGURE 6.7: STRUCTURE FOR A RULE-BASED SESSION

INTRODUCTION		
	RELATIONAL RULE	**PROCEDURAL RULE**
Engage the attention of the learners	• Curiosity-evoking situation/problem	• Ask questions, demonstrate procedure, and describe its operation
Arouse learner interest and motivation	• Curiosity-evoking situation	• Describe procedure to be learned and the range of applicability
Establish your instructional purpose	• Understand/apply principle, relationship between concepts	• Emphasise efficiency and reliability of procedure.
Preview session	• Inquiry-directions: expository - outline	• Preview procedure in chunks
BODY		
	RELATIONAL RULE	**PROCEDURAL RULE**
Recall prior knowledge	• Review relevant concepts	• Review component concepts, sub-procedures, or related principles
Process information	• Present/ introduce relationship; state in principle form; demonstrate application of principle	• Simplify complex procedures or situations that require procedure into steps in procedure, order of steps, how to evaluate the correct application • May elaborate over iterations
Focus attention	• Direction and size in change of one variable when other variable changes	• Critical characteristics of situations requiring procedure, key cues to transitions between steps, keywords of each step, cues for correct completion of procedure
Employee learning strategies	• Mnemonic rule statement, diagram of relationship or some other learning strategy	• Job aid, mnemonic for order of steps
Practice	• Predict, explain, and control changes in concept(s) based on change of another; recognise situations where rule applies; and determine whether rule was correctly applied	• Identify situations requiring procedures, order of steps, completion of steps, and correct completion of procedure
Evaluate feedback	• Review relevant concepts • Information on where rule is applicable, outcome of application	• Correct answer with explanation, checklist or rating scale, video feedback
CONCLUSION		
Summarise and review	• Major steps in procedure, relationship to principle, appropriate situations for application	
Transfer knowledge	• To problem solving, more complex procedures • Emphasise utility of procedure in terms of reliability and efficiency	
Remotivate and close		

Adapted from Delahaye (2000).

A Problem-Solving Session

Problem-solving sessions are commonplace in training programmes and are defined as focusing on skills to combine previously-learned rules. This type of session yields new learning, because the learner is able to react to problems of a similar class in the future.

One of the most effective strategies for training in problem-solving involves the presentation of carefully-sequenced problem sets. The first set of problems should be the most fundamental of those to be learned. Trainees may learn these rules well in advance of the problem-solving instruction or just prior to it. After learners have received instruction on selecting and combining the rules to solve a class of problems, then you may provide additional rules and combine these rules with the earlier ones to solve a larger class of problem(s).

A simulation can be used in a problem-solving session. A simulation is an activity that attempts to mimic the most essential features of the reality by allowing learners to make decisions within the reality without actually suffering the consequences of their decisions. Case studies and case problems may present a realistic situation and require the learner to respond as if they were the person who is solving the problem in reality.

We suggest that you use the sequence set out in **Figure 6.8** when conducting a problem-solving session.

A Skill-Based Session

There are three generic types of skills that you may be required train on. First, the most basic type of skill involves gathering information (usually by sight) and acting on it (usually with some type of muscle movement). This is called a *psychomotor* skill.

The second type of skill involves *procedures*, or *psychomotor activities* linked in a series. The order of the psychomotor activities is crucial. Aspects of driving a car (starting up, turning a corner) are examples of procedural skills. The main learning aid here is a job breakdown or checklist that specifies the order in which component psychomotor skills must be performed.

The third and more complex type of skill involves *diagnosis*. All forms of troubleshooting and problem definition involve diagnostic skills. Discovering the reason why a car will not start is an example. The main learning aid is a logic chart, or algorithm.

If you know the types of skills included in a session, it will help you in two important ways:

- You become more aware of the aspects of the skill that should be emphasised (for example, order in procedures, logic in diagnosis)
- You are reminded of the appropriate learning aids that should be prepared while planning the session.

FIGURE 6.8: STRUCTURE FOR A PROBLEM-SOLVING SESSION

INTRODUCTION	
Engage learner attention Arouse learner interest and motivation	• Present a challenging and interesting problem in a novel manner
Establish instructional purpose	• State the class of problem that the learner will learn to solve
Preview session	• Point out that problems will become increasingly complex throughout the session
BODY	
Recall prior knowledge	• Explicitly review relevant prior knowledge; rules, declarative knowledge, and strategies • Suggest ways that learners can reorganise knowledge in a more effective form • Attend to similarities/differences in other problem-solving learning
Process information	• Provide simplified, prototypical versions of the problem first • Verbalise task requirements • Provide model, think-aloud • Decompose the problem into sub-goals
Focus attention	• Isolate critical attributes in the given state and state goal
Employee learning strategies	• Generalise networks and analogies • Monitor success of solutions • Ask guiding questions and provide hints • Represent problem in alternate forms • Use print or other media as a form of external storage
Practice	• Practice identifying and clarifying given and state goal • Practice decomposing the problem • Practice evaluating adequacy of a provided solution • Practice with well-defined problems first
Evaluate feedback	• Model the solution process or provoked models of solution • Give hints or ask questions • Provide information on efficiency and effectiveness of solution
CONCLUSION	
Summarise and review	• Restate critical attributes of the problem class • Summarise effective strategies • Suggest ways of organising knowledge for storage and retrieval
Transfer knowledge	• Find similar problems outside the classroom • Explicitly state when strategies may transfer to other problem types
Remotivate /close	• Review the importance and breadth of what has been learned
ASSESSMENT	
Assess performance	• Test ability to solve similar but novel problems, both well-defined and poorly defined • Test ability to isolate critical attributes of the goal and given states • Test ability to evaluate others' solutions • Test ability to justify solutions
Feedback and reinforcement	• Identify whether problems are in pattern recognition, decomposition, explaining solution, etc.

Adapted from Delahaye (2000).

When applying a theory-session model, you must sometimes contrive an activity that enables you to decide whether or not the trainee has attained the training objective.

The situation is a little easier when working with a skill-session model, because the trainer can actually see the trainee performing the task and applying the content of the session directly. In the skill-session model, the physical activity (the behavioural component of the objective) is what the session is all about.

When planning a skill session, you should break down the task into a series of closely-linked steps of physical activity. If the trainee practices this series over and over, he/she will become more proficient at the task (as measured in time and quality). Consequently, the basis of any skill session is a task analysis – a breakdown of a task into skill steps.

Task Breakdown
The task breakdown is usually written directly from information gathered during a training needs analysis. It is basically a step-by-step definition of the task, arranged so that each skill step is a building block on which to place the subsequent skill steps. Adequate performance of all steps ensures adequate learning of the task.

In addition, the breakdown should support each step with explanatory points, which answer the "how", "why", "when" and "where" and describe also the vital tasks involved in the task. Explanatory points should also emphasise safety aspects.

Research shows that a trainee should be able to perform the specified task in less than 10% of the total length of the sessions. Thus, if the trainer has a 40-minute session, he/she will probably have time to present, and the trainees have time to learn, a 4-minute task.

The Training Objective(s)
When you complete the task breakdown, you will find that you have already done the basic work toward preparing the training objective(s). You should make the training objective(s) of the session clear.

We now explain the structure of a skill session for a simple task. Like the theory-session model, a skill-session model has three component parts:

INTRO-DUCTION	BODY				CONCLUSION
	Show	Show and Tell	Check for Understanding	Practice	
	4-step segment				

The Introduction

There are four tasks that you should consider in the introduction:

- **Orient:** Announce the topic of the skill session, and then show trainees how this particular task fits in the total process. You should not make the explanation too detailed. If the skill session is a follow-up to a theory session, you should summarise the knowledge gained in the theory session, preferably by using questioning techniques

- **Motivate:** Why is this session so important? Why should the trainees perform the task in the manner you have specified? The answers to these questions must be logical, and not just "because the instruction manual says so". You should show the trainees that the acquisition of the skill to do this task is important to them

- **Measure current knowledge:** This is the most important component of the introduction. How does the trainer know that trainees can use a screwdriver correctly? Do they have basic keyboard or typing skills? At times, the trainer may have to find out whether there are any left-handed trainees on the programme. This usually occurs when certain physical/directional manipulation is necessary

- **State complete training objective(s):** State the objective(s) clearly and precisely. You should include a time standard within which the trainees must complete the task. This gives the trainees something concrete to aim at and makes it easier for the trainer to judge whether or not the instruction has been successful. Furthermore, the trainees thus have an easily remembered standard that they can take back to the job. If the end-of-training standard differs from the standard required after subsequent practice on the job, point this out to trainees and specify both standards.

The Body

Where trainees are learning a simple task, the body of a skill session consists of four complete and separate steps:

- **Show:** You should perform the task as set out in the task breakdown within the time limit set in the statement of objectives. This gives the trainees an easy introduction to the task and also gives them a mental picture and a standard to work toward. This demonstration is silent, but you can draw attention to particularly important points on safety. The length of this component depends on the task. When you have finished this step, you should quickly tidy up the work area in preparation to start the task again

- **Show and Tell:** You should SHOW and TELL each skill step as set out in the task breakdown. Emphasise safety factors and particularly difficult or tricky parts. You should stress each skill step, and pause between each so that the trainees know that every skill step has a separate identity

You need to make sure that every trainee can see the "show and tell" clearly. You may encounter the problem of left-handed *versus* right-handed trainees. If this happens, stand the right-handed trainees behind you and place the left-handed trainees in front. Make provision for the trainees to ask questions, and constantly check that they all understand each step or explanatory point as you progress

You must be aware that you are also a model. Throughout the session, you must follow all the correct methods and maintain good housekeeping and safety standards

- **Check for understanding:** This is the initial feedback (both for you and for the trainees). A useful technique here is to ask the trainees to name each skill step. You could actually perform the task to the trainees' instructions. Do not let one trainee name all the steps – give all trainees an opportunity. The trainer must be certain at the end of this stage that all the trainees know the steps and key points, and make sure the trainees stress the importance of all the safety features mentioned during the session. When you are sure that the trainees know all the skill steps, they are ready for the final stage

- **Practice:** Trainees should practice for at least 50% of the total time allocated for the body of the session. Thus if the skill session body is 20 minutes, then the practice step alone must last at least 10 minutes. Before the trainees begin the practice step, you should have provided them with three basic items:

  ○ A task breakdown sheet. This should show each step and the explanatory points for each step. Include drawings, if they will make the points clearer

  ○ The correct tools and equipment to complete the skill. Check that these operate within the safety requirements

  ○ Sufficient material. The trainees will most probably need three or four attempts before they become proficient within the standard stated in the objective. Therefore, provide sufficient material for the task to be carried out a number of times

You should supervise the trainees continually throughout the practice period and be vigilant for unsafe practices, untidy housekeeping, and incorrect methods. Errors should be corrected in a constructive manner, and you should watch for a trainee who is confused or lost, and spend more time with them.

The practice step is your opportunity to give individual instruction, so make the most of it. The previous three steps (show, show and tell, and check for understanding) are group-oriented, so you have to aim at the average trainee. You can use the practice step to help learners who are experiencing difficulty with the skill and to give learners who have mastered the skill additional challenging tasks to maintain their interest.

The Conclusion
You should briefly review the steps and key points (using questions). You can write these on a white-board for emphasis and to encourage trainee participation throughout the conclusion. In particular, check:

- Whether they found any of the skill steps particularly difficult. This will reinforce these steps for the trainees and let the trainer know which steps to emphasise next time
- Whether they have discovered any new or different techniques. This is a fertile field for ideas for the next time and also gives the trainees a sense of having contributed. If they create a realistic alternative technique, they will leave the session with that particular skill greatly reinforced. In addition, this quick check can identify trainees who identify possible shortcut techniques during training and decide to do it "their way" back on the job. Frequently, the trainer can point out to the trainee why the shortcut is not acceptable and prevent negative outcomes such as increased costs for the organisation, to (in extreme situations) permanent injury or death for the employee.

You should review briefly the standards of time and workmanship, and emphasise the most important safety factor; check if there are any questions and provide a definite finish to the session. Some of the guidelines you should follow when delivering a skill-based session are shown in **Figure 6.9.**

SELECTING APPROPRIATE TRAINING METHODS

We have so far focused on your overall instructional strategy. We now consider the next design decision that you have to make: What methods of learning should be used to achieve the learning objectives and fit into the instructional strategy? You have a large choice of methods to select from.

Group-Oriented Didactic Learning Methods

Most formal training events take place in a group setting. Therefore, during the course of your career, you are likely to use a number of group-oriented training methods. These methods are didactic in nature and place a strong emphasis on your expertise knowledge of the subject matter and your delivery skills. They include:

FIGURE 6.9: CHECKLIST FOR CONDUCTING INSTRUCTION

INTRODUCTION
• Did you clearly and precisely state the session objective(s)?   • Did you include time quality standards in objective(s)?   • Did you use past experiences to introduce the session?   • Did you check current knowledge?   • Did you motivate the group?
BODY
Show
• Did you do the job in a competent manner?   • Did you observe the time factors, good methods, safety and housekeeping?
Show and Tell
• Did you show and tell one skill step at a time?   • Did you stress key points (pause between skill steps)?   • Did you ensure that all trainees could see clearly?   • Did you follow the breakdown (no backtracking)?   • Did you observe correct methods, good housekeeping, and safety?   • Did you make adequate provision for trainees to ask question?
Check Understanding
• Did you ask trainees to describe skill steps and key points?   • Did you perform the task to trainees' instructions?   • Did you ensure that all trainees know how to do the task?
Practice
• Did you have everything ready and properly arranged?   • Did you correct errors as they occurred with constructive criticism?   • Did you ensure correct methods, good housekeeping and safety factors?   • Did you structure adequate trainee practice?
CONCLUSION
• Did you briefly review critical steps and key tasks?   • Did you ensure trainees were aware of the standards expected?   • Did you ask for new ways to perform the task?

• **Lectures:** We define a lecture as a talk or verbal presentation given to a small or large audience. Your objective is to convey aspects of your knowledge to the learners, which they are then expected to absorb and retain. The absence of any involvement, other than listening by learners, means that the process is essentially a passive one, and you have little or no opportunity for the group to interact. In order to be effective using this method, you need to be an expert on the subject and communicate this with authority to the audience. You should ensure that the lecture does not become a monologue, but rather something that your learners can identify with and participate in.

- **Briefing Groups:** Briefing groups are often used in training and non-training situations because they are an effective means of two-way communication. Briefing groups provide a mechanism for cascading information. This allows for discussion within groups; managers can get immediate reaction and feedback. The characteristic of a briefing group is this continuity of communication and feedback

- **Formal Talks:** Formal talks, presentations and lessons are very popular training methods. The concentration level of the learner will most likely vary depending on the individual, the content and the skill of the trainer. This method is quite effective provided it is supported by handouts to highlight the significant learning points. It is preferable that you also provide practise for learners so you reinforce the learning event.

- **Demonstrations:** You can use a demonstration, followed by a practice session, when you are conducting manual and social skills training. In a demonstration, you show the complete exercise (the overview) and then the individual components. The trainees then copy your individual movements one at a time and you correct mistakes. You and the participants can then discuss each learner's performance and provide feedback and guidance. You must ensure that all the learners can see the demonstration. This is very often overlooked

- **Seminars and Workshops:** You should use a seminar or workshop with small groups of learners (ideally no more than 15). The method of instruction you use should be Socratic rather than formal instruction, with the whole group working out answers to a series of questions. Your role will differ between a seminar and a workshop. In a seminar, your role is to achieve a predetermined result. Therefore, you will take more control. In a workshop situation, the focus is on tackling real questions, where there are no predetermined answers and so you will use a more facilitative style in the workshop content. Both methods will be effective (if skilfully set up and facilitated). The learners are required to work out the answers for themselves; therefore, they perceive ownership of the situation. Learners are then more likely to remember what they have learned and you are more likely to achieve transfer.

Figure 6.10 presents the advantages and disadvantages of these more didactic methods from your own perspective and that of your learners.

FIGURE 6.10: ADVANTAGES & DISADVANTAGES OF GROUP-ORIENTED, DIDACTIC LEARNING METHODS

Learning Method	Description	Trainer Perspective	Learner Perspective	Applications	Participant Involvement	Group Size
Lecture	Structured, planned talk. Usually accompanied by visual aids - slides, OHPs, flipchart	• Suitable for large audiences where participation is not needed • Content and timing can be planned in detail • Structure needs to be planned carefully and should be lively or audience will lose attention • Audience input should be considered in the form of seminars • High level of control over time and content • Multiple applications	• Lively style needed • Communication of material may be limited if no provision of feedback to lecturer • There may be low levels of retention and poor interaction by learners	• Wide range of training options	• Very low	• Unlimited
Briefing Groups	Trainer or panel of experts provide the salient facts or a "brief" on given topic which then forms the basis of a question and answer session	• A relatively simple process to implement • Requires very good facilitation skills to manage the Q&A session	• Fast pace • Good involvement in the process • Challenges participants • Success depends on trainee quality • May be too short to be informative	• Fact-finding • Problem-solving	• Medium	• Up to 20

Learning Method	Description	Trainer Perspective	Learner Perspective	Applications	Participant Involvement	Group Size
Demonstrations	Free exchange of info/opinions A "controlled" discussion may follow a planned path, the leader controlling the agenda; an "open" discussion may mirror members' priorities May be time-consuming	• May be time-consuming, especially if discussion wanders or "process problems" emerge • Attitudes may harden not adjust • Especially suitable for development/ adjustment of attitudes/opinions • Highly practical and directly applicable	• Individual participation may be affected by group composition • Offers feedback to trainer on learning achievement • Promotes group cohesion	• Develop manual skills • New process systems and procedures	• Low / High	• 1-10

Learning Method	Description	Trainer Perspective	Learner Perspective	Applications	Participant Involvement	Group Size
Formal Talks	Formula-based "teaching" session: Tell – how to do Show – how to do Do (supervised practice) Review process and results	• For introducing skills, usually in line with a planned breakdown of small sequential practice stages • Skill may be best addressed as a whole, rather than in parts, but lengthy stages 1 and 2 yield memory problems • Typically, follows some other form of training, the skills to be learnt being those of application	• Design / balance of session important • Confidence is built by mastery and link-up of stages • Provides a vehicle for feedback to instructor • Time constraints can be eliminated with reference to the learning process	• Multiple applications	• Low	• Unlimited
Seminars / Workshops	Means of exploring specific topic by researching aspects in advance and exchanging information through reports and discussion with other group members	• Require strong facilitation and knowledge of the issues • Very appropriate for conceptual and theoretical issues	• Places a lot of responsibility on individuals. • Encourage different perspectives to emerge. • Success is dependent on participants' knowledge	• Lots of application to professional work areas	• Medium	• 10-20

Group-Oriented Experiential Learning Methods

Your learning objectives may require that you use more experiential learning methods. These methods factor in the experience of the adult learner and they allow for significant amounts of participation by the learner in the learning event. Experiential learning methods make significant demands of your facilitation skills. There is a strong focus on process and significantly less on your subject matter knowledge. As you develop your confidence as a trainer, you will need to become more competent using methods such as role-plays, case studies, in-tray exercises and brainstorming.

Role-plays
Role-plays are very useful in a training situation. They usually involve presenting the trainee with a scripted scenario or situation and asking them to act out a particular role with the intention of reaching a conclusion. If you are to gain the maximum benefit from a role-play in a learning situation, it is important that the incidents you include as part of the role-play are realistic. You will need to give yourself time to prepare an outline brief of the personalities involved and ensure that the circumstances closely reflect those encountered in the working environment. The brief you prepare should be sufficiently detailed to make it clear to your learners the learning issues involved. It should also be sufficiently flexible so that the learner can improvise and give it a personal interpretation.

Role-plays need careful facilitation. The objective of the role-play is on behaviour, not on the acting talents of the learner. You will need to brief your learners on what they should look out for and focus them on the relevant content and process issues. You can ask your trainees to assume the role of observers and to record their observations of the behaviour demonstrated. You should provide your learners with a structured observation sheet to enable them to record systematically their observations.

Case Studies
These are very frequently used in management training and development programmes and are a very popular and effective method. Case studies are built around the notion that the trainee is presented with a record of a set of circumstances, which may be based on an actual event or an imaginary situation.

There are three variations of the case study method that you might find appropriate:

- A case study, where you provide trainees with a set of facts, real or imagined, and their task is to diagnose a particular problem(s)

- Case studies where the learner's task is to identify problems but also to go into problem-solving mode and generate appropriate solutions
- Case studies that provide the learner with both the problem and the solution but ask the learners to be evaluative, comment on the actions taken and assess the implications.

The variation that you will use will depend on your learning objectives and the capabilities of your learners.

The complexity of the issues will dictate whether you incorporate the case study into the training programme as a short 30 to 60 minute exercise or opt for a more complex learning event. With managerial grades. your course might be built around the case study itself and last for several days.

Irrespective of the case study variation that you use, the learning will be achieved by providing information on an issue or series of issues. This information might be in documentary form, (such as a report) or it could be communicated through oral or visual means (such as a video or slide presentation). Once your learners have been provided with the raw data to examine, you can begin the process of analysis.

"In-tray" Exercises
This method is most relevant in the context of management or graduate training. "In-tray" exercises consist of a paper-handling simulation based on the contents of a typical company employee's in-tray. The learning objective is for the trainee involved to be projected into the position of the person responsible for dealing with the in-tray items and then to resolve all the work it contains. On completion of the exercise, you will review the learner's progress and provide feedback.

You can use 'In-tray' exercises in two situations:

- As a diagnostic tool to discover how the group member would handle the work outstanding in the tray
- As an evaluative method to test how well the trainee would put into effect the skills learnt on the training course.

In the first situation, each learner is given a series of items to sort through and take action on as they feel appropriate. The exercise would also be carried out independently. The final step is to reconvene as a group to review the decisions or actions taken and to assess their effectiveness.

The approach is similar where the in-tray is used as an evaluative method. The items in the in-tray – files, letters, and memoranda – are reviewed individually and action taken by the person involved. The main difference lies in the fact that, prior to undertaking the task, the trainee will be given advice on the best means of dealing with the particular problems that the tray highlights. You will judge the trainee on their ability to handle the complexity in the exercise. It is important to emphasise that providing the feedback at this stage of the exercise is an essential ingredient in the learning process.

You will need to give a significant amount of time if you propose to use an in-tray exercise.

Brainstorming

Brainstorming is essentially a loosely structured form of discussion. Its main function is to provide you with a practical means of generating ideas without participants becoming embroiled in unproductive analysis. Its success rests on two important principles:

- The first is founded in synergistic theory, that a group can provide more high quality ideas by working together than the same people would produce working independently. This is because the group interaction produces cross-fertilisation, in which an idea presented on its own, which normally would be dismissed as impractical, is adapted, adopted and improved by someone else to provide a more feasible approach

- The second principle is that, if a group is to produce ideas, it is imperative that subjecting these ideas to evaluation too early on does not inhibit creative thinking. Creative thought passes through three stages: the generation of the idea; the evaluation or analysis of that idea; and the application of the idea to the chosen situation. If others sit in judgement after each idea is proposed, then analysis by paralysis sets in and the flow of ideas dry up. Creative thoughts can be stimulated in an environment where judgement is postponed *after* all the possible solutions have been provided.

There are six ground rules for running a brainstorming session.

- **No criticism**: The free flow of ideas can only take place where there is no fear of being criticised. Criticism in this context is given a wide interpretation, so that this will clearly preclude an outright attack on a proposal, but it also extends to cover indirect ridiculing of someone's idea or being very patronising about it. It is also important *not* to imply that an idea has no merit by ignoring any contribution or by betraying cynicism through such non-verbal gestures as a dismissive shrug or raised eyebrows

- **Encourage ideas**: In order to ensure that there are enough ideas for cross-fertilisation to take place, the group must feel that their contributions are valued. The emphasis should be on the *quantity* of suggestions and not the quality. There will be sufficient opportunity at the evaluation stage for individuals to voice their feelings about any particular suggestion

- **Equal participation**: It follows that, if everyone should feel that their suggestion is worthy of consideration, then everyone should be entitled to put forward their ideas. The fairest way to prevent one or two more dominant group members from monopolising the group is to establish a system where each person is asked for a contribution in turn. This might make the process more regimented but this is more than compensated for by the involvement of the whole group

  If a member of the group is unable to make a suggestion at any point, this should be indicated by the individual concerned and should be accepted without comment and the process continued. (It is quite likely that while no idea springs to mind this time round, subsequent recommendations might trigger a thought for the next time)

- **Free association**: In order to gain the maximum number of suggestions, there should be no boundaries on what is suggested. Any idea (no matter how outrageous or far fetched it might seem) is worthy of consideration. The logic behind this is that an idea, which seems completely impractical, could provide the basis of a worthwhile idea in somebody else's mind

- **Record all ideas:** It isn't just the suggestions that are important but also the opportunity to reflect on them in the hope of inspiring further ideas. In order to allow this to happen, all the ideas should be recorded on a flip-chart or white-board, and in the words used by the participants. Otherwise, further clarification could interrupt the flow of thought and be viewed by some group members as seeking justification before acceptance

- **Allow time to incubate:** Once the ideas have been set down, there should be some time to contemplate suggestions.

Figure 6.11 presents a summary of the advantages of each method from your own perspective, and those of trainee, and the learner.

One-to-One Learning Methods

You are most likely to use 1:1 learning methods in an on-the-job training context. They are frequently used for management training and development or where you are training operators on production skills. The more frequently used 1:1 methods include coaching, mentoring, counselling and performance discussions. We discuss the practical application these methods in **Chapter Ten**.

FIGURE 6.11: ADVANTAGES & DISADVANTAGES OF GROUP-ORIENTED EXPERIENTIAL LEARNING METHODS

Learning Method	Description	Trainer Perspective	Learner Perspective	Applications	Participant Involvement	Group Size
Action Learning Sets	• Involve a group of people convening to bring to the set real work problems • They act as comrades in adversity, supporting and challenging each other • Each participant works on their problem between set meetings and brings new information and solutions back to the group	• Degree of interdependence of group members • Trainer can help to establish learning set or act as learning set adviser • Adviser can offer support or help line and guide process if needed • Can achieve high-level objectives	• Typically the group meets once a month for half a day over a period of six to nine months • Learning through questioning is very powerful • Learners learn at own pace	• Complex problem-solving • All managerial skills	• High	• 4-6
Action Maze	• Similar to a case study, but uses printed instructions to guide a group through to a pre-determined conclusion • Choices and options are offered at certain stages, rather than a pathway • Set situations will result from the choices • Discovery of preferred paths is the main outcome of this exercise	• Can be useful for problem solving or decision-making • Requires careful design • Allows participant interdependence • Time-consuming and difficult to produce	• Incorrect decision-making can result in high levels of learning – learning from mistakes is good! • Learners who make the most incorrect decisions learn the most	• Problem-solving • Decision-making • Managerial skills • Supervisory skills	• High	• Small group syndicates

Learning Method	Description	Trainer Perspective	Learner Perspective	Applications	Participant Involvement	Group Size
Brainstorming	• Creative ideas from participants • Group is allowed to submit ideas or suggestions and none are rejected • No discussion and no value judgement are made at this stage • Subsequently all ideas can be sorted and assessed in any way • Exploration can produce existing results	• Allows trainer to quickly gather information as to the levels of knowledge of the participant • Allows the generation of a lot of ideas in a short space of time and creates a climate of creativity • Very effective and simple procedure to use	• Good fun and very creative allowing a lot of participant input with no discussion • Most people can contribute without much effort • Participants feel a sense of ownership of the ideas	• Problem diagnosis. Team-building Creative thinking	• High	• Up to 10
Business Case Simulations	• Dynamic exercises or case studies – usually involving coming to terms with a situation then managing it via a set of imposed decisions. • Computerised models offer complex data and often decisions that interact.	• Interactive element generates enthusiasm, notably when teams are in simulated competition • Can be linked with team development • Model can be challenged as unrealistic	• Offers practice in management – observation, analysis, judgement, decision-making, etc • Can instil confidence	• All aspects of management development	• Very high	• 6-8

Learning Method	Description	Trainer Perspective	Learner Perspective	Applications	Participant Involvement	Group Size
Buzz Groups	• Small groups, often formed after an input session, answer a set question or complete a set task and report back to the trainer or the rest of the group	• Avoid one group giving all the answers and leaving nothing for the other • Very participative and a larger number of contributions can be offered in a short space of time	• Helps rapid knowledge gains and starts trainee thought processes • Good group support engendered			
Case Study	• Examination of events or situations (often real-life usually aimed at learning by analysing the detailed material, or posing and defining solutions for problems	• Especially useful for analysis of existing /proposed systems • Can incorporate exercises • Simple cases may be unrealistic • Difficult to reproduce an exact duplicate of the working environment • Time-consuming to prepare	• Opportunities exist for both exchange of views on "what matters" and problem-solving	• Management development • Executive training	• High	• 10 max
Exercise	• Carry out a particular task along prescribed lines • Often a test of knowledge earlier delivered to learners	• Exercise must relate to the working environment, what attainable objectives • Some form of assessment can give an idea of how much has been learnt by the end user	• Highly active form of learning; satisfies needs for practice to apply knowledge or develop skill • Testing gives confidence	• Many applications	• High	• Unlimited

Learning Method	Description	Trainer Perspective	Learner Perspective	Applications	Participant Involvement	Group Size
Experiential Exercises	• Client-centred approach to individual, group and organisational learning that engages the learner using the elements of action, reaction, transfer and support	• The trainer's role is to act as a facilitator to enable the construction of knowledge, skill, attitude and value from the direct experience	• Is a learner-centred focus that draws upon personal experience as the vehicle to access knowledge, skills and attitudes and provide for planned and emergent learning	• Personal development	• High	• 6-8
In-Tray Methods	• Often used in time management training • Can use a simulated in-tray with many tasks and the participant has to order the tasks and allocate times, explaining the reasoning behind decisions • Can also be used to simulate a bigger exercise using a set of tasks where participant has to decide which to delegate, interpret, and carry out sets of instructions, all with interruptions and other distractions • After each exercise the results are analysed and discussed	• Requires very careful planning and thought • Appraisal can be time-consuming • Can be complex or simple, low theoretical base and very practical • Immediate knowledge application provide good insights into work	• Very participant-centred • High level of transfer • Must be realistic otherwise will have negative reactions	• Time management • Planning skills • Supervising skills • Clerical skills	• High	• Small groups

Learning Method	Description	Trainer Perspective	Learner Perspective	Applications	Participant Involvement	Group Size
Role Play	• Enactment of role(s) in protected environment • Asked to suspend self-reality and adopt other roles	• Mainly used to practice face to face skills (selling) combined with review critiques from trainers and/or other learners	• Unless disciplined, can cause embarrassment • Degree of reality of design is an important factor for participants • Can be good for video feedback	• Interpersonal skills • Counselling • Negotiating • Human resource management	• High	• 6-8
Simulations	• Any large simulation exercise that attempts to represent a high degree of reality, often also termed business or management "games" • Games often have rules, players and are competitive	• Need to be careful about possible unexpected outcomes due to the levels of reality in the simulation • Can be good to allow a high degree of participant interdependence • High levels of planning and preparation needed Useful as an exercise towards the end of a programme to consolidate practice of previous narrow skills thus developing complex skills	• Allow more complex scenarios to develop that are close to real life yet allow practice and mistakes to occur in a safe environment	• Any supervisory management development initiatives	• High	• 8-10 max

Learning Method	Description	Trainer Perspective	Learner Perspective	Applications	Participant Involvement	Group Size
Syndicates	• Larger tasks and exercises involving planning and preparation • Dividing the main group into smaller groups with separate rooms • Asked to discuss tasks and solve or identify a specific problem; followed by a review and evaluation	• Allow group sharing, exchange and support • Opportunity for more in-depth work than buzz groups • More opportunity for quieter members to contribute over time	• Allow group to develop its strength and identity due to larger complex project			

Coaching

Coaching is most frequently used to develop managerial skills and prepare leaders for more senior positions. You may be asked to perform the role of a coach, although this role will usually be performed by managers. If you are a direct trainer, you may have to coach operators in a production skills training content or in areas such as handling customers.

Coaching can be either an informal or formal process. Coaching as an informal process is an everyday occurrence in organisations. When managers are asked if they coach their staff, very often the reply will be that they do not because they do not associate their assistance in helping the employees with the term coaching but simply as "part of the job". Formal coaching is used as a learning experience for employees and is considered one of a manager's most important responsibilities. Managers often find it difficult to adopt a formal coaching role due to: lack of time, inappropriate managerial style or lack of coaching skill on their own part.

Mentoring

Mentoring is a similar process to coaching, in so far as the employee can seek guidance and advice in terms of expertise, experience and understanding. A mentor is usually from another line function and will not be the direct manager of the learner and is usually a few more levels senior. This eliminates any possibility of conflict in terms of the development of, or problems encountered by, the individual or protégé.

It is preferable that the mentor is given clearly defined terms of reference – for example, who makes the ultimate decision if the mentor considers that the employee needs to attend a formal training session to support the informal on-the-job learning? Does the direct line manager allow the learner to attend, even though the suggestion did not originate with the direct manager? Can the manager insist on the employee's attendance? Constraints, if they exist, should be communicated to the mentors when they take on the mentoring role.

Mentoring can be used with new graduates who are participating on fast-track training programmes. It is also of high value in the development of supervisors and managers.

Counselling

Counselling is often not considered a training method, although it has many components to it that facilitate learning, including discovery, acceptance of responsibility and willingness to change.

Counselling can take many forms in training situations – for example, a manager may "counsel" an employee if a performance level is not being reached or as a result of a misdemeanour of some kind. Another example is if an employee is experiencing emotional or financial difficulties, or if there were "outward" signs of stress.

Counselling skills are important skills for managers and form part of their development process. The essential skill in counselling is that of actively listening and not relating one's own experience, and thereby assisting the individual to sort out the problem. Counselling does not mean offering advice or anecdotes, which concentrate on one particular response to such problems but instead offering employees alternative solutions so that they can make choices and arrive at their own decisions. Counselling should enable the employee to make decisions and, in some cases, assist in the release of potential energy for change and development for the organisation's benefit.

Whereas coaching and mentoring are job-related, counselling may cover a wider range of issues and difficulties, including problems outside the working environment that could affect the standards of the employee's performance. It is important for managers to recognise their capability with regard to counselling, and to know when it is necessary to encourage and advise the individual to seek professional counselling outside the organisation. Unless a manager is professionally trained as a counsellor, giving advice and guidance can sometimes lead to further problems.

Counselling may be a once only session, or it may be conducted over a lengthy period, depending on the particular problem.

Counselling should create a freedom to express a problem in an atmosphere of confidentiality. There are inherent challenges however, because a manager may have to decide at some point to break the confidentiality because the knowledge he/she has learned about the individual could impact on the organisation in some way – for example, an employee might confess to a misdemeanour that could have an adverse affect on the organisation and its profitability.

Performance Discussions
Performance discussions can be learning-oriented. The developmental component of performance discussions depends on the manner in which they are carried out. They have a number of development dimensions. They are an important mechanism to encourage and develop managers to achieve performance standards. Performance discussions should be ongoing. Many performance discussions occur in an informal way as part of the work that an employee undertakes.

Performance discussions are more effective when the performance is assessed against previously set and agreed criteria. An open dialogue has to be created to allow the exchange of ideas without fear of recrimination or the threat of job loss or demotion, and positive outcomes will only be achieved if both the manager and the employee can be honest with each other.

Job Attachments and Secondments

Job attachments to a variety of departments are considered an excellent method of developing managers' and graduates' skills. They also help them to discover the areas in which they want to make their main career. Traditionally, technician and graduate engineering apprentices have to work in a variety of departments for a period of six months or so in each. The attachments frequently include sales and finance, as well as the specialist areas of plant maintenance, production, research, and design and product development. This breadth of experience is necessary, if graduate engineers are to gain membership of one of more chartered institutions.

The Japanese practice of rotating young professionals through many departments is widely extolled as producing well-rounded general managers. The Japanese tend to spend several years doing a real job in each department, so they usually are in their 30s before gaining their first management appointment.

Secondment is another form of attachment but differs insofar as it involves moving from one location to another, usually to another organisation or at least to a different site. Secondments are frequently used to develop professionals who may need experience in another organisation or professional context to enhance their skills. Secondments are valuable because they allow for cross-fertilisation of ideas.

Team-Based Learning Methods

Action Learning
Action learning is increasingly used in supervisory or management development. It seeks to avoid the pitfalls associated with more formal methods, because it uses the actual job of managing and supervision as a vehicle for learning. Action learning is associated with Revans, who holds that learning should begin with the everyday management of problem-solving.

Action learning focuses on both the individual and the team. Through an action learning process, learners actively challenge one another's ideas, they encourage each other to espouse theories and perceptions that they may not have voiced to date and the process helps learners to consciously think about other ideas and concepts that may be applied.

You should consider using action learning when:

- You want to develop managers to solve complex problems and to challenge organisational assumptions
- You are sure that you have the commitment of your organisation's leaders to time resources and people to the process

- The problem or opportunity is a genuine one and not some form of puzzle
- You wish to achieve team and organisation learning objectives.

Action learning can achieve a number of purposes, including:
- To voluntarily work on problems of managing and organising
- To work on problems that involve the set members
- To analyse individual perceptions of the problem in order to provide other perspectives and identify courses of action
- To take action that is reported back to the learning set to allow further reflection
- To support and challenge members to encourage effective learning and action
- To raise awareness of group processes and encourage improved teamwork. The learning set sometimes has a facilitator who helps members develop the skills of action learning
- To encourage three levels of learning:
  ° About the problem
  ° About oneself
  ° About the learning process and "learning to learn".

If you consider using action learning as a method of learning, there are six elements that you should consider.

Element 1: Forming Action Learning Groups
One or more action learning groups (also known as action learning sets) are formed. Each group is composed of four to eight members from different functions or departments. By diversifying its membership in this way, the group can take advantage of different perspectives in addressing organisational problems. Each group includes learners who care about the problem to be addressed, who know something about the problem, and who have the power to implement the solution recommended by the group or to monitor the work of others in implementing that solution.

Element 2: Undertaking Projects, Problems or Tasks
One of the fundamental beliefs underlying action learning is that learners learn best when they take meaningful action to solve important organisational problems and then reflect on and learn from the actions taken. Several criteria are used to determine whether a problem is appropriate for an action-learning group to address:
- *Reality:* The problem must be current, be of genuine significance to the organisation, and require a tangible result by a specific date so that the investment of time and funds is justified

- *Feasibility:* The problem must be within the competence of the group to solve
- *Richness in potential learning:* The problem must provide learning opportunities for the group members and its solution must offer possible applications to other parts of the organisation.

Element 3: Questioning and Reflecting

Action learning focuses on the right questions rather than the right answers. The assumption is that what people *do not know* is as important as what they *do* know. In action learning, the group members tackle a problem by first asking questions that clarify the exact nature of that problem; next they reflect on the problem and identify possible solutions; then they choose that action to take.

The classic formula for action learning is $L = P + Q + R$, where L is learning, P is programmed instruction (knowledge in current use, in books, already in one's mind, and so on), Q is fresh questioning and r is reflection (pulling apart, making sense of, trying to understand).

When the members of an action-learning group begin to address a problem, they ask and answer the following questions:

- What goal is the organisation seeking to accomplish?
- What obstacles are keeping the organisation from accomplishing this goal?
- What can the organisation do about the obstacles?
- Who knows what information is needed?
- Who cares about having a solution implemented?
- Who has the power to implement the solution?

Element 4: Making a Commitment to Action

There is really no learning unless action is taken on the problem that a group addresses, and no action should be taken without learning from it. The group members either must have the power to implement their solution(s) or must be assured that others will assume responsibility for implementation. Action enhances the learning, as it provides a basis and anchor for the critical dimension of reflection.

Implementation is part of the contract between an action learning group and the organisation. If the group members merely prepare reports and make recommendations, their commitment, effectiveness, and learning are diminished. Unless a solution is implemented and the group members reflect on that implementation and its effectiveness, there will be no evidence that something better or different can be done. Consequently, there will be no indication that real learning has taken place.

Element 5: Discussing what has been learned
Solving an organisational problem provides immediate, short-term benefits to the organisation. The greater, long-term benefit, however, is the learning that the group members acquire about themselves, about the effectiveness of their group, and about ways in which that learning can be applied throughout the organisation. Therefore, time must be set aside for group members to discuss what they have learned as individuals and as a group and how that learning can be used in other parts of the organisation.

Element 6: Analysing the Learning Experience
It is advisable for each action learning group to have a facilitator (also known as a set advisor). This person may be either a member of the working group or a non-member, whose sole task is to help the group members reflect on what they are learning and how they are solving problems. The facilitator assists the group members in analysing how they have listened, reframed the problem, provided feedback to one another, handled differences, fostered creativity, and so on. He or she should be competent in working with the processes vital to action learning: questioning, emphasising, learning, avoiding judgement, focusing on the task, and providing air time (time to talk) for every member. If no facilitator is involved, the group must still analyse their learning experience for themselves.

There are a number of practical issues that you may need to consider when implementing action learning as a method. These steps that follow are advisable if you are to maximise the potential of the method:

- **Step 1 – Hold an information workshop:** An organisation-wide workshop shows both managers and non-managerial employees how action learning works. External consultants or knowledgeable staff members explain and demonstrate the basic principles and dynamics of action learning

- **Step 2 – Establish Projects:** One or more projects involving organisational problems are identified to be addressed by action learning groups. The projects chosen are ones that will be 1) meaningful to potential group members and their jobs and 2) important to the organisation as a whole. The problems must be ones for which employees can offer several viable solutions, not ones that could be better solved by experts

- **Step 3 – Form Action Learning Groups:** Action learning groups are formed, each consisting of four to eight members from diverse backgrounds and representing different kinds of functional expertise. A facilitator also may be assigned to each group, although this is not absolutely necessary. If a facilitator is assigned, that person should be someone whom the members do not already know, so that he or she can act independently of the group's culture

- **Step 4 – Work on Problems:** Each action-learning group meets on a periodic basis (daily, weekly, or every two weeks) over a period of several weeks to several months. Each meeting requires a full day or a few hours, depending on the nature of the problem being addressed and the constraints of the members' schedules and responsibilities

- **Step 5 – Record Findings:** An action group's learning is developed as a result of discussing and resolving its problems. In each group, the members use such techniques as feedback, brainstorming, reflection, discussion, and analysis to reach a solution. What they discover and experience during this process is recorded

- **Step 6 – Reflecting on the Work:** After a group completes its project, its members reflect on their work, either with or without the assistance of a facilitator. Their objective is to learn as much as possible about how they identified, assessed, and solved the problems; what increased their learning; how they communicated; and what assumptions shaped their actions.

Figure 6.12 provides a summary of the ground rules for operating an action learning set.

Figure 6.13 provides a summary of the advantages and applications of one-to-one learning methods.

Technology-Based Methods
Open Learning
Open learning is used increasingly in organisations. The earliest open learning approaches were texts of the '"teach yourself" type and postal correspondence schools. Many colleges now run open learning centres in parallel with more traditional courses. Some companies have set up open learning centres, so that employees at all levels can follow a variety of vocational and general education courses.

The growth in open and distance learning reflects a change in working practices. First, fewer employers are prepared to give day release to employees and, even if they do, the employees may not feel able to do their jobs in four days a week. Secondly, employees frequently have evening commitments that prevent them from attending conventional courses; many people prefer to study on their own with occasional lectures and tutorials.

FIGURE 6.12: GROUND RULES FOR OPERATING AN ACTION LEARNING SET

- Ground rules may be developed by members
- Ground rules may be changed following discussion by the members
- Equal time should be allotted to each member
- Action plans should be agreed
- All members should make a commitment to attend
- Each member's project is dealt with in turn
- Members need to develop the skill of listening and receiving information
- The facilitator should clearly explain what he or she is looking for from the presentation so that the other members can focus their attention
- Feedback should be conducted in a constructive and supportive spirit, which may require the development of these skills
- Issues discussed in the set should be confidential
- It is valuable when identifying a problem to be used for action learning to be clear what it is about and what measures are going to be used to judge the level of achievement.
- Identify the benefits associated with addressing the problem. If you cannot identify any then there will be little motivation to resolving the issue and the energy will dissipate.
- Choose a problem that is important to you and your organisation. If the problem is perceived to be trivial then it will not occupy your attention and energies nor will lit be something the organisation will actively support in terms of time and resources.
- Set yourself benchmarks to assess your progress in resolving the problem; this may also be done through consultation with other people who may have a vested interest in your quest.
- Try and forecast possible difficulties that might arise, and work out strategies for overcoming these. One of the reasons the problem exists is probably that there are a number of difficulties that have previously prevented any action being taken on the problem.
- It is essential to the success of the action-learning programme that there is commitment and openness across the organisation and particularly from the top. Without support, attempts to address problems will be stifled and pushed to the periphery where they will be forgotten about.

Adapted from Beard and Wilson (2002).

One of the disadvantages of any open-learning package is that the learner may drop out because of the lack of personal contact on an ongoing basis either with a tutor or other learners. However, the more progressive open-learning providers have developed high-contact programmes to overcome this.

FIGURE 6.13: ADVANTAGES & DISADVANTAGES OF ONE-TO-ONE & TEAM-BASED LEARNING METHODS

Learning Method	Description	Trainer (Manager) Perspective	Learner Perspective	Application	Participant Involvement	Group Size
Action Learning	• Learners work in teams to solve problems • Teams are called learning sets • Learning sets are facilitated	• Focuses on organisational problems as the basis for learning • Contributes to the development of teamwork in organisations • Suitable for complex problem situations	• Participant fully involved in the learning process • Learning from other members • Strong focus on reflection	• Team development • Complex problem-solving • Management and executive development	• Very high involvement by learner	• 4-6 participants
Coaching	• One-to-one or one-to-many • Primarily job/skill-related • Occurs within work context and environment	• Can view it in a corrective or developmental way • Provides an opportunity to develop managerial skills • Fosters effective working relationships • Effectiveness depends on skill of each • Time-consuming and demanding emotionally	• Opportunity to role-model effective behaviours • Builds effective relationships with manager • Can facilitate effective performance • Requires openness and motivation to learn • Depends on capacity to accept and act on feedback	• All areas of management supervisory and professional development	• Very high level of learner involvement	• It can be 1:1, although it is possible to have group coaching

Learning Method	Description	Trainer (Manager) Perspective	Learner Perspective	Application	Participant Involvement	Group Size
Counselling	• Focus is on personal development and enhancement of coping skills • Focus on self-directed or directed by counsellor • May occur in an informal and formal way	• Can be used by trainer (manager) to address performance issues • May be used to enhance self-esteem and task self-efficacy • Helps establish an open relationship with learner • Has application to a range of work/performance situations	• Facilitates learner to engage on self-reflection • Increases learner self-awareness • Enhances learner's self-efficacy and self-esteem • Promotes self-development processes	• Many aspects of career development and personal development	• Very high learner involvement	• 1:1 process
Job Attachments and Secondments	• Focus is on new job and/or organisational experiences • Of significant duration and intensity	• Can be used to test learner in a range of situations • Encourages organisation to plan proactively a manager's future development • Helps to develop an understanding of customer and suppliers • Can be used to address a plateaued career	• Provides learner with new and broadening experiences • Attachments can be stretching and challenging • Can act as a career development strategy	• Management executive and professional and graduate development	• High involvement	• Not applicable

Learning Method	Description	Trainer (Manager) Perspective	Learner Perspective	Application	Participant Involvement	Group Size
Mentoring	• One-to-one or one-to-many • Focus is on non-job issues • Usually career or psychological	• Can facilitate learner's career development • Facilitates mentee learning quickly about organisation • Helps prepare managers for succession	• Learn quickly about the organisation • A source of support in psychological to Lerner • Helps advance learner's career	• Many aspects of management and career development	• Moderate to high but not necessarily continuous	• Usually 1:1 relationship
Performance Discussions	• Annual review of performance and development • Development planning related to job and career	• Encourages learner (manager) to be concerned about subordinate's development • Performance discussion takes place in context of job • Developments linked to career and job	• Opportunity to plan future development in a systematic way • Links development to job dimensions • Encourages discussion about development issues	• Very appropriate for supervisory, manager and executive development	• High level of learner involvement	• 1:1 process

Programmed Learning, Computer-Based Training And Interactive Videos

These represent specialised forms of open learning. In **Programmed Learning**, students are tested when every point is made, either by a write-in or multiple-choice question. The aim is to ensure that the student normally answers the question correctly, but that the questions are not trivial. Programmed learning can be presented either in books or on machines. The problems are that programmes take a long time to write and that few authors can achieve the appropriate adult-to-adult tone.

Computer-based training is automated programmed learning. It has the advantage that it is relatively easy to write branches that fill in gaps or correct errors in the student's knowledge. The disadvantages are that a computer screen holds relatively few words and that writing requires a skilled trainer.

Interactive video is programmed learning combined with moving pictures. It is potentially a very powerful teaching medium. Effective programmes have been written on social skills, such as how bus drivers should deal with difficult passengers. However, at present there are several technical limits to the amount of material that can be presented on a disc.

Figure 6.14 presents the advantages and limitations of project and technology-based methods from your and your learner's perspectives.

BEST PRACTICE INDICATORS

Some of the best practice issues that you should consider related to the contents of this chapter are:

- The T&D annual plan, and plans at unit and operational levels are implemented through well-chosen learning experiences and processes across the organisation
- The T&D process ensures active involvement of stakeholders throughout the design, delivery and evaluation of planned learning experiences
- Such experiences include not only formal training and education programmes, but also a wide range of development methods and processes that can be tailored to the needs of individuals and teams
- Learning initiatives to enhance and improve performance continuously, respond in appropriate ways to identified T&D needs
- Best practice is regularly incorporated into the design and delivery of planned experiences. Major initiatives are benchmarked to ensure excellent and efficient use of resources

FIGURE 6.14: ADVANTAGES & DISADVANTAGES OF TECHNOLOGY-BASED METHODS

Learning Method	Description	Trainer Perspective	Learner Perspective	Applications	Participant Involvement	Group Size
CD ROM	• Compact Disk Read Only Memory	• Offers a means of delivery for CBT programmes; Each disk offers high capacity optical data storage, which becomes a reference source equal to many books • Special hardware needed • Limited to retrieval of stored data • CD writers are now much more readily available, allowing briefing providers to press their own CDs	• Allows the learner to learn at his/her own pace • Use of images can offer a variety of learning techniques in the learning process • Retrieval can be in text, picture and sound form making for an interactive and varied form of learning that seems to be self-motivating	• Knowledge based areas	• High	• Small

Learning Method	Description	Trainer Perspective	Learner Perspective	Applications	Participant Involvement	Group Size
Computer Based Training (CBT)	• Learner-managed coverage of programmed material, usually involving keyboard and screen • Learner uses keyboard in line with screen instructions, calling forth information and responding to questions • Moves to introduce Artificial Intelligence (AI) with the prospect of "talking with the machine" - using the machine as a tutor and managing one's own learning process - are not yet commercially available but may develop	• Many varied uses • Equipment may be expensive • Present levels of technology make logic-based programmes most reliable. • Care should be taken to ensure the material is appropriate (i.e. extensive evaluation before use). • Screen material can be complex and include animation. • Good for presenting technical data • Compatible hardware and software needed • Tutorial help should be provided	• CBT can offer workplace simulations, and can link with videotape to provide still or moving pictures • Can offer the learner an insight to applications in practice. • Addition of artificial intelligence allows "dialogue" with learner; learner responds to computer question, computer interprets response and adjusts its own programme – hence offering flexible learning process	• Skill and manual type training	• High	• Small

Learning Method	Description	Trainer Perspective	Learner Perspective	Applications	Participant Involvement	Group Size
Computer Conference / Newsgroups	• These provide specialist information on specific topics	• Exchange of ideas can be carried out using this medium • Connection to the Internet is required and the associated costs should be considered	• Newsgroups' contributors tend to act as tutors and answer questions posted to the newsgroup quickly • One question posted can be responded to by many other people, providing a great variety of styles that and user can apply to specific situations	• Knowledge areas primarily	• High	• Small
Web-Based Learning	• Learning *via* the Internet and the World Wide Web – ever-increasing as an available resource • Extensive research should be carried out into find appropriate web sites	• Both hardware and software can be expensive and connection fees should be considered along with associated running fees • Care should be taken so that end-users do not use the Internet as toy or download inappropriate information • Evaluation against learning objectives should also be carried out	• Allows users to learn at their own pace and in their own time • Exciting way to learn as the resources are extensive and tend to present information in a clear manner • However information provided on the Internet is not always attributable and sources should be verified before use • Most web sites allow users to email site provider and gain further information	• Mostly knowledge applications	• High	• Small groups

- Induction and basic skills training at all organisational levels are the shared responsibility of managers and mentors, with relevant support from specialist training and development staff
- High quality induction and basic skills training are well integrated. They are systematically and consistently applied across the organisation for all new entrants, and for those new to jobs and roles
- T&D coverage meets needs for continuous development and flexibility, and for change. It ensures timely responses to new business activities and processes, and to the emergence of critical issues in the workplace
- Career planning and development is an integral part of the organisation's T&D strategy to stimulate and enhance performance in the workplace
- Benchmarking can also help you identify learning methods and activities that may be valuable in your organisation. To do this, you should:
  - Identify clearly the activity or process where there is a need to improve performance in your organisation
  - Identify a similar process either elsewhere in your organisation, or in another organisation, where they achieve more satisfactory outcomes. Concentrate on finding a similar process or activity, not content. Think creatively – for instance, when the UK Prison Service wanted to improve how it dealt with queues of prisoners it benchmarked its process with the Post Office Counters
  - Analyse how people in your organisation learn to deal with the process, and how people in your selected benchmark organisation learn to deal with the same process
  - Consider how the learning process in the benchmark organisation could be transferred to your organisation.
- You should balance your learning methods in any one session to ensure that there is a good combination of active and passive methods.

Reflections on the Training & Development Scenario

Once you have established what you wish to achieve through learning, you need to select the most appropriate method. There is no formula for this – the most appropriate method will vary according to the particular circumstances of the organisation, the individuals, and the learning objective.

Factors you will need to consider are likely to include:

- How many people share the need? If there are only a few people to be trained, it may not be worthwhile investing in an elaborate learning method, or in producing a tailored in-house design

- Is it a one-off learning need, or is it likely to be on going? For instance, in the introduction of a new performance appraisal system, you may choose one method for the initial "sheep dip" to help all existing staff learn the new procedures, and then produce a different version to cater for the smaller groups of new staff who are new to the organisation or newly promoted into managerial roles

- How quickly do people need to learn? The organisation may need everyone to learn a new procedure very quickly. This is likely to restrict the choice of learning method

- Is the objective about learning something brand new to the organisation? This makes it unlikely that on-the-job coaching will be an option, unless you adopt a cascade approach. Would there be time for this?

- What is the organisation's learning culture and style? If people are used to formal classroom learning, they will react differently to, for example, a combination of computer-based training and learning sets. It may be appropriate to change learning methods, perhaps as part of a more general culture change, but you need to consider the impact of the learning method as well as the content.

- What are individuals' learning styles? Everyone has his or her own preferred method of learning. Can you offer a range of options so people can choose what best meets their needs? Is there a prevailing learning style?

- What resources are available? This includes not only cash, but also time for people to learn and any trainer or coach time that may be needed. It may also include facilities such as computer terminals, other equipment and rooms.

- What is the nature of the learning needs? Is it knowledge or skill-based? Learning a skill generally requires more practice than acquiring knowledge.

As well as formal training courses, the range of learning activities you can select from include:

- Structured on-the-job training and coaching
- Individually-directed learning, including reading and using open learning materials
- Computer-based learning
- Interactive video or CD-ROM
- Job shadowing
- Secondments
- Special projects
- Delegated work
- Standing-in for manager or supervisor.

For each of these activities, you will then need to consider whether it should be:

- Run internally or externally
- Tailored or off-the-shelf
- Run by specialist trainers or from among the line managers
- A single block of learning or a modular approach
- Involve a single learning method or combination of methods.

Chapter Seven

PREPARING VISUAL & WRITTEN MATERIALS FOR TRAINING

LEARNING OBJECTIVES

On completion of this chapter, you should be able to:

- List the main reasons for using visual aids in the delivery of training and development

- List some of the criteria and rules that you should follow when preparing visual aids

- Explain the advantages, disadvantages and appropriateness of different visual aids

- List the criteria that should be followed when preparing and writing training documentation and materials

- Explain the structure and format of different training documents, including training procedures, job aids and training handouts.

A Training & Development Scenario

John was a Training Manager for a large computer manufacturing plant employing over 3,000 people. The company was extremely busy and was constantly updating current products and introducing new products. It was engaged in on-going recruitment of general operatives and, because of the scarcity of staff, they were recruiting non-national workers who had some language difficulties. John was getting numerous complaints from the Quality section, implying that training was ineffective as employees were making too many mistakes, resulting in costly rework and damaged materials. In production meetings, complaints were mounting against the credibility and professionalism of the training department.

John decided to take steps to address the issues and instigated an investigation to get to the root of the problem. After a thorough analysis, he discovered that the training procedures were being written by the Engineering Section – as a result, the language used by the engineers was highly technical and jargon-ridden.

He consulted with the engineers, who were quite defensive and argued that the operatives should be able to understand the procedures. "The engineers in the parent company in the US wrote up these procedures and a lot of time and effort and travel went into producing these materials", they said. They suggested that John should try to prepare the operatives and teach them English. The operatives were quite defensive and refused to use the documentation, declaring it ineffective and incomprehensible.

There was a complete stand-off between the two sections and John was finding it difficult to work forward on the situation. He examined the procedures and discovered that the language used was too detailed and specialist.

This created a conundrum: if he criticised the operatives, he could patronise and alienate them but, if he gave negative feedback to the engineering department, it could seriously damage internal customer relations.

INTRODUCTION

In the two previous chapters, we discussed and explained a number of core components of the training design process. A frequently-ignored area of expertise concerns the use of visual aids in the training situation and the preparation and use of training documents to support the training, to reinforce learning and to ensure effective transfer of learning.

We first consider the use of visual aids in training situations, when you should use them and the types of visual support that are available. We then focus on the preparation of written training materials. We give you advice on how to structure your writing and how to write for training audiences and we provide specific guidelines on the preparation of four types of training documentation:

- Training procedures
- Job aids
- Training manuals
- Training handouts.

VISUAL AIDS IN TRAINING

You will most likely have to prepare some form of visual aid and learning materials to supplement and support your training activities.

Using Visual Aids in Training

Visual aids are used in training events because they facilitate effective communication. Visual aids are defined as "any training tool used to emphasise, clarify and support key learning points". There are many reasons why learners use visual aids, just as there are many types of visual aids.

Visual aids help learners process and retain data. In addition to enhancing comprehension and memory, visual aids can heighten the persuasive impact of ideas because they engage trainers actively in the learning exchange. The trainer's credibility and persuasiveness are enhanced by use of effective visual aids. With these functions in mind, it should be noted that visual aids should be simple, clear and professional. The purpose of a visual aid is to augment the training message, not replace it or distract from it.

Computer graphics make it easier to supplement the trainer's main ideas with visual materials. Each type of visual aid communicates information in a different way. In general, visual aids such as slides, photographs and posters can help an audience feel the way the trainer does. They can enhance the emotional dimension of a training session. On the other hand, descriptive or written materials can help an audience think the way the trainer does. Numbers and charts reinforce cognitive processes; photographs reinforce affective processes.

Although visual aids can be excellent supports if used properly, they can detract from the message and presentation, if used improperly. The following example outlines good and poor practice in respect of visual aid.

Example 1:

Agenda

- The external environment has become more complex and hostile. Several new markets have arisen over the last decade.
- We have seen six new entrants to our traditional market, all directly copying and competing with us.
- We have several options we must consider.
- I think we should concentrate on the emerging markets and reduce our investments in our traditional markets as we can potentially increase our revenues by over 50% given similar efforts.

Agenda

- Business Environment
- Likely Competition
- Several Options
- Justification
- Summary

Slide 1 has a number of disadvantages. The size of the font is too small. Even when this is enlarged to full size and projected, this slide will be difficult to read unless you are very close to it. There are too many words per line. Although there is no set formula to determine the optimal number of words on any given line or slide, bullet-points should be used as conceptual guides, not as notes from which to read.

Slide 2 in this example uses a larger type font and can easily be seen. The points made are short, consistent and easily taken in at a glance. An important point to remember about presenting a slide like this is that the trainer should read all five points through once before going back up to the first point to further elaborate. If he/she does not do this, what can happen is that as he/she reads the first point and then proceeds to discuss it, many people will be reading down the rest of the list and they will not be listening to what the trainer has to say. Learners like to know what is coming and find it easier to listen if we have a conceptual framework up-front. Therefore, the trainer should direct people's attention quickly down the list once, then bring them back up to the first point for discussion.

If developed in Microsoft PowerPoint, the text can be made to appear line by line. This is a good approach because it avoids information overload.

There is evidence to indicate that visual aids are very valuable in a training situation. In fact, visual aids:

- Shorten meeting time by up to 28%
- Shorten the time to understand concepts and increase comprehension by up to 73%

- Increase participant interaction and motivation by up to 80%
- Make your message 43% more persuasive.
- Achieve group consensus more frequently (70% *vs.* 58% of the time)
- Affect decisions made (favourable decisions are given more often to presenters who use audiovisual aids than those who do not)
- Make the presentation up to 50% more memorable
- Accelerate learning, retention and recall by 55% to 95%.

Figure 7.1 presents some of the questions you should ask yourself when preparing visual aids for a training session.

FIGURE 7.1: PREPARING VISUAL AIDS: SOME QUESTIONS

- Is it large enough to be seen by everyone without straining?
- Is all the printing short and neat?
- Is the visual aid colourful and involving? Studies show colour highlights can aid recall of information.
- Can I see the visual aid without blocking my audience's view of it? Will I be able to maintain good eye contact with my listeners while using the visual aid?
- Can I avoid reaching across my body or waving the visual aid in front of my face if I am using an overhead projector?
- Can I avoid distracting my listeners by keeping the visual aid covered or out of sight before and after I use it?
- Can I avoid making the visual aid the most important aspect of my session? Will it be more than just an ornament?
- Am I comfortable with using the visual aid? Have I practised with it so that using it is natural and it does not breakdown the flow of ideas in my speech?
- Have I made the necessary arrangement for special visual aids in advance?
- What will I do if the visual aid fails to work? Am I prepared for unexpected contingencies such as a burned-out projector bulb, a corrupted computer file or a room that cannot be darkened?
- Have I planned for assistance or volunteers in advance if they are needed?
- Will a pointer be needed?
- Will all the charts be secured so I don't have to hunt for them on the floor in the middle of my session?
- Am I using a variety of visual aids to increase my listeners' interest?
- If I'm using handouts, can I adjust to the distraction caused by passing them around?
- Can I compete with listeners who will read the handout rather than listen to me?
- Are my visual aids professional; neat, attractive and accurate?
- Can I speak over the noise of a projector or other machine?
- Can I translate complex numbers into pie charts or bar charts or line graphs for easier comprehension?

When considering the use of visual aids, you need to be aware of the following issues:

- **Apply psychology to the training session:** Learners are not perfect. All individuals have physical and psychological limits to their ability to pay attention, and to perceive visually and aurally. Physically, therefore, the trainer should make sure that his/her visual aids are large, bright, clear, etc. Psychologically, learners have attitudes, beliefs and expectations all of which affect their ability to attend, listen and recall. Finally, remember that although the trainer has very likely been working on the session for quite some time, it is the first time for the learners

- **Less is more:** Fewer and larger elements in a display mean more information grasped by the learner. If the trainer presents 20 pieces of information and only 10% is retained, he/she has successfully communicated only two pieces of information. If, on the other hand, he/she presents no more than five pieces of information, and 80% is retained, then they have doubled the information communicated to four pieces. Either way, the trainer is not going to be able to get all of the information across, so he/she should save something for next time

- **Learners want both information and stimulation:** The trainer should not fall into the trap of thinking that his/her job as a trainer is to show the learning group that they know more about the topic than they would ever care to know. What they should do is to get the learning group interested in knowing more about the topic and then give them a few bits that they can grasp, digest and use

- **Reduce working-memory load on the learner:** In visual aids, the trainer should not use acronyms or symbols that need to be defined. This requires learners to do double the work. Also, let spatial and contrast relations work. Remember that blank space on a slide is not necessarily wasted space.

When to Use Visual Aids in Training

There are five situations where visual support can make an effective contribution to any training situation:

- **Where the subject matter is complex:** In situations where the topic is complicated, or deals with abstract issues such as ideas or concepts, using well-constructed visuals can help clarify the incomprehensible

- **Where there is a need to show relationships:** It is much easier to show linkages using a visual format than to attempt to describe the same relationships verbally. Similarly, where there is a requirement to show how one process relates to another, the simplest method is to use a visual medium such as a flow-chart in preference to a lengthy description

- **Where statistical information is involved:** Learners may find figures and financial data difficult to grasp, and even those who have a head for statistics will find that there comes a point where their mind cannot process the data involved. Visual presentation offers a solution to these problems by allowing one set of sales figures, for example, to be displayed alongside those for the previous quarter. This reduces the strain on the memory and allows the group to concentrate on the learning points, which can be distilled from the data

- **Where reinforcement should be given:** If a point is worth making, it is worth remembering. Using visual support gives added impetus to the trainer's verbal message by highlighting the key points or issues that he/she wants the group to retain. This can be achieved by enhancing each point visually as it is made or by including an occasional summary in visual form

- **Where you wish to maintain interest:** One of the primary purposes for using visual support is to maintain the learner's interest in the topic. Using carefully selected visual aids will extend concentration spans and increase understanding. The visual medium must be selected carefully. If over-used, the visual aids will not only fail to assist concentration but they will become the principal cause of distraction.

You will also need to consider three other factors.

- **Cost:** The group size and the subject matter might have some influence on the financial resources available. If the programme of training is going to be run regularly for a high number of participants, and for a considerable period, it makes good economic sense to invest in visual aids that are durable and easy to use

- **Group Size:** The medium chosen must be the most suitable for the numbers attending. A flip-chart might be an effective method of communicating ideas to a group of eight but it is unlikely to be appreciated where 30 or 40 are involved

- **Facilities Available:** It makes good sense to use a visual medium that fits in with the equipment and facilities available. The use of computer graphics may be an excellent idea of itself but, unless the hardware exists to relay the data on the course, it will be money and effort thrown away.

You have a number of options in terms of visual support for the training situation and should choose between them carefully.

Flip-charts

Flip-charts are simply large pads of white paper stapled together and punched with holes for displaying on an easel.

Most flip charts are about 25" x 32" (635mm x 813mm) in size, although smaller versions are available for desktop easels. It is a good idea to incorporate a blank page between different pages of the chart in any event. This prevents the group attempting to discern the next part of the chart through the current page.

If you expect to carry out a number of calculations or to prepare bar charts or other graphics, it is also possible to obtain flip charts printed with feint squares invisible from a distance but ideal as a guide for the trainer.

When using flip charts, you should make sure that an adequate supply of suitable marker pens are available and that they work. Writing on flip charts is an important skill. You need to think of what you want to write in advance and then visualise it magnified four times larger. The larger the group, the larger the lettering needs to be.

When writing on the chart you should always stand to the side of the easel. You should stand to the left side, if you are right-handed, and to the right side, if you are left-handed. This keeps obstruction to a minimum. Obstruction can also be a problem when you speak and write at the same time. Although this appears to save time, it means that the group will be reading what is being written rather than listening to what is being said. This is even more likely to happen when the voice is muffled by speaking to the flip-chart not to the group.

There are a number of advantages of using a flipchart in a training session. It is possible to prepare many charts and drawings in advance: they can be taped to walls for reference during the training session. They are relatively inexpensive and very portable, they facilitate note taking and they allow the trainer to focus on key learning points.

Figure 7.2 provides a summary of guidelines that you should be aware of when using a flip-chart in a training situation.

Overhead Projectors

The overhead projector (or OHP) is one of the most versatile mediums for visual presentation. At its simplest, it is a metallic box containing a lamp that projects the image from a transparency placed on top, through a series of lenses and mirrors to a screen beyond. As the lens has a fixed focal length, the image projected is controlled by the lens-to-screen distance. Usually, it is necessary to experiment by moving the OHP backwards and forwards to establish the clearest image.

A major difficulty to overcome in using an OHP is the "keystone" or wedge shape, caused by the OHP not being at 90° to the screen.

The result is that the image is distorted by being wider at the top than it is at the bottom. This can be overcome by either tilting the screen forward from the top or by raising up the front of the OHP.

FIGURE 7.2: TIPS FOR USING FLIP-CHARTS IN TRAINING

- Use two charts, so as not to stay on one side of the room.
- Two charts has the advantage of allowing participants to take notes from one chart while ideas are being written on the second.
- Two charts allow participants to see the relationship between two ideas.
- Avoid writing too much on one page. Write large enough for people at the back of the room to see.
- Use vivid colours. Use colours that can be easily seen.
- Check pens before lecture. Use broad tip pens for better visibility.
- Make sure chart stands have sufficient paper.
- Check to see that sheets on the pad have not been written on already.
- Look frequently at the group while writing.
- Before the programme, outline any diagrams that will be required, lightly in pencil.
- Turn the page or tear it off when finished covering the points.
- Place a blank sheet of paper between prepared charts so that the sheets underneath do not show through.
- Write neatly, quickly and legibly.
- When recording participants' ideas, use their own words. Ask their permission to use alternative phrases.
- Record short phrases; ask participants for ways to summarise lengthy ideas.
- Ask participants to record ideas.

Transparencies/Slides

You should take considerable care over the preparation and presentation of OHP transparencies. Transparencies are only as good as their originals. It is imperative that the best possible originals are used to generate transparencies and that these originals are kept separate for use on later courses if needed.

Transparencies should be bold, simple and easy to read. Any lettering must be large, and graphics should be colourful. It is advisable to put transparencies into cardboard frames or mounts that prevent acetates from sticking together.

Three additional techniques can add a professional touch to the use of transparencies:

- **Masks:** These are constructed from card, taped to the frame and then open like miniature windows to show information in sequence

- **Reveal:** The "reveal" is a method of controlling the amount of information that a group sees by placing a piece of card or paper over the transparency and "revealing" data as it seems appropriate. It is ideally suited to lists or diagrams where too much information would provide a distraction. For the "reveal" to work effectively, try placing the card or paper under the transparency rather than over it, so that the weight of the transparency will hold the card in place
- **Overlays:** These are a series of transparencies that can be used one on top of the other to build-up a process or complex sequence gradually. They frequently use different colour and film to highlight or contrast the different areas of the process.

You should follow these guidelines when you decide to use transparencies in a training situation:

- Decide the number of transparencies: there is a tendency to use too many
- Get to know the equipment before the training starts
- Use colour to add emphasis
- Pre-focus the projector before participants arrive
- Place transparency on the projector before turning it on
- Turn off the projector before removing the transparency
- Avoid the "keystone" effect (when the projected image is not perfectly square on the screen)
- Do not talk to the visuals
- Do not get in the way of the image.

You can use transparencies very effectively in the training situation, since they are:

- Simple to use
- Transferable
- Easily prepared in advance
- Suitable for most sized groups
- Display diagrammatic data well.

It is also possible to create a transparency in front of a group of trainees, based on their input.

However, transparencies are not suitable for large amounts of text. In addition, the OHPs used to present them can be distracting and noisy, as well as being prone to machine failure and they require a minimum projection distance of three to four metres from the screen in order to avoid blurring, which limits the size of room in which they can be used.

Videotapes

The use of video as a means of providing visual support has increased dramatically over the last few years. There are two ways in which using video can assist the trainer:

- By providing a pre-recorded training film for the course
- As a means of showing a record of a trainee's actions on the course.

In its first form, the video acts as an alternative to films or slides. As training videos have become more popular, the range and quality of them has risen. As well as the major training video providers, a number of trade associations have produced their own training videos. Many large companies have also subsidised their own training by making videos and these can often be hired out by other interested parties at a nominal charge.

Video feedback

Video camera equipment is now within the capability and budget of most training departments. It provides you with lots of opportunities – for example, where previously a participant had simply been told by the trainer about any verbal or non-verbal behaviour, now video feedback offers proof of performance.

When using feedback in training, you should inform the trainees:

- Everyone will have the opportunity to be taped
- Doing it right is not necessary or even expected. They are there to experiment with ideas, to help each other, and to find ways to further increase effectiveness
- It is normal to be nervous when being filmed. Successful experience helps build confidence
- It is better to make mistakes here and to learn from them, than out on the job where the consequences can be serious.

Computer Graphics

Advance in computer software has influenced the way training materials can be prepared and displayed. Computer graphics make possible to create presentations that, only a few years ago, would have been regarded as too costly or complex.

If you plan to use computer graphics, you should consider the following issues:

- Trainees respond best to a trainer who uses technology as an aid, not as a crutch
- Simple relevant computer-generated graphics (pie, bar, column, line charts) aid retention

- Animation is most effective in simple forms – for example, bar charts that grow or text revealed line by line
- Graphic transitions (wipes, fades, etc.), combined with animation, work better for retention than transitions or animation alone.

White Boards

Whiteboards have gloss covering, which permits multi-coloured dry marking pens to be used and wiped away. Whiteboards:

- Accommodate expansive models and diagrams
- Are inexpensive compared to other visual aids
- Permit quick reinforcement of the spoken word
- Makes added emphasis more easily possible than coloured chalk/pens
- Get attention and allow the trainer to focus on key ideas
- Stimulate participation and progressive development of ideas
- Allow "on the spot" illustrations with a picture or a diagram
- Facilitate note-taking by trainees.

Disadvantages associated with the use of whiteboards include:

- Trainers must turn their backs on the group to write and so eye contact is lost with trainees
- Trainer may end up talking to board instead of the group
- Time is lost when erasing
- Once erased, the data is lost
- Visibility can be a problem
- May make participants feel like "school children"
- May expose trainer's inability to spell or vocabulary defects.

PREPARING WRITTEN MATERIALS

You may need to prepare different types of training material for use in a training situation. These can include preparing handouts, writing training instructions, preparing a summary of a training session or, at a more advanced level, you may have to write a training manual or set of training procedures.

There are five basic steps you should follow when preparing effective written training material. We have labelled these the Five Ss (see **Figure 7.3**). These five Ss are sequential, in the sense that each step builds upon the preceding step. The first three steps involve preparation, the fourth and fifth focus on the written material itself.

FIGURE 7.3: THE FIVE SS APPROACH TO PREPARING EFFECTIVE WRITTEN TRAINING MATERIAL

Formulate **STRATEGY** for specific learning groups	Develop a clear **STRUCTURE**	**SUPPORT** your points with evidence	Combine ideas with engaging **STYLE**	**SUPPLEMENT** with relevant information and answers to questions

Formulate a Specific Strategy

Identify the Purpose

Before collecting information or writing notes, you should clarify the general purpose for writing the training document. Is your purpose to motivate, inform, persuade, demonstrate or teach? Your purpose will affect the structure of your message and how it supplements your ideas, as well as the style of the training session. That is why it is important to identify your general purpose first.

The specific purpose should be easy to determine, once you have identified the general purpose, by asking "What do I want my trainees to learn?" or "What behaviours or attitudes do I want my trainees to adopt?". Each specific purpose determines how you tailor the remainder of the session to meet the needs of the audience and the demands of the situation.

Tailor the Message to the Specific Audience

The success of your written training materials is partially dependent upon your learners' understanding and receptivity. The key to developing an appropriate message is to understand their knowledge of the topic, their attitude toward the message and their expectations of the presentation. If they already know what you are tying to teach them, they will become bored and disengaged. You should start with what they already know, and then expand on it. Remember that learners retain more information, if the material is associated with something they already know, rephrased, repeated and reinforced with visual aids and limited to three to five new ideas. Motivated trainees retain more, so early in the message you should explain how they can use the information or why it is important for them.

It is also important to consider the attitudes of your learners to the training message. Less-motivated learners do not learn as readily as eager learners. If learners are less motivated, you should start the written material by establishing common ground or recognising similar values. For more uncommitted learners, it is important to develop a two-sided message by presenting both sides of an issue. In this way, you can assure them that you have researched the topic or situation effectively, that you have all of the relevant information and that you can appreciate both sides of the argument. You should use strong arguments with plenty of supporting material and choose more neutral or abstract language as ideas are developed.

FIGURE 7.4: ONE-SIDED *VERSUS* TWO-SIDED MESSAGES IN A TRAINING SITUATION

Use a one-sided message when:	Use a two-sided message when:
• The learner already favours the position	• The learner initially disagrees with the position
• The learner is not well-educated on the topic	• The learner is well-educated on the training message
• You require a public commitment from the learners	• You will experience counter-persuasion on the training message

Research suggests that the best way to present a two-sided message is to give the arguments that support your position first. You should organise those arguments, beginning with the weakest and ending with the strongest. Then present the opposing argument, beginning with the strongest and ending with the weakest. In this way, you take advantage of the learner's tendency to remember the most recent thing they read: the strong supporting argument and the opponent's weak argument.

Meet the demands of the situation. Some situations clearly demand more formal written materials. More formal language choices and more correct sentence structure are demanded by formal situations. You should determine the expectations of your learners and adapt the language to suit them. Most experts agree that the language should be one step more advanced than that of your training audience.

Develop a Clear Structure

Grab the Audience / Training Group

You should give the trainee a reason to read on. Give them a road map to follow. You should begin with an introductory statement or two. In general, an effective introduction does three things:

- It catches the learner's attention and sets a tone for the message
- It provides your learners with a reason for reading
- It gives your learners a road map or quick sketch of the message.

Work from the assumption that others do not understand, and have no reason to read to or understand what you mean

Thus, there is a need to spend a considerable time and effort in providing others with information that could increase their interest and their motivation to read on, while continually checking that the trainees are reading and understanding the written material. It is important to give readers an outline of plans so they can know what to expect.

Next, choose an appropriate organising pattern
Organisation is critical because it affects comprehension of the written message. Your learners will retain more when messages are organised. Organisation also affects the trainer's credibility as a writer. A writer who is organised is viewed more positively than one who is not. Organisation affects attitude change. Learners are more likely to be influenced by a viewpoint if it is organised. Finally, an organised message is more likely to be retained and thus to influence the learner's behaviour. **Figure 7.5** presents some common patterns of organisation in writing.

There are many patterns of organisation to choose from. In general, you should order thoughts using dimensions like time, direction, causal process, problem-solving sequence, complexity, space or familiarity. A related technique is to organise material as a series of answers to typical questions.

As you plan the message, consider the learners' orientation. The main question to ask is "What do my learners already know or think?" Start from that point, then move closer to the desired knowledge or point of view.

Written training documents vary in the amount of detailed information that can be conveyed in a single effort. Most learners prefer three main points, but many learners can remember up to five main points. Seven chunks of information are about the limit of a person's immediate short-term memory at any one time. Since learners must remember what you have written if they are to act on it, dividing a training session into no more than five major chunks should make ideas easier to remember.

FIGURE 7.5: COMMON PATTERNS OF ORGANISATION IN WRITING TRAINING MATERIAL

Pattern	Explanation
Chronological	Traces the order of events in a time sequence (such as past, present and future)
Spatial	Arranges major points in terms of physical distance or direction from each other
Causal	Develops ideas from causes (such as diagnosing a problem from its causes) to effect or results to cause (such as from its symptoms to the problem)
Topical	Enumerates aspects of the topic (such as size, colour, shape or texture)
Monroe's Motivated Sequence	Follows a five-step process: • Gaining attention • Showing a need • Presenting a solution • Visualising the results when the solution is implemented • Calling for action to implement the solution
Familiarity - acceptance order	Begins with what the learner knows or believes and moves on to new ideas
Inquiry order	Develops the topic in steps the same way you acquire the information or solve a problem
Question - Answer	Raises and answers a series of learner possible questions
Problem - Solution	First establishes that a problem exists then develops a plan to solve the problem
Elimination order	Surveys all the available solutions and systematically eliminates each possibility until only one remains

Adapted from Carlorio *et al.* (1997).

Use Transitions or Signposts to Signal Your Progress

It is important to give the learners a "road map" at the beginning of the written message. You should then continue to help trainees through it. To do this, you should signal when the attention is to move from one idea to another by summarising the first idea, then forecasting the new idea.

In written form, you can signal transitions by indenting, numbering or using bullets to highlight information. You can call the learner's attention to keywords with italicised or bold print.

Conclude on a High Note

Two important psychological concepts are at work when preparing written training communication – primacy and recency. Primacy relates to the first impression received and recency is the last. Learners tend to remember the first and last things they read or hear in messages. You establish an initial feeling in the introduction that colours the rest of the training document and the impression created during the conclusion influences the learner's overall evaluation of the written message. Since these are the most important segments of the session, they warrant the most preparation.

Summarise Ideas for a Final Time
Research shows that this kind of reinforcement helps trainees retain information. Normally, learners remember less than 20% of what they hear or read. If you do nothing to prevent it, within 24 hours, the loss will be 50% of what is heard; within 72 hours, the loss have risen to 85% to 90%.

If you preview the information in the introduction, reinforce it in internal summaries, and then summarise it in the conclusion. This will increase the odds that the audience will remember key ideas. Reviewing events and notes can increase retention by as much as 400%.

The last statement you make after the summary can take a variety of forms. You can call for action, reinforce a learners' commitment to action, or establish feelings of goodwill. For example, you might emphasise legitimacy by highlighting several authoritative quotes, by emphasising the "I am here to help" message, by predicting conditions in the future, by underscoring the utility of an idea through emphasis on its bottom-line impact, or by using an emotional appeal to have increased commitment and loyalty.

Figure 7.6 presents some examples of introductions and conclusions.

FIGURE 7.6: TYPES OF INTRODUCTIONS & CONCLUSIONS

There are many different kinds of introductions and conclusions you can choose when preparing written training materials. When you select an introduction or conclusion, you should question whether it orients the audience to the purpose and clearly signals the beginning or ending of the written training material.

- Refer to the subject or occasion
- Use a personal reference
- Ask a rhetorical question
- Make a startling statement
- Use a quotation
- Tell a humorous story
- Use an illustration
- Issue a challenge or appeal
- Use suspense
- Appeal to the reader's self-interest
- Employ a visual aid
- Refer to a recent incident
- Compliment the reader
- Request a specific action

Support Key Points

There are many reasons to use supporting materials or evidence as you develop training material. Research indicates that supporting material make a significant difference in the impact of ideas. This is true, even if you are not well-known to the learners or if they find your credibility moderate to low. The impact on trainees will probably be more permanent if you use supporting materials. Theorists are concerned with getting more information than other trainees do. It is important to cater for their needs by providing back-up notes.

What kind of support should you choose? Many kinds of supporting materials are available. Messages are strongest when they are built upon a variety of supporting materials. The following are some of the issues you should consider:

- If you have low to moderate credibility, written and theoretical evidence will probably increase persuasive effectiveness
- There seems to be minimal difference between emotional and logical evidence
- Using evidence is usually better than not using it
- There seems to be little difference between biased sources and objective sources in their final impact on a learner
- Good writing may improve the potency of evidence, usually when sources of the evidence are unknown or have low credibility
- Evidence can reinforce the long-term effectiveness of persuasion
- Evidence is most effective when learners are not familiar with it
- People are more likely to believe evidence that agrees with their own position
- Highly dogmatic people are more affected by evidence than are less dogmatic people
- Evidence produces more attitude change when the course and source qualifications are provided
- Trainers with low credibility are perceived as more credible when they cite evidence in written learning materials
- Using irrelevant evidence or poorly qualified sources may produce the opposite effect to what the trainer intends.

Using an Appropriate Style

In all kinds of training documents, a fundamental aim is to convey information clearly and persuasively to the receiver. In writing, this is made a little more difficult by the fact that the reader is usually elsewhere when the message is being composed. Thus, it is essential that all training documentation is appropriate in tone and easy to understand and that the message be clear, concise and persuasive.

Most readers of training documentation do not have time to peruse long-winded documents. Therefore, the first aim should be to write uncomplicated sentences and use a direct, no-nonsense style. Although, there is no such thing as a "correct" sentence length, long, heavily-qualified sentences make the writing difficult and time-consuming to read. However, a series of very short sentences with the same structure and stress pattern can be very monotonous. The ideal style is one in which there is some variation in sentence length, but where sentences are generally short. An average sentence length of 15 to 20 words is a good rule of thumb to follow.

Here are some ways of giving impact and vigour to sentence structure:

- **RULE 1: Use the Active Voice:** All well-written documents use a mixture of active and passive constructions, but with a preference for the active voice. In the active voice, the agent of the action is the subject of the sentence. In the passive voice, the person or thing to whom the action is being done is the subject of the sentence. The agent is either named later in the sentence or not named at all. There are two reasons for preferring the active voice. First, active constructions are more dynamic and usually contain fewer words. Second, they always name the agent of the action, so the reader is not left wondering who was responsible

- **RULE 2: Use Personal Pronouns (when appropriate):** Quite often, when writing formal training documents, it is advisable for the writer to maintain a distance between him/herself and the reader, or to be cautious in putting forward proposals or recommendations. In such cases, it may be best to use impersonal constructions. Although an impersonal style can be off-putting, it is generally acceptable in training documents

- **RULE 3: Do Not Use Jargon, Write Plainly:** Writers use jargon or long, inflated words because they think it makes them appear more impressive or dignified. However, readers may simply fail to understand the message. *The Concise Oxford Dictionary* defines jargon as "words or expressions used by a particular group or profession" but also as "barbarous or debased language" and "gibberish". Jargon can be acceptable when used in the right context, but it becomes confusing or meaningless when used incorrectly. Quite often, it is necessary to use some jargon, particularly when writing technical documents. Each profession has its own special terms and it makes sense to use these when writing for fellow professionals. However, professional phrases will probably be completely unintelligible to a layperson. This is why the writer should try to reduce jargon as much as possible in training material aimed at non-specialists. It can also help the reader if a glossary of unfamiliar technical terms is provided

- **RULE 4: Avoid Long, Pompous Words:** English is very rich in synonyms, that is, words that have nearly the same meaning. In place of the word home, for example, you could use *abode, domicile, residence* or *habitation.* However, *home* is the simple, ordinary word, normally used in conversation. The others have their place, but sound too formal or pompous in most training documentation. As a general rule, therefore, using "big" words – it is better to use simple, plain words instead

- **RULE 5: Use Verbs Instead of Abstract Nouns:** Another way of invigorating a piece of writing is by removing abstract noun phrases and putting equivalent verbs in their place. An abstract noun may be recognised by endings such as *-ment, -tion, -ance, -ence*, etc. Overusing these phrases can make a document seem slow and lifeless. In contrast, the verbs from which they come denote action.

All the rules so far help towards achieving a clear, direct and plain style. Conciseness is increasingly valued as a quality of effective training documentation. It not only aids clarity but also saves on stationery, storage space and typists' time. The following rules will help you to reduce words still further without in any way reducing the impact of your training message:

- **RULE 6: Avoid Wordy Phrases:** There are many long-winded phrases in English, which perform the function of prepositions or adverbs. Replace these with one or two simple words

- **RULE 7: Avoid Redundancies:** In both speech and writing, we often use words that repeat an idea. Sometimes these words are justified because they add an important emphasis or qualification. Usually, however, they add nothing to meaning, in which case they are said to be redundant. In another type of phrase, the same word (usually a pronoun or conjunction) is repeated unnecessarily. A third type occurs when adjectives and adverbs are used without justification.

- **RULE 8: Use Words in their Correct Sense:** One form of loose writing is to confuse words that are the same or similar in sound but different in meaning (accept - except; continual - continuous; council - counsel; elicit - illicit; stationary - stationery). Often it is the simplest words that cause most problems. Take care with: have - of; lead - led; of - off; raise - rise; its - it's; loose - lose; quiet - quite; their – there - they're. Equally troublesome are words that are close in sound and meaning but different in tone. Care must also be taken with words that have a more restricted application in writing than in speech. These include less (often confused with fewer in colloquial speech), between (confused with among), amount (confused with number) and aggravate (confused with annoy)

- **RULE 9: Avoid Colloquial Expressions:** Another form of loose writing is the use of colloquial idioms and expressions, words and phrases that belong to informal conversation but are not accepted in formal business and technical writing. Contradictions should also be avoided, as they, too, are considered to be part of colloquial speech. So it is better to write cannot, do not and will not, for example, instead of can't, don't and won't.

- **RULE 10: Use a Friendly, Understated Tone:** It is the tone of the piece of writing (cheerful, patronising, serious, etc) that conveys the writer's attitude to both subject matter and reader. Choosing words to convey this tone is often a matter of following well-established conventions. Sometimes it may not be easy to maintain this understated tone. Nevertheless, the safest course is to remain polite and to let the facts speak for themselves.

Supplement by Preparing Different Types of Training Documents

We have covered some of the general guidelines involved in writing learning objectives and lesson plans. However, in order to supplement your learning, you may need to prepare a number of documents. In this section, we focus on other training documents that you may have to produce, such as training procedures, job aids and training manuals.

Training Procedures

Training procedures are frequently used during on-the-job and technical training situations and are often required by external regulatory agencies. When preparing training procedures, you should observe the following guidelines:

Objective
To provide a guide to writing procedures by covering format, design, style and control.

Format
- **Consistency:** Unlike job aids, procedures should not be produced in different sizes and formats. Their primary purposes are for training and reference. Rather than acting as on-the-job reminders, a consistent procedure format allows users to track down information easily

- **Left-Hand Facing Margins:** Procedures should normally be held in binders so that they can be opened flat with both left- and right-hand facing pages visible. Print the procedures only on the right-hand pages, and use the left-hand ones for producing any relevant charts, diagrams, forms, etc. that are referred to on that page of the procedure. Photo-reducing these will enable you to add pointers and comments
- **Columns:** The columns on the left should be used for section and subsection numbering, and those on the right for cross-referencing and highlighting revisions
- **Reference Numbering:** Some sort of standard company-wide reference numbering system is necessary for most companies, but it should be kept as simple as possible and existing codes, which people already know, should be used.

Design
- **Objective Section:** This should tell the learner what the training procedure covers, and what any user of the procedure should be able to do
- **Design Steps:** For each operation in the procedure, ask:
  - What is being done now? What else might be done instead?
  - Who does it? Who else might do it instead?
  - Where is it done? Where might it be done instead?
  - When is it done? When might it be done?
  - How is it done? How else could it be done?
  - For each operation, identify the information, equipment and materials necessary for the operation to be performed
  - For each operation, identify and, where appropriate, design the output format
  - Identify clearly, by job title, who performs and who may authorise each operation
  - Sequence the operations, highlighting any parallel or alternative operations. Flow-charts are easy to follow and understand
  - Consider the treatment of exceptions. You may want to put these in an appendix rather than in the main procedure
  - Consider whether to repeat information that is held elsewhere, or just cross-reference it. Remember that all procedures should be able to stand alone and enable the user to perform the operation

Key Design Criteria
Identify clearly any important factors and their impact on the operations. These might include: Legal requirements; Safety

precautions; Security; Confidentiality; Quality control; Management information requirements; and Job flexibility requirements.

Style
Sections and Paragraphs:
- As far as possible, each section or subsection should be given a separate, unique heading. Consistent text enhancements (capitals, underlining, bold print) should be used to identify them
- A numeric section numbering system should be used
- Each process or action should be a separate line or paragraph.

Choice of Words:
- Use the imperative or present tense, second person (you)
- Terminology should be kept consistent – for example, do not refer to both "billing" and "invoicing" of the same process. Frequent repetition of the same term is stylistically acceptable
- References to forms, procedures, and reports should be made using their title and any reference number
- Language appropriate to the user should be used – technical jargon is appropriate only if the user will understand it.

Control:
- **Review and Approval:** All procedures should be reviewed by the user and approved by the immediate supervisor. Procedures that span several areas of operation should be approved at the appropriate level of authority
- **Updating:** The users should notify the procedure writer of any on-going revisions that are needed
- The procedure writer should immediately revise the procedure to incorporate any major changes – for example, new equipment, new format of input or output, new or significant changes in activities
- The procedure writer should review the procedure regularly in order to include any less urgent changes –f or example, new job titles, minor changes in activities
- Revised papers should be re-issued to all procedure-holders with a covering note indicating the changes; for extensive amendments, reissue the whole procedure.

Central Monitoring
If the master copies of all procedures are held centrally, they can be monitored to:
- Identify any duplication of activities

- Highlight areas where procedures do not exist
- Ensure proper approval and authorisation
- Ensure that they are kept up-to-date
- Check consistency of writing.

Job Aids

You may also need to prepare written job aids for employees to reinforce training in a task or procedure.

Job aids are more detailed than job descriptions or even procedures, but normally only cover a single task. Their function is to remind the learner of what needs to be done. Therefore, they must be written with the learner constantly in mind, and must take account of his/her previous knowledge, or lack of it. They are particularly useful for critical or infrequent tasks, and are often written as checklists, flow-charts, decision trees or step-by-step instructions. Whatever format is chosen, the following structure is useful to ensure no major points are missed:

- **Preparation:** What needs to be known or done before the task can be performed? What information, materials or equipment need to be available? Diagrams may sometimes be helpful
- **Start-Up:** Any preliminaries to the task, including commissioning of equipment into operation
- **Task:** All steps, in order of performance. Only essential details should be included, but enough to enable the task to be completed
- **Close Down:** Finishing procedures, including any decommissioning of equipment, recording of results or reporting to other people.

Language must be clearly understood. Over-elegant sentences should be avoided, phrases that cover a single point will be followed more easily. If your learner's reading ability is limited, step-by-step diagrams should be used to give instructions.

In order to ensure that the job aid is as foolproof as possible, it should be tested out on typical employees beforehand.

Since job aids exist to help the learner actually perform the job, they should not be filed away in a manual. They are more beneficial pinned on the wall above the piece of equipment to be operated or stuck at the front of a record or log book.

Presentation is very important. Job aids that illustrate the use of equipment should be bright, easy-to-read posters, laminated for cleanliness and durable. Even job aids for clerical procedures should be covered in transparent protective material, if they are to be used frequently. Size is also important, as A5 or card size reminders, which fit an employee's personal filing system, are more likely to be carried and referred to regularly.

Training Manuals

Training manuals usually consist of collections of related procedures. It is helpful to include reference aids such as contents pages and indexes, which are easy to include and keep up-to-date.

If the procedures are well-established and unlikely to change frequently, it is useful to have sequential page numbers through all the documents; otherwise the page reference has to include the procedure number too.

FIGURE 7.7: CONTENTS PAGE OF A TRAINING DEPARTMENT MANUAL

Ref. No.	Procedure
A-326-010	Introduction
A-326-011	Identifying training needs
A-326-012	Preparing the training agenda
A-326-013	Recording and conforming course nominations

In this example, the second page of *Preparing the training agenda* might be page 8. However, if each procedure was numbered separately, it would be page A-326-102/2.

Indexes are more complicated. They can be done manually, by scanning each page and picking out the main point, but this is tedious and time-consuming. Fortunately, they can also be created using word-processors to find key words. Updating indexes is also a major job. You not only have to make references to the changed elements of the procedures, but the revised text may also have caused page-numbering changes. Since it is often necessary to re-create the index completely each time there are changes, it is sensible to restrict indexes, if possible, to well-established procedures.

Training Handouts

You will frequently have to prepare training handouts to:

- **Reinforce the message:** The trainer can provide an outline of the presentation for trainees to note down points or questions, and use for discussion or future reference. For example, when the trainer makes a PowerPoint slide presentation, he/she can distribute the note pages so that trainees not only have a record of the slides but also can make notes beside each slide. Thus, participants avoid having to spend a lot of time copying down notes and asking the trainer to stop before moving onto the next slide

- **Explain and organise a group activity:** Employees can follow the instructions and steps given in the handout
- **Access learning:** The trainer can provide a question sheet, for example, after a video, to test how much employees have learnt and how they might apply the new information. The first questions might test their memory and understanding of the material, but the last one might ask them how they might use this information on the job. This last question can pull everything together and generate a practical discussion.

When preparing handouts, you should follow these guidelines:

- Use short sentences to give clear simple instructions or ask questions
- Consider using a mix of "closed" questions and more general "open" questions. Closed questions require people to retrieve detailed information - for example, from a manual or video. Open questions require them to express their own ideas and opinions, and encourage people to think about and discuss the material
- Provide one or two questions that force people to select relevant information and apply it to their job situations
- Limit handouts to a page – it makes them easier to read and use
- Test out instructions or questions by having someone else read them for possible confusion or ambiguity. Which instructions or questions are not clear? Which questions need more space for answering? Do employees need more explanation or guidance on a particular task?

We conclude this section with some tips in **Figure 7.8** that you can follow when writing training materials.

FIGURE 7.8: TIPS FOR WRITING EFFECTIVE TRAINING MATERIALS

1. Develop a **strategy** for your target group. Try to develop the purpose of the training material and fit in the language and approach to suit the needs of your learners.	• What do I want my readers to absorb? • Understand your specific audience • Start with what they already know and then expand on it
2. Have a **structure** Start, grab their attention Middle, organise your material End, summarise ideas	• You need to grab the attention of your trainees. Explain the WIIFM process. What is in it for me? • Give them a road map or a sketch of the message • Outline your plans to the reader to keep them on track • Make sure the material is properly organised, it is more likely to be retained
3. Support ideas with examples, pictures and anything else that will help get your message across	• Factual evidence can back up the credibility of the written material
4. Create a consistent **style** throughout your materials, using the same type, graphics etc, to create uniformity. Attractive: balanced; uncluttered; Make it look interesting; Avoid graphics that make the document untidy	• Develop precision – avoid sloppiness • Make sure that grammar is correct • Have the facts right • Write as if you are the reader • Avoid ambiguity – write for the alien!
5. You should **supplement** your training materials with appropriate documentation.	• Avoid too many documents • Ensure that the policy or procedure is professionally produced • Ensure that you reference the supporting documentation appropriately

Plan

The actual task of writing is very time consuming and needs complete concentration. You need to plan well and develop an effective structure in advance. This will keep you on track when your attention wanders. If you do loose concentration, take a walk; it does wonders for the brain.

Use Plain, Direct Style

A plain style helps the trainer write quickly and avoids the problem of using flowery language to impress. Group sentences into well constructed paragraphs. Each paragraph should deal with one topic only and there should be a clear progression from one paragraph to the next. A paragraph should be regarded as a link between one idea and the next.

Precision

The first draft of any writing needs revision. You are bound to make mistakes and omissions. It is a good idea to distance yourself from the document and cool off for a bit. A time gap allows you to be more self critical of the material written. Try to get someone else to critique your work. This provides an independent viewpoint. Listen to advice as they could recommend very useful changes and even give you more ideas.

Make sure your sentences have only 15 to 20 words

Use the active voice – more dynamic and contains fewer words

Maintain a distance between yourself and the reader

Avoid jargon

Avoid long pompous words and wordy phrases

Use verbs instead of abstract nouns, e.g. Preparation = Prepare; Assessment = Assess

Verbal Perfection

Make sure the words chosen accurately express the ideas

Ask yourself if the word conveys the right meaning without creating confusion

Use of Space

Avoid cluttering up your training instruction

Frame each page with good size margins, at least two centimetres left and right and three centimetres top and bottom

Avoid long and unbroken stretches of text

Leave spaces of readings

Sub-sections in the text can be inset or indented to make them stand out

Paragraphs

Good paragraphs can make it easier for the reader to follow

Each paragraph should cover a single main issue and should be 6 to 8 lines long

Use signposts to make the first sentence of each paragraph lead into the main point of the next paragraph

Fonts

Chose plain, legible fonts

Avoid different fonts in the same text

Use **bold**, *italic* and <u>underline</u> for emphasis, but use them sparingly

Numbering

Number all pages clearly and consistently

BEST PRACTICE INDICATORS

Some of the best practice issues that you should consider related to the contents of this chapter are:

- Visual aids and written training documentation can enhance your professionalism as a trainer and the professionalism of the training function

- Do realise that visual aids are not, of themselves, the message, merely an effective means of reinforcing your training message

- Do not over-use visual aids on a training programme. They inhibit trainee participation and create information over-load

- You need to achieve an appropriate balance in the visual aids you use. Do not over-use one particular aid

- Make your visual aids interesting. Make use of colour. It attracts and retains the attention of learners

- Use written materials such as a training handout to reinforce your learning. Make sure that the document is an appropriate length and complexity, given the abilities and current knowledge of your learners

- Distribute training documentation before the training, if you require some advance preparation on the part of learners. Be concerned with the structure of your documentation and where possible write the material in the active voice.

Reflections on the Training & Development Scenario

He created a facilitated focus group session consisting of members of the Engineering Dept and the Operators group to try to iron out the difficulties.

The group worked very well and it was decided to set up a training programme to learn a co-ordinated approach to designing training procedures. A cross-functional team process was inculcated into the programme and worked very effectively. The engineers streamlined their writing to take into account the experience of the operatives and the operatives helped the process considerably.

The Quality section was also involved in the process to help ensure that the relevant information was being processed. A pilot scheme was set up and further training programmes were implemented on how to write clearly, avoid jargon and present in an easily assimilated fashion.

Chapter Eight

UNDERSTANDING THE PSYCHOLOGY OF TRAINING DELIVERY

LEARNING OBJECTIVES

On completion of this chapter, you should be able to understand:

- The psychological dimensions of the training design and delivery process

- Some of the interpersonal needs that learners have in a training situation

- The components of the interpersonal communication process

- The dynamics of the communication process and the psychological and perceptual barriers that you may encounter in a training situation

- Some of the psychological and behavioural features of your learners that you need to consider in a training programme situation

- The core concepts of transactional analysis and its implications for your communication approach in a training situation

- The dimensions of non-verbal behaviour and its relevance to training

- The role of the physical environment and its influence on trainer communications and interaction with learners

- The different styles that you may exhibit as a trainer and their influence on learner behaviour

- The concepts of group dynamics and their relevance to understanding behaviour in group training situations

- Some of the psychological dimensions of preparing learners for a training event.

A Training & Development Scenario

As the trainer responsible for the two-day Induction Programme in a Financial Services Company, you deliver the introductory module on the first day and two other modules during the programme.

It is always critical to set up the group for success at the first session. On this particular Monday, you are faced with 12 new employees. It seems that three of your inductees are going to be challenging over the next two days:

• Claire, a mature employee, has already voiced her opinion that she is very familiar with the financial services industry and that she does not see what she will gain from attending this programme

• John, a school leaver, has not spoken at all and seems to be intimidated by the whole group

• Jackie, a new employee in the Marketing Team, has been talking non-stop and dominating the morning's discussion.

Your task: How will you manage these three challenging trainees during the course of the programme?

INTRODUCTION

We have already considered some of the psychological dimensions of the learning process. In **Chapter Three**, we discussed the principles of learning, characteristics of the adult learner and the role of motivation and retention in the learning process. When you perform an instructor or facilitator role in the delivery of training, the emphasis is on communicating understanding. In this chapter, our focus is on explaining some of the more important dimensions of the oral communication process, including the roles that sound, accent, pitch, projection and pace will have on your effectiveness as a trainer. We consider some of the vocal problems and barriers that you may encounter.

Psychology provides a number of important concepts that you can use to understand how communication works in a training situation. We consider the importance of understanding the role of interpersonal style, locus of control, tolerance of ambiguity, the needs of learners in a group-training situation, your style as a trainer, the role of transactional analysis in explaining your interaction with trainees.

Psychology can help you to understand how the physical characteristics of the learning environment will impact on your effectiveness as a trainer and the extent of interaction between you and the learners. You may also, from time to time, encounter difficult trainees who seek to challenge your position or are unwilling to participate in a learning event. We explain the psychological characteristics of each type and outline strategies to deal with them.

The psychology of groups is useful in explaining how consensus and conflict emerges in a learning group as well as informing us about group cohesiveness and the types of roles that learners may perform in a group-learning event. We will outline some strategies that you can use to deal with these issues.

UNDERSTANDING THE COMMUNICATION PROCESS

Your focus (*raison d'être*) as a trainer should be to communicate accurately, achieve understanding and demonstrate empathy with your learners. This will ensure the development of a positive interpersonal relationship between you and your learners. Your ability to communicate effectively is a core competency, as training delivery is an intense interpersonal situation.

In a training situation, your learners need to understand your message and its meaning. There are a number of ways in which the meaning of the message and the process of understanding can be lost:

- **Coding the Message:** This is the "language" that you use to convey the message, it can be verbal or non-verbal (visual aids)

- **The Medium of the Message:** In training, the primary medium used to transmit the message is your spoken word. Audiovisual methods can also be used. It is important to choose the most appropriate medium to deliver your training message

- **Distortion:** This refers to the way in which the meaning of the message is lost – for example, your language is inappropriate to your learning group or contains jargon that your learners may be unable to decode or to decode correctly. Learners may also decode incorrectly because of prejudice, preconceived ideas or because your body language or use of voice is incongruent with what is being said. Many learners only hear what they expect to or want to hear

- **Noise:** The distractions of interference in the environment in which training communication takes place – for example, physical noise like passing traffic, or psychological noise like tiredness or frustration, or perhaps cultural noise, if trainees are drawn from a number of countries.

These barriers can result in the key points you wish to make not being correctly absorbed and understood by your learners. The potential existence of these barriers demonstrates the need to ensure that you receive feedback from your learners. Feedback is important to you because it enables you to test your learners' understanding, so that you can react to the feedback you receive. As a skilled trainer you should be concerned with feedback at two levels:

- **Rapport:** Your participants will provide feedback with their body language, general interest level and level of interaction with you during the training session. You will need to develop an understanding of body language to interpret how engaged your learners are in the learning process

- **Questioning:** You will introduce activities that will "test" your learner's understanding of the subject matter. This may take the form of questions, formally during the session, informally at the end of the programme or at break times, or in an exercise that uses the ideas covered during the session. Effective questioning is useful in creating a connection between you and your learners.

Psychological Dimensions of Interpersonal Communication

If you adopt an appropriate interpersonal communication style, you will enhance the level of learning that takes place during a training session. Effective interpersonal communication is likely to engender feelings of support, understanding and co-operation from your learners.

The research on interpersonal communication highlights two important problems that you are likely to encounter if you use poor interpersonal skills in a training situation:

- **Defensiveness:** Learners may feel threatened or detached as a result of your communication message. They will focus on self-protection and will channel energies into constructing a defence rather than focusing on listening and learning. In a more intensive form, your learners are likely to exhibit anger, aggression, competitiveness and, in some cases, avoidance

- **Disconfirmation:** You should avoid a situation where your learners feel incompetent, unworthy or insignificant as a result of your interpersonal communication style. If this is the case, adult learners in particular will spend time trying to re-establish their self-worth, and trying to portray self-importance rather than focusing on listening and learning. In an extreme form, it may result in showing off and self-centred type behaviour. It may also result in the psychological withdrawal of the learner and a loss of motivation. The "jug and mug" style is often associated in a negative way with the school environment.

The psychology of communications literature provides principles for use when communicating in a direct training situation – see **Figure 8.1**.

FIGURE 8.1: PRINCIPLES OF EFFECTIVE INTERPERSONAL COMMUNICATION

Principle	Elements of Principle
Effective interpersonal communication will focus on the problem and not on the learner	• Focus on problems and solutions • Separate the learner from the behaviour • Learners react to problem-centred communication in a positive way • Avoid expressing personal opinions or feelings about the behaviour and attitudes of learners
Effective interpersonal communication is based on congruence or exactly matching your verbal and non-verbal communications to what your learners are thinking and feeling	• Honest statements are better than artificial or dishonest statements • You should engender trust with your learners • Learners will usually react positively to honest communication • The more honest you are, the more likely your learners will adjust psychologically
Your interpersonal communication in a training situation should strive to be descriptive	• Describe events and behaviour as objectively as possible • Be prepared to discuss your reactions to the behaviour of learners • Describe the objective consequences that are likely to result from particular behaviour • Be prepared to discuss alternative or additional behaviours • Focus on alternative solutions, not on who is right or wrong
You should strive in your training communications to validate, rather than invalidate, learners	• Your communication should arouse positive feelings • Do not adopt a superior position; it tends to project you as superior and others inferior • Do express agreement with a good contribution from a learner • Be willing to tolerate, even welcome, criticism and other views • Avoid using over-generalised statements • Do not show indifference in your communications with others
Your training communication should be specific and useful	• Specific statements are generally considered more valuable • Do not make extreme or outlandish statements
Effective training communications is conjunctive, in that it flows smoothly and is joined to previous messages	• Ensure that there is an equal opportunity for each learner to contribute • Do not interpret for your learners • Avoid extended pauses in your communication • Do not seek to control the contributions of your learners • Ask questions that are based directly on a learners' previous statement
You should take ownership of the statements you make in a training situation	• Take responsibility for the statements you make • Acknowledge the source of ideas if they are not yours • Convey the message that you are involved and not aloof • Show a willingness to invest yourself in the training relationship
Effective training communications require listening	• Listen and respond effectively to the statements of your learners • Make eye contact with your learners and show interest/attention • Exhibit appropriate body language such as head nods • Avoid actions that suggest you are bored • Ask lots of questions and paraphrase • Do not over-talk; make smooth transitions between your role as speaker and customer • Use mirroring, pacing and leading techniques

Adapted from Carlopio *et al.* (1997).

PSYCHOLOGICAL ASPECTS OF YOUR VOICE

Your voice is the medium for carrying the message to your learners. If you use it correctly, it can be a powerful instrument. However, in order to make it a powerful instrument, it is important that you practice. We know from research that there are seven dimensions of your voice that are important in training:

- **Sound:** What we hear when we talk is very different from the sound received by others. This is because the jawbone acts as a diaphragm and the sound vibrates through the air passages connecting the mouth and ears. In such circumstances, it would be little wonder if the voice was not distorted. Learning is compromised when the learner has to strive to hear what the trainer is saying. You need to ensure that your voice is easy to hear

- **Accent:** No sooner has the initial shock of hearing yourself worn off than it is replaced by anxiety over diction and accent. Unless your accent is so marked that what is said is completely unintelligible, then accept it as part of your personality. In fact, take it one stage further and turn it into a positive characteristic

- **Projection:** You can use your voice to grab the learners' attention. This does not mean that you should shout or bellow. Being aggressive is not the same thing as being powerful. (It is possible to attract interest by speaking in little more than a whisper. If your voice is barely audible the group needs to listen carefully to hear what you have to say). Assessing the correct volume level is not always easy. You are closer to the sound source than anyone else in the room and this may give a misleading perception of volume. The key issue is to make full use of an innate ability to adjust volume to suit the circumstances. For example, when you are talking to someone standing directly opposite him or her, your mind will automatically gauge the level of volume necessary to carry his or her voice comfortably. You can compensate for distance by looking at the last row of trainees rather than those immediately at the front. The result will be that your voice will be projected to reflect this, and the sound will be carried, and be audible to the whole room

- **Pace:** Your mind has the ability to process information far quicker than the mouth is capable of delivering it. The average person speaks about 50 words per minute. The net effect of this is that, unless the information being communicated is very complicated, it is easy for the mind to use its excess capacity to think about other matters. If this mental jaunt is to be prevented, then it is essential that the pace of your delivery is correct. If the pace is too slow or measured, it creates the impression that the trainer is plotting the context as he/she speaks, which is unlikely to inspire confidence. On the other hand, if the delivery is too fast, transmitting too much information, for too long, so the mind gives up attempting to process the barrage of data and just switches off. Getting the balance right means thinking about the information being communicated. New or complex ideas should be delivered at a slow, steady pace with opportunities for participants to register the information and check their understanding. Where the information being communicated is background information, facts learners should already know, or scene-setting details, then they can be provided at a faster pace. A number of factors influence the pace of your communication:

○ *Number of Trainees:* The more trainees there are the longer it will take to communicate and have trainees register their response to your message – hence, the dictum "more space, less pace". As participant numbers increase, the trainer should slow down delivery to check the response that the message is producing

○ *Nerves:* Tension increases the pressure to get the experience over as quickly as possible. The greater the tension, the greater the acceleration

○ *Interest:* The degree of interest the trainer has in the topic will slow down or speed up the communication accordingly. The more enthusiastic the trainer is, the faster the delivery

○ *Time:* Where time is not at a premium, the trainer can afford to meander through the material. In most cases, though, you will be racing against the clock and through the material

• **Pitch:** A common criticism made against trainers is that they are "monotonous" or one-toned. In reality, it is impossible for anyone to communicate using a single tone and even the simplest conversation would use between 10 and 20 different notes. However, when training or speaking in formal situations, trainers tend to use a more limited scale of five to eight notes. Perhaps, by constant rehearsal and repetition of the training material, you have lost the highs and lows that would occur quite naturally when the words were spontaneous. In some cases, it is a deliberate style – you feel that to add too much inflection would make a serious topic too dramatic. Whatever the reason, varying the pitch of what is said helps you to retain learners' interest In some cases, pitch changes are not intentional but occur because of stress. Tension in the body manifests itself through tension of the vocal cords. These shortened, and "highly strung", vocal cords then cause the all-too-frequent strangulated voice or an embarrassing vibratunal effect. When the trainer is tired, the reverse happens and the cords lengthen and sag. The solution is to be conscious of what causes these pitch changes and what effect these can have on the learning group

- **Pauses:** Trainers generally underestimate the power of the pause. The most effective trainers have learnt to master the art of silence, and comedians depend on it for their livelihood. The inclusion of a pause before a punch line is the essence of comic timing and serves a similar purpose in training situations. Trainers often feel self-conscious about using pauses, because they believe that a pause might be considered a sign of nervousness or indecision on their part. In most cases, such fears are unfounded, providing that these pauses are not unnecessarily elongated. You can use pauses in the training situation in a number of ways:

  ° *Before Speaking:* A pause allows time for the trainer to gather his/her own thoughts and for the group to prepare themselves for the further content

  ° *As Punctuation:* Use a pause to paragraph speech or increase understanding: "So there are two types of question we can ask (pause). These are (pause) training questions (pause) and testing questions (pause)"

  ° *Highlighting:* When a point is of vital significance but can be easily overlooked or misunderstood, pausing at the right moment can amplify the meaning – for example, greater emphasis can be achieved by saying: "You must ... *not* (pause) on any account (pause) ..." rather than "You mustn't on any account ..."

  ° *After Disruption:* If a question has been asked or the trainer's flow has been interrupted, pausing after dealing with the issue signifies that the matter is now at a close and that the trainer is returning to the original discussion

  ° *Learning Styles:* Some learners are reflectors and need some silence to reflect on questions before speaking. Using pauses gives you the opportunity to help them participate

- **Emphasis:** With any training approach, the key to success is to use it sparingly, and emphasis is no exception. There is generally little to be gained from emphasising every other word in a verbal communication, any more than you would wish to underline every other word that you write. The idea is to make the essential learning points or key messages as obvious and memorable as possible. Emphasis can be provided by stressing certain areas of content, enumerating or listing and by making an assertion.

Some Vocal Problems Associated with Training

There are four vocal problems common to many training situations:

- **Fading:** Faders are trainers whose sentences are so long that, by the time they reach the end, they barely have enough strength left to draw breath. The result is that the last part of the sentence is very faint

- **Mumbling:** Mumbling generally occurs when the trainer is unsure of what he/she is saying and therefore wishes as few people as possible to hear it

- **Gabbling:** Gabbling occurs when a trainer either (1) omits words and/or syllables or (2) runs all the words together into one long sentence. In an attempt to return to a less exposed environment, the content is completely incomprehensible, but it does have the advantages of cutting speaking time down by half. Consciously slowing the pace and concentrating on diction can address this

- **Mufflers:** Muffling is another response to pressure. The most common cause of muffling for trainers is talking with your back to the group and addressing flip-charts or overhead transparency images instead of trainees. Other forms of muffling include placing your hand in front of your mouth, speaking through clenched teeth or just speaking too softly.

Adopting an Appropriate Training Communication Style

Very effective trainers have an appearance of effortlessness. They have such a command of their material that it appears that they are completely at ease. The research tells us that most learners prefer a conversational style. This does not mean that you should not prepare. There are, however, significant differences between giving a training session and holding a conversation:

- **Formal speaking is more highly structured:** It requires more detailed planning and development. Specific time limits may be imposed and the trainer does not have the advantage of being able to respond individually to listeners

- **Formal speaking requires more formal language:** Slang, jargon and poor grammar all lower trainer credibility, even in informal speech situations. Listeners usually react negatively to poor language choices. In fact, many studies show that some kinds of language, such as obscene language, dramatically lower a trainer's credibility

- **Formal speaking requires a different method of delivery:** The trainer's voice must be adjusted in volume and projection, posture must be correct and distracting mannerisms and verbal habits must be avoided.

Preparing your Thoughts and Ideas

Once you have carefully considered strategy, structure and support, you should prepare your training notes. To do this, simply write key points in a rough outline, following the structure chosen. What is done next depends on the focus of the training. Most often, the trainer will speak in a conversational manner that is not memorised or read; this is referred to as extemporaneous speaking.

Conversational skill in a training situation is desirable because it is perceived as natural and flexible; it applies to most situations. To prepare, copy key words on note cards to stimulate memory; standard pages are often distracting. You should write out quotations, statistics or anything that requires exact wording. You can highlight places where you intend to use visual aids, pause for questions or present an exhibit. To rehearse, you should go through the speech and phrase ideas in language that seems natural. It is also acceptable to phrase ideas with different words each time. In fact, this increases the conversational quality of the training because the words will be typical of oral style and natural expression. It will help develop flexibility, allowing you to adjust to different wording and flow of ideas.

If the training situation is very formal and demands precise wording or exquisite prose, you should prepare a word-for-word manuscript to memorise or read. You should rehearse with the manuscript, trying to achieve as much natural flow in the dialogue as possible. This form of training is rare. You should avoid using written scripts or memorisation for training situations, because it disrupts the natural flow of conversational style and breaks your eye contact with the learners. In addition, because manuscripts are prepared in written form first, they usually take on the style of written language, so that it will sound like written rather than oral speech to your learners.

Verbal style differs from written style in the following ways:

- The average sentence length is shorter (about 16 words) in conversation
- Vocabulary is more limited in speaking than in writing; fewer than 50 words make up almost half of the total vocabulary we use when we speak
- Spoken vocabulary consists of more short words
- Speakers use more words referring to themselves such as "I", "me" and "we" ("I" and "you" make up almost 8% of the words used in speaking); listeners rate this as more interesting
- More qualifying terms ("much", "many" and "a lot") and closure terms ("none", "never" and "always") are used in speaking

- More phrases and terms indicating hesitation are apparent in speaking ("it seems to me", "apparently", "in my opinion" and "maybe")
- Fewer precise numbers are used in speaking
- Speakers use more contractions and colloquial expressions ("can't", "wouldn't", "golly", "wow" and "chill out").

UNDERSTANDING DIMENSIONS OF NON-VERBAL INTERPERSONAL STYLE

So far in this chapter, we have focused on the verbal communication process. We will now turn to dimensions of interpersonal style. There is strong evidence from research that shows, if you match the non-verbal communication of your learners, then your capacity to motivate, influence and achieve learning goals is significantly enhanced. Research conducted by two Australians, McPhee and Andrewartha, reveals six very important dimension of non-verbal influence (see **Table 8.2**). These concepts are very relevant to understanding your effectiveness in a training situation. They argue that every person generally displays some of the behaviour patterns on each side of the continuum, although we are more likely to lean more strongly towards one end or the other. They do not advocate that one end is better than the other; they simply reflect different aspects of non-verbal communication traits.

THE LEARNER'S PERCEPTUAL SYSTEM

How learners form concepts, explain ideas and evaluate things is very much influenced by how they perceive the world. Our brains are designed to perceive the outside world, using visual auditory and tactile means. Most learners have a favourite or preferred mode of perception and it is likely to be more consistent than the other two. A learner's assessment of people and things varies according to their perceptual system and the training situation is subtly influenced by this preference. Where a group of learners have a perceptual style that matches that of the trainer, they are said to be on the same wavelength. In contrast, where the two perceptual systems are mismatched, it is likely that misunderstanding will occur in the training context.

FIGURE 8.2: NON-VERBAL COMMUNICATION STYLES

DIMENSION 1	Exaggerators	Understators
Characteristics	• Blow things out of proportion • Mountains out of mole hills • Enthusiasm, energy • Noticeable reaction to events • When things are good, they get excited and demonstrative • When things get bad, they react strongly and negatively • Emphasis on body language and voice tone • Dominate meetings • Excellent creative communicators	• Play things down • Make molehills out of mountains • Little body language • Minimum voice inflection • Quiet and shy • Can be overlooked • Handles crisis quietly • Unflappable and immovable in the face of disruptions/distractions • Excellent calm, consolidating managers and leaders • Perceive exaggeration as being over the top
Matching	• Get on well with other exaggerators as they are on the same wave length • Mismatched with understators	• Get on well with other understators as they relate well to them
Communicating with Others	• Tone down their interaction and relax their communication style, otherwise they risk being seen as lacking emotional control or having an unbalanced viewpoint	• Put more energy and drama into the interaction to gain better attention. Otherwise will be perceived as less powerful and less certain by others, even passive
DIMENSION 2	The Self Evaluator	Other Evaluator
Characteristics	• Assess their contribution and behaviour in a critical and evaluative manner • Tend to overlook others' contributions and behaviour • Too much responsibility for delegated tasks and become over-burdened • Very demanding of themselves and take responsibility for others • Blame their own behaviour • Can be highly stressed	• Evaluate contributions from others and allocate blame to others without examining their own role • Like to discuss third party errors • Have blind spots about their own input
Matching	• Less effective with other self-evaluators because each person tends to blame their own behaviour • Need to look outside their own situation	• Quite effective with other evaluators as they engage in a blitz of blaming others. The relationship can deteriorate if the topic of blame is between the two of them
Communicating with Others	• Need to assess others' impact on the situation and stop blaming themselves	• Need to critically appraise their own input in order to enhance their development

DIMENSION 3	Initiators	Responders
Characteristics	• Like introducing new concepts/taking the lead in communicating • Produce ideas • Assume the dominant position • Good in leading teams • Can be too directive • Good at starting tasks, not at finishing them • Good at giving ideas, assistance, reactions, involvement and interference	• Like others to take the lead • Like to understand every aspect of the situation before responding to others' initiatives • Less comfortable in isolated roles, but are good in supportive roles • Excellent democratic and participative leadership style • Good at completing tasks and finishing them
Matching	• Get on well with responders in a complimentary and matched relationship • They can become jammed or get into conflict with other initiators; this can result in a competitive relationship	• Get on well with initiators with whom they have an understanding • Have difficulties with other responders, as there is a tendency for no one to take the lead
Communicating with Others	• Need to step back from taking the lead automatically and allow others to take charge • Need to stick to the task and complete it	• Need to step out of their zone of comfort and push themselves into the limelight • Need to develop their tolerance for ambiguity and accept initiatives without using in-depth analysis constantly
DIMENSION 4	Rapid Processor	Gradual Processor
Characteristics	• Process ideas rapidly • Respond quickly to events • Like to get all the information at once and are frustrated by delays and changes • Impatient with slow people • Like major tasks challenging and full of elements • Get bored with slow-moving tasks with little risk or challenge • Never miss an opportunity and rush headlong into mistakes	• Become overwhelmed with too much data • Like to process information gradually and digest it thoroughly before absorbing the next piece • Like well-defined and focused tasks • Dislike high pressure and high change situations • Never make impulsive mistakes, yet they can lose out on golden opportunities
Matching	• Get on well with other rapid learners and can rush off in a tangent with other rapid processors • Can find gradual people too slow to deal with patiently and this leads to misunderstandings	• Get on well with other gradual learners, but are perceived as being too slow by rapid processors
Communicating with Others	• Need to slow down a little and leave more time for thought and preparation • Need to be less impetuous and reactive	• Need to be encouraged to move more quickly and to develop confidence in risk-taking activities

DIMENSION 5	Detailed Examiners	Conceptualisers
Characteristics	• Examine each specific element crucial to the tasks • Love complex detail • Effective in terms of developing a project once it has started • Enjoy focusing on nitty-gritty detail	• Like the overall concept or the "big picture" • Don't like getting involved in detail • Can overlook important detail because they are more interested in concepts
Matching	• Get on well with others who pay attention to detail, yet are needed by conceptualisers to help complete projects.	• Get on well with other "big picture" people • Mismatched with detailers, as they perceive them as being over-meticulous and obsessed with the trivial • Need to tolerate and respect the need for operational thinkers who need to get involved in detail to complete tasks
Communicating with Others	• Need to relinquish their obsession with detail and tolerate ambiguity • Need to develop an understanding of how to get outside the detail and learn to look for the "big picture"	• Need to respect the importance of grasping detail and not overlooking it

DIMENSION 6	Linear Thinker	Lateral Thinker
Characteristics	• Carefully ordered, sequential and one-directional thought process • The first thing leads to the next and so on to the logical conclusion • Like methodical tasks and set routines and clear guidelines • Like to do things by the book and tend to be inflexible with changes • Uncomfortable with ambiguous tasks	• Variable in their thinking and planning, can move from one aspect of the problem to another without an obvious connection and can initiate ideas from everywhere • Exhibit innovative and creative thought processes • Can handle several different tasks simultaneously • Relate well when ideas are presented ambiguously or in a random fashion • Have variable routines and have so much flexibility that they are hard to tie down
Matching	• Get on well with other linear thinkers who think methodically and sequentially • Don't get on well with lateral thinkers, who they think are scatter-brained, illogical and disorganised	• Don't get on with liner thinkers and perceive them as rigid, inflexible, non-creative and boring
Communicating with Others	• Need to respect the need for other types of communicators and to understand that thinking laterally is vital and productive	• Need to put some order into chaos to gain the respect of the linear thinker and should try to understand their perspective and desire for order

Adapted from Carlopio *et al.* (1997).

The modes found include:

- **Visual Mode (Seeing):** Visual learners see the idea. They are mainly influenced by a visual perspective and prefer to think in visual images. They may use more visual words such as "see", "clear", "look" and so on. It is their visual discrimination that helps them to absorb the training message – in general, they prefer to see it, read it, study a diagram and examine it visually. Visualisers respond best to pictures, images, slides, overheads, taking notes, as well as visual word pictures. Visualisers relate naturally well to others who are also visual. They are less effective with auditory and tactile learners. In a real sense, they speak a different language. With visual learners, it may be helpful to not talk as much, but to find pictures, images and other ways of showing them what is being said. About 70% of the population has a visual perspective

- **Auditory Mode (Hearing):** Auditory learners listen to the concepts and prefer to sound out their ideas. They tend to use language with more auditory elements in it, using words like "noise", "listen", "hear", "sounds like" and so on. They like listening to conversations, the sound of their own voice, and respond to discriminations in pitch and intensity. As learners, they talk things through conclusively. In a team-learning situation, they like to talk things over and sound people out. The tone of voice and sound of things is often quite important to them. Auditory learners relate naturally well to others who are auditory. They are less effective with visual and tactile people. With auditory learners, it may be necessary for you to talk things through more and use less visual presentation. About 20% of the population has an auditory preference. Effective questioning techniques can assist the auditory learner absorb the training message

- **Experiential Mode (Touching):** Experiential learners like to "grasp the concept", to "chew it over" and "get in touch with their ideas". They tend to rely on their intuition, being involved and experiencing in a "hands on" manner, rather than listening to or looking at things. They prefer good practical exercises in a learning situation instead of watching and listening. As learners, they often understand things intuitively, without necessarily being able to describe their reasons. This type of learner relates naturally well with others who are experiential. They may be less effective with visual and auditory learners. With experiential learners, it is helpful to look for examples that describe the concept in concrete terms and help them to have some experience of what is being presented. Only 10% of the population has an experiential perspective. Role-plays can be quite useful in terms of helping the experiential learner absorb the training message.

UNDERSTANDING TRAINING COMMUNICATION / USING TRANSACTIONAL ANALYSIS & THE "JOHARI WINDOW"

Transactional Analysis

Berne developed a psychological model of understanding individual behaviour based on the Freudian theory of the id, ego and super ego. An understanding of transactional analysis is very useful for the trainer because it provides an insight into why learners interact, behave and communicate the way they do in certain group situations.

Berne believed that we are made up of three parts, the Parent part, similar to Freud's super ego, the Adult part, related to the ego and the Child area closely linked to the id. In more detail:

- The **Parent** ego state contains the behaviours and attitudes that a person has developed from his/her parents, including values, prejudices and rituals, etc. One way of becoming aware of the parent ego state is to list the adjectives that come to mind when you think of real-life parents (critical and dominant or nurturing and kind, helpful and even cynical). It will be quickly apparent that the parent ego state is composed of two parts: A Nurturing Parent and a Critical Parent

- To become aware of the **Adult** ego state, list the adjectives that come to mind when you think of adults (logical, understanding, fair, just, analytical). The adult state collects information and has a realistic perspective. The adult may respond critically and analytically to information, or may respond to the relevant information and look at ways of improving irrelevant information

- To become aware of the **Child** state, describe child-like behaviour (fun-loving, childlike, childish, mischievous, and carefree). Again, two parts of the child state emerge: A Free Child, which is natural, spontaneous, and creative, and the Adaptive Child, which is compliant and rebellious. The Adaptive Child responds to the perceived presence of a Parent, externally or internally.

In any interaction in the training environment, each participant will be operating from one of his/her three parts and addressing one of the other party's parts. The trainer needs to stay in the Adult part at all times.

FIGURE 8.3: USING TRANSACTIONAL ANALYSIS IN TRAINING

A participant has been forced to attend a presentation skills course.

Many years ago, I was running a presentation skills course and all the participants bar one appeared highly motivated, enthusiastic and eager for learning. I noticed that one individual was sullen and exhibited closed body language. The message being transmitted was that of the Adapted Child, compliant by their attendance but rebellious in their response to me as a trainer. He was quite disruptive and negative and his behaviour was starting to affect other group members. My natural response as a trainer was to jump into Critical Parent mode, point out the learner's transgressions and eject him from the programme.

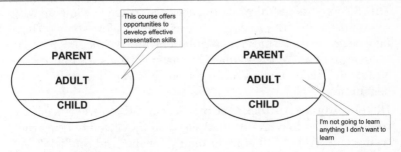

Berne believed that if we persisted in the parent/child mode the conflict could not be resolved. The trainer needs to keep in the adult state in order to help the learner to an adult state and this breaks the destructive cycle.

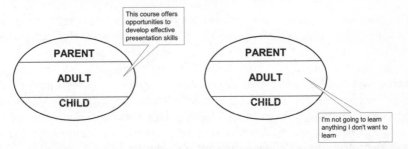

However, this would have damaged the nurturing atmosphere of the programme. I broke the group into small groups for a learning exercise and managed to speak to the truculent learner on his own. I discovered that Mike was new to the organisation and had given his first presentation to his new team the previous week. He had put a lot of hard work into making the right impression. After the presentation, he went back to his desk and checked his email, to discover a terse note from his new boss ordering him to attend this particular course. His boss had not taken the time to give him constructive feedback and had forced him to attend a programme that he had come to perceive as a punishment. He was taking his aggression out on the course. I appealed to his natural Adult state and pointed out the advantages of the programme to his career development. He moved into the Adult state and developed highly effective presentation skills and made a valuable contribution to the learning of the other course members. This transaction is outlined in the diagram above.

Adapted from Berne (1964).

The following transactions can be of value in a training delivery situation:

- **Developing a Creative Atmosphere:** The trainee and learner use their Child state, if the need is to solve a problem and brainstorm all possible solutions. The trainer needs to generate an atmosphere of trust and creativity, where learners are "free-wheeling" and coming up with ideas so the playful child ego state is in action. Once the ideas have been generated, then the Adult state needs to sort out the relevant and practical ideas

- **Developing a Responsible Parental Learning Interaction:** This response is useful when trainees are trying to come up with solutions to difficult problems – for example, safety issues. They may be generating rules and regulations and developing plans for the maintenance of their rules. The need is to ensure that rules are observed. This behaviour may be seen as Parent-like and demanding

- **Developing an Adult Learning State:** If the trainee needs to resolve conflict in a group situation, then they need to bring the trainees into the Adult state to reduce tension and conflict. The Adult-mode interaction is useful when the trainee wants to calm people down, create a logical perspective or when the trainer wants to focus on technical information.

The trainer needs to be aware that staying in the Adult mode without dealing with the creativity of the Child state and the nurturing ability of the Parent state, can be counter-productive.

In many training situations, it is necessary to make an assessment of the learners. Transactional analysis can contribute to this assessment in an objective and systematic way. The following profiles of learners have been identified in training environments – each presents a different scenario and the approach that transactional analysis suggests that you should use

- **Profile 1: Critical Parent:** This profile tends to present a trainee who is difficult to work with. This trainee can come across as hardworking, moralistic, judgemental, may be authoritarian in some interactions and may be perceived as looking for attention and approval

- **Profile 2: Adopted Child:** This trainee is often found in traditional organisations, where managers tend to treat other employees as children and foster a dependency relationship. These managers use an autocratic management style that disempowers the individual

- **Profile 3: Free Child:** Child-dominant trainees tend to be lively and enthusiastic in a training environment. They project charm and creativity in their interpersonal style but do not respond well to rules and regulations and have a strong need to be liked by the group. They need to be controlled by the trainer as they can hijack the learning event by creating too much humour and too few learning opportunities

- **Profile 4: Adult:** This profile presents a trainee who is logical and objective. They possess a logical and factual perspective, which can be perceived as boring and intimidating to other trainees. Their relationship with other trainees tend to be unsatisfactory and, consequently, they may have difficulties working in group learning situations

- **Profile 5: Parent/Adult:** This profile gives the trainee the facility to move quickly from Parent to Adult. These trainees are hardworking and very high achievers. Their strengths are their ability to create a logical perspective and separate opinion from fact

- **Profile 6: Critical Parent & Free Child:** In this profile, the charm of the Child adds intuition and creativity to the power of the Adult. The tendency of the Parent state to curb the creativity of the Child state can be reduced to create a situation of rationality.

As a trainer, you need to stay in the Adult state, particularly if you have to handle difficult participants or conflict situations.

ASSERTIVENESS BEHAVIOUR IN A TRAINING CONTEXT

Your ability to behave assertively in a training situation is an important dimension of your overall effectiveness as a trainer. Researchers use the concepts of life positions as the basis to understand assertive behaviour. You need to know how to influence trainees and how to protect yourself against the attempts of trainees to influence you in an inappropriate way. This skill is particularly important in learning situations where maintaining your authority and position may be difficult in the face of strong resistance – for example, in senior management development situations where managers feel they do not need to learn.

Life positions theory envisages four types of behaviour: aggressive, assertive, passive and defensive behaviours. These are presented in **Figure 8.4**. The characteristics of these different behaviours are:

- **Aggressive Behaviour:** Aggressive behaviour is a very strong style and is used by people to win where the other person loses. The aggressive person wants to achieve his/her own personal agenda at all times. This behaviour needs to be used tactfully and very sparingly. The aggressive person's mind frame believes strongly that they are OK, "I'm right, you're wrong", "I'm the boss, I will decide".

Aggressive people demonstrate the following types of behaviour:

- ○ Strong violent emotions
- ○ Judging others negatively while presenting themselves in a positive light
- ○ Blaming others and putting people down
- ○ Using threatening body language, finger pointing, invading body space, etc.
- ○ Manipulation techniques

FIGURE 8.4: LIFE POSITIONS MODEL OF BEHAVIOURS

ASSERTIVE	AGGRESSIVE
I'M OK YOU'RE OK **Adult Part**	I'M OK YOU'RE NOT OK **The Parent** **Unacceptable Aggression**
PASSIVE	**DEPRESSIVE**
I'M NOT OK YOU'RE OK **The Adapted Dutiful Child** **Unacceptable Submission**	I'M NOT OK YOU'RE NOT OK EITHER **The Adapted Rebellious Child** **Cynicism and Depression**

Source: Harris (1995).

- **Passive Behaviour:** The second behaviour is the Passive type. Their view of the world is that they are *not* OK. They generally exhibit a type of martyrdom and feel that everyone else has an easier life than they do. When confronted with issues, they are inclined to say nothing and internalise the issues as a personal chastisement. They usually exhibit the following characteristics:
  - ○ Being a victim
  - ○ Putting up with all sorts of things in order not to rock the boat
  - ○ Holding back and not speaking up
  - ○ If they overuse this behaviour, they can end up internalising their communication difficulties and make themselves ill.
- **Depressive Behaviour:** The third style of behaviour is known as the Depressive style. This individual exhibits a life attitude "I'm not OK but you're not OK either" and is not fun to be with. We all

know examples of the depressive approach to life, who usually exhibit the following characteristics:

- ○ Constantly complaining about everyone and everything
- ○ Never in good humour; a negative approach to everything
- ○ They use distractive criticism constantly.
- ○ They can be very dangerous in a training environment and need to be managed appropriately by the trainer.

- **Assertive Behaviour:** The ideal behaviour is assertive behaviour – the type that we would all like to exhibit all the time. Assertiveness is all about standing up for your own rights without infringing on the rights of others. The assertive person:
  - ○ Can get their view across clearly, calmly rationally
  - ○ Remain calm and controlled in highly charged and conflicted situations
  - ○ Can admit when they are wrong and apologise accordingly without grovelling

Assertive individuals are honest, have strong self-respect, and have respect for others. They are open, have high self-esteem, are into win-win situations and adopt Adult-type behaviour. Their life view is "I'm OK, you're OK", "I am not better or worse than anyone else".

TRAINER INSTRUCTION STYLE

Each trainer has a unique trainer style. Some trainers have a stronger preference for setting up and directing learning activities, others are more comfortable helping learners to share and interpret their reactions to a learning event, others are better at helping the learner to generalise concepts and, finally, some trainers like to help learners to apply how to use learning in their own situations.

There are four generic trainer styles:

- **Instructor:** The instructor enjoys setting up and directing the learning activity. The instructor is most comfortable giving directions and taking charge of the learning activity. The instructor prefers to tell the learners what to do, is well-organised and self-confident, and concentrates on one item at a time. He/she provides examples, controls learners' participation, and uses lectures effectively

- **Explorer:** The Explorer is most comfortable helping learners to share and interpret their reactions to a learning activity. He/she is a good listener who creates an open learning environment, encourages free expression, and ensures that everyone is involved in the discussion. The Explorer is open to non-verbal cues and shows empathy for the feelings and emotions of learners. The

Explorer is accepting of learner's reactions and encourages self-directed learning

- **Thinker:** The Thinker is most comfortable helping the learner generalise concepts from the reactions to a learning experience. The Thinker help learners to categorise, organise, and integrate their reactions into theories, principles and generalisations. The thinker focuses on ideas and thought rather than feelings and emotions. He/she acknowledges different interpretations and theories. Independent thinking is encouraged, based on objective information. The Thinker assists learners in making connections between the past and the present. The Thinker is often a practised observer of the learning activity

- **Guide:** The Guide is most comfortable helping learners to apply how to use new learning in their own situations. The Guide prefers to involve trainees in activities, problem-solving, discussions and evaluations of their own progress. Experimentation with practical application is encouraged. The Guide encourages trainees to draw on each other and the trainer as resources. He/she acts as a facilitator to translate theory into practical action. The Guide focuses on meaningful and applicable solutions to real-life problems and encourages achievement participation.

An alternative trainer-style model is provided by Gilley *et al.* (2003), in **Figure 8.5**, in which they identify five instructional styles, each reflecting different beliefs about the learning process.

FIGURE 8.5: THE TWO CONTINUUMS OF THE TEACHING / LEARNING PROCESS

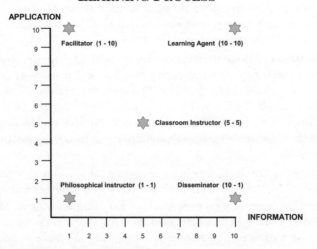

Source: Gilley *et al.* (2002).

- **Classroom Instructor (5-5):** If you use this style, you attempt to integrate information and application. However, instruction often occurs in a safe, non-life-like environment. Additionally, the information you delivery is moderate in complexity and application is relegated to role-playing or simulations. Consequently, the amount of learning that occurs is slight and is easily forgotten when employees return to the job. Learning takes place at the lowest common denominator for the learning group, and deep awareness and understanding are not likely

- **Facilitator (1-10):** If you use this style, the experience of the learners is personalised. New ideas, facts, concepts and theories are not emphasised. The learner must possess an adequate understanding or have relevant application in order for meaningful awareness to occur. The primary focus of this approach is to deepen the learners' existing knowledge level and to crystallise the learners' experiences. When this is accomplished, the learners' experiences become a source of knowledge and a benchmark for comparisons. Training is often active and interesting, and is most effective when basic knowledge already exists

- **Learning Agent (10-10):** If you use this style, you believe that information and application are equal partners in the learning acquisition process. This style differs from classroom instruction in that the emphasis on information and application are equally paramount and are at the highest possible level. You must be skilled in several learning methods and be expert in the discipline. By focusing simultaneously on information and its application, the integrator of learning can demonstrate concern for the learner and for the material, and promote a healthy relationship between them

- **Philosophical Instructor (1-1):** This style of instruction is often valued for its intrinsic intellectual satisfaction. As a trainer, neither content nor experience is emphasised. Philosophical issues are often addressed using this style. Gratification is received through cognitive exchanges, but few new ideas or facts are presented. This style required intelligent learners and instructors in order to be effective. Training programmes using this style are difficult to design because few, if any, learning objectives are stated

- **Disseminator (10-1):** If you use this style of instruction, you assume that learning is primarily a process of disseminating information and memorising. The most common method of presentation is lecturing. Disseminators often use a few examples to demonstrate application. You do not give significant consideration to the experience of the learner. You assume that learners can absorb ideas, facts, concepts and themes. They may complete tests or examinations to identify how much they have learned.

The style you adopt will depend on the characteristics of your learners. A specific issue that is highly relevant is the maturity of your learners in a learning or training situation. If your trainers have low maturity, then it makes sense to be more instructor-oriented, and to guide and advise, to demonstrate and prompt. Where your learners have high levels of maturity, you can adopt much more facilitative behaviours. These behaviours are summarised in **Figure 8.6**.

FIGURE 8.6: LEARNER GROUP MATURITY & TRAINER BEHAVIOUR

Style	Trainer Behaviour	Learner Situational Maturity	Trainer Relationship Behaviour
Guiding	• Directing, order, tell the way • Setting, persuade, "get on board" • Guiding, advise, show the way • Prompting, incite, prime	**Low**	• Distance, maintain remoteness • Recognising acknowledge accord, notice / supporting, prop up, carry the weight • Sustaining, nourish, keep from falling
Coaching & Empowering	• Consulting, seek information • Helping, assist, aid • Realising, set free, "make over to"	**Moderate**	• Responding, show sensitivity to • Encouraging, urge, make bold • Withdrawing, pull back from discontinue giving
Creating Responsibility for Learning	• Resorting, a stock to be drawn on • Participating, having a share in • Collaborating, work in combination with others	**High**	• Respecting, having regard/esteem for • Warmth, show affection, liking for • Maturity, bear the same relations to others

UNDERSTANDING NON-VERBAL BEHAVIOUR

Each time you interact with other people, you draw conclusions about them from what they say and do. Some of these conclusions will be right and some will be wrong. Equally, they are drawing conclusions about your behaviour. Even though these impressions are shaped and reshaped on an on-going basis, much of what you think about other people will be informed by your first impressions of them.

When you meet people for the first time, your senses work flat out to process all the information you are taking in about them:

• You can see what they look like

- You can hear what they are saying
- You can feel the handshake
- You can study their body language and gestures.

All this information is taken in and rapidly processed by your senses. You reach tentative conclusions about them. You decide whether you like or dislike them, trust or distrust them. And equally they are drawing conclusions about you.

All this happens very early on in the encounter and is the basis for the 90:90 rule which states that: *People form 90% of their lasting impressions in the first 90 seconds.*

Non-verbal communication can be transmitted through:

- Skin colour: Blushing, turning white, flushed
- Minute muscle changes: Eyes, mouth, jaw-line
- Lower lip changes: Straight from the subconscious
- Breathing changes: Subtle.

You can use non-verbal behaviour or body language skills in a training context to:

- Make yourself more effective in meetings and 1: 1 situations
- Make more effective presentations
- Get more information out of appraisals, interviews and negotiations when selling or counselling
- Present yourself effectively in appraisals and interviews and when negotiating or selling
- Make yourself more approachable.

FIGURE 8.7: BODY LANGUAGE DIMENSIONS

	POSITIVE WORDS		
I N C O N G R U E N T	Negative Body Language Positive Words **Contradictory**	Positive Body Language Positive Words **Effective**	**C O N G R U E N T**
	Contradictory Positive Body Language Negative Words	**Hostile** Negative Body Language Negative Words	
	NEGATIVE WORDS		

Source: Schultz (1958).

ESTABLISHING RAPPORT

This helps to build trust and helps move people away from suspicion towards openness and mutual trust. There are a number of ways you can do build rapport:

Mirror, Pace and Lead

- **Mirror:** One way to understand the other person's non-verbal communication is to "mirror" their body postures, gestures, facial expressions and mannerisms. Unconsciously, we do this anyway; if you do this consciously, it tunes you into the feeling state of the other person, making you more aware of how they feel.

- **Pacing:** Pacing is a set of behaviours that you can use to gain and maintain rapport for a period of time, while interacting with another person. If you are having a longer conversation with someone – for example, an interview or appraisal – you can mirror their continuous body language – this is called "pacing". With both mirroring and pacing, it is important that you soften the gestures you make, so what you are doing does not become obvious to the other person

- **Leading:** The third step in the sequence is "leading". After you have paced the person you are in conversation with, and have established rapport with them, you can change their body language, by gradually changing yours. So you can change someone from tense and uptight to relaxed or bored, or from withdrawn to alert and interested or critical and negative to positive, etc

Eye Contact

We all know that if we want people to listen to us, respect us and take us seriously, we need to "look them straight in the eye". However, we also know that it is rude to stare. Another point to consider is that direct eye contact often feels too strong and aggressive, or sometimes too embarrassing and personal. One way to get around this is to focus somewhere near the eyes, but not make direct eye-to-eye contact. It is comfortable to make eye contact with an individual between 50 and 70% of the time.

Posture

Your posture, and the way you carry yourself, communicate a lot of non-verbal information and even say something about your general outlook and attitude to life.

Use of Space

The distance that people generally maintain between themselves and other people can be broken into four main categories:

- **Intimate Distance:** Ranges from touching to 0.5 metres and is the distance used with someone you have a close affectionate relationship with. Sometimes when you have to use this distance with strangers – for example, in a lift or a crowded room – it can make you feel uncomfortable (that is why most people just watch the floor numbers as the lift goes up and down)

- **Personal Distance:** Ranges from 0.5 metres to 1.25 metres and is the distance that you use when you are talking with casual friends or colleagues at work

- **Social Distance:** Ranges from 1.2 metres to 2 metres and is the distance you use when you are conducting impersonal business, such as when you are dealing in a bank

- **Public Distance:** The distance that you use when you are addressing an audience in a formal setting, usually at least 3.5 metres.

By matching the distance to the setting, you will send the proper signals to the other person, and, in this way, reinforce your verbal communication.

Vocal

When you speak, your voice carries a great deal of information that is not included in the words you use. This additional information is called "paralanguage". It includes: Vocal quality; Projection; Pace; Pitch; Energy; Volume; Pronunciation; and Pauses.

Paralanguage is important in face-to-face communications, but especially important if you are a trainer. Most trainees like to hear a voice that sounds interesting and friendly as well as being:

- **Pleasant:** Suggesting that the person has an agreeable manner

- **Natural:** Using simple, straightforward language and avoiding technical terms and jargon

- **Alert:** Giving the impression that the trainer is wide awake and interested in what you have to say

- **Distinct and clear**

- **Expressive:** A well-modulated voice at a normal tone, neither too loud nor too low. The pace should be moderate (news-reader pace, which is about 150 words per minute) and there should be variety in the tone of voice to add colour and vitality to what is being said.

UNDERSTANDING THE BEHAVIOUR OF YOUR LEARNERS

As a trainer, you must continuously recognise that you are dealing with people, who differ in terms of their psychological characteristics and behaviour. Some learners are co-operative and highly motivated, others are more likely to be disruptive and may be motivated to create conflict within the learning group. There is research indicating the different types of learners you are likely to encounter in a training situation, including:

- **The Talking Terror**: In his most irksome form, this learner is a loud mouth that dominates the group and monopolises any discussions. In a less irritating, but equally disruptive form, this learner is the constant chatterer who has always had something similar happens to him/her. Whatever manifestation the talking terror might appear in, the group will be looking to you to maintain control

  Although the end result may vary somewhat, the cause of Talking Terror is invariably the consequence of insecurity. The talker often feels that he must prove himself before the trainer and/or group. Consequently, this learner may spend much time trying to demonstrate to the group a depth of knowledge in order earn respect. Or this learner may be seeking approval by showing his enthusiasm for the topic under discussion (the "eager beaver"), or he may just want to be noticed by the group as someone worthy of attention and acceptance (the "chatterbox")

- **The Great Griper:** Although a certain amount of constructive criticism is often encouraged on training courses, the problem with the "Great Griper" is that he regards every discussion as an opportunity to air his grievances about the company, the people he works with, the conditions he works under – in fact, anything at all. If this learner is allowed the chance to raise his "pet peeves", the general negative approach can completely undermine the enthusiasm of the rest of the group

- **The Moaner:** A variation of the Great Griper is the "Moaner", whose pet phrase is "Ain't it awful?". This state of mind can become infectious if there are a number of people from the same area of an organisation on the course, so you need to deal promptly with this behaviour. You should ask Moaners to specify the issues as openly and honestly as possible. In the final reckoning, it might be best if they leave the course, but only as a last resort. If there is only one Moaner, peer pressure will often resolve the situation. However, where the group as a whole has serious concerns about its organisation, it is often best to introduce a short sharp session to allow them to get it off their chest – you are unlikely to make much progress until they have left that baggage behind

- **Doubting Thomas:** The "Doubting Thomas" is a variant of the Great Griper, wit the difference that, while the Great Griper often has only one or two areas of sensitivity, the Doubting Thomas has developed an all-encompassing cynicism. Once again, if this negative attitude is allowed to develop, it can be contagious and cast doom and gloom over the whole group

  Invariably, the Doubting Thomas is someone with a number of years' seniority, whose his attitude may be the product of seeing many bright ideas tried and fail. Perhaps some of the ideas that were never given a chance were his, which explains why he is less receptive to the ideas of others. Finally, it might be that the sceptic (young or old) feels that he might not be able to master these new approaches, processes, or procedures and therefore regards them as a threat best eliminated by dismissing them.

- **Head Shaker:** A variant of the Doubting Thomas, who continually uses head-shaking as a form of non-verbal behaviour to indicate disagreement with the trainer and/or dislike with some of the ideas being discussed. The trainer can deal with this situation by:
  - Ignoring the individual altogether
  - Focusing on the trainee who is making the contribution
  - Confronting the trainee, "Frank, I see you shaking your head. Do you want to share your reaction with the rest of the group?"

- **The Conspirators:** Unlike the preceding categories, conspirators cannot work alone – they need to join forces with one or more people. Despite their title, their actions are rarely sinister, but arise from the manner in which they can be seen absorbed in their own private discussion in total disregard of those around them. Often the purpose of the conversation is to clarify a point that one of the party is uncertain about but, if the behaviour occurs immediately following a break, it is likely to be to conclude a conversation started earlier

- **The Whisperer:** The "Whisperer" is a variant of the Conspirator. There are a number of reasons and solutions for whispering:
  - *Boredom:* Encourage the whisperer's involvement
  - *Lack of understanding:* Implement a strategy to help the learner's understanding
  - *Small talk:* Insist that small talk be reserved for the break. Peer pressure can be used to enforce this.

  The "power of silence" will often stop whispering, especially if combined with good eye contact

- **The Arguer:** An "Arguer" derives satisfaction from challenging the trainer – maybe he just enjoys an argument, or perhaps he is aggressive by nature. You should:

- ° Stay calm and do not get upset or drawn into a protracted confrontation or stand-off
- ° When a correct statement is made, express agreement
- ° When an incorrect statement is made, open up the discussion to the group for a correction: "What do the rest of you think"?

- **The Pot Plant:** The "Pot Plant" is so called because, apart from sitting in the group and looking decorative, he seems to contribute very little to the group except a touch of additional colour. There are all sorts of reasons why a Pot Plant might remain silent or withdrawn from the group, including inhibition and lack of motivation or interest in the topic

- **The Busy Body:** This trainee ducks in and out of the training session taking messages, rushing to the phone, etc. Address the situation by doing the following:
  - ° Before the session, get agreement to hold calls
  - ° Schedule training away from the site
  - ° If person is important, stop the training session and ask the busybody when he/she will be available
  - ° Reschedule the session, if necessary.

- **The Jolly Jester :** It may seem hard to believe that anyone could take exception to a "Jolly Jester", who brings a smile to everyone's face and can always be counted upon to have a merry quip to meet every occasion. In fact, it's his capacity to find humour in any situation that appears eventually to drive the remainder of the group insane. In moderation, his sense of humour can be a considerable asset and can help to break down barriers, to relax the group and to build up camaraderie. However, when subjected to frequent or prolonged exposure, the group lives in constant fear of saying something that might give rise to innuendo, double entendre or provide the cue for a joke.

  It is unlikely that a Jester will ever realise the anguish that he/she causes through insensitive remarks or inopportune humour. In fact, if the problem was pointed out to him, the chances are that he would be devastated, since his driving aim is to be "one of the lads" and accepted as part of the group

- **The Know-it-All:** There will usually be one or two very talkative people who wish to "show off" their knowledge, although sometimes they know little but just like to chatter (the "empty vessel"). Strategies for dealing with a Know-it-All include:
  - ° When asking a question, make eye contact elsewhere to allow other learners an opportunity to become involved

- ○ If a Know-it-All is talking at length, wait for a pause, briefly summarise, refocus and move on
- ○ Ask a tough question to slow them down.
- **The Quiet One:** The most likely cause of quietness is that the student is either timid or bored. Body language and other behaviour should help to identify to which category they belong
  - ○ Encourage the timid ones with easy questions and bolster their confidence
  - ○ Involve the bored ones by letting them participate in exercises, plan a session or even give a presentation
- **The Latecomer:** The most likely cause of lateness is a lack of motivation to attend. In dealing with a Latecomer:
  - ○ Focus the group away from door
  - ○ Acknowledge the presence of the Latecomer when they arrive
  - ○ Don't stop training to review
  - ○ Off-line, ask the Latecomer what would make the training session important enough for them to want to be on time
  - ○ Ask the Latecomer to do some task.
- **Early Leaver:** Some participants have a habit of leaving early, due to work or other pressures. In dealing with Early Leavers:
  - ○ At the beginning of the session, check to see whether everyone can stay until the end
  - ○ Don't confront the Leaver in group
  - ○ Check off-line to see why they leave.
- **Broken Record:** This individual is there only to make the same point over and over again. They can cause major disruption to the flow of the programme and can irritate the other trainees. In dealing with this type of trainee:
- Assure them that the idea is written into the group memory
- "Why don't we take three minutes now to hear what you've got to say ... then perhaps you can let go of it".

We offer some guidelines for dealing with the more difficult learner types in **Figure 8.8**.

FIGURE 8.8: GUIDELINES FOR HANDLING DIFFICULT TRAINEES

Type	Guidelines
Talking Terror	• Look for an opportunity to intervene. This may be a pause for breath or a moment's hesitation. Think or agree with the talker (few talkers will want to interrupt this vote of support) and then, having regained the group's attention, press home your advantage by redirecting their concentration elsewhere. For example: "Yes, Max, that would make sense. Does anyone else know of ways that we could achieve this?" • Check your understanding and then move on. For example: "Just a moment Max - so what you are saying is X, Y, Z. Has anyone else got a view on this?" • Speak to him/her during a convenient break and explain that you are pleased that he/she is participating but that you want to involve other members of the group in the discussion • Channel his/her energies elsewhere. Ask him/her to record all the ideas generated by the group on to a flip chart or seek his/her assistance as a technical operator of equipment or as an observer for the purposes of an exercise
Great Griper	• Allow him/her his/her say once. Let him/her clear it off his/her chest and then move on. "Fred, I can see that you feel strongly about this. Supposing we set aside three minutes now to discuss this and then let's agree to drop the matter until after the course?" • Turn the problem round and ask him what he would do about the problem and what action he would take. It could be that a simple solution does exist, in which case why hasn't he acted upon it?' "Fred, you've explained the problem to us. What would you want to see happen to resolve it?" • Acknowledge the gripe without accepting its validity and then take some form of positive action to lay it to rest. "I can appreciate why this might upset you, Fred, so let's get together at lunchtime and see if we can draft a memo to the MD/Sales Director/Chief Executive and get this sorted out"
Doubting Thomas	• Gain acceptance step by step. First by getting agreement that if an idea or process did work it would justify the time and effort spent learning it. If this is forthcoming, albeit reluctantly, the next step is to suggest that the Doubting Thomas agrees to suspend his judgement until the course is over and the end result can be evaluated • If the Doubting Thomas does not believe there is merit in the process, ask him/her to be specific about why he/she believes this and then seek his/her acceptance that the only way of proving who is right and who is wrong is by giving the process a fair chance
Pot Plant	• The approach that you take will depend on what you feel causes the Pot Plant's lack of participation. In all cases, the response should be to find a suitable opening to get the Pot Plant involved • If you assess his/her reluctance stems from insecurity, build up his/her confidence before the group by directing a question towards him/her when you know he/she will be able to answer it • Where the non-involvement is through lack of motivation, it could be that the Pot Plant doesn't appreciate how the topic relates to him/her. Take time to demonstrate the subject's impact (you might also consider whether a more stimulating training approach might help) • If the root cause for withdrawal is an inability to articulate ideas, this can be quickly remedied by phrasing questions in a way that draws a response without requiring a full explanation • For those whose preference is to listen rather than speak, it is for the trainer to accept that there can still be involvement without over-active participation.

Type	Guidelines
Jolly Jester	• The means of keeping control is to adopt the view that prevention is better than cure. Once he has begun a witty story, it becomes almost impossible to cut him/her off mid-flow. So the moment he/she appears to be laying the foundation for a joke or humorous tale, explain that there will be ample opportunity during the breaks or lunch to regale the group with anecdotes but that training time is at a premium. "Sorry, Martin, I know that we would all love to hear what happened when you went for an interview but unfortunately we haven't the time now. Perhaps you could buy us all a drink at the end of the session and tell us then" • Alternatively, use peer pressure to discourage him/her from making unwarranted interruptions.
Conspirators	• If the reason for the conspiratorial conversation appears to be to improve understanding, it may be that you are not explaining the material thoroughly or that there is some confusion. In either case, you will need to ask those involved whether a problem exists • When the discussion appears to be unrelated to the training, there are four possible approaches: • If the conversation seems to be coming to a close, ignore it and carry on • Stop talking and look at the conversationalists so that they become conscious that they are distracting you. If this doesn't happen immediately, wait and often someone else on the course will interrupt on your behalf • Ask them if there is an issue they would want to explore with the rest of the group (in practice, this is difficult to say without sounding like a school-teacher) The better approach is to acknowledge that they have matters they wish to pursue but that they will have the opportunity to do so in 30 minutes when they break • Using the name of one of the conspirators, pose a question to them as if oblivious of their current conversation, "Chris, are there any other ways we might ...?"

Dealing with Personal Conflicts

Occasionally, personality conflicts arise in learning situations. It is a challenge for any trainer to remember to draw upon their questioning, listening and feedback skills, in order to maintain or create the correct learning environment. Sometimes learners may come to a new situation, believing that they already know everything and resent being told what to do. Other times, trainees are not comfortable in their jobs and may act quiet or withdrawn. There are many reasons why a trainee may relate negatively in a training situation. However, your task as a trainer is to manage this difficult communication dynamic effectively. We suggest that you might use the troubleshooting process in **Figure 8.9**.

FIGURE 8.9: A TROUBLE-SHOOTING PROCESS FOR DEALING WITH DIFFICULT TRAINEES

Step 1: Get Yourself Out of the Way

Before attempting to influence a change in trainee behaviour, the trainer must first know his/her own feelings and get them out of the way. This is a critical step if the trainer is going to regain control of the situation. Ask:

- How am I feeling right now? Am I angry, hurt, cynical, confused, or frustrated?
- What do I really want from the trainee? Is it critical to the training process or just for my personal needs?
- Is what I am doing right now getting me closer to what I want? Is my current behaviour helping to resolve or perpetuate the situation?
- If not, what else could I be doing? Well, since I am accountable, it's up to me to try something different. Be willing to set your personal emotions aside.

Once the trainer has risen above personal needs, it is time to think about the trainee.

Step 2: Brainstorm the Possible Causes of the Behaviour

The trainer should start by getting clear what the specific behaviour is that is causing the difficulty. Next, brainstorm the possible causes of this behaviour. It should be remembered that the trainee is a human being with complex emotions. Look for the underlying beliefs or fears that may be the cause of the surface behaviour.

Step 3:   Confront the Situation with your Trainee

Now it's time for the trainer to talk to the trainee. Start by speaking plainly and directly about the behaviour, but be specific and accurate.

Next, ask open-ended questions about possible causes of that behaviour. List ideas about possible causes and ask if any of them might be true.

When the trainee responds to questions be ready to power listen for the 'true' message. Make sure to create connection with the trainee and find the places where it is possible to relate to them or agree with their point of view.

Step 4:   Negotiate an Agreement to Get Back on Track

The trainer should use his/her skills to give effective feedback to the trainee. Consider what is required and then ask the trainee to work towards building an agreement.

It may be necessary to remind the trainee of the original contract, which both the trainee and trainer signed. If there is a broken agreement at issue, be willing to review the signed contract and ask the trainee to honour his/her initial intentions.

Give the trainee encouragement and support for getting past the difficult issues, by using listening and feedback skills.

UNDERSTANDING FEEDBACK: THE "JOHARI" WINDOW

The "Johari" Window is a useful device when you are in learning situations that involve giving and receiving feedback. Two psychologists, Joseph Luft and Harry Ingham, originally developed the Johari Window model. This model is viewed as a communication window in which an individual gives and receives information about him/herself and others.

FIGURE 8.10: DIMENSIONS OF THE "JOHARI" WINDOW

		SELF	
		Solicits Feedback	
		Things I Know	Things I Don't Know
GROUP	Things they know	**ARENA**	**BLIND SPOT**
Self-disclosure	Things They don't know	**FACADE (Hidden Area)**	**UNKNOWN**

Source: Hardingham (1998).

The model can be perceived as a window where the information moves from one pane to another as the level of mutual trust and the exchange of feedback varies in the training group. Consequently, the size and shape of the panes will vary from time to time.

The **ARENA** pane consists of things that "I know about myself" and which "the group knows". This area promotes open exchange of information, since the behaviour is public and available to everyone. As the level of trust increases within the group, more information, particularly personal information, is shared

The **BLIND SPOT** contains information that "I don't know about myself" but which "the group may know". As an individual begins to participate in the group, they unconsciously communicate all kinds of information that is picked up by others – verbal cues, mannerisms, the way they say things, their style of relating to others. Individual insensitivity to their own behaviour and what it may communicate to others can be quite surprising and disconcerting. The trainer needs an insight into their own blind spots, otherwise they risk damaging the learning process

The **FACADE** or "hidden area" contains things that "an individual knows about him/herself" but of which "the group is unaware". For whatever reason, they keep this information hidden from others. They may fear that, if others knew of their feelings, perceptions and opinions, they might be rejected, be attacked or hurt, so they withhold this information. A trainer needs to share some of their private information with learners to make a connection and to create rapport. This requires strong levels of self-confidence.

The **UNKNOWN** contains things that "neither myself nor the group knows about me". Some of this may be so far below the surface that the individual may never become aware of it. Other material, however, may be below the surface of awareness of both the individual and the group but can be made public through an exchange of feedback. This may include such things as early childhood memories, latent potential, and unrecognised resources. Since the internal boundaries can move vertically and horizontally as a result of soliciting or giving feedback, it should be possible to have a window in which there would be no unknown, but it is unlikely that individuals will ever know everything about themselves.

Reducing the blind spot involves moving the vertical line to the right, since this area contains information that the group members know about the individual but of which he/she is unaware. The only way he/she can learn of it is to get feedback from the group. To encourage this, the trainer needs to develop a receptive attitude and actively solicit it in any way that the trainer will feel comfortable in giving it.

ARENA	BLIND SPOT
FAÇADE	UNKNOWN

ARENA	BLIND SPOT
FAÇADE	UNKNOWN

Reducing the FACADE involves moving the horizontal line down. Since this area contains information that individuals have been keeping from the group, the trainer can reduce it by giving feedback to the group or individuals about reactions to what is going on. Thus, the group does not need to guess about or interpret the meaning of a person's behaviour.

You will notice that, while reducing their Blind Spots and Facades through self-disclosure, giving and soliciting feedback, individuals are at the same time increasing the size of their Arena or public area. In this process, some people create an imbalance by tending to do much more of one than the other, which may affect their effectiveness in the group and others' reactions to them. The size and shape of the Arena, therefore is a result of both the amount of feedback shared and the ratio of giving *versus* soliciting feedback.

By examining four different window shapes, we can see how extreme ratios in terms of giving and soliciting feedback may appear to others in the group:

A   B   C   D

| A | BS | | A | BS | | A | BS | | A | BS |
| F | U | | F | U | | F | U | | F | U |

- **Ideal (A):** The size of the Arena increases as the level of the group awareness increases, facilitated by the exchange of feedback. The large Arena suggests that much of the trainer's behaviour and communication is above board and open, so there are fewer opportunities for interpretation (or misinterpretation) of an individual's behaviour. It is not necessary to have a large Arena with everybody, although when in a group or in significant relationships, many of an individual's feelings, perceptions and opinions are public, and there is less need for "game playing"

- **Interviewer (B):** The large Facade suggests a trainer whose participation style is to ask questions of the group without giving information or feedback – for example "What do you think about this?", "How would you have acted in my shoes?", "How do you feel about what I just said?". The person wants to know where other people stand before committing him/herself on issues and it is hard to know where he/she stands. He/she may eventually evoke reaction or irritation, distrust and withholding, or may confront him/her with a statement similar to "You are always asking me how I feel about what's going on, but you never say how you feel yourself"

- **Bull in a China Shop (C):** This window with a large Blind spot indicates a person who gives feedback but solicits very little from others. Their participation style is to tell the group what he/she thinks of them, how he/she feels about what is going on in the group, and where he/she stands on group issues. Sometimes they may lash out at individuals or criticise the group as a whole, believing that they are being open and above board. They may appear insensitive to the feedback given to them, not hearing what group members tell him/her or may respond in a way that makes the group reluctant to continue giving him/her feedback – for example, get angry, cry, or threaten to leave. They are unlikely to know how they come across to other people, appearing to be out of touch or evasive. The result of this one-way communication (from him/her to others) is that they persist in behaving ineffectively as they do not know which behaviour to change

- **Turtle (D):** This window represents the person who does not know much about him/herself, nor does the group know much about them, as he/she neither gives nor asks for feedback. They may be the silent member or the "observer", insulating him/herself within a shell, which makes it difficult for others to know where he/she stands or where they stand with him/her. When confronted about their lack of involvement, they may respond with "I learn more by listening". The turtle's shell keeps people from getting in, and him/herself from getting out, by not providing the group with any data to which they can react.

The purpose of soliciting feedback, providing self-disclosure and giving feedback is to move information from the Blind Spot and the Facade into the Arena, where it is available to everyone. In addition, through the feedback process, new information can move from the Unknown into the Arena. A person may have an "Aha!" experience, when they suddenly perceive a relationship between a here-and-now interaction in the group and some previous event, which could be called "insight" or "inspiration".

It is not an easy task to give feedback in such a way that it can be received without threat to the receiver. It requires practice in becoming sensitive to other people's needs and being able to put yourself in their shoes. The effective giving and receiving of feedback relies on acceptance of yourself and others. As this acceptance increases, the need to give feedback that can be construed as evaluative or judgmental decreases.

STRUCTURING THE PHYSICAL LEARNING ENVIRONMENT

A major issue that will determine the effectiveness of your learning event is the seating arrangement that you use and where you will position yourself in the learning situation.

Your Position in the Training Plan

You should consider your own position at the beginning of a learning session. Will you stand behind a podium, sit in a chair with no barrier between you and the participants, stand at the front and move around a little, or will you first take one position and then shift to another? The answers to these questions depend on the atmosphere required, the nature of the opening activity, and what makes you feel comfortable.

Using a podium provides a degree of formality and emphasises your authority. a podium is appropriate for formal presentation occasions, like the opening of a conference for the beginning of an induction course for new staff. On the other hand, sitting in a chair with no barrier between you and participants indicates an informal relaxed approach with open discussion. If you choose to stand at the front and move around, the atmosphere is less relaxed and more purposeful; in particular, by moving towards participants, you encourages their contributions and involvement. Quite often, you will need to take up one position in order to make any introductory remarks, then shift to another position for the opening activity.

Seating Position of Learners

There are numerous ways of laying out a training room. We suggest seven alternative layouts that you can use in a training situation. Some commentators argue that there are two primary layouts that are especially useful because trainers have discovered that they are particularly effective.

The V-shaped Layout
This is illustrated in **Figure 8.11**. It gives all participants a clear and unobstructed view of the facilitator and the overhead projector screen. Trainers like the V shape because it gives the learners a better view of each other and the front of the training room. However, it requires a significant amount of space and you will usually need breakout tables to use for small group work.

FIGURE 8.11: THE V-SHAPE LAYOUT

Formal U-Shaped Style

The U-shaped pattern is mainly used for facilitation sessions, which involve a presentation or demonstration supported by visual aids. The U-shape allows the facilitator to walk into and move around the U, to increase his/her contact with participants and encourage involvement in discussion or practical exercises. Participants at the rear of the U may, however, be too far from the screen, flip-chart or video. Small group work can also be difficult to organise, and you may need to move furniture to provide the necessary pace for learners. **Figure 8.12** presents the formal U-shape style.

FIGURE 8.12: THE FORMAL U-SHAPE LAYOUT

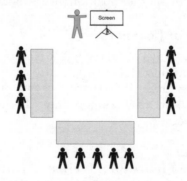

The Group Style

Furniture set out in a small group-style indicates an emphasis on group work and encourages an informal atmosphere and exchange of ideas. If the facilitator has to make a formal presentation, however, this arrangement may lead to a lack of attention among some participants and side conversations may develop in some groups.

FIGURE 8.13: THE GROUP-STYLE SEATING LAYOUT

Figure 8.14 presents a variation of the group style. The placement of separate groups at each table facilitates the transition from large group work to small group sessions, since the participants don't have to move for subgroup work, as they are already at their individual workshop tables. If the content of a training programme requires considerable small group work, then this payout should probably be selected over the V or the U arrangements.

FIGURE 8.14: A VARIATION OF THE GROUP-STYLE LAYOUT

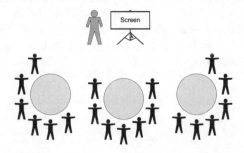

Team Conference Style
The team conference style, consisting of tables in a complete square, is best used when the facilitator is working with a team and acting more as a team leader. This arrangement encourages an atmosphere of teamwork and allows participants to work together and share information easily. However, it can be limiting in terms of creating sub-groups.

FIGURE 8.15: THE TEAM CONFERENCE-STYLE LAYOUT

Conference / Lecture Style

Rows of tables and chairs indicate a formal conference or lecture session where large numbers of participants need to be accommodated and not much audience participation is expected. This arrangement provides a high degree of control but there is a lack of opportunity for participants to interact. If the facilitator wants some participation in this setting, he/she needs to encourage and provide opportunities for interaction – for example, by providing a question and answer period and encouraging people from the back to contribute. The facilitator is in control and participants cannot communicate easily with each other. This layout is similar to classroom conditions and adults can be intimidated by the connection with school. It is conducive to a facilitator-led interaction with "jug and mug" connotations.

FIGURE 8.16: THE CONFERENCE / LECTURE-STYLE SEATING LAYOUT

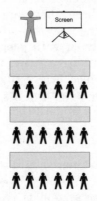

Complete Circle
By sitting in a circle with participants without tables, the facilitator can eliminate barriers and create greater participation. However, some participants may be intimidated by over-exposure and limit their contributions – see **Figure 8.17**.

FIGURE 8.17: THE COMPLETE CIRCLE SEATING LAYOUT

Seating Position of Learners
Another important preparation decision is how you divide participants for any group work. In particular you may want to mix people and avoid putting participants from the same work-area together.

One of the things participants look forward to when they attend a training session is to get a break from the same old faces, views and problems. Working with participants from their own work-area may detract from their enjoyment and the productivity of the group. It may also lead to conflict and disruption when feelings, suppressed on the job, are set free in the "safe setting" that a training session can provide.

A related issue to consider here is whether the trainer wants participants to choose where they sit. Communication and the effectiveness of the training may be adversely affected if, at the beginning, participants only sit with people they know. One way to ensure a mix from the start is to write out participant name-cards and place them on the tables before they arrive. Not only do the trainer and participants benefit from the mix, but the trainer also avoids a cliquish atmosphere from the beginning.

Equipment

Most important of all, the trainer should set up and check in advance the equipment to be used.

Make sure the projector system is ready and the slides can be seen, the video has been rewound and is ready to start at the beginning, so there will no technical hitches to disrupt the session. Check the lighting, and whether it can be adjusted – for example, for showing slides or a video. The trainer should also check the ventilation – a room that is stuffy or very warm may lull participants to sleep, especially if the trainer needs to talk for much of the time. **Figure 8.18** presents a summary of a number of issues that you need to consider.

FIGURE 8.18: PHYSICAL LEARNING ENVIRONMENT CHECKLIST

Room	Overhead Projector	Audio or Video Equipment	Flip Charts	Participant's Materials	Facilitator's (Trainer's) Materials
• Tables? • Chairs? • Sign on door? • Temperature? • Refreshments? • Electrical Outlets • Other (specify)	• Positioned correctly? • Extension cord? • Extra bulb? • Focus adjusted? • Projector screen • Room light OK? • Positioned? • Stand for tables • Other (specify)	• Video player? • Correct size tape? • Monitor? • Screen size proportional for room size? • Extension cords? • Video recorder? • Video camera? • Appropriate connecting cables? • Audio player/recorder • Speakers? • Microphone? • Other (specify)	• Extra paper? • Magic markers (washable vs. permanent)? • Masking tape? • Easel(s)? • Other (specify)	• Handouts? • Name tags? • Coffee or other beverages? • Extra paper? • Pencils? • Other (specify)	• Leader's guide? • Evaluations? • Video tape(s)? • Overhead transparencies? • Temporary transparency marking pen or pencil? • Transparency "write-on" film? • Other (specify)

PREPARING LEARNERS FOR THE LEARNING EVENT

The period before the learning event is an important one. You can view it as a time to inform and notify learners of the learning event and to foster an environment of trust, openness and participation by the learners in the learning.

Whether trainees have been "sent" to the programme, or are coming voluntarily, it is vital that they know its objectives and how it is to be conducted. Effective notification procedures are essential in underlining the programme objectives. Notification is also a useful way of requiring some pre-learning reading or work to be done, and this can allow more use of the timetable for learning.

The pre-programme period is also a time for the learner and line manager to review the programme objectives and to make sure that the learner can draw the most out of the experience. As pointed out in earlier chapters, the active involvement of the line manager will be an important factor in facilitating learning transfer.

Your tasks in the pre-programme period might include:

- **Needs and Expectations:** The pre-programme period is a good time to carry out a training needs analysis by meeting the line manager and potential trainees one-by-one. This prepares the participants for the content of the programme and generates buy-in and commitment. It also gives the trainer the opportunity to tailor the training content to suit the needs of the target group. Further, it assists in getting a general feel for the learning objectives and for each learner's strengths and opportunities for development. It is not always possible to carry out such an in-depth analysis so, failing this, it is a good idea to carry out a "concerns and expectations" exercise with the group at the start of the programme. Again, this gives the trainer a chance to get a fix on each individual and to give them a quick opportunity to make their training group specific

- **Creating the Right Learning Atmosphere:** Preparing the learners also involves creating the right learning environment. You need to generate a feeling of trust, openness and participation in the group. Sometimes, it is important to establish a confidentiality clause in the course. Learning new skills can be quite a vulnerable thing for an adult so anything that happens within the training environment should be kept within it.

Figure 6.1 presents a summary of ice-breakers, energisers and buzz groups you can use to create an appropriate learning atmosphere.

UNDERSTANDING THE ROLE OF GROUP DYNAMICS IN A TRAINING CONTEXT

Most formal training takes place in group settings. These groups may range in size from four participants to possibly 20.

When a group comes together, they may be doing so for the first time. It is unusual for a training session to be conducted with a well-established work group. Given this, it is important that you understand the dynamics and interactions of small groups when they meet for the first time. The cohesiveness of your learners will depend on the group's backgrounds, their emotional maturity, emotional needs and the extent to which they come from the same business unit or organisation.

Four dimensions of group dynamics are important in order for you to more fully understand how learning groups may function:

- The development process through which groups evolve
- Learner needs within the group
- The phenomenon of consensus or agreement within a team
- The types of team roles that learners may adopt in team learning situations.

Group Formation

According to Tuckman, groups generally evolve through four stages of development: forming, storming, norming and performing:

- **Stage 1 – Forming:** When a group comes together for the first time, they are naturally apprehensive about why they are there and what is to be achieved. Learners are somewhat polite, guarded, even nervous and uncertain. You need to create an atmosphere of trust and participation, by breaking the ice and creating buy-in

- **Stage 2 – Storming:** Once the group get to know each other, a certain jockeying for position occurs. Tension and emotion can run high and disagreements can occur on how the task has to be completed. The Storming stage is important because, if it is successful, it unites the group and gets them focused on using effective working structures and procedures. As a trainer, you need to adopt a supportive role here and be skilled in using conflict resolution skills assertively. A leader could emerge at this state. The group can then move on to the Norming stage

- **Stage 3 – Norming:** Conflict and hostility starts to be controlled and an emerging sense of harmony pervades. The group comes together as a co-ordinated unit, trust emerges in a leader and they develop norms of acceptable behaviour. However, it is important to note that over-adherence to group norms can result in a negative phenomenon of group-think. You need to give plenty of encouragement to keep up momentum at this stage

- **Stage 4 – Performing:** The group needs to progress effectively through the first three stages, before it can arrive at the Performing stage, where it puts all the energy and focus into achieving its task.

- **Stage 5 – Mourning / Ending:** The final stage is Mourning/ Ending, where the task has been accomplished and it is time for the team to disband. The trainer needs to address any outstanding issues at this stage and ask for feedback.

Understanding the stages and typical problems associated with working with groups can help you to identify proactively problems occurring in groups and deal with them appropriately. **Figure 8.19** summarises some of the activities that you can undertake to manage the group formation process.

FIGURE 8.19: BEHAVIOURS OF THE GROUP: FACILITATOR / TRAINER TIPS

Stage	Characteristics	Trainer Implications
Forming	• Initial entry of members • Confusion, uncertainty • Feeling out others • Assessing the situation • Getting acquainted	• Establish ground rules • Create environment • Establish buy-in • Stage expectations • Goals, vision
Storming	• Tension and emotion high • Hostility and in-fighting may occur • Discussion about tasks, alternatives and possible actions • Clique formation • Feeling trapped • Demotivated	• Clarify objectives • Supportive role • Facilitate conflict resolution assertively • Get group to solve problems
Norming	• Group comes together as a co-ordinated unit • There is a balancing of forces • Trust is established in leader • Emerging sense of harmony	• Encourage positive norms • Discourage negative norms • Discourage excessive "group-think" • Watch for spillage to storming
Performing	• Emergence of a well-functioning group • Group able to deal with complex tasks and handle disagreements • Group structure stable	• Give plenty of encouragement • Keep up momentum • Do not relax • Beware of "group-think"
Mourning / Ending	• Team disbands • An important stage for many temporary groups, including project teams and committees • There may be feelings of sadness experienced at the end	• Address outstanding issues • Ask for feedback • Offer praise and rewards • Create networks or arrangements to meet in the future

The Needs of Learners in Group Situations

It is a generally accepted principle of social psychology that people need other people and that they will seek to establish compatible relationships with others in social interactions. The group context of a training situation has to accommodate these needs in order for learners to work effectively in team situations.

Schutz (1988) put forward a classification of these needs:

- **Inclusion:** The need to include others (expressed inclusion) and the need to be included by others (wanted inclusion)
- **Control:** The need to control others (expressed control) and the need to be controlled by others (wanted control)
- **Openness:** The need to form close relationships with others. Learners may be expressing openness towards other people and/or wanting openness to be expressed towards them.

In the context of a learning event, you will need to address these needs effectively

- **Inclusion Needs:** Learners need to understand why they are on the course and whether other group members will accept them. You can resolve inclusion issues in the following way:
  - ° Open the programme with introductions and allow people to establish, identify and place themselves and each other
  - ° Use learner's names
  - ° Use pre-course information
  - ° Use an effective room layout
  - ° Make good eye contact
  - ° Include late comers smoothly
- **Control Needs:** Once learners feel they are on the right learning programme, control issues come into action. Learners need to know who is in charge, their own levels of control and responsibility for outcomes. You need to understand control issues, as they can be very disruptive if not addressed correctly. Control issues can be addressed by:
  - ° Structuring groups and tasks to ensure full contribution
  - ° Divide and re-divide big groups into sub-groups to avoid cliques and power plays
  - ° Using skilful facilitation skills
  - ° Avoid power-based confrontations
  - ° Use conflict diffusion skills
- **Affection Needs:** Learners are concerned with how much respect, recognition, feedback and interpersonal contact they can get from each other. They need to know that their self-esteem will stay

intact. If you manage inclusion and control issues effectively, you will allow learners to explore affection issues for themselves.

You need to keep a professional distance from the group in order to help them manage their needs. You cannot become part of the group.

Group Consensus and Agreement

The issues of how consensus and agreement emerges in a group are well-studied. Harvey (1974) proposed the Abilene Paradox to explain how groups frequently take actions that contradict what they really want to do and that defeat the very purposes they are trying to achieve. He also proposed that groups sometimes find it difficult to manage agreement, which can have very negative consequences for the functioning of a group.

Many training situations involve the use of group learning processes. Therefore you need to be conscious of the symptoms of the Abilene Paradox in team learning situations. **Figure 8.20** summarises some of the issues that you can look out for.

FIGURE 8.20: SYMPTOMS OF THE ABILENE PARADOX IN A TRAINING SITUATION

1.	Learners feel pain, frustration, and feelings of impotence or sterility when trying to cope with the problem. There is a lot of apparent conflict.
2.	Learners agree privately, as individuals, as to the nature of the problem or learning task.
3.	Learners also agree, privately, as individuals, as to the steps required to cope with the problem.
4.	There is a great deal of blaming others for the conditions they are in.
5.	Learners break into sub-groups of trusted friends to share rumours, complaints, fantasies, or strategies relating to the problem or its solution.
6.	Learners fail to communicate their desires and beliefs to others accurately. They are likely to communicate just the opposite of what they mean.
7.	Learners make collective decisions that lead them to take actions contrary to what they personally and collectively want to do.
8.	As a result of such counterproductive actions, learners experience even greater anger, frustration, irritation and dissatisfaction with the organisation.

If these symptoms are manifest in a group-learning situation, then you will need to make reference to it in your feedback on how will they accomplish the learning task. You may also need to intervene in the learning task when they experience a major roadblock.

Group Roles in Learning Situations

Learners tend to adopt different roles in a learning situation. Belbin, who has conducted extensive research in this area, proposes that learners in a group situation may perform three types of roles:

- **Action-oriented Roles:** Shaper, Implementer and Completer-Finisher
- **People-oriented Roles:** Co-ordinator, Team-worker and Resource Investigator
- **Cerebral Roles:** Plant, Monitor, Evaluator and Specialist.

You can observe these roles in team learning activities. The characteristics of these nine roles are explained in **Figure 8.21**.

FIGURE 8.21: BELBIN TEAM-ROLE TYPES & LEARNING PREFERENCES

BELBIN Team-Role Type	Contributions	Allowable Weaknesses	Learning Preferences
Plant	• Creative, imaginative, unorthodox • Solves difficult problems	• Ignores incidents • Too preoccupied to communicate effectively	• Small group learning situations • Free-form rather than highly-structured • High-level training situations
Co-ordinator	• Mature, confident, a good chairperson • Clarifies goals, promotes decision-making and delegates well	• Can often be seen as manipulative • Off-loads personal work	• Leading small group discussions • Good at facilitating and gathering ideas • Likes a high level of involvement in training
Monitor-Evaluator	• Sober, strategic and discerning • Sees all options • Judges accurately	• Lacks drive and ability to inspire others	• Preference for more structured learning situations • Likes summaries and key points • Less inclined to participate in small group activities

BELBIN Team-Role Type	Contributions	Allowable Weaknesses	Learning Preferences
Implementer	• Disciplined, reliable, conservative and efficient • Turns ideas into practical actions	• Somewhat inflexible • Slow to respond to new possibilities	• Preference for highly-structured learning situations • Generally receptive to ideas and the expert knowledge of the trainer • Likes practical-type training situations
Completer-Finisher	• Painstaking, conscientious, anxious • Searched out errors and omissions • Delivers on time	• Inclined to worry unduly • Reluctant to delegate	• Likes detail; prefers systematic and well-structured learning situations • Likes to be in control of the learning • May like the training to proceed at an even pace
Resource Investigator	• Extrovert, enthusiastic, communicative • Explores opportunities • Develops contacts	• Over-optimistic • Loses interest once initial enthusiasm has passed	• Likes small group training situations • Will bring energy to the training event • May be difficult to retain their interest
Shaper	• Challenging, dynamic, thrives on pressure • The drive and courage to overcome obstacles	• Prone to provocation • Offends people's feelings	• May not listen very effectively to trainer • Will have a strong desire to get involved and challenge the trainer • Will likely have strong opinions and will need to be managed carefully
Team-worker	• Co-operative, mild, perceptive and diplomatic • Listens, builds, averts friction	• Indecisive in crunch situations	• Will listen carefully to what the trainer has to say • May have a dislike of ambiguous training situations • Will be effective in small group activities
Specialist	• Single-minded, self-starting, dedicated • Provides knowledge and skills in rare supply	• Contributes only on a narrow front • Dwells on technicalities	• Will bring a level of expert knowledge to a learning event • Will be concerned with the technical expertise of the trainer • May have difficulty accepting ideas that do not fit in with own knowledge base

BEST PRACTICE INDICATORS

Some of the best practice issues that you should consider related to the contents of this chapter are:

- The training situation is one where an understanding of the psychological characteristics of individual or groups will be beneficial to your effectiveness as a trainer

- Training is an arena of communication, where trainees are given cues that help them learn and training content, such as diagrams, recall modes, key behaviours and advanced organisers

- Non-verbal behaviour plays an important role in explaining your effectiveness as a trainer, so you must be skilled in reading and interpreting it

- Communication in a training situation is about perception, expectation, making demands and achieving understanding

- Many training situations involve group communications, which are more complex, more likely to involve conflict, require you as a trainer to balance control with flexibility and to promote consensus and decision-making

- Learners have different needs in group training situations. These include sharing, integrating, encouraging, progressing, asserting. There will also be task dimensions such as starting information exchange, decision-making and action planning

- You should adapt an instructional style that reflects the maturity of your group, their comfort in learning situations, their existing knowledge and their expectations of you as a trainer

- You should design the layout of your training room to reflect the training objectives you wish to achieve. You will also need to consider the physical limitations of the training room and the duration of your learning event.

Reflections on Training & Development Scenario

Managing Claire: You will need to seek an opportunity to reassure Claire that the company values her expertise. You may get this opportunity at the first coffee break. A good way to recognise her experience, and to change her attitude to the Induction Programme, is to tell her that you would really value her inputs. You can reinforce this message when you are presenting, by asking Claire for her views and expertise. In addition to this intervention, you should outline to Claire the unique aspects of this company that will be explored at the Induction Programme.

Managing John: You will need to introduce some small group exercises to encourage John to participate. He will be more likely to contribute in a paired discussion or a triad discussion. If he speaks in front of the whole group, give him lots of positive feedback (head-nodding, smiling, verbal encouragement). In the small groups, make sure that John is not paired with Jackie! Throughout the two days, you will need to make an effort to encourage John – for example, at lunch breaks, etc. If you help him to break into the group, he will have lots to contribute.

Managing Jackie: During group discussions, you will need to intervene directly with Jackie. She will keep talking if you do not interrupt her. You can say "Thank you very much for that contribution. Now, does anyone else have another view?" In a small group session, you could approach the group that Jackie is in and suggest that she takes the notes. This will give the others a greater opportunity to participate. It might be appropriate to say to Jackie at a break that you really appreciate her inputs, but you would also like her to give others a chance to contribute.

Chapter Nine

DELIVERING EFFECTIVE TRAINING: CORE COMPETENCIES

LEARNING OBJECTIVES

Upon completion of this chapter, **you** should be able to:

- Understand the differences between an instructor and facilitator approach to training

- Describe the core competencies that you require to be an effective instructor and facilitator

- Describe the steps involved in on-the-job training instruction

- Understand the factors that you have to consider when making a training presentation to a small or large group of participants

- Understand and use a number of different questioning techniques in a range of training situations

- Understand the role of listening in a training context and be able to practise active listening

- Understand the purpose of feedback in a training situation and be able to use a range of feedback techniques

- Be able to facilitate training situations and use a range of facilitation skills and behaviours

- Prepare written training materials that suit the specific learning purposes you wish to achieve

- Understand and apply a number of non-verbal communication skills in a training situation.

A Training & Development Scenario

You are the Training & Development Manager of one of the country's leading companies supplying a diverse range of electronic, analytical and computational products and services. It has always been characterised by high innovation and quality, and for its positive values related to managing its people.

By the mid-1980s, a combination of external pressure meant that the company managers had to become more strategic in their culture and abilities, capable of responding to the macro issues the company was facing, both as individuals and as members of a company-wide management community. The managers come mainly from a technical background, and fewer than 40% have any formal business education. Most have worked for years in an extremely successful company, where costs received little emphasis. They are also used to the autonomy and local cultures of the company's functional matrix management system. With key markets on the decline, new technology needing heavy investment, major competition from small companies and low-cost foreign combines, and costs rising rapidly within the company, these managers must now quickly learn new attitudes and become much more entrepreneurial in their abilities and outlook.

Working with a national business school whose reputation for high quality, effective business programmes is excellent, you now have to design a company-wide management development programme aimed at senior middle managers, aged 30-40, with 10 years or more of service in the company, a technical background and education, and responsible for 20-50 people. Promotion prospects are decreasing, so it is important that this programme is not seen as a promotion ticket, but as a way of improving managerial competence in current roles. Key criteria for the programme are:

- It must be business-focused, cost-effective, have the involvement of senior management, and reflect corporate issues
- It must be capable of being delivered by each of the company's regional training teams, and within their resources
- It must emphasise manager's responsibility for self-development, and stimulate them to a real commitment in this respect
- Teamwork must be a key feature of the design, so that participants learn from and support each other in the learning processes
- The programme must focus on making the target population more effective in their current role.

Task: What training style should you adopt to address the issues outlined in this scenario? How could you use feedback in this learning situation to facilitate the quality of learning?

INTRODUCTION

We focus in this chapter on the core competencies you require to deliver effective training. If you are a direct trainer, you are likely to perform an instructor role, either in an on-the-job or course context. You may also be required to adopt a more facilitator role, which requires the use of a different mix of the competencies that we consider in this chapter. The competencies that you require whether you perform an instructor or facilitator role: instructing, questioning, listening, facilitating, giving and receiving feedback and the role of non-verbal behaviour competencies.

THE DELIVERY CONTINUUM: INSTRUCTION TO FACILITATION

Most direct training activities that you will be required to undertake will fall within the continuum: instruction to facilitation. Below we outline the key features of each concept.

Instruction

When you perform an instruction role, you are involved in programmed learning. This requires the direct transmission of predetermined learning objectives. The delivery task you must perform is to follow the key steps of instruction:

- You are expected to have, and to follow, a set of learning objectives for all parts of the learning event
- You are expected to be comprehensive, yet keep things simple. You are expected to specify what you expect to achieve, to sequence the material and to practice it, to show and tell and to test that these learners are performing to the level you require
- Preparation is a key task that you will be expected to undertake, involving developing materials, presentations and simulations and appropriate tasks to ensure that all objectives are addressed
- You will need to give consideration to how best to create, and maintain, the interest of your learners. Instruction is a didactic activity and your materials will need to be engaging, your tasks and activities motivating and your training room instruction engaging for your learners
- Instruction requires you to be concerned with modelling. You should provide learning through imitation, "Do it the way I do it". You will also need to be concerned with managing the retention of information and procedures
- Timing is an important issue, keep everything in perspective
- Practice and feedback are core elements. They enable you to manage trial and error. You will need to ensure that practice is

realistic and reflects the actual job conditions. Practice will allow you to reinforce the correct ways and eliminate those that are not.

We know from research that effective instructors possess five important characteristics:

- Consistency, managing repeated delivery of the same training activity
- Very organised and focused on detail, in order to ensure that all aspects of the instruction process are effective
- Cognisant of, and taking account of, the learning abilities of your training group
- Demonstrating patience with the core element of the instruction process, which is showing and telling, trial and error
- Maintaining objectivity in assessing the knowledge, capabilities and behaviours of learners.

You will realise that some of the core principles of instruction create tensions and conflict with the principles of adult learning that we outlined in **Chapter Three**. Adult learners may find the instruction context difficult for a number of reasons:

- They are more likely to vary in terms of experience
- They are likely to get bored easily with didactic and instructor type sessions
- They dislike feeling exposed and seek to avoid embarrassment
- They are likely to feel vulnerable in feedback situations
- They may have negative perceptions of the training room situation, largely derived from their experience at school
- Sometimes they have a dislike of being "taught".

Therefore, you may prefer to adopt an alternative approach; nonetheless, the nature of your learning objectives may require that you adopt an instructor style.

Facilitation

Facilitation is at the other end of the continuum, involving the use of a range of techniques and methods that enable your learners to discover, to participate and to experience. Facilitation is a role that direct trainers are increasingly required to perform, primarily because of the needs of adult learners and the changing nature of learning activities in organisations, which are increasingly complex and are most amenable to being taught using an facilitator style.

When you perform in the role of facilitator, you manage the learning process through the use of participative methods and reflection on experiences that you share with the learner. You do not assume that learners are empty vessels to be filled up, but are capable and come to the learning situation with capacity for ideas and current skills.

As a facilitator, you will be very concerned to establish and maintain rapport with your participants. You will need to foster an atmosphere of trust, where your learners are free to share opinions and ideas. If you can achieve this atmosphere, you will have eliminated many of the barriers to effective learning. As facilitator, you will be concerned to balance the training content with the process dimensions of your learning group. In order to be fully effective, you will need to develop a good relationship with your learners and fully involve them in activities that facilitate learning.

There are six dimensions of facilitation that you may be required to perform during a training session:

- **Planning:** You will be concerned to clarify the aims of the learning and the goals. This will most likely be a joint activity

- **Meaning:** You will be concerned to ensure that participants understand what is going on, so that they will be able to relate it to their own experiences

- **Confronting:** This is a difficult task, but may be necessary. You may need to get your learners to face up to things that they generally tend to avoid. You will need to raise the learners' consciousness of key issues

- **Feelings:** Learners will have feelings and emotions about the learning task, so you will need to think about how to manage them

- **Structuring:** This is a more formal dimension of your role as a facilitator, where you will be concerned with the structure and form in which the learning should take place

- **Valuing:** This dimension is concerned with attempts to build a supportive atmosphere. Your aim here is to ensure that participants feel empowered and that you are meeting their needs and interests.

Instructors are generally required to specify right or wrong. This is less likely to be the case with facilitation, where facilitators are usually required to give feedback on ideas, capabilities and behaviour – note, however, that this is less likely to be in a context where there is a need to specify a "one best way".

In order for you to be an effective facilitator, you will need to be effective on the following competencies, which we address in this chapter, and have already addressed in **Chapter Seven**:

- Understand individual development and group processes and dynamics. You are less concerned with the subject matter knowledge that you possess

- You will need to understand where your learners are likely to encounter difficulties in learning and how you can facilitate progress
- You will spend a lot of time creating a positive environment for learning. You can achieve this by using some of the participative methods we considered in **Chapter Six**. Your aim is to develop a supportive, but challenging, relationship
- You will keep the learning process on track, using a combination of questioning, probing, challenging and feedback. Therefore, you will need well-developed interpersonal skills. To interact effectively with your learners, you will need to develop empathy, integrity, and responsiveness and be emotionally stable
- The flip-chart is central to your activities as a facilitator. You will use it to set tasks and summarise, and to get the learners to prepare their presentations. In this context, your skills in listening, questioning and challenging are also important
- You will need to be skilled to observe and respond with effective feedback, which is central to your effectiveness as a facilitator.

Figure 9.1 provides a summary of the problems that may arise when you are performing either of these roles and some of the strategies that you can use to deal with them.

DEVELOPING EFFECTIVE TRAINING COMPETENCIES

We have outlined the continuum of roles that you may be required to undertake in order to deliver training effectively in an organisation. We have made reference to a number of skills or competencies that you require to be effective. We will spend the remainder of this chapter focusing on three training situations and the competencies that you require in order to perform them. **Figure 9.2** provides an outline of these training situations and the underpinning competencies.

FIGURE 9.1: PROBLEMS ENCOUNTERED WHEN PERFORMING INSTRUCTION & FACILITATION ROLES

	Problem	Cause	Potential Solution
Instruction	• Learners find the instruction too dull • Little buy in from learners • Too contrived and non related to experience • Not keeping on track • Little chance for learners to question and consolidate • Pitched at an inappropriate level • Too directive and authoritarian • Little or no feedback from learners • Poor presentation style, material and handouts • Lack of preparation and knowledge	• Too much information and lack of variety in presentation style • Mandatory attendance rather than discretionary • All theory and no practice • Instructor not able to judge pace • Too much instruction and lack of confidence to open up to questioning • Lack of preparation and little knowledge of learners • Does not know learners needs • Lack of time to involve learners • Too rigid an approach • An inexperienced trainer	• Vary style within training room • Define and convey clear aims and objectives • Prepare and make time to get to know learners • Keep to time-table • Encourage participation in use of ice-breakers, room layout and practice • Review, improve materials and make changes • Work on presentation style • Encourage questions and be prepared to answer them • Enhance confidence and start with smaller groups • Get to know job and do 'train you' type training
Facilitation	• Poor group dynamics • Some learners are over-talkative or very quiet • Learners fears, personalities and attitudes • Difficulty in keeping facilitation focused on objectives • Difficulty to keep session on track • Facilitator is not competent • Different capacities among learners • Lack of learner motivation • Learning objectives not clearly specified	• Difficulties in selecting learners • Facilitator does not have skill to recognise and involve others • Lack of briefing and preparation of learners • Objectives not clear; poor time management • Poor prior planning of the learning • Lack of experience; new to facilitation role • Problems in responding in different ways to learners needs • May relate to reasons for training and/or the selection process • Lack of prior preparation	• Investigate learners and do some work to enhance dynamics • Tactfully stop talkative people and get all to contribute • Create a safe environment in which learning can take place • Allow time for reviews and have questions and answer sessions • Prior planning, think about timings • Develop facilitation skills • Respond flexibly to needs of learners • Focus on conditions in workplace which may enhance motivation • Take time out to define learning objectives

FIGURE 9.2: TRAINING ACTIVITIES & ASSOCIATED COMPETENCIES

Key Training Activities		
On-the-Job Training Instruction	**Making a Presentation to a Small/Large Group**	**Facilitating a Learning Situation**
• One-to-one interaction • Just-in-time • In the workplace • Structured • Very clearly defined learning objectives • Focus on content and reason	• Formal training situation • Focus on content • Highly-structured • Knowledge transfer • Less interaction from audience • Didactic	• Focus on process • Less structured • Driven by learner concerns • Group-oriented activity • Highly-dependent on skill of facilitator • Understanding of group dynamics
Trainer Competencies		
Listening	**Questioning**	**Feedback**
• Attending • Note-taking • Active listening • Networking • Summarising • Paraphrasing • Clarifying	• Asking questions • Responding to guidelines • Types of questions • Effective / ineffective questions • Questioning approach	• Different types of feedback • Giving and receiving feedback • Self-awareness • Understanding the motivational aspects • Understanding others
Non-Verbal Behaviours		
• Body language • Handshake • Sitting on the edge of the chair • Sitting back with arms folded • Crossing arms • Shrugging shoulders	• Head expressions • Eye contact • Smiling • Winking • Raising eyebrows • Blushing • Flushed • Lower lip changes • Breathing changes	• Physical proximity • Distance between people • Indication of liking and disliking • Intimate distance • Social distance • Personal distance • Public distance • Constantly looking at the wrist watch

On-the-Job or Job Training Instruction

On-the-job training is distinguished from other forms of training in that it is:

• Carried out at the work site

• Delivered while the learner is engaged in performing work tasks and activities

• Usually conducted on a one-to-one basis between the trainer and the learner.

We make a distinction between unplanned and planned on-the-job training. Unplanned on-the-job training is ineffective as a training practice – research shows that people cannot learn a detailed task simply by watching others. If the training is unplanned, it is unlikely that it will be organised around what the learner needs to know and do. Learners who observe activities in a poorly-organised work environment will find it difficult to make sense of what they are supposed to be learning and/or understand how the various elements of a task fit together.

If you wish to conduct a structured on-the-job learning, it is important that you base it on a thorough analysis of the work and that you use a high performer as the basis for your analysis. You should use the results of this analysis to demonstrate to a trainee what to do, to tell them about the content of each task and why each task is important.

Organisations are increasingly using experienced employees to act as trainers. Therefore, it is important that you train the employee in how to be an effective trainer. It is also important that you tailor your approach so that the learner has an opportunity to watch or observe, to ask, then perform and solicit feedback. On-the-job instruction is usually conducted with a small number of trainees. It is likely to be, in many cases, a 1:1 situation.

The popularity of on-the-job training is primarily due to the many advantages it has over off-the-job training. We consider it to have five important advantages:

* The trainee learns the actual duties and responsibilities that he/she will be required to perform
* The trainee learns in the actual working environment
* Some productivity takes place during training (although low initially)
* A close bond between the trainee and trainer may be created
* The often-prohibitive costs of off-the-job training (travel, lodging, seminar fees, etc) are avoided.

For these reasons, it is not surprising that trainers look to on-the-job training techniques to satisfy most training needs.

The most common form of on-the-job training is job instruction training (JIT). This method became popular as far back as World War II. It involves you instructing a small group of trainees in the actual work environment on key skills and knowledge that are necessary to perform a task or job.

On-the-job training (OJT) is appropriate:

* When the employee is required to engage in performance immediately, rather than simply acquire information. You can use OJT to demonstrate to trainees how to perform a task in a work-

setting, thus helping to reduce the transfer of training problem that is likely to occur if the training takes place off-the-job

- When time is a critical issue, or when you have limited time to organise effective off-the-job instruction
- When you have one trainee, or a small number of trainees, rather than a large cohort.

You should not use an on-the-job strategy, if there are health and safety issues in respect of the trainees or other employees. It is also unwise to use it where it may undermine a learner's credibility with customers.

We propose a four step approach to job instruction training:

- **Step 1. Prepare the Trainee:** Important points you should remember when preparing the trainee for training include:
  - ° Realise that the trainee may be anxious. Some anxiety is normal, although too much anxiety may hamper the learning process. Anxiety can be reduced by spending more time getting to know the trainee and assuring them that the objective is to help build skills and confidence. You can take other steps such as comfortable seating and lighting, creating a friendly atmosphere, smiling and using the trainee's names, encouraging the trainees to talk and ask questions and demonstrating enthusiasm about the task you are to complete
  - ° Find out what the trainee already knows about the job. Discuss relevant experiences the trainee may have had and determine how similar those experiences are to the job or task being taught. You should check the trainees' current knowledge, identify any taps in knowledge and explore similar training or situations the trainees have experienced
  - ° Put the training into context, by telling the trainees what the job/task is about. Explain how this job/task fits into wider work or the organisation / section and explain how the training relates to the job and other training sessions
  - ° Let the trainee know what is expected, by explaining the desired performance level in straightforward and unambiguous terms
  - ° Communicate the training plan. Let the trainee know what is in store for him/her (explain the training schedule, who will conduct the training, etc)
  - ° Arouse the trainees' interest, by explaining why this skill/procedure is so important and what the trainees will gain from acquiring it and by stating clearly the training objective, giving the trainees something to aim at

- ° Introduce trainees to all the materials, tools, equipment and new words they will encounter in the session.
- **Step 2. Present the Training:** The training can begin once the trainee has been prepared. Key points in this step include:
  - ° Go slowly, and explain thoroughly each step, one element at a time. For each step, clearly state its importance
  - ° Avoid jargon and technical terms. Speak in terms that are easily understood and make sure everything you say is understood. Be receptive to any questions from the trainee
  - ° Take your time. The trainee may be seeing the task for the first time. Train at a much slower pace than you would actually perform the task under normal working conditions
  - ° Show the overall task. Complete the task following precisely the procedure you identified in your task analysis; put all the steps into context; give the trainee a mental picture of what they have to do; and talk to the trainee establishing the critical points throughout. Summarise at the end
  - ° Stress the key points, correct procedure, and safety features. Relate what you are doing to the trainee's past experience.
  - ° Check understanding by repeating the task, with the trainee telling you what to do at each step. Ask questions that get them thinking. Check that they understand why you are performing in this order. Correct any errors as they occur and review the correct procedure. Encourage them to ask questions. Summarise the operation in a second run-through.
  - ° Repeat the job or task. Go through the task as many times as necessary to ensure that the trainee understands the process. Again, solicit questions from the trainee. Make sure the trainee understands there are no "dumb" questions.
- **Step 3. Tryout:** During this step, the trainee actually performs the task or job. Important considerations for this step include:
  - ° Play a coaching role, while the trainee tries out the task or job. A good coach strives to build skill and confidence in the learner, and provide feedback throughout the task. Feedback should be both positive (when the learner does the task correctly) and developmental (when the learner is having trouble with a task)
  - ° If the learner is having difficulty, use constructive criticism to overcome problem areas
  - ° Do not let the trainee form bad habits. Even though different people may perform a job or task slightly differently, look closely for inefficient methods or procedures and correct them immediately

○ Communicate with the trainee throughout the tryout. Ask questions to assess the trainee's understanding of what is being learned. Again, solicit questions

○ **Part Practice:** Let the trainee work through that stage. Have them tell you what they are going to do before they do it. Ask questions to establish they know why they are doing it that way. Encourage them to ask questions throughout. Give praise and constructive feedback. Have them to the task again, without having to tell you about what they are doing. Help them review their performance. Repeat the task with several different examples. Check their confidence and competence.

○ **Whole Practice:** During this component the trainee completes the while practice. Help them review overall performance Return to part practice for areas that are incomplete or need special attention. Repeat whole task with several different examples. Repeat whole task with several different examples. Start with simple and work up to more difficult.

• **Step 4. Follow Up:** The final step of the JIT technique takes place when the trainee begins to perform the job or task independently. Your job as a trainer continues until the trainee's performance continually meets expected performance levels. During this step:

○ Remember that the trainee may run into unexpected problems. Be accessible and approachable

○ Check back occasionally to make sure that things are running smoothly and to ensure that bad habits have not crept in to contaminate the learning

○ Continue to give feedback to the employee. Let them know that you are receptive to new ideas and suggestions that may make the job easier or more productive

○ Issue them with any notes or manuals

○ Check whether they found any of the steps particularly difficult

○ Ask for any questions on the process they have covered

○ Identify to whom, and where, they can go for further help

○ Summarise the whole process covered

○ Point out that this is the best method from a number of possibilities. Explain why some alternative methods have been tried but rejected

○ Check whether they have discovered any new or different techniques. Try out methods suggested by trainees. Do they produce acceptable results?

○ Suggest that they keep an open mind about any possible improvements

° Briefly review the required job performance standards for time, quantity, quality and safety.

Making a Formal Presentation to a Small or Large Group

A second training task you are likely to perform is making a formal training presentation within the context of a training course. You are still performing in an instructor mode. We explain some of the steps that you should consider when enhancing your presentation skills. Mastering the skills to make an effective presentation does not come easily.

Generally, the more rehearsal, the better. One or two rehearsals is usually not enough to master new material. It is a good idea to rehearse the presentation under simulated conditions – in a similar room, with listeners who can give suggestions for improvement. Mental rehearsing, by running through the presentation and the scene in your mind, is also effective. You should time the presentation to determine whether it is necessary to cut or expand the ideas. We know, from research, that practising a training presentation for short periods of time over the course of several days is more successful in reducing anxiety and improving memory than concentrated practice. Distributed practice is more efficient and yields better results than massed practice when mastering your training presentation skills.

There are a number of issues that you should pay attention to:

- **Practice Using Visual Aids:** This will help you to get used to handling visual aids and give some idea of how long the training will take with the visual aids. You should prepare for the totally unexpected. Consider the situation where the roar of an overhead plane drowns out your voice? What if the microphone goes dead, a window blows open, or the room becomes extremely hot? Compensate for minor disruptions by slowing the rate, raising the volume a little, and continuing. You will encourage listeners to listen to your message rather than be temporarily distracted. For other disruptions, a good rule of thumb is to respond the same way you would if you were in the audience. Take off your jacket if it is too hot, close the window, raise your voice if listeners cannot hear you, or pause to allow a complex idea to sink in.

- **Channel Your Anxiety:** You should also think about how you will channel your anxiety as you practice. It is common for trainers to report feeling anxious before they speak, it is normal. To manage anxiety, you should channel it into positive energy. Prepare well in advance for the training – develop ideas, support them and practice delivery. This way, even if you are anxious, you will have something important to say. It may help to visualise the speaking situation by closing your eyes, relaxing and thinking about how it is going to feel and what the audience will look like as they watch. You should expect to feel a little momentary panic as you get up to speak, it will evaporate as you progress into the speech. But remember that anxiety about speaking never really goes away. Most experienced trainers still get podium panic. The advantage of experience is that it gets easier; trainers learn to cope by converting their anxiety into energy and enthusiasm, which gives you an extra sparkle as you speak

- **Convey Controlled Enthusiasm for the Training:** Studies of effective trainers used adjectives such as flexible, co-operative, audience-oriented, pleasant and interesting. But only a few of these adjectives related to the content of the presentations. Enthusiasm is the hallmark of a good trainer. Learners will forgive other deficiencies, if you obviously love the subject and are genuinely interested in conveying that appreciation to the learners. Posture, tone of voice and facial expressions are all critical indicators of your attitude. Although enthusiasm is important, it must be controlled and should not be confused with loudness. Avoid bellowing or preaching at learners – it is enough that you can be easily heard and that your tone is sufficiently empathic to convey meaning effectively

- **Delivery:** Delivery should be used to enhance your training message and to maintain learner attention. Eye contact is the most important tool for establishing audience involvement, as it makes learners feel as if they are involved in a one-on-one, semi-private discussion with you. In Western culture, we value directness and honesty; one of the expressions of these values is direct eye contact.

You can enhance the overall quality of your training presentation if you follow a set of guidelines like the ones that we suggest in **Figure 9.3**.

FIGURE 9.3: GUIDELINES FOR TRAINER INTERPERSONAL EFFECTIVENESS

Use of Words	Tone of Voice	Body Language
• Avoid jargon and abbreviations	• Vary pace and volume to avoid monotony	• Dress appropriately, be and look efficient
• Use everyday familiar words, take care with regional colloquialisms	• Use a natural speaking voice, acting is difficult to maintain	• Move naturally
• Keep sentences short and simple	• Don't worry about having a regional accent, it can add interest	• Don't worry unduly about mannerisms, but beware of those that distract
• Talk at a level the audience will understand, but don't patronise or talk down to them	• Speak louder than usual, try to throw voice to the back of the room but don't shout, this strains the voice and deafens small groups	• Use the eyes to communicate the messages
• Paint verbal pictures by using examples, analogies and metaphors	• Over-emphasise and accentuate syllables	• Don't read notes and don't start at the ceiling or floor
• Make frequent use of summaries	• Sharp increases or decreases in volume will aid listening	• Look at the whole group, not just at the friendly faces
• Signpost the way ahead, tell them what's coming next	• Speak slower than usual (when individuals are nervous they tend to go faster)	• Smile and convey enjoyment and enthusiasm about the subject
• Don't apologise or use negatives	• Develop the art of the pause, use it to emphasise the main points	• Move about occasionally and use hand gestures to reinforce points
• Stress the positive and sell the benefits	• Watch out for a tendency to gabble; pronounce each word fully	• Put down marker pens, pointers etc, don't play with them
• Put forward what's in it for them	• Project enthusiasm, keep a sparkle in the voice	• Use open posture to convey confidence
• Steer clear of talking about statistics - put them on an overhead projector and reinforce with a handout	• Vary the tempo for different audiences and at different times in your talk	• Empty pockets of loose change so that you it can't cause distraction
• Take care to avoid filter words with no meaning "Er", "Um", "Know what I mean", "like"	• Don't drop the voice at the end of sentences	• Don't wear distracting jewellery such as noisy bracelets, beeping watches, earrings that catch the light
• Repeat key phrases	• Speak clearly and precisely, don't mumble	• Avoid clutching the lectern until the knuckles show white
• Carefully script the opening and then memorise it; A positive opening will give both trainer and trainees confidence	• Emphasise the key words in the message	• Be properly groomed before commencing, then there will be no need to tug your hair, play with clothes or scratch
• Always end with a high spot that leaves them wanting to hear more		• When being questioned, look directly at the questioner; pause and look down when considering an answer; look directly at them when giving your answer
		• Keep hands in front ready for action; don't put your hands in your pockets, or on your hips; don't fold your arms
		• Walk slowly to the front, look at the group, smile and take a few deep breaths before starting
		• Be poised, be courteous, be sincere and above all, you should be yourself

Facilitating in a Training Context

As you become more experienced as a trainer, you will most likely move away from an instructor style and perform a more facilitation style. Your role as a facilitator is to help the group to carry out an agreed task. You do not do the task for the group, but make it easier for the group to do its work.

The task in a group is a group task. The main difference between an individual tackling a task alone is that only the individual need relate to the task. In a group, each member has to relate to the task but also has to relate to every other member while doing so. In a group, many differences and similarities can exist – age, sex, background, culture, class, etc. To a greater or lesser extent, these differences and similarities can interfere with, or assist, the group in tackling the task. Group-members will be trying to work at the task, while at the same time trying to have their needs met arising out of the differences and similarities – for example, need to be accepted, to dominate, to complete, to assist, etc.

As a facilitator, you have to be aware of the task that the group has undertaken and at the same time be aware of needs that members have. These needs must be acknowledged and responded to in order that the task is done. To be effective in conducting a facilitated session, there are five practical functions that you should complete:

- **Space:** As a facilitator you are the person responsible for ensuring that the space where the group will work is in order – enough chairs, light, heat, etc

- **Helping the Group to Settle:** Your task is to help the group to feel secure enough to be able to tackle the task. You may do this by breaking some of the barriers and helping to build a climate of trust – introductions, a brief comment from each, an ice-breaker, etc. You must demonstrate consistently that you accept each member and trust the group to complete the task

- **Ensure that the both Task, and Constraints, are clear:** At the beginning of the group session, you should help the group to be clear about the task and the time-frame within which the task has to be achieved. Is the task to share experiences, explore attitudes, arrive at a decision, plan an action, present a proposal? Each member has a contribution to make, so time should be thought of as a shared resource

- **Direct/Facilitate the Discussion:** This is your main task and it is during the discussion that a range of skills is helpful, including your ability to listen, clarify, empathise, challenge, support, summarise, and question

- **Manage Time:** You need to help the group to be aware of time as the discussion continues, so that the task is complete within the time allotted.

Some Skills to Ensure Effective Facilitation

To be an effective facilitator, there are a number of important skills that you are expected to use, including:

- **Listening and Empathy:** Learners need to feel they are being listened to and that their ideas and concerns are recognised as worthy and important contributions. You need to listen attentively to all participants, maintaining eye contact with each speaker; contributions need to be responded to and perhaps recorded for all to see. Discussions need to build on earlier statements; if they do not, it may be helpful to summarise the points, which have been overlooked. It is also essential that you avoid discrimination and, for example, develop alternatives to the exclusive use of male pronouns (he, his, him) – such as 'he or she' or alternating use of male and female – in written and oral presentations. This can be essential to the trust and safety of some learners whose contributions are especially important to obtain because they have been systematically ignored in the past, in other settings, if not in the group at hand. Confidentiality is another issue that influences trust levels – if personal histories or opinions are aired, it may fall to you to make sure the learning group agrees about what "confidential" means in this case

- **Validation:** Learners need to feel validated as equal and important members of the group. You should not be the only one who generously (but honestly) offers comments like "I'm glad to see you here" or "I like that idea", etc

- **Acceptance:** Learners need to feel accepted. You should provide opportunity for everyone to introduce himself or herself, if they are not familiar with each other. It is not enough for you alone to know everyone's names and personal background

- **Trust and Safety:** Learners need to feel a sense of trust and safety in the group. It is especially important that negative comment be interrupted by you (or other group members). Non-verbal behaviours can communicate a "put down" too; not looking at certain people, or looking bored, can hurt more than words. Butting into a discussion before someone has finished undermines trust; so do side conversations. Comments that imply the superiority of one sex, race, economic class, ethnic group or age group over others are destructive of trust and safety, even though the victim of the remarks probably will not feel safe enough to express the hurt. The learner will probably have intended no harm at all; nonetheless, you should be prepared to interrupt such remarks, tactfully but promptly and firmly

- **Participation:** Learners need to feel that they are able – and expected – to give suggestions, to lend support, and to take the initiative. It is very difficult to learn how to be a more effective participant in social issues, if training activities encourage passivity. In order to counteract the passive model of learning, which comes from years of sitting in lectures, you need to be encouraging, appreciative and welcoming of each learner's contribution

- **Ask for Help:** For most adults, groups have a competitive atmosphere, which make it unsafe to admit that they need help. But the success of a learning group depends on the success of every member in developing skills. So it is essential to be able to ask for help when it is needed, for encouragement when an activity seems difficult or challenging and for appreciation when there are new accomplishments. You can help by modelling these behaviours (by doing them yourself for all to see) or by making a statement encouraging learners to ask for help

- **Life Experience:** Learners need to know that their life experiences are an important and valuable resource to be drawn upon and shared for their own learning and the group's learning as well. In particular, those people with less formal education need to be reassured that what they have learned through experience is just as valid and worthwhile (it may be helpful to say this explicitly). Activities and discussion questions should invite sharing of experiences

- **Free Release of Ideas:** Learners need processes that allow for the free release of their feelings and thoughts. Again, a well-planned activity will provide encouragement for this, with plenty of time for discussion. Activities are the stimulus and the shared experience provides a basis for focussed discussion and decisions about how to implement new procedures or ideas

- **Humour and Fun:** Learners need an atmosphere where they can be taken seriously, while at the same time allowing for laughter, humour, errors and flexibility. Lightness and fun have an important part to play in learning; if people are enjoying themselves, they are also probably open to new ideas. If they are feeling comfortable enough to risk making mistakes, they are likely to experience much more rapid learning

- **Resolve Conflicts:** Learners need processes that allow for resolution of conflicts without somebody winning at another's expense. When you identify a situation in which two learners' ideas are in conflict, it is usually not good enough to point to a "right answer" – it is important to recognise the valid components of the other answer and to strive for a solution that taps the best of both learner's ideas

- **Evaluate Learning:** Learners need the opportunity to evaluate their learning and express their satisfaction, dissatisfaction or suggestions for future improvement. This is one of the most important ways in which the learners can take charge of their own learning by guiding the development of future learning plans. Accomplishments deserve to be shared and frustrations need to be communicated, rather than being turned back in on the learner

- **Worthwhile Activity:** Learners need to feel they are engaged in a meaningful and important activity. In school, we were expected to take it on faith that what the teacher had to say was important. However, in the workplace, it is essential to explain the purposes of learning activities and useful to allow participants to question, clarify and even change the purposes at the start of an activity to ensure that they are motivated and committed to the activities

- **New Ideas:** Learners need to develop new ideas about the facilitator/participant relationship. In school, the teacher determined content, directed learning, maintained discipline and judged performance. The teacher was older, stronger and usually wiser. There is a tendency to expect the same of facilitators, even if that isn't appropriate. The facilitator may have chosen the content, but with group input about needs, objectives, and preferred methods. The facilitator creates opportunities for the group. Rather than presenting an image or someone who knows it all, the facilitator can be someone who is eager to learn, with a lot of good ideas about how to learn, where to find out, and how to acquire new skills

- **Mutual Responsibility:** You and your participants share a mutual responsibility to achieve the desired learning. You can emphasise the democratic nature of learning and can help participants be aware that they are in charge of their learning, that it is their business being conducted, and that each person has contributions to make. You may find times when participants are effectively taking control of their own learning, so that you can literally slip into a back seat or become another participant, in the interest of building independence among the learners

- **Overcoming Old Patterns:** Learners sometimes need help to overcome old patterns of passivity and feelings of inadequacy. In a discussion session, ask for the thoughts of those who haven't spoken yet or set a guideline from the beginning that no one speaks twice until everyone has spoken once. It may help to check out in a 1:1 the concerns and reservations of those who hold back

- **Relating to "real" situations:** Learners need to know how a learning activity relates to "real" situations. Even if the learning activities use the actual problems and situations that the group is confronting, it is important to help participants make their conclusions explicit. This can be done in discussion sessions by raising such questions as "Exactly how will we use the ideas that have come up today?" or "Are we willing to try this new procedure on a regular basis?"

- **Check for Attention:** Even the best of learning plans will not hold the attention of participants 100% of the time. You can use the attention level as a gauge of how well things are going. When energy droops and people begin to fidget, it is a signal to check whether things are repetitive, off the point or boring. You can also ask the group what is going on. Usually, learners will know what's up and take question as an indication of your respect for them, a reminder to them that they can share the situation to meet their needs. Raising the question implies a willingness by you to be flexible – to change the schedule activity, to have a break, to make (or elicit) a summary of what has just happened or to lead three laps around the building

- **Locating Learners:** Learners need to understand where in the planned sequence of activates the group has reached. An agenda should be posted and/or distributed, explained and referred to periodically. This can help to reduce feelings of being lost and also helps the participants to decide when it is most appropriate to raise a particular question or concern

- **Learners in Control:** Learners need to have real control over how they spend their time. The agenda should include time estimates for each activity. If necessary, these times can be debated or reviewed at the start. A time schedule is only helpful if it is used. You need to keep an eye on the clock or appoint someone else to do this. If an activity looks like it will run over time, the group should have the opportunity to decide whether to cut it short, drop a later item, or extend the session to include everything. You should try to make realistic time estimates for learning activities, allowing adequate time for the sort of discussion that allows participants to understand and incorporate new skills and information. To some extent, you can move things along and keep discussions tightly focused, but decisions to run over time or omit parts of the agenda should be made by the group. If a sessions are on a tight time schedule, it may be useful to time individual contributions to a discussion.

DEVELOPING YOUR QUESTIONING SKILLS

We have discussed three training tasks that you may be requested to undertake from time to time. We have made reference to specific skills that you will need to possess in order to carry out these tasks effectively. We now explain the role of questioning skills and a range of questioning techniques that you can use. In **Figure 9.4**, we set out the key elements of the questioning competency.

FIGURE 9.4: QUESTIONING: ASSOCIATED KNOWLEDGE, SKILLS & ATTITUDES

Competency: Questioning		
Knowledge	**Skills**	**Attitudes**
• Types of questions • Purpose of questioning • When to use questions in a training situation • Differences between asking a question	• Sequencing questions • Phrasing questions • Timing of questions • Creating conditions where questions can be asked • Credibility of the trainer in terms of knowledge • Creating rapport	• An open mind • Respect for the learner • Receptivity and approachability • A willingness to respond to questions

Why Use Questions in a Training Session?

We propose that competency in asking and responding to questions is important for a number of reasons. We also highlight some of the issues involved in practising this competency effectively. **Figure 9.5** provides a summary of the advantages and limitations in using questions in a training session.

Types of Questions that you can use during a Training Session
To be an effective trainer, you must learn to question for understanding. You must always be an observer of the trainee's behaviour and be willing to "check out" the trainee's emotional state and measure learning. The following questioning techniques can aid you in assessing the progress of learning. They are presented in **Figure 9.6**.

FIGURE 9.5: USING QUESTIONS IN TRAINING SESSIONS: ADVANTAGES & DISADVANTAGES

Advantages	Disadvantages
• Breaks the ice and start a dialogue • Helps check knowledge and understanding on what's been covered • Gives trainees more confidence in the ability to use the material • Satisfies special needs and interests of individuals • Provides a guide to trainees' initial knowledge on the topic • Involves the group at an early stage • Stimulates the trainees to think things through • Can be used to encourage reluctant participants to talk • Helps explore attitudes, opinions and feelings • Introduces group participation and variety • Maintains trainees interest in mid-session lull • Uses the group's knowledge • Ensures the trainer doesn't bore them by telling them things they already know • Channels the session in a direction • Gives you feedback on how well trainees are doing • Provides a means of assessing progress to date • Stimulates active learning, thus ensuring greater understanding and retention of the material	• It may prove difficult to handle the group • The atmosphere may become disorderly and noisy • It is easy to go off on tangents and not cover the training points • One person may dominate and answer all the questions • It can be time-consuming, taking longer to cover the material • Trainees with an action-oriented learning style may become frustrated • Gives the opportunity for the self-opinionated to "get on their soapbox" • The trainees may lack knowledge and feel they have nothing to contribute • The trainees may hold back from fear of the reaction of other trainees or you • They can be frustrating because they only give wrong or stupid answers

FIGURE 9.6: DIFFERENT QUESTION TYPES IN TRAINING: PURPOSE & FORM

Question Type	Purpose	Question Form	Illustrations
Open	To establish rapport	Contact	Introductory questions / comments to establish the first superficial relationship and to put respondent at ease, e.g. reference to mutually shared experiences, unusual leisure interests; Please tell me about ...
	To explore broad background information	General	How do you feel about ... What do you think about ...
	To explore opinions/ attitudes	Opinion-seeking Trailer	Making a broad comment on a subject and then pause in anticipation of a response (i.e. the question is hidden)
Probe	To show interest / encouragement	Non-verbal noises	"Ummm?", "Er?", "Ah", "Oh?", "Hmmm?", together with appropriate facial expressions (smiles, raised eyebrows) and head movements

Question Type	Purpose	Question Form	Illustrations
		Supportive statements	"I see ...?", "And then ...?", "That's interesting ... (tell me more)"
		Key word repetition	Repetition of one or two words to encourage further response
		Mirror	Repetition of short reply as a query, "Why?", "Why not?", allied to various non-verbal signals
	To seek further information	Simple interrogative	"How do your responsibilities now compare with those in your last job?"
		The pause	"How do you mean?", "Can you tell me more about that?"
		Comparative	"What would you do if ...?", "How would you feel if ...?"
		Extension	"Why do you feel that way?", "Do you have any other reasons for feeling as you do?"
		Hypothetical	"You think that ...?", "It seems to you that ...?", "You feel that ...?"
	To explore opinions/attitudes	Opinion investigation	"As I understand it ...?", "If I've got it right ...?", "So what you're saying is ...?"
	To demonstrate understanding / clarify information already given	The reflection	
		Summary	
Closed	To establish facts/information	Yes/no response	"Are you ...?", "Do you ...?", "So what you're saying is ...?"
		Identification of person, time, location, number	"How many people do you have reporting to you?", "How long did you have that job?"
Counter-Productive	To prompt desired answer	Leading	"I take it you believe that ...?", "You don't really think that ... do you?", "You must admit that ...?", "Isn't it a fact that ...?"
	To confuse or mislead	Marathon	Asking a question in a rambling, incomprehensible way
		Trick	"Do you think that this is the right answer?"
			Two or more questions presented as a package. "You did say you wouldn't mind being away from home occasionally? Oh, and you do have a current driving licence, don't you?", " I presume it's clear? And, by the way ...?"
		Ambiguous	"What about games?"
	To prevent respondent saying anything	Rhetorical	Answering your own questions, "Do you ...? Of course you do. I always say that ...?"

We will now talk about some specific questioning approaches that you can use in a training situation. You can use the following question formats to enhance the quality of the learning event:

- **The "To the Group" Question:** In this situation, you ask a question and then wait for an answer from the group. This allows the trainees to think and encourages involvement in the learning process. If there is no immediate answer, you should not rush in; sometimes, a pause is useful and silence has the potential to stimulate the thinking process. If you do not get a response, then ask a direct question of some member of the group

- **The Direct Question:** You can throw out the person's name and then ask them a question. By stating the name first, you ensure that you get their attention

- **The Combination Question:** This question is useful to gain the training group's attention, so you ask the question of the group, then give the entire group time to think and than name a specific participant to answer it

- **Closed-Ended Questions:** These questions require an answer consisting of a yes/no or a single word response from the trainee. Closed questions save time and direct trainees to a single answer – for example: "Do you know how to start up the Aligner?" or "Do you know the safety requirements for this module?"

- **Open-Ended Questions:** These questions require an answer longer than a yes/no or single word response. In general, more information is gained about what the trainee does or does not know by asking open-ended questions. For example: "What are the steps to start up the Aligner?", "What are the consequences of not following the safety requirements?", or "What is the purpose of the task you are presently doing?"

- **Follow-Up Questions:** Quite often the trainee finds a way to leave you wondering whether they really understood the subject. Follow-up questions help you, and the trainee, understand more about what the trainee knows. Here are some examples: "What do you mean when you say …?" or "How do you know that's true?"

- **Redirected Questions:** These questions are questions that are asked by the trainee to you, where you then relay the question back to the trainees. This challenges the trainees' willingness to engage in a critical thinking process

- **Probing Questions:** Information given by trainees may need to be explored in more detail – make sure that you probe further if you are not clear about an answer. "How many sessions have you carried out?", "Are you responsible for all aspects of training?", or "What responsibility do you have for testing understanding?"

- **Comparisons:** Getting trainees to compare their experience in different training situations are often very useful. "What are the major differences between working in the sales department rather than in production?"

- **Behavioural Questions:** You may pose this type of question to yourself or the group – for example, what would you say or do in particular situations. Be specific. "When one of your trainees performance deteriorated, what did you do?" or "What did you do in your last job to contribute towards teamwork?"

It is important to emphasise that the ultimate purpose in posing questions is to receive an answer and to lead to a wider understanding by the learners. The objective is not for you to impress the group with the extent of your knowledge, nor to highlight the lack of knowledge on the learner's part. Questions should be framed in a way that do not embarrass or threaten a learner.

Some Appropriate Questioning Techniques

There are a variety of ways of *not* asking questions in a training context but the three most often encountered are:

- **Creeping Poison:** This is where questions are asked in sequence around the group so that an individual can predict that a specific question will be addressed to them. This is an inadvisable method, because it leads to increased pressure – group members can become so preoccupied about the question that they will face that concentration becomes difficult as they await their turn under the spotlight. Additionally, those who have already answered a question may feel that they need not pay attention since the danger of being asked an additional question has receded. However, the advantage of sequential answers is that everyone has an equal opportunity to answer questions and that no one is overlooked or victimised

- **Heart Failure:** Sometimes referred to as "3P" questioning, which stands for "pose, pause and pounce", "Heart Failure" is the opposite of Creeping Poison. This is where a trainer questions individuals in the group without any prior warning. The random nature of the questioning technique means that the group has to "keep on its toes" and pay attention; the disadvantage is that the pressure of being put on the spot can result in blind panic, the mind going blank, or an ill-considered or garbled answer

- **Popcorn Questioning:** Popcorn questioning is less direct and so a less threatening method of questioning. In this approach, you pose a question to the whole group and, as with popping corn, allow the group to heat up gradually, answering questions as soon as they feel confident to do so. By providing the right environment and encouraging a response, answers should be "popping up throughout the group". Popcorn questioning is useful where individual group members may feel inhibited or where the intention is to enhance team spirit and gain greater participation. The approach is less formal but care must be taken to avoid the same people answering questions each time.

Responding to Answers Provided by Learners

Skill in framing questions in the right way is only part of your skill in questioning in a training context. The second major factor is in responding to the answers that learners give.

When an individual answers a question, it is important for you to realise that the group will be looking at how that answer is received and how they would feel if they were in the respondent's shoes. Insensitivity on the trainer's part in handling responses can discourage the group from any further participation. How you react to answers and then respond to them is an important component of your questioning competency. You need to:

- **Acknowledge every contribution:** Every response deserves some acknowledgement. Ignoring a contribution is an indication that the response was unworthy of comment and will discourage that person and the rest of the group

- **Always acknowledge answers immediately:** Whether the response is correct or incorrect, you should always acknowledge immediately. Failure to do so could result in learning points being missed or incorrect responses being assumed to be correct

- **Acknowledge correct responses:** Where the response provided is what was required, you should commend the responder, repeat the answer given and emphasise or expand upon the issue, moving on to further questions if appropriate. For example, "Thank you John. That's an excellent point. Financial considerations are not the only factor; human factors must also be taken into account. Can anyone think …?"

- **Broadly correct responses:** If the answer given is broadly correct, emphasise the correct elements and seek further information about the remainder. For example, "Yes, the cost element is one factor here but are there any others we need to consider?"

- **Do not dismiss incorrect answers:** You should not dismiss incorrect responses without due consideration. Try to find something in the answer given that could be of merit. One approach is to acknowledge the answer given, explore the reasons for reaching that conclusion and/or empathise with the respondent.

Then either (1) re-state the question to provide an opportunity to the individual to correct that answer or (2) put the answer given, to the group for comment – for example:

1. "Michael, I can understand why throwing complaining customers out might be one way of dealing with the problem but do you think it would provide the best approach to handling customer complaints?"

2. "So, Michael, your suggestion would be to throw complaining customers out to discourage further customer complaints. Does the group agree that this would be the best approach to handle customer complaints?"

- **Where the answer doesn't make sense:** Many learners understand the question asked, but find it difficult to put their thoughts into words. If the problem seems to stem from the inability of the learner to articulate their thoughts, the solution might be to help clarify the underlying meaning and check back. For example: "Alan, if I understand you correctly, you would want to see more involvement, is that right?" The objective is to clarify or paraphrase the individual's ideas, not to ignore them and impose your own

- **Where the response is completely irrelevant:** In some cases, the answers given seem to bear little resemblance to the question asked. Before you start to question your sanity, or that of the group, you should check that the question was understood and, if not, re-state it in a clearer form. The cause might be that some trainees are answering a question that they think you ought to have asked or that they believe you will be asking. In other words, their thoughts have outraced the issues under discussion. A response to this would be to thank them for their contribution and indicate that the topic will be covered at a later stage or that it touches on matters outside the boundaries of the present topic. Such as, "Thank you Derek , but you are way ahead of me. That's a good point that we will be pursuing later. Could you make sure that I cover it when we look at the topic in the next session?"

As well as being able to ask questions, effective training requires that you are able to answer questions too. It is always a wise idea to establish at the outset when you intend to deal with any problems or questions and, providing the group is made aware of the approach that you will be using, this is largely a matter of personal choice.

There are a number of reasons for asking a trainer questions. The most obvious reason is to seek an answer to a particular issue:

- **Genuine request for information:** If the question is a genuine request for information, you should answer it concisely and check with the questioner that this provides an answer that meets their needs. If further clarification is required, this can either be given instantly, or you can suggest that the matter could best be discussed during a suitable interval

- **Testing credibility:** The object of asking a testing question is not about understanding but to probe your knowledge and expertise. Often, the questioner already knows the answer but wants to see how you handle the question. If this is the case, your credibility depends on your honesty. Trainers are not expected to be the fountain of all knowledge but it is often felt that, if they admit that they don't know, they will lose all credibility. This is not the case: It is infinitely better for you to remain silent and be thought a fool than to open your mouth and prove it beyond all doubt. If you don't know – you shouldn't bluff. If you fake an answer and are found out, it will cast doubt upon everything that has been said so far. On the other hand, if you are confident enough to admit that you don't know, this implies that you feel sure of the accuracy of everything else you said. Providing the questioner doesn't seek basic information that you should know, the best approach is for you to congratulate the questioner on raising an important issue, admit that an answer does not readily spring to mind and promise to provide a definite response tomorrow, or after the course or later on (you must ensure the promise is fulfilled). The rule here is "if in doubt, find out"

- **Displaying knowledge:** The purpose of the display question is to impress upon others how knowledgeable the questioner is. All the learner is looking for is confirmation of your intelligence in front of the group and, providing the facts are correct, you can win them over by flattery. "Now that's an interesting question". If the information is not accurate, you need to take considerable care to reinforce those areas that might lead to misinformation

- **The sidetracking question:** The objective of the sidetracking question is to move the learners' attention into an area that holds greater interest for the questioner. This might be deliberate or unintentional but, in either case, you should resist the temptation to be led off the track. For example, "We will be looking at just that problem tomorrow morning, Rose, so it might be better to save that question for then"

- **Challenging questions:** Sometimes referred to as the "Gotcha question", it often takes the form of using information provided by you earlier to contradict the views currently being stated. Your response in this situation is very important. The rule here for you is to never take the criticism or challenge personally, even if (or particularly if) it is meant that way! The correct approach is to pause, admit that the point is an interesting one, and use the time gained to think carefully about your response. If you can't justify what has been said, then do not try to. Defending the indefensible will mean that, far from winning the person over, you will convince the rest of the group of the validity of your concern. Instead, you should admit your mistake and emphasise the correct solution. Equally, if there is a good reason for the inconsistency of the answers, you shouldn't use this as an opportunity to score points. If you belittle the questioner in front of the group, at best he will be alienated, at worst he will seek revenge later. You should demonstrate that you are above such things and thus you will gain the respect of the whole group.

Some of the guidelines you can follow when asking questions are presented in **Figure 9.7**.

FIGURE 9.7: GUIDELINES WHEN ASKING QUESTIONS IN A TRAINING CONTEXT

- **Make sure that the question is clear:** It is impossible to answer anything correctly if you don't understand the question. Jargon and technical language should be avoided, which might not be understood and the question phrased unambiguously
- **Keep it short:** There is little point in asking a question so long-winded or confusing that the respondent has to ask for it to be repeated. Where a question is complicated, it should be broken down into digestible chunks
- **Keep it fair:** The person questioned should be able to answer the question from the knowledge gained on the course or from knowledge he could reasonably be expected to have already.
- **Do distribute questions evenly:** The question should be tailored to suit the person questioned. Part of keeping it fair is making sure that individuals don't feel that they are being victimised and that questions aren't always addressed to them. Questions are occasionally used as a method of keeping particular group members alert and under control. Although this is an acceptable approach, it should not be carried out in a manner that leaves anyone feeling "picked upon"
- **Don't ask 50/50 questions:** Ask questions that require an answer to be thought out, and not just guessed at. Avoid questions like "Which would you press, the red button or the blue button?"
- **Don't ask vague questions:** Questions like "What is the first thing you would expect to see in any office?" are too broad to be of any value. Questions should be precise enough to indicate the knowledge required to answer correctly
- **Don't seek public confessions:** It is unfair to expect a response to questions such as "Has anyone here ever been ill through stress?". Questions such as "What sort of illnesses can be attributed to stress?" or "What sort of effects can stress produce?" will often result in a wider and more enthusiastic response
- **Don't ask questions reminiscent of the classroom:** Classroom questions are those questions that can be completed in one word, such as "We call this a ...?" with a pause for the group to provide a response
- **Don't answer the question:** Trainers are often so concerned that they won't get the answer they want (or worse yet, any answer at all) that they finish up answering the question themselves. You shouldn't give up too easily. If the group does fail to react, it might be that they don't understand what is being asked, so you should phrase the question in another way.

USING LISTENING TECHNIQUES TO DELIVER EFFECTIVE TRAINING

Your second core competency is listening. Your purpose in listening is to make a conscious effort to hear what is really being said, with the intention of creating connection with the trainee and diagnosing their current emotional state. Listening requires you to:

- Be open to discovering the trainee's true meaning
- Facilitate the trainee having the experience of "feeling" heard and understood.

Listening is a skill you will use quite a lot when facilitating. In **Figure 9.8**, we set out the key elements of the listening competency.

FIGURE 9.8: LISTENING: ASSOCIATED KNOWLEDGE, SKILLS & ATTITUDES

Competency: Listening		
Knowledge	**Skills**	**Attitudes**
• When listening is required • Nature of active listening • Value of listening • Listening in the learning	• Managing silences • Reading the non-verbal dimensions of learning • Attending to the learner • Showing that you are listening • Giving affirmation	• Belief in development • Respond for learner • Neutrality • Empathy • Openness to active listening • Genuine interest in people • Content is not the only focus

It is generally considered that trainers are poor listeners. Research suggests that they test in the low 25% of skilled listeners. They are likely to immediately forget 75% of what another person has said. Reasons for not being skilled listeners include:

- A lack of formal training in listening
- A historical awareness that trainers get the attention and that talk is power (listening, therefore is not thought of as powerful)
- A tendency to use spare auditory/thinking capacity inappropriately
- Concentration is blocked due to "external" barriers
- Receptivity is blocked due to "internal" barriers.

Defensiveness leads to ineffective communication. Therefore, it is very important that you build and maintain a supportive climate for communication. Supportiveness can be increased where you:

- Indicate your desire to understand and gain more information
- Take a problem-solving approach instead of a judgmental one

- Are spontaneous and direct
- Express empathy
- Have an open attitude and are willing to experiment with ideas, attitudes and behaviours.

Figure 9.9 sets out examples of good and poor listening in a training context.

FIGURE 9.9: EXAMPLES OF GOOD & POOR LISTENING BEHAVIOUR IN A TRAINING CONTEXT

Poor Listening Skills	Good Listening Skills
• Assuming that you know what the other person is going to say and not concentrating • Thinking of what you want to say next • Concentrating on how the speaker looks rather than on what they are saying • Tuning out people you do not agree with • Daydreaming when the other person is speaking • Pretending that you understand when you do not • Not clarifying things that are unclear	• Clearing away thoughts and feelings from previous events • Giving the speaker your full attention • Checking that you have heard accurately • Giving encouraging signals • Not "switching off" when you hear something you don't agree with • Re-stating what you think you have heard if you are not sure about it

The following represents a model that you can use to facilitate listening in a training situation

- **Step 1: Consciously decide to do the work of Power Listening:** Focus 100% of your attention on the learner. Shift physical position so that the learner can access all the information they need. Make eye contact and be in a position to observe the learner's body language. Separate from external distractions such as the phone, beeper, and tools or work the learner is currently engaged in

- **Step 2: Suspend your "internal" judgements:** Temporarily let go of your assessment of the learner or the subject matter. Put him/herself in the other person's position. Be willing to ask "What if he/she has a valid point?"

- **Step 3: Scan for the "unseated" message and other clues:** Pay attention to the learner's non-verbal clues, to determine the underlying meaning in the message. Scan regularly for: pauses in breathing; eye movement; emotion; voice level and tone; facial expressions; intuition

- **Step 4: Ask clarifying questions:** Ask open-ended probing questions that will assist him/her in getting beyond the surface meaning. Whenever your intuition says "there's something more here" or "there's something which isn't understood", you should be willing to ask questions like: "What exactly did you mean, when you said ..."

- **Step 5: Summarise understanding of the learner's "true" message:** Endeavour to capture understanding of the "true" message in one straightforward and focused sentence. Deliver it as an open-ended question, such as: "It seems as though you felt embarrassed by not performing the process correctly yesterday and now you are reluctant to learn today's objective. Is that correct?" If you have captured the essence, the learner will feel assisted, as well as listened to. Even if you are off the mark, the learner will answer the question in a way that will take you closer to the truth.

Active listening requires the possession of a number of important skills, as well as the avoidance of pitfalls. The more important dimensions of active listening are presented in **Figure 9.10**.

FIGURE 9.10: ACTIVE LISTENING: SKILLS & PITFALLS

Skills	
Summarising	• Drawing together several things a speaker says to make one statement. • Example: "So, you are saying three things, one ..., two ..., three ..."
Clarifying / testing Understanding	• Checking that what is said is understood. Includes opinions, facts, decisions etc. • Example: "So what you are saying is that you will not be available on that Friday because of other commitments"
Reflecting a feeling	• Picking up on the implicit or explicit feelings expressed by a speaker and demonstrating an understanding or acceptance of these. • Example: "It sounds like that was a very exciting time"
Paraphrasing	• Repeating back to the speaker a little of what was said either in her/his own or similar words. This "prompt" encourages people to continue. • Example: "So, what was happening at work was confusing"
Explaining	• Giving an interpretation of previous statements. • Example: "It could be that what happened was ..."
Open-ended Questioning	• Asking questions that will encourage further disclosure. • Example: "It could be that what happened was ..."
Encouraging	• Thanking people for their contribution and offering praise. • Example: "What happened then?", "How did that affect you?" • or • Using sub-speech to indicate an ongoing understanding of what is being said. These serve as indicators to continue, that the listener is prepared to listen a little longer. • Example: "Mmm ... uhuh ... yes ..."

Skills	
Silence	• Allowing time between what a person says before the facilitator speaks. Silence can encourage a speaker to continue and can indicate absorption of what is being said.
Linking	• Statements / questions / comments can be linked by the facilitator using short sentences indicating interest, support and encouragement to continue. • Example: "And then?"
Pitfalls	
Over-analysing	• Interpreting the speaker's motives. • Result: Prevents the speaker discovering your motives independently. Facilitator may be inaccurate and/or seen as a know-it-all
Parroting	• Repeating parrot-like what the speaker says. • Result: The speaker gets annoyed and may feel that s/he is not being listened to
Over-expansion	• Adding to what was said. • Result: the speaker may feel misheard
Omitting	• Ignoring relevant facts, feelings or events. • Results: The speaker may feel misheard
Exaggerating	• Intensifying the feelings expressed, or the importance of what was said. • Result: The speaker may have to repeat or contradict the facilitator
Under-scoring	• Underestimating the intensity of the emotion expressed. • Result: The speaker may feel unimportant or that s/he has made an irrelevant contribution
Rushing	• Anticipating what the speaker will say next and saying it for her/him. • Result: This prevents the speaker from working at their own pace and he/she may feel manipulated
Lagging	• Failing to move on with the speaker to the next item. • Result: Speaker may become frustrated
'Solution seeking'	• Facilitator is trying to find solutions to problems or concentrating on what he/she is going to say and consequently is not paying attention to what is being said.
Listener's needs	• Listener is so caught up in his/her own needs and viewpoints that he/she is unable to get past them to listen
Poor environment	• Lack of privacy, noise, unpleasant surroundings

USING FEEDBACK IN A TRAINING CONTEXT

The third core competency for effective training is giving and receiving feedback. The purpose of effective feedback is to build and maintain relationships with learners and to promote learning. In **Figure 9.11**, we set out the key elements of the feedback competency. Feedback is a competency that you will use a great deal in conducting on-the-job instruction or in facilitating.

FIGURE 9.11: FEEDBACK: ASSOCIATED KNOWLEDGE, SKILLS & ATTITUDES

Competency: Feedback		
Knowledge	**Skills**	**Attitudes**
• Why feedback? • The feedback process • When to use feedback • Individual reaction to feedback • Psychological aspects of feedback • Types of feedback	• Interpersonal skills • Skills to give and receive feedback • Creating conditions for effective feedback • Concerning self reflection	• Respect for learner • Belief in development • Responsibility for development • Constructive feedback enhances learning

Feedback is information about the results of someone's actions. The purpose of feedback in a training context is to build and maintain relationships with learners and to promote learning. Immediate and direct feedback can help you to:

• Acknowledge and reinforce behaviour that meets the job requirement expectations

• Negotiate for a change in behaviour that does not meet the job requirement expectations.

Trainers often fail to give learners honest, direct and descriptive information on how their behaviour impacts on the success of the training. Consequently, learners do not know how others feel, and trainees and trainer do not learn how to interact with each other more effectively. Without feedback, the trainee will not know how they are doing. Without feedback, you cannot make improvements to the material or delivery. When giving feedback, you should:

• Give acknowledging feedback and reinforcement for something well done

• Acknowledge trainees' responses, whether correct or incorrect, as attempts to learn and follow them with accepting, rather than rejecting, comments

• Reinforce or reward responses with a smile, a favourable nod, and a little attention

• Provide a tangible token for successful completion of a particularly difficult or time-consuming task

• Provide enough "marking off points" that trainees will know where they are in the training and how they are progressing.

You need to avoid situations where you:

- Cause a learner to feel humiliated or embarrassed. It can make a trainee "shut down", lose enthusiasm or stop learning
- Publicly talk about your trainee's progress
- Compare one trainee to another
- Laugh at a trainee's efforts
- Tell the trainee by word or deed that their questions are stupid
- Assume the trainee is not as capable as you would wish. Using statements like: "You couldn't possibly understand the answer to that question"
- Chastise your trainee for failing.

Some Feedback Techniques For Trainers

There are many different ways to give trainees feedback. The use of feedback is dependent on the type of training situation you are conducting. You will be required to give lots of feedback in a facilitation situation. There are various approaches, but the following can be effective :

- **Immediate Verbal Feedback:** Typically used in 1:1 training situations where you have the opportunity to deliver the feedback personally to the trainee. Immediate feedback needs to be delivered for acknowledging and reinforcing actions. This can take the form of a smile, a nod, a "good idea" comment, and so on. It is important that you are consistent and acknowledge performance, so that the trainee will feel successful and build confidence. It can be detrimental to a trainee to be ignored or passed over when they have contributed during the day. Immediate feedback needs to be given on a regular basis throughout the entire training session. If trainees are not doing what they should be doing, they need to be informed up-front. Do not save everything until the end. Clear things up as you go. Whatever the feedback, let trainees know where they stand.
- **Written Feedback:** While verbal feedback is the most effective feedback in a training situation, because it gives the trainee an opportunity to ask questions, it takes a considerable amount of time. Written feedback is an alternative. Criteria for written feedback should be determined by you before the session and communicated to the trainee at the beginning of the lesson. Written feedback needs to be accurate and specific to the topics outlined in the training.

There is evidence that trainers often fail to give trainees feedback for the following reasons:

- Lack of formal training in observing and becoming aware of the interpersonal dynamics of a training situation
- History of receiving poor feedback when the content of the message was personal and intended to be punishing or corrective
- Tendency to think of feedback as either "positive" (the good news) or "negative" (the bad news). This results in trainers wanting to avoid the negative feedback or viewing it as unhelpful. Surprisingly, many trainers also avoid or "brush off" the positive feedback, by saying "I was just doing my job" or "It was nothing, really"
- Fear that a trainee's feelings may be hurt
- Fear that the trainee will get angry and disrupt the training.

Whatever feedback you provide in the training content should be:

- **Helpful:** The bottom line is that the purpose for giving feedback must be to build an effective training relationship; it must be helpful not just for you, but for learners as well
- **Appropriate:** The subject of the feedback must be within the context of the training programme itself. A good common sense rule is to ask the following question: "Does this behaviour have something to do with the training relationship?"
- **Well-timed:** Feedback is most effective when given at the earliest available opportunity. It is important not to let too much time elapse and not to let feelings or emotions build up
- **Solicited:** It is far better for feedback to be solicited, rather than imposed. When the receiver of feedback has given permission, they are more open to hearing the information. It is even better when the method for giving and receiving feedback has been formally established between the trainee and trainer
- **Accurate:** It is imperative that the information about the behaviour be descriptive, specific, verifiable, and neutrally presented. You should describe the actual behaviour with facts and information that will allow the receiver to verify the event, actions or words said
- **Personally-owned:** The behaviour itself can be interpreted several different ways, depending on who observed it and their values, beliefs and experiences. Therefore, it is important for the feedback to be personally "owned" by the giver as their unique response to the behaviour.

Figure 9.12 presents a model for giving and receiving feedback.

FIGURE 9.12: A MODEL FOR GIVING & RECEIVING FEEDBACK IN A TRAINING CONTEXT

Steps	Giving Feedback	Receiving Feedback
1	**Identify the behaviour in descriptive, specific, accurate and non-threatening terms:** Openers: "I've noticed ...", "Do you remember ..." Example: "Do you remember this morning's session, when I was in the middle of presenting a report, you said, "Michael, that's enough, please sit down"	**Listen to the statement without evaluating it:** You should listen for enough details to identify the specifics of the event, situation or behaviour that is being identified. Allow the speaker to talk without interruption
2	**Ask for verification from the receiver:** Openers: "Do you remember that ..." Example: "James, do you remember?"	**Test the validity of the information:** If you can't remember the event, situation or behaviour, ask for more information. Then check it out for accuracy. Otherwise, you should only acknowledge neutrally that you are aware of the situation/event
3	**Express the effects of this behaviour:** Openers: "As a result, I feel ..." Example: "As a result, I felt humiliated in front of my peers. Later, I started to feel angry."	**You should put yourself in the other person's position:** Let go of the need to see things as "right" or "wrong", and ask does he/she have a valid point? How would you feel if the situation were reversed? The speaker should be allowed to talk without interruption
4	**Express your expectations of the future:** Openers: "In the future, I would prefer ..." Example: "In the future, I would prefer you come to me before the meeting and tell me that you have a long agenda and you need me to keep my report short, or you could even ask me in the meeting to wrap it up in a minute so we can move on."	**Be open to concrete suggestions of future action and be willing to brainstorm possible alternatives when asked:** Be willing to ask clarifying questions, however, they should not take over the conversation, but let the trainee finish. You should indicate what the feedback means by paraphrasing your understanding of the speaker's request
5	**Ask the receiver to work on a joint agreement and ask them for feedback:** Openers: "What would work for you ...", "Do you have any feedback for me?" Example: "James, would you be willing to agree to either of my requests? What would work for you?", "Do you have any feedback for me?"	**Be willing to formulate a plan that works for both trainer and trainee, and give feedback when asked:** Give your point of view or fill in the details as needed. Should the trainee continue the behaviour, change the behaviour or agree to disagree. If you cannot come up with a plan, ask the giver of the feedback to help determine how to be more effective in the situation

USING NON-VERBAL COMPETENCIES IN A TRAINING CONTEXT

We consider non-verbal competencies to be an important dimension of effective training, underpinning the three previous competencies we have discussed. Although you communicate with your voice, you also communicate with your whole body. Non-verbal behaviour represents a powerful communication tool. Research reveals that only 7% of the meaning participants derive from a trainer's message comes from what is said; 38% is derived from voice and 55% from body language. Gestures, mannerisms, and expressions can have a major impact on the receipt and understanding of a message.

In **Figure 9.13**, we present the key dimensions of the non-verbal communications competency.

TABLE 9.13: NON-VERBAL COMMUNICATION: ASSOCIATED KNOWLEDGE, SKILLS & ATTITUDES

Competency: Non-Verbal Communication		
Knowledge	**Skills**	**Attitudes**
• Purpose and role of non-verbal communication • Reading non-verbal communication • Types of non-verbal communication	• When to use particular non-verbal cues • Responding to non-verbal cues • How your non-verbal behaviour influences learner reactions	• Attend to non-verbal communication • Self awareness • Interest in people • Openness and responsiveness

Receipt of a Training Message

It is impossible for people to learn when they are nervous, and equally it is impossible for trainers to teach when they communicate nervousness. This does not mean that trainers must avoid training until such time as you can do so without a degree of stress; an element of tension is essential and inevitable in many training situations. What it does mean, though, is that the effective trainer must aim to look relaxed and be in control, even when the reality is a little different. You can do this in a number of ways

- **Smile:** The simplest and most effective way of demonstrating that you are friendly and approachable is by smiling. This should be a natural relaxed smile, not a nervous giggle, and certainly not a maniacal grin, which makes trainees wonder what is in store for them. The less relaxed you feel, the more important smiling becomes

- **Handshakes:** Handshakes are a conventional means of breaking down barriers. Your handshake should not be so flaccid that it is asking the participant to shake a wet fish, nor so firm that it becomes a trial of strength

- **Posture:** The way in which you stand can also provide a very clear indication of the way you are feeling. Appearance should indicate that you are in control

- **Demeanour:** Your whole approach should be one of openness and assurance. Being self-assured is not the same thing as being conceited. Nothing said or done should make trainees feel inhibited, embarrassed or patronised

- **Appearance:** It is often said that first impressions are lasting impressions and that you never get a second chance to create a first impression. When trainees attend a course, they generally have formed some opinion of what they expect to see. Appearance will form an integral part of this expectation.

Understanding the Training Message

The clarity of your training message being communicated, and the conviction with which it is received by others, can be significantly influenced by the non-verbal signals transmitted during the presentation.

Eyes

The eyes are the most conspicuous channel of communication. In normal conversation, the parties communicating will maintain eye contact for 25% to 35% of the time, and their eye blink rate will be approximately once every 3-10 seconds. During group training, eye contact reduces dramatically and the blink rate increases.

However, listening conventions suggest that eye contact and active listening work in unison. People assume that, if someone is looking at them when they are talking, then that information is intended for them. If, on the other hand, their eye contact is elsewhere, it is felt that the speaker and their message can be disregarded.

This can frequently be seen in group training sessions where a question is addressed to the group and eye contact is made with the group as a whole. The result is a delayed response or no response at all. If the same question is asked while looking at an individual, that person will feel compelled to answer or acknowledge it.

If eye contact is so crucial, why do so many trainers find it difficult? The answer undoubtedly is that because it is so powerful a gauge of feelings that people instinctively avoid eye contact in case others see how nervous or anxious they really are. In actuality, this absence of eye contact confirms that the avoiding party is scared. Gaze behaviour of influential personalities shows that they make more frequent eye contact and hold this contact for a great deal longer than normal.

Far from interpreting the lack of eye contact as diffidence on your part, trainees will see it as demonstrating a lack of confidence, an intention to hide feelings or some form of deceit.

Arms and Hands

Possibly the greatest difficulty you encounter when presenting material is what to do with your hands. In normal conversation, hands might not merit a second thought but somehow, in making a presentation, hands suddenly seem to acquire the capacity to move independently of the rest of the mind or body. They can be seen tying themselves into knots, ferreting about in pockets and discovering nasal orifices they would not dream of exploring ordinarily in polite company.

What is it that causes this transformation? Nervous tension results in excess energy to the system, which needs to find a satisfactory outlet. In the absence of any obvious opportunity to work off this energy release, the body uses the only alternative available, which is to seek out something to toy with.

The following hand movements should be avoided:

- **Grooming:** There is nothing intrinsically wrong in ensuring one's tie is straight or hair is in place. However, continuous patting and primping becomes irritating

- **Fiddling:** As a rule, this involves small objects such as buttons, watches, and rings, though other forms include toying with marker pens, paper clips and elastic bands. If you are conscious of being a "fiddler", you should reduce the temptation by keeping jewellery, pendants, necklaces, badges, cuff-links, to a minimum. Equally, you should keep well away from easily manipulated objects, such as loose change in trouser pockets

- **Stroking:** Akin to fiddling is comfort stroking, which invariably takes the form of stroking ear lobes or neck, though more advanced forms include folding arms across the body and hugging oneself

- **Wringing:** Hand-wringing is a common occurrence and appears to an audience as a plea for clemency (which it often is)

- **Scratching:** Of all the hand gestures, it is scratching that produces the most powerful response from a training audience. The cause of this scratching seems to stem from a tingling sensation in the nerve endings brought about by a change in the body's chemistry. The effect is to set the speaker into frenzied scratching, soon mirrored by the rest of the room.

When to Use Hand Movements

Hand gestures should only be used to provide greater understanding to a training group. They should have a purpose, should be natural and should be deliberate.

Many trainers believe that if they make vague hand movements, these will be less obtrusive and therefore more acceptable. Small jerky movements only serve to heighten your self-consciousness. If you want to move your arms, you should do so intentionally and obviously.

The main purposes for using hand movements are as follows:

* **Reinforcement:** Hand gestures are at their best when they are used to reinforce what has been said verbally. In fact, it seems to be impossible to ask for directions without receiving a verbal description together with a demonstration of winding roads and undulating hills reinforced by hand movements. This process of supporting what is said verbally by using hand movements adds a further dimension to any training presentation and can be viewed as an alternative form of visual aid

* **Emphasis:** Emphasising hand gestures differ from reinforcement gestures in that they do not attempt to describe a situation but rather to stress its importance. Pointing a finger, table-thumping and chopping the air are all examples of emphasising hand movements. Providing these movements are not over-used, they can help communicate to the group the important learning points.

Feet, Legs and Body

Your standing with learners and their attitude towards you can be strongly influenced by the way that you physically stand before the group. It is very difficult to convey an impression of controlled confidence when you are standing cross-legged and wobbling from side to side. The most authoritative posture is still regarded as standing upright. Not only does this provide good eye-contact with the learners and a command over the room, but it does not constrict the diaphragm in ways that sitting can. An acceptable compromise is to sit on the edge of a solid table. This can have the effect of making the atmosphere less formal without inhibiting vocal projection.

Where an upright stance is used, care should be taken to make it look relaxed and comfortable. Trainers should not look like wooden soldiers nor stand like reluctant nudists with hands clasped in front of their body. Moving about can, in certain circumstances, stimulate and refocus the group's attention. Equally, movement can become the source of considerable distraction and annoyance – however, this is up to you to judge.

FIGURE 9.15: WAYS OF INCREASING THE VALUE OF NON-VERBAL COMMUNICATION IN A TRAINING SETTING

Voice
- Vary your inflection, pace, intonation and pitch (lower pitch is preferable)
- Vary the length of passes
- Avoid a sarcastic tone because it usually backfires
- Breathe!
- Watch the back of the room to check whether participants can hear

Eye Contact
- Good eye contact is vital. Eye contact shows that you know your material. It also allows you to "read the audience"
- Look at the group (People who are perceived as sincere look at their group at least 64% of the time; those who are perceived as insincere look at their group only 21% of the time)
- Look around the group gracefully. Share with whole room
- Use your eyes to encourage quieter members to talk - look at them expectantly, but relieve them if they do not respond
- To increase eye contact, limit reading. Do not read from a training manual.

Facial Expression
- Be friendly
- Smile when appropriate
- Look confident
- Enjoy oneself and have fun with the group

Stance and Movement
- Show energy, yet control. You should be yourself. If you are awkward with your hands, use a lectern, clipboard, and lots of visuals
- Move into the group for emphasis and variety. Walk purposefully
- Consider where to stand, cover both sides of the room
- When asking questions, use the aisles or move into the group
- End strong. Do not start "packing up" material during the participants' final exercise

Gestures
- Be natural and comfortable with participants
- Use gestures to emphasise key points and spice up conversation
- Use gestures to demonstrate relationships between key points

Overall Body Language
- Show enthusiasm and energy during the programme
- Use your whole body to manage disruptive behaviours - eyes, gestures, movement, etc.
- Hold up your hand to stop someone who interrupts another participant
- When the group wanders, move to the flip-chart and use your hand to refocus the group back to the goal or issue
- Step between two participants who are arguing to cut off their eye contact
- Move to a position in the room where participants must look across others and include them in their eye contact when they speak to you.

BEST PRACTICE INDICATORS

Some of the best practice issues that you should consider related to the contents of this chapter are:

- Even where you have prepared to a high level, you are likely to be nervous before a training situation. If you are a skilled trainer, you will be able to control and harness this nervous energy and translate it into enthusiasm and activity

- Use appropriate delivery skills. Show interest and enthusiasm. Establish good eye contact, use positive gestures and natural movement, make sure your language is understandable and do not try to impress your learners with technical jargon

- Find out about your learners. Do some of this work before they attend but, at the beginning of the programme, you should clarify expectations. Find out what they already know. Ask questions to get the learners involved and interested

- Present the main points of your training session. Tell them what you intend to do and say. Provide an overview that emphasises the main skills and knowledge and explains the process aspects of the learning

- Continually ask questions to involve your learners and check their understanding. Questioning not only gets your learners involved but it provides you with immediate feedback on the effectiveness of the training. You should also encourage questions and feedback from your learners

- Make sure that you provide enough time to discuss new knowledge and practice new skills. This practice component is particularly important in job instruction

- Be professional at all times and pay attention to your body language and the body language of your learners.

Reflections on Training & Development Scenario

This training scenario is a demanding one in terms of the skills it demands of you as a trainer. First, you are dealing with an experienced group of managers - in some cases, well-educated. They will likely possess a high level of trainability and comfort in training situations. The learning objectives are ambitious and, in many cases, require small group learning. There is a particular requirement that learners take responsibility for development. These requirements indicate that you will use a more facilitative rather than instructional style. If you use a facilitation style, it will help you to address effectively a number of issues:

- A facilitation approach will allow the learners to meet and to interact in an instructional, non-directed way. It will also encourage the managers to explore their learning objectives and to clarify expectations
- It will help to ensure a teamwork approach to the learning process. They are more likely to interact with each other, when the trainer is facilitating rather than instructing
- Facilitation places considerable onus on the managers to take ownership of the learning process to enhance their self-awareness and to develop their skills as managers
- Facilitation enables the trainer to enhance his/her credibility with a high profile manager group.

There are a number of reasons to use feedback as a developmental tool:
- It can increase the self knowledge of managers
- It encourages self-development because it can identify opportunities for improvement
- It promotes collaboration through the involvement and use of feedback from peers and the trainer
- It provides information on individual development needs and in the priority order of these needs.

Chapter Ten

THE MANAGER AS TRAINER & DEVELOPER

LEARNING OBJECTIVES

On completion of this chapter, you should be able to:

- Understand the contribution that the manager can make to training and developing staff in organisations

- Explain the positive and negative features of developmental relationships

- Explain the different training and development roles that the manager may perform in an organisation

- Explain the different types of coaching activities that a manager performs

- Explain the skills and strategies that the manager can use to mentor employees

- Explain the steps that can be taken by the manager to use performance reviews for development purposes

- Explain the characteristics of coaching and how to use it in a corrective and developmental context

- Explain the value of counselling in a developmental context

- Outline the value of a personal development plan and explain its key components.

A Training & Development Scenario

You are asked to provide advice on how the performance review process outlined in this scenario may be enhanced to make it more developmental.

XYZ Limited has operated a performance review process for the past five years. The system was designed by the HR manager in consultation with key managers within the organisation.

Each manager and supervisor is required to conduct an appraisal interview with every member of staff on a yearly basis. This typically lasts for approximately 30 minutes. Managers and supervisors are required to rate employees on issues such as drive and energy, attendance and punctuality, initiative and innovation, attitude, judgement, communication effectiveness and quality of work. When major disagreements occur about the ratings, the HR manager reviews the documentation and, in exceptional cases, adjusts the appraisal rating.

Management have come to the conclusion that neither managers nor employees are particularly enthusiastic about the process. Managers feel that the process requires them to "play God" in rating employees on a highly subjective set of measures, largely associated with personality characteristics that do not appear to have particular relevance to performance and development. Managers and employees received little or no training on how to conduct developmental performance reviews. There is little clarity about what the company expects to achieve from the process. Most employees dislike the appraisal interviews, which they feel provide an opportunity for managers to pick on their faults rather than focus on the future and emphasise development issues.

INTRODUCTION

We have considered the roles and skills of the trainer in facilitating training and development in organisations. We have identified and described at various points the role of the manager in developing employees. We give more consideration to the roles of the manager as a trainer and developer of staff in this chapter.

We consider the manager to be an important stakeholder in influencing and determining the effectiveness of T&D in an organisation. Typically, managers perform a number of important T&D roles. They may carry out on-the-job training, they may be involved in both corrective and developmental coaching, they may act as formal and informal mentors and they may undertake developmental reviews.

We consider the personal development plan to be an important component of effective development. We explain the issues you should consider when constructing a personal development plan. We consider each of these development dimensions in this chapter.

DEVELOPMENTAL RELATIONSHIPS & THE MANAGER

The process of training and developing staff in organisations does not take place in a vacuum but occurs as a response to the environment in which an individual works. The manager is a major component of the learning environment. Managers influence the nature and direction of an individual's development, and also have responsibility for the learning and development climate. We firmly believe that individuals are responsible for their own learning, although the manager has a major role to play.

There are three distinct developmental relationships that a manager can adopt in respect of developing his/her direct reports

- **The Usurper:** In this relationship, the manager seeks to take over fully the responsibility for a direct report's development. This is a role that may be appropriate for the manager to play at the initial stage of a direct report's development. It may also be an appropriate role to perform where the learner has low trainability, less learning maturity and is relatively inexperienced. But this role should be no more than a temporary role for a manager

- **The Supporter / Sharer:** This relationship is a more positive and constructive one from both the perspective of the manager and the direct report. Both manager and direct report maintain a constructive dialogue on development and both have different development responsibilities. The manager provides the opportunities for development and the direct report has the responsibility for taking and using them. There is a strong sharing of ideas and discussion of development needs. Manager and direct report are likely to discuss development actions and address both organisational and personal needs. The supporter / sharer role is a demanding role for both parties to play. It requires a sharing of ownership, a strong level of motivation by both parties and a level of agreement on the development needs that are to be addressed

- **The Abdicator:** The third developmental relationship is the abdicator. A very advanced development relationship could evolve from supporter / sharer to abdicator over a period of time. The manager in this case abandons the interface. There are a number of implications that can flow from this withdrawal of responsibility by the manager. If the direct report is mature, then this role offers the potential for the direct report to take increased ownership for development activity. It allows the direct report to self-direct his/her learning and self-manage the process. However, the direct report may ignore the organisational agenda and focus primarily on individual development needs. Where the direct report possesses less maturity and emotional resilience and has not fully developed his/her learning skills, it is likely that limited development may take place. This is a risk that the manager may have to take.

Figure 10.1 provides a summary of the three roles.

Line managers are "key players" in promoting training and development. One of the fundamental tenets of Human Resource Management is that managers should take responsibility for the "people management" as well as the "task management" aspects of their role. This is in contrast to the situation where responsibility for training and development is "hived off" to development specialists and trainers or is perceived to be the responsibility of training departments. There is a strong rationale for this approach – simply that managers are in day-to-day contact with their employees, they know the job role and are aware of the direct report's strengths and weaknesses. Therefore, they are ideally placed to take an active role in the development of their direct reports, whose performance they are expected meant to manage.

The problem with this is that managers often tend to be task-driven and do not possess the people management skills necessary to take on a significant developmental role. Nevertheless, many organisations now expect line managers to take a degree of responsibility for employee development, and are putting in place supporting systems to ensure that this happens. Sometimes, 360-degree appraisal is used, and staff development responsibilities are being written into job descriptions and appearing in managers' performance objectives. In addition, organisations are trying to provide managers with the skills they need to take on these responsibilities.

FIGURE 10.1: CHARACTERISTICS OF THREE DEVELOPMENT RELATIONSHIPS

Dimensions	Usurper	Supporter / Sharer	Abdicator
Development Activities			
Articulation of needs	• Prescribed by the manager	• Joint discussion of needs	• Direct report drives this issue
Identification of solutions	• Manager prescribes what needs to be done	• Manager seeks the views of the direct report	• Direct report decides what actions, if any, need to be taken
Espousal of benefits	• Manager makes the arguments on the benefits which are usually organisational	• Manager and direct report discuss both potential organisational and individual benefits	• Direct report makes the decision about the potential benefits
Development experience as source of ideas	• Manager articulates his/her experience of development	• Both manager and direct report experience are relevant	• Direct report experience is relevant primarily
Locus of thinking and reflection	• Manager does the thinking and reflection	• Manager and direct report think and reflect on the issues	• Direct report will engage in self reflection
Level of risk	• Low risk, manager protects the direct report	• Manager and direct report agree on the risks to be taken	• High risk, provided the direct report takes some development initiatives
Conditions for Effectiveness			
Level of experience	• Inexperienced novice direct report	• At mid-stage in terms of work experience	• Highly-experienced direct report
Level of self-efficacy	• Low self-efficacy and confidence to initiate development	• Moderate confidence and self-efficacy; needs to acquire more experience	• Very high self-efficacy and confidence to achieve
Level of motivation	• Strong motivation by the manager; direct report less motivated to undertake development	• Good level of motivation by both manager and direct report	• Can be highly motivated; however could possibly loose interest in development altogether
Level of learning awareness	• Limited learning awareness; and less knowledge of learning styles and preferences	• Learning awareness is evolving; experimentation is likely to identify learning preferences	• Strong learning to learn skills; a self-managed learner

Dimensions	Usurper	Supporter / Sharer	Abdicator
Level of dependency	• Very high dependency on the development actions of manager and commitment to progress	• Shared relationship. Manager and direct report depend on each other to achieve outcomes	• Little or not dependency on manager; direct report is a free agent in terms of development
Development Outcomes			
Responsibility	• Transactional arrangement only; aim is to move towards shared responsibility	• Shared responsibility; manager for the opportunities; the direct report for the learning	• Learner has primary responsibility for development • Strong learning motivation
Level of learning	• Relatively less learning. Inhibits growth and learning long term	• Good steady and incremental growth and development	• Potentially strong development and growth focus

---

Training & Development Roles of Line Managers

- Appraisal of performance
- Appraisal of potential
- Analysis of development needs and goals
- Recognising and facilitating developing opportunities
- Giving learning a priority
- Using everyday activities for learning purposes
- Establishing learning goals
- Accepting risks in subordinate performance
- Monitoring learning achievement
- Providing feedback on performance and learning
- Acting as a model of learning behaviour
- Using learning styles to facilitate meaningful learning
- Offering help, support and counselling
- Direct coaching of employees.

Typical responses from line managers when faced with the news that they share responsibility for the development of employees under their supervision range from comments like "I'm paid to manage the job, not train people. That's what we have a training department for!" to "Can you send Joe on an interpersonal skills course? He must learn how to deal with people".

The question arises as to why line managers are reluctant to become involved in T&D. The research evidence suggests that line managers may not have staff development clearly specified in their job description and performance objectives; that they lack the skills necessary for needs assessment, course selection and evaluation, and they may prefer to defer to centralised training departments where expertise is seen to rest. This system of expertise is often likely to be perpetuated by a centralised training department concerned with justifying its own existence.

Whatever the rationale for resistance, line management involvement is considered critical to the success of T&D. Many of the reasons for this have been articulated already in **Chapter Two** but, in summary, the increasing pace of organisational change requires that decision-making be taken closer to the work being done. It is line managers who are most continually involved with employees, know their development needs, understand their part of the business better than anyone else, and are in the best position to evaluate the results of employee development activity as it relates to the current and future work of the work group.

Whatever the rationale for resistance, it is easily overcome if top management makes T&D a high priority. Shifting both responsibility and authority, in addition to resources, for T&D to line managers can have significant influence on line manager behaviour. If coupled with appropriate development of the skills needed, this can produce positive outcomes.

There is general agreement as to the dimensions of the line manager's role for employee development. It involves giving active support to the role of employee development in the organisation. Setting aside time to think about and engage in employee development activities can do this. Short-term workload should not be accepted as an excuse for failure to allow employees to participate in T&D – this merely demonstrates the manager's lack of ability to plan and manage human resources. Second, managers should engage in regular, formal need assessment activities with their staff. Often the most appropriate forum for this is with the work team; at other times, it is with individual employees. The development and updating of the "personal development plan" should be seen as an opportunity to reinforce the message of continuous development that is inherent in the philosophy of employee development.

This suggests that managers themselves will need new skills: to coach, to assess training and development needs and to evaluate T&D activities that have been conducted, as well as the increased management skills needed to work with a workforce that is continually developing and changing its own skill base. Therefore, they must be active participants in the employee development process.

There is evidence that the optimum developmental relationship requires the espousal and implementation of a number of important values and actions by the manager, including:

- Manager and direct report work with a natural curiosity and the manager is continually concerned about the learner
- Manager direct report agree some form of explicit or implicit learning contract
- Real issues and problems are worked on and used as vehicles for learning
- Feedback on self-performance is encouraged and practiced
- Learners are considered to have a valuable contribution to make to the process of learning
- Learners are trusted to learn for themselves
- Responsibility for learning is shared with learners
- The manager offers resources to learn
- Learners continually develop and are encouraged to develop
- Learner and manager have joint responsibility and power to make development decisions
- There is a climate of genuine mutual care, concern and understanding
- The focus is on fostering continuous learning, asking questions, and the process of learning, and learning is at the pace of the learner
- The emphasis is on promoting a climate for deeper, more impact learning that affects life behaviour
- There are no teachers, only learners, in the developmental relationship.

MENTORING & COACHING

Mentoring and coaching are two development processes that you will most likely use in a T&D role, either as a trainer or as a manager. We provided a brief definition of these concepts in **Chapter One**. We explain in more detail the differences between both concepts now.

Coaching is a process in which an individual (usually a manager) interacts with another (direct report) to teach, model, and provide feedback on technical, professional and interpersonal skills and behaviours in a future-focused constructive way. The coach seeks to use everyday experience to improve performance.

Coaching, as a development tool, performs important functions:

- To enable the direct report to recognise their own strengths and weaknesses

- To encourage the direct report to establish targets for future performance improvement
- To monitor and review the direct report's progress in achieving targets
- To identify any problems that are likely to impact performance and progress
- To assist the direct report in generating alternatives and developing development action plans
- To enhance the direct report's understanding of the work context
- To assist the direct report to realise their potential.

Mentoring is a process that deliberately pairs a person who is more skilled or experienced with one who is less skilled or experienced (the protégé or mentee) in order to transfer skills and experience in a focused, effective and efficient manner. The skills transferred may be job-specific, technical or professional, generic or career-oriented. The reporting relationship is "off-line" – that is, not between a manager and his/her direct report.

Many trainers consider mentoring to be a career management tool used by organisations to nurture staff. Mentoring generally involves the giving of advice and guidance or in providing a role model. Mentors focuses on the development of the learner, giving time and attention beyond the role boundaries of the manager. Development usually takes place "as required" at a pace to suit the individual.

Mentoring processes usually include the following elements:

- Determining which goals, needs and opportunities of the organisation can be supported by increased skills and experience
- Developing strategies for pairing employees in a mentoring relationship on the basis of skill deficits in the employee and the presence of those skills in another
- Securing some form of agreement for each pair that defines the roles, focus and duration of the mentoring relationship.

Mentors typically carry out tasks such as teaching, tutoring, coaching, modelling, serving as a sounding board, demonstrating, listening, reflecting on the contribution of the mentee, giving feedback, counselling and guiding. The role is therefore all-embracing and requires a strong skill set.

Informal mentoring occurs in many organisations. Although it is a positive process in that it enables individuals to form natural pairs, mentors often choose mentees who are very much like themselves and impress their beliefs and styles on the protégé or mentee. It is possible that learners with strong development potential may be left out of these informal relationships.

There is evidence indicating that the creation of an effective mentoring relationship is a function of personality, so some organisations have adopted a facilitated mentoring strategy. This process is an overall structure and series of activities that enable the creation of a mentoring relationship. The process is available to any individual who perceives that he or she has potential for development and is willing and motivated to take more responsibility for personal and management development

Coaching and mentoring processes are appropriate to use in a number of situations:

- **Performance Improvements:** Coaching is appropriate where performance improvements are needed, when someone starts a new job task or procedure or where someone is initiating a professional development process

- **New Organisational Skill Requirements:** Mentoring and coaching are useful processes where organisations are concerned about the future skill needs of the organisation, as they can contribute to developing these skills

- **Inefficient Formal Training Processes:** Typical formal training courses are aimed at the average learner. It is common on many formal courses to find that participants have widely varying skills and knowledge and so a significant proportion of training content may not be relevant to a participant. In a coaching or mentoring situation, the learning is precisely targeted to the learner's specific needs. When this specific focus is clearly defined, they are very effective for learning

- **Speed of Traditional Formal Learning may be too Slow:** Formal learning events may not be scheduled at a time to suit the demands of the organisation for new skills. Training departments may only provide courses at a particular time. Coaching or mentoring strategies may be appropriate to address issues in the short-term and to meet skill requirements in a timely fashion.

Figure 10.2 shows the main differences between coaching and mentoring.

FIGURE 10.2: DIFFERENCES BETWEEN COACHING & MENTORING

Criterion	Coaching	Mentoring
Primary Focus	• Main focus is the task, the job, the professional skill or expertise	• Main focus is the career, the individual and the organisation
Content of Process	• Emphasis is on knowledge, skill, attitudes, values and performance	• Emphasis is on capability, self-esteem, self-efficacy, potential, career planning
On-line / Off-line	• It is primarily a line manager role carried out in the work context • It is, therefore, an "on-line" activity	• It is primarily an experienced manager or professional role carried out either inside, or outside, the organisation and is usually not related to immediate work activities • The mentor is not the direct manager, therefore the relationship is best when conducted "off-line"
Key Driver of the Process	• The coach is the primary driver of the process, and he/she sets the agenda for knowledge and skill development • The coach usually sets the time and requirement for coaching	• The mentee, or protégé, is the primary driver of the process • He or she decides when to avail of the relationship and for what purposes • The expectations and obligations of each party may be specified in a mentoring agreement
Time Focus	• Coaching is generally a short-term process • It typically addresses a short-term need and it may occur in a reactive or proactive manner	• Mentoring is typically a longer-term relationship - often "for life" • Many mentoring relationships may exist for many years
Nature of Learning Processes	• Strong emphasis on feedback to the learner • Emphasis on correction and/or desired behaviours • Feedback and discussion processes are primarily explicit • Feedback may be directive and instructional • Learning process is concerned with deepening of knowledge or skill	• Feedback and discussion processes are primarily collaborative • Strong emphasis on questioning, listening and reflecting • Feedback and discussion primarily about implicit, intuitive issues and behaviours • Less emphasis on correction, more concerned about broadening thinking, building confidence and/or development of self

The Manager as Coach

Coaching involves helping another person systematically and deliberately to develop skill and knowledge. It usually involves personal development in terms of attitudes and motivation. Some commentators argue that the role of coach is an amalgam of four other roles that are usually performed by a manager:

- **Appraiser:** This role focuses on what development is required, what the performance standards are and the preparation of a development plan to achieve them
- **Supporter:** This role is concerned with creating opportunities, providing support, services and recourses and counselling and helping the direct report with problems
- **Communicator:** This role is concerned with giving balanced and constructive feedback. The coach offers advice and suggestions, develops positive relationships and is an information source
- **Motivator:** This role focuses on encouraging, giving recognition, challenging, articulating expectations and understanding the needs of the direct report or developer.

Figure 10.3 presents a summary of key dimensions of the coach in a training and developmental context. These represent the more commonly-emphasised roles.

FIGURE 10.3: DIMENSIONS OF COACHING IN A T&D CONTEXT

- **Experiential Coaching:** This takes place when the coach is observing or sharing the individual's on-the-job activity. The coach can guide the work performance encourage, give feedback and "model" the appropriate skill
- **Reflective Coaching:** The coach asks questions about the individual's performance in the development area so that the key aspects of the experience can be recalled and thought about. This may produce new angles and insights for the person being coached. It can often produce significant leaps forward in learning
- **Guideline Coaching:** This approach involves the coach in explanation or in giving rules and guidelines. It is the instruction element of coaching
- **Trial Coaching:** The coach gives the individual the chance to try out a new skill. Both parties manage the degree of risk in the trial. It is an opportunity to test and experience in relative safety, as a preparation for the real thing
- **Coaching as Preparation for Learning:** If the individual is to have a development opportunity in the near future, the coach can help maximise the learning by discussing it beforehand. If the person is able to attend a course, for example, the coach manager should spend time checking what learning they both would like to occur on the course. It will help the learning motivation of the learner to share hopes, enthusiasm and expectations.
- **Coaching as Learning Reinforcement:** New learning needs reinforcement and the coach can be instrumental in helping achieve this. If the individual returns from a course with new skills and knowledge, for instance, it is vital for the coach to discuss it. Together, they check what has been learned, what else needs to be done, how the coach can support the development and how much of their plan has been accomplished. Opportunity to practice is essential.

Types of coaching include:

- **Individual *versus* Group Coaching:** Coaching is primarily a 1:1 activity and most managers generally coach on an individual basis. However, coaching can also take place with groups or teams, since some people find working on a 1:1 basis uncomfortable and are most comfortable with groups or teams. However, in order to be an effective coach, you first need to be comfortable working on a 1:1 basis. Like all skills, it takes practice to increase your competence and feel comfortable with the coaching process

- **Hands-On Coaching:** "Hands-on" coaching is appropriate than you are training new or inexperienced staff. Your role as a coach is to demonstrate and explain new tasks, activities and procedures and then observe direct reports putting them into practice. Your tone and manner need to be sympathetic, motivational and patient. The hands-on coach will typically say:
  ° "I am going to tell you exactly what to do"
  ° "I will show you how to do it"
  ° "That was good (not so good or indifferent)"
  ° "Now try it again"

- Hands-Off Coaching: "Hands-Off" coaching is used with experienced staff or when trying to develop superior performance in someone. You will rely almost entirely on questioning to enable learners to improve and to take responsibility for doing so. At the same time, the learner is developing the mental attitude necessary for success. As a hands-off coach, you will typically say:
  ° "Can you tell me what your performance objectives are?"
  ° "How can you improve?"
  ° "Can you show me?"
  ° "How does it feel?"
  ° "Can you imagine what success might be like?"
  ° "Can you describe it?'"

- **Qualifier Coaching:** "Qualifier" coaching may be used when helping learners who are studying or training for a professional qualification to develop a specific piece of knowledge or expertise for their studies. As a qualifier coach, you need to:
  ° Explain clearly the standards and performance criteria required for the specific qualification desired
  ° Enable the learner to collect appropriate evidence for assessment
  ° Liaise effectively with other people supporting the learner's qualification
  ° Provide the learner with technical input, support or expertise.

The Components of Coaching

The coaching process usually follows a five-stage process:

- Statement of purpose
- Objectives and options
- What is happening now
- Empowering the learner
- Review of performance.

We will briefly describe these components. Later, we will describe the specific components of corrective and developmental coaching and the specific issues that pertain to each one. The components are:

- **Specifying the Purpose:** In a coaching relationship, it is important to define the purpose of any coaching session for those involved. For example:
  - ○ "How much time have we got?"
  - ○ "What is the purpose of this session of you?"
  - ○ "What are you looking for from me?"
  - ○ "What can I *not* coach you on?"

  It is important to spell out exactly what the learner sees as the purpose of each coaching session, rather than the coach prescribing it. If the learner encounters difficulties answering these questions, then the coach should help the individual to clarify the learning purpose before embarking on any actual coaching. This helps create a sense of ownership in the learner in his/her own development

- **Exploring Objectives and Options:** It is important for the learner to identify his/her own objective(s), option(s) and indeed goal(s). Your role as coach must be to keep the learner on track and help them to measure progress – but the goals must be relevant and realistic and owned by the individual.

  A trusting and honest relationship between you and the learner is fundamental, if real progress is to be made towards the achievement of goals. You should help the learner to identify their objectives by asking questions, such as:
  - ○ "What is your ultimate goal?"
  - ○ "How realistic is that objective?"
  - ○ "What do you want to achieve in the short- /medium- /long-term?"
  - ○ "When do you need to achieve this goal by?"
  - ○ "Is it realistic?"
  - ○ "How will we measure your progress?"
  - ○ "What will you feel like when you achieve your goal?"
  - ○ "What would achieving this goal mean to you?"

In asking these questions, you act as a motivator in building enthusiasm for the personal benefits that the learner will gain from the coaching. The agreed objectives should be SMART:

- ° *Specific:* The objective should clearly state exactly what the learner should be able to do after completing the activity
- ° *Measurable:* The objective should indicate the level of performance the learner is required to achieve
- ° *Achievable:* The target should be realistic and attainable
- ° *Relevant:* The target should be appropriate to the situation
- ° *Time-bound:* The goal should include the timescale over which the change should occur

The Focus of the Coaching Session

Once you and your learner have begun with an objective or goal in mind, both of you need to establish the current level of performance. You need to ask judgemental questions that help to raise the awareness of your learner and focus him/her focus on the gap between the current and the desired level of performance. You need to pay close attention to the answers, and to explore further with the learner, if the responses are not specific enough. The following are examples of questions you can use for this "reality check":

- "What is happening now?"
- "What has been done so far?"
- "Who is involved?"
- "What is your contribution?"
- "What are the current results?"
- "What stopped you from achieving more?"
- "What are the barriers in relation to your goal?"
- "What, if anything, have you done to overcome these obstacles?"
- "What would you do differently now?"
- "What are the opportunities open to you in relation to your goal?"
- "On a scale of 1 to 10, how would you rate your current level of performance?"

Open questions encourage the learner to dig deep within him/herself and not rely on you to come up with all the answers. They can be supported or followed-up with questions to explore further.

Empowering your Learner

Empowerment is a way of giving more responsibility to your learner. As coach, you must remain accountable for the overall results and the performance of your learners. However, from the commencement of coaching, it should be the learner who is primarily responsible for his or her own development. Learners who are empowered in a coaching situation can identify what objectives they need to meet and therefore what options they have in order to close the gap between their current performance and the desired performance.

Empowering questions in a coaching context include:

- "What are the different alternatives?"
- "What else could you do to improve your performance?"
- "What options do you have?"
- "What are the pros and cons of each option?"
- "Which would give the best results?"
- "Would you like a suggestion?"
- "What would you do differently if you could start all over again?"
- "How much trust do you have in your ability to do it?"
- "On a scale of one to ten, what is the likelihood of your succeeding with this idea?"
- "What are here advantages / disadvantages of this approach?"
- "What plan of action will you implement?"
- "How can I (the coach) help you?"

You will need good interpersonal skills to help a learner through these empowering questions. It is advisable to start on a positive footing and to ask what has worked so far. Out of empowering should come an agreed plan of new tasks, actions and activities of the learner to carry out.

Review of Coaching Session

You will need to observe and review the learner's performance and compare it against an agreed standard. You should offer constructive feedback and ensure that such reviews are on-going.

Typical questions to ask during a review include:

- "What were you trying to achieve?"
- "What worked well for you during the performance?"
- "What could have gone better?"
- "What would you do differently the next time?"
- "What are the next steps in your action plan?"

Finally, your coaching style should be designed to build self-confidence and in particular to encourage learner autonomy.

Coaching has the potential to offer numerous benefits to the learner, the coach, the training department and the organisation.

Figure 10.4 is a summary of the key benefits that you can articulate in order to justify the implementation of a coaching strategy.

FIGURE 10.4: BENEFITS OF COACHING

Learner
- The recognition of the importance of the line manager
- The development of their skills
- Higher job satisfaction, as they improve their performance
- Greater interest in, and sense of responsibility for, their work
- A growing ability to take on a greater variety of tasks

Coach
- A more successful and productive department / team
- Greater confidence when delegating tasks to your staff
- Development of your own management skills
- A growing reputation as a "developer of people"
- Exposure to new ideas and perspectives from your staff

Organisation
- Encourages instant and ongoing feedback about performance
- Improves manager and staff relationships and communications
- Provides a cost-effective means of staff development
- Greater value for money from formal training

Training Department
- Encourages line managers to think about their T&D role
- Takes the emphasis away from formal, course-based learning
- Enhances the learning transfer process and potentially enhances the status of the training function
- It takes some of the burden off you as a trainer
- It facilitates a speedy response to learning and training needs
- A realisation that the training department must act in partnership with line managers and learners

We now consider two coaching situations: corrective and developmental.

Conducting Corrective Coaching

Corrective coaching is an important dimension of a manager's role because it focuses on developing skills for effective performance in your organisation. It involves meeting with your direct report where you focus on correcting a pattern of behaviour and improving overall job performance. Corrective coaching is important because, if it is used effectively and not just at performance review time, it can lead to significant improvements in individual job performance. Most important from the manager's point of view, corrective coaching can prevent small problems developing into big ones.

Corrective coaching has three major advantages for the manager:

- It is a tool for giving regular and direct feedback to your direct reports. Through coaching, you can keep direct reports "on track" with their regular assignments and the special tasks or projects you have delegated to them

- It is a source of information and skills. You can learn more about, and from, your direct reports because good corrective coaching involves two-way communication. By using constructive feedback in coaching sessions, you can also encourage the development of positive work relationships

- It provides opportunities for you to develop and practise your interpersonal and management skills.

It is important that corrective coaching has benefits for your direct reports. Three specific benefits can be identified:

- Direct feedback on performance problems and opportunities for improvement. If you coach constructively, direct reports can turn a mistake or work problem into a learning situation

- Stimulus to direct reports who may just be cruising along. Corrective coaching shows your concern for what the direct report is doing and your attention can improve their performance

- Opportunities for employees to develop their own problem-solving skills. A good coach will not impose solutions but, through discussion, will help direct reports to sort out their own problems and make better decisions.

Figure 10.5 provides a summary of corrective coaching guidelines that may be followed by the manager or by a trainer when they are required to perform a corrective coaching role.

FIGURE 10.5: CONDUCTING CORRECTIVE COACHING: GUIDELINES FOR ACTION

1. **Identifying Coaching Goals:** Before you discuss a performance problem with a direct report, take the time you need to plan and prepare. Decide what you want to accomplish through the coaching session – what are the specific outcomes you want to see, such as the direct report making a specific commitment to change or improve something

2. **Prepare for Coaching Session:** Gather the information that you need, decide upon the time/place for your discussion and communicate this to the direct report

3. **Express your Desire to Help:** Welcome the direct report and explain that you want to ensure good two-way communication in the workplace. This meeting is an opportunity to clarify and discuss your own and your direct report's expectations and views. Begin by focusing on positives – informing your direct reports that you appreciate the things they do well makes them more open to receiving feedback on performance problems

4. **State the Problem and its Consequences:** Based on the facts of the situation, describe the problem that has led to this coaching session. At the beginning of the session, it is important to be objective and factual and to use descriptive rather than evaluative

statements. Be relaxed and open-minded. Don't jump to conclusions and be prepared to discuss the direct report's expectations. After stating the problem you might refer to some of the consequences – for example, other people being affected, work delayed, customers upset, and so on. You should not overlook your own feelings as they relate to the issue – what has been the impact of this problem on you – and share those feelings with the direct report

5. **Reach Agreement that a Problem Exists:** Obtaining the direct report's agreement that a problem exists is the most important, and often the most difficult step, in the corrective coaching process. If you continue without gaining agreement, additional difficulties will arise and you may need to return again to try to secure agreement. One way of gaining agreement is to point out the gap between the standard or what you expect and the person's actions and behaviour. Once you have agreement that a problem exists, emphasise this agreement so that it is clear to the direct report

6. **Discuss Causes of the Problem:** Determine the facts by asking information questions like "What happened ...", "What time ...", "Why did you do that?". Encourage the direct report to talk about the problem while you listen and try to see the situation from his/her point of view. In addition to asking questions, you might steer the coaching session by interrupting occasionally and using reflective statements such as: "So you think that ...", "Does this mean that ...". These statements reflect back to direct reports the picture they are presenting and check your understanding of what has been said. They may also stimulate your direct report to expand on a point or help you guide them to the next stage in the coaching session

7. **Discuss Possible Solutions and their Benefits:** Move the discussion from talking about the past to talking about the future, from talking about things that have gone wrong to how to prevent them from going wrong again. With a direct report who needs more direction, you may narrow down the possible solutions by discussing two or three options: "What do you think would be better ...?". Don't forget to discuss how the direct report will benefit from taking the actions you suggest

8. **Agree upon Actions:** On the basis that employees generally respond well to a personal approach, you might tell the direct report something about how you see things and your own experience related to this problem. Here, you can demonstrate your own involvement as a person rather than someone judging at a distance. However, try to avoid telling your direct report that they "should do such and such" or "should have done such and such". Too many "should"s can make you appear rigid and pedantic. The responsibility for changing his/her behaviour is not yours: it lies with the individual. This is why your direct reports needs to be involved in making decisions and agreeing upon future action. In this way, he/she will be more committed to these decisions or actions. End this session on an encouraging note and show how direct reports can benefit from taking the actions agreed upon. Identify a target for future performance and arrange to discuss the issue again at a future date so that you can provide support and monitor progress

9. **Document the Session:** You need to document the session. Then you will have a record to refer back to later, particularly if there are any further coaching sessions or if disciplinary action may be necessary. Document the solutions or actions agreed upon and the date of the follow-up meeting

10. **Follow-up on the Session:** Consider how you might follow-up on the corrective coaching session. When and how often do you need to check on progress? How will you recognise achievement or change? If you reward the behaviour, it is most likely to be repeated. What will you do if the problem continues?

Created from Beard and Wilson (2002), Sheal (1999) and Evenden and Anderson (1992).

Developmental Coaching

Some of the skills we have discussed in respect of corrective coaching equally apply to developmental coaching, although a number of additional considerations apply to the effective implementation of developmental coaching:

- **Customisation of the Coaching Relationship:** Coaching can be customised to the unique needs of the direct report / learner being coached. Both the content (what is learned) and the process (when, where and how it is learned) can be customised. Thus, unique needs can be met in one process. Another consideration in choosing coaching is how well a customised learning approach fits with the organisational culture

- **Just-in-Time Coaching:** When the development need is urgent, coaching can be arranged more quickly than other learning modes such as classroom training, university courses, or action learning

- **The Value of Coaching:** Coaching is recommended when an employee's time is more valuable than the cost, such as with senior executives, financial gurus, and other key individuals. Coaching tends to provide the maximum learning for the time invested, because the learning is continuously tailored exactly to the topics and the level of the person being coached

- **Confidentiality:** Coaching generally takes place in the context of a close, trusting relationship, where it is safe to discuss sensitive personal and business issues. For managers, in particular, it provides a confidential and objective sounding board for issues that they may be reluctant or unable to discuss with other members of their team

- **Skill Focus of Coaching:** Developing coaching is a particular useful way of enhancing a range of skills such as the following:
  - Interpersonal skills, including relationship building, tact and sensitivity, assertiveness, conflict management, working across cultures, and influencing without authority
  - Communication, including listening skills, presentations, and speaking with impact
  - Leadership skills, including delegating, coaching and mentoring, and motivating others
  - Certain cognitive skills, such as prioritising, decision-making, and strategic thinking
  - Self-management skills, including time management, emotion and anger management and work-life balance.

Figure 10.6 sets out what you need to consider when establishing a developmental coaching relationship.

FIGURE 10.6: DEVELOPMENTAL COACHING: DESIGN CONSIDERATIONS

Identifying the Learners who will Benefit from Coaching

Organisations should develop specific criteria for determining who will receive coaching. The following questions should be considered when selecting learners:

- Is there a genuine development need?
- Is that development need linked to business performance?
- Is the issue something the individual has control over, or is it symptomatic of a larger organisational problem that needs to be addressed on a broader scale?
- Is the person open to learning and feedback?
- Is the person motivated to learn and change?
- Is coaching the most appropriate development solution given your understanding of the problem?

Selecting and Training the Coach

An effective coach requires two key qualities:

1. It is important to make sure that the coach can relate to the person and the world that person lives in. Find out how well the coach has worked with others in similar situations by asking the following questions:
    - What kinds of people have you worked with? What results did you achieve?
    - Where do you do your best work? With what kinds of people and topics do you work best?
    - Who would you turn down and why?

2. A coach should be able to walk a person through all the important steps of learning. The following questions are useful in assessing a coach's appropriateness to the learning process:
    - How will you determine what the person needs to work on?
    - How will you help the person learn new ways to do things?
    - How will you ensure they get results?

You may consider using either an external or internal coach. External coaches are most appropriate:

- When you need rapid learning and behaviour change. Few organisations have internal coaches with the depth of skill and experience that is readily available among external coaches. This is especially the case for management development
- For dealing with direct reports who are resistant to change or who are cynical toward the coaching process. There is less risk if an external person fails as a coach
- For relatively confidential or sensitive issues, where the person does not want an internal person involved
- When internal coaches are unavailable or in different locations.
- When internal coaches do not have the particular expertise that is desired
- When an objective, independent viewpoint is critical

In contrast, internal coaches are most appropriate in these cases:

- As part of regular, ongoing development activities, such as supporting a specific development programme
- When deep knowledge of the personalities or relationships among a given cast of characters is important
- When knowledge of organisational politics or how things really get done inside the organisation is critical

Initiate the Coaching Relationship

Contracting: There are several aspects of contracting:
- The first focuses on the content, outlining the purpose of the coaching, establishing specific learning goals, and setting clear expectations for how and when performance will improve
- The second is procedural, defining various stakeholders and their roles, as well as clarifying guidelines for confidentiality and communications
- Finally, contracting involves financial arrangements, such as fees, expenses, and billing schedules in the case of an external coach.

The contracting process can begin by identifying the key stakeholders, usually the coach, the person being coached, that person's superior boss or designated organisational sponsor, and an appropriate human resource contact. The coach should discuss expectations, roles and responsibilities with each stakeholder.

Coaching Sessions: There are typically three parts to an effective coaching session:
- *The Opening:* In the very first meeting, the opening is a chance to clarify expectations, solidify the working agenda, and get to know each other. This may be the first time the coach and the participant meet face-to-face, although they have usually been in communication with each other in arranging the coaching process. The coach needs to pay particular attention to building trust and rapport by understanding what the person hopes to accomplish through coaching. In subsequent meetings, the first part of each session allows time to re-establish that rapport, catch up on what has happened since the last session, and prioritise the agenda for the day
- *Practice:* The middle segment is the heart of the coaching process. Here, through hands-on practice of real-world situations, instruction, modelling, feedback, and discussion, the coach facilitates the kind of learning that participants can carry back with them to the workplace
- *Action Planning:* It is relatively easy for participants to leave each session with new insights and skills and a genuine motivation to put them into action. Participants should visualise exactly what will happen when they try to put a new behaviour into action. When do they plan to do it? How will they remember to do it? What will get in their way? What will they do to stay on track? How will they evaluate the outcome of their new action? How will they get feedback from others? When will they try it again? How will they modify or build on what they tried the next time they use it?

Development Activities Between Sessions: Between coaching sessions, participants are expected to apply what they have learned. Attention to this is essential for breaking old habits and establishing new ones. Participants need to be encouraged to push their comfort zone on a daily basis.

Created from Kraiger (2001), Evenden and Anderson (1992) and Gunnnigle (1999).

Corrective *versus* Developmental Coaching

It is likely that in your role as manager you will perform both corrective and developmental coaching. Both processes have the potential to develop the employee. **Figure 10.7** provides a summary of the assumptions and differences between corrective and developmental coaching.

FIGURE 10.7: DIFFERENCES BETWEEN CORRECTIVE & DEVELOPMENTAL COACHING

Corrective Coaching	Developmental Coaching
Direct reports resist change and the coach's task is to motive them to develop	Direct reports are motivated to learn and grow; the coach's task is to tap into that motivation to develop
Coaching needs to start with a thorough assessment of needs analysis, so direct reports have an accurate picture of themselves and their development needs	Insight is a never-ending discovery process that is nurtured throughout the entire coaching process; all that is necessary to begin is a good starting point
Coaches need to provide feedback to the direct reports they coach	Although feedback from the coach may be helpful, the coach's primary role is to help direct reports improve their ability to nurture deeper insights by gathering their own feedback
Coaches have a more objective understanding of the issues than the direct report	Both coaches and direct reports have important insights and information. By working together, they can put together a more useful picture of what is happening
Coaches need to be experts in a given topic, in order to teach it to direct reports	Coaches need to be experts in how direct reports learn so they can help direct reports actually change behaviours and become more effective. One of the most valuable things a coach can do is help direct reports learn how to learn for themselves
Coaching takes a lot of time and effort	Coaching is about finding leverage so that direct reports focus on the one or two things that will have the greatest payoff
Coaching is about fixing problem behaviours (as assumption that often leads to a focus on the past)	Coaching is about improving future performance; it works best when the focus is on understanding what works for the direct report, what does not work and what they will do the next time they are in the same situation

Adapted from Kraiger (2001).

The Manager as Mentor

A mentor is usually a more experienced and senior person than the mentee. Mentors are likely to be technical or professional experts or middle or senior managers and are more frequently drawn from within the organisation.

Mentors usually perform a number of important roles. Typically, they provide one or more of the following:

- Guidance on how to acquire the necessary knowledge and skills to do a new job
- Advice on dealing with any administrative, technical or "people" problems

- Information on "the way things are done around here" – the culture and its manifestations in the shape of core values and organisational behaviour
- Help in obtaining access to information and people within the organisation
- Coaching in specific skills, especially managerial skills such as leadership, communications and time management
- Help in completing projects – not by doing it for the mentee but by helping them to help themselves
- A parental figure, with whom mentees can discuss their aspirations and concerns, and who will lend a sympathetic ear to their problems.

There are a number of roles that mentors may have to fulfil:

- **Mentor as Coach:** Coaching can help in developing new skills in the mentee, can give constructive and considered feedback and can offer an insight into management practice. It works best when the mentor is supportive and offers friendly encouragement
- **Mentor as Counsellor:** Counselling can help mentees explore and resolve problems and difficulties they may be facing in a confidential setting. However, it is important to remember that you are not a trained counsellor and any issues that you cannot handle should be passed to an expert
- **Mentor as Role Model:** Mentors, by their behaviour, can demonstrate the acceptable standards of conduct and impart "the way things are done around here", particularly in the case of new recruits. They can also be seen as someone who has "trodden the path" already.

It is important that the focus of the mentoring is on helping the mentee to learn. While direct advice and instruction from the mentor can be helpful, it is important to ensure that mentees learn to think for themselves and that the mentoring process does not, either intentionally or unintentionally, create a dependence where they just blindly follow the mentor's instructions and cannot take action without advice.

Mentoring is likely to suit managers who are interested in the development of others and who enjoy sharing their knowledge and experience with them. Not all managers are likely to make good mentors. It requires a considerable amount of time commitment, emotional resources and sustained effort.

Selecting Mentors and Initiating a Programme

There are a number of issues that you and your organisation should consider implementing a mentoring programme.

Selection of Mentors

This is a critical task, because it determines the success of the programme. You should select as mentors those who are interested in other people and, in particular, in their development. When choosing a mentor, the following qualities are important: experience, breadth of knowledge, technical proficiency, credibility, respect for confidentiality and status. The mentor needs to be completely trustworthy, so that it is possible for the mentee to discuss career and personal issues knowing that they will be held in strict confidence.

If the right kind of mentor does not exist in your organisation, you should look outside. You can find mentors in Universities, colleges, similar organisations, or your own professional association. Most people worry about asking someone to mentor them without remuneration. Remember that most people consider it a privilege to help others develop and are flattered to be asked to participate in other people's career development. They understand that being asked to act as a mentor is a way of building their own career and profession. The pay-off for the mentor is that as their protégés develop, so will their own network and sphere of influence.

When you are choosing a mentor, the following are some of the questions that need to be asked (from the perspective of the mentee):

- Do I want someone with similar, or contrasting, work experience to me, or a mixture?
- What type of background and experience do they possess?
- Do I want a mentor with a similar, contrasting, or specific management style?
- Do I want to work with someone of the same or a different gender?
- Should they be based in the same building or site, or could I travel easily to another location to meet them?
- Do I want to work with someone with a wide knowledge of the industry or with a deeper understanding in a specialist area?
- Will I have ready access to them, or will they be too busy to meet me at short notice?
- How well do they know my line manager?

Development of Mentor Skills

In order to be an effective mentor, the mentor should be capable of identifying the strengths and opportunities for development of the mentee. The mentor needs to be skilled in motivating the mentee to develop – it may be necessary to have coaching skills to provide specific skill development. The mentor should also be able to provide networking opportunities for the mentee to access other influential people, as well as education and development resources and opportunities. The skilled mentor needs to be able to listen actively, question effectively, understand differences in learning style and adapt their mentoring style to the learning style of the mentee. The mentor may need to challenge assumptions and ensure that they give enough time to the protégé. Mentors need to be self-aware and capable of self-analysis and two-way feedback.

Establishing Ground Rules and Preparing the Mentoring Contract
If your mentoring programme takes place in a formal context, then it may be your role as trainer to make a formal allocation of mentor and mentee. If, however, mentoring takes place on an informal basis, then the mentee will probably have to seek out and approach a suitable mentor. However arrived at, from the perspective of the organisation, it is important that the contractual dimensions of the relationship are made explicit from the outset. Some of the issues include:

- Identify and explore the expectations of both mentor and mentee
- Agree the overall objectives of the mentoring relationship
- Agree on what each other's roles are within the relationship
- Consider what will be covered and what will not
- Decide how mentor and mentee will give each other feedback
- Discuss any involvement of the mentee's line manager
- Decide who will be responsible for organising meetings
- Decide when and where mentor and mentee both meet
- Decide on how long mentor and mentee will generally meet for
- Discuss on-going informal contact with each other
- Agree on the structure for mentoring meetings
- Agree on the breadth of confidentiality
- Decide on the overall duration of the relationship
- Agree on an opt-out clause after a certain timeframe (usually three months), if the relationship is not working out
- Decide on the processes to be used when there are disagreements and conflicts.

Benefits of Mentoring

Mentoring can bring benefits to the manager who performs the role of mentor, the learner as mentee or protégé, and the organisation – generally, and particularly to the training function. **Figure 10.8** summarises the benefits for all of the parties.

FIGURE 10.8: BENEFITS OF MENTORING

Mentee	Mentor	Organisation	Training Function
• A smoother adjustment to a new role or position • Help in acquiring more quickly and comprehensively the skills and knowledge that they need • Help with the necessary choices in the development of the careers • Access to someone more senior than themselves, other than their line manager • A greater understanding of both the formal and informal workings of the organisation	• Increased motivation and self-esteem brought about by the mentoring role • Greater respect and recognition from staff in the organisation • An opportunity to hone and improve their own management skills, particularly advisory and supporting skills in a safe environment • An opportunity to learn about the perspectives and views of others less senior than themselves and in other parts of the organisation • A chance to influence and improve communications with others in the organisation	• An opportunity for staff to be encouraged, supported and motivated to reach their potential • A greater job satisfaction, morale and commitment by mentors and mentees to their work • Improved work performance of mentees • The transfer of the organisational values to mentees • Leading to a morale stable culture • Improved communications through linking different departments and levels within the organisation • Established routes for effective career development that can aid the recruitment of high calibre staff	• Involvement of managers in the process of developing employees • Capitalising on those managers who are interested in the development of others and who enjoy sharing their knowledge with others • Raising the status of training and development with key individuals within the organisation • Ensuring a balance between formal group focused training and individualised training • Involving learners in decisions about training and development and ensuring partnership

FIGURE 10.9: EFFECTIVE MENTORING: PRACTICE GUIDELINES

Identify Mentoring Needs: You need to consider the current situation. What are your department's needs in terms of career planning, graduate development, job certification or vocational qualifications? What do individual members of staff need to learn during the next year? What do your new employees need to learn? Who needs to learn a new skill? Who can teach particular skills?

Assess Whether Mentoring will Work: Are the conditions for a mentoring relationship favourable? If there is a lack of management commitment, you or someone else could make a presentation on mentoring. If there are no rewards for mentoring currently, your organisation might find a way to reward mentors through the performance review system or some other recognition process

Identifying the Potential Mentor: As you think about your staff, try to match your potential mentors and those who need to learn. The best matches occur between mentors and staff who share similar jobs, and work in close proximity to each other so they can easily get together. You should identify managers who are already functioning as informal mentors – managers who seem to have the motivation and some experience of mentoring. You might also consider which of your senior management team might benefit from taking on mentoring responsibilities

Discuss with Potential Mentor: Meet with the potential mentor and discuss the purpose and benefits of a mentoring relationship. At the beginning, you need to find out whether the person really wants to be a mentor. Mentors and mentees should always be volunteers. Not all experienced staff may wish to share their know-how. Indeed, some may enjoy the advantage that superior knowledge gives them and want to withhold important job information. If you think this might be the case, you should not use that manager as a mentor, or explain very clearly what is required and monitor the mentoring relationship carefully. You also need to draw out any concerns or fears the prospective mentor might have. If these concerns are not discussed at the start, they can undermine the process

Discuss with the Mentee: You should meet with the employee(s) to be mentored. Discuss their strengths, interests, specific skills that may need to be developed. Explain the purpose and benefits of mentoring as a development tool. Mentoring involves people working together, it is a mutual exchange, and employees should know that they are just as responsible for the success of mentoring relationship as the mentor. In particular, mentees must be prepared to consider their own areas for improvement and be willing to learn. The motivation of the mentee to learn is an important judgement call that you will have to make

Arrange for Training: To ensure that the mentoring relationship gets off to a good start, it's useful for both mentors and mentees to attend a briefing or introduction to the mentoring process. By working together on tasks like needs assessment and development planning, both parties can forge their working relationship, clarify expectations, and ensure that they are "singing from the same sheet"

Agree Development Plan: Work on the mentees' development plans might start at the briefing session or the introduction to the mentoring process. These discussions between the mentors and mentees often need more time and require consultation with other people involved – for example, the mentees' supervisors, the training or personnel departments, or other organisations where mentees may have a field trip or short assignment

The Initial Meeting: The first meeting is very important. Mentor and mentee should find out about each other in terms of general background, professional training, time in the organisation, career history, key skills and knowledge. It is important that all elements of the mentoring contract are clearly agreed upon. It is recommended that the initial meeting should occur on a four to six week basis for the first six months to establish the mentoring relationship. Every effort should be made by both parties to keep to the meeting schedule. The duration each meeting should be for 1 to 2 hours per month.

Structuring Follow-Up Meetings: The overall duration of a formal mentoring relationship tends to be from six months to two years. It is desirable that it be for at least six months. In between meetings, both mentor and mentee should contact each other to check on progress, ask questions and deal with any relevant issues. When mentor and mentee meet for the next and subsequent meetings, the following issues should be considered:

- Decide and agree what you want to get out of the meeting
- Review progress since the last meeting
- Establish what has been learnt
- Focus on making progress on a specific issue:
- Establish what the issue is
- Explore what is causing it
- Consider it and discuss possible ways forward
- Seek suggestions and, if needed, offer advice
- Agree a way forward
- Summarise conclusions and actions
- Agree on a time and place for the next meeting.

Adapted from O'Connor (1999).

Problems with Formal Mentoring Relationships

The establishment of formal mentoring relationships in organisations is a difficult one. It is not uncommon for mentoring relationships to fail or to under-perform, for reasons that include:

- **One or both members in the relationship find it difficult to get along with the other:** Mentor or mentee may not like one another because they hold widely differing views, or simply there is a clash of personality. If this arises, then it should be addressed as early as possible – both should review the relationship to date and discuss whether it is with trying to resolve differences and start again, or indeed whether to call on the opt-out clause and agree to part. It may be worth involving another person, such as a member of the personnel department in these discussions and decisions

- **Someone breaches a confidence:** This can lead to a lack of trust on the part of the other, resulting in an ineffective mentoring relationship. If the spread and depth of confidentiality has not been previously negotiated, then this should be discussed immediately. If a confidentiality clause is already in place, then both mentor and mentee need to sit down and discuss the reasons behind the breach of confidence and how to ensure it does not happen again – there may be a need to renegotiate the mentoring contract again

- **Mentoring takes up more time and is more demanding than originally anticipated:** If the mentor or mentee cannot commit the necessary time and attention, or is continually cancelling and re-scheduling meetings, particularly at short notice, then frustration is likely to develop. Furthermore, this behaviour will send a negative signal about the importance of the relationship. If this is simply due to poor time and diary management, then revisiting the time aspect of the mentoring contract and agreeing in advance to a programme of meeting dates over a considerable time-frame – say, six months – may work. However, if the reason is a genuine lack of time, then both parties need to consider whether it is worth seeking another mentor/mentee

- **Neither party is really interested in maintaining the mentoring relationship:** This occurs when the mentor and the mentee become complacent – eventually, the partnership dissolves due to lack of interest. This can arise if the relationship has run its course, in which case the mentoring has reached its natural conclusion. But if this is not the case, then both need to make more of an effort in terms of general input, setting objectives and goals, agreeing action plans and arranging a programme of meetings, etc. in order to maintain a sense of overall purpose to the relationship

- **The mentee has unrealistic expectations about what the mentor can offer:** The mentee views the mentor as someone of considerable standing in the organisation, and as such, someone who should be able to "pull strings" and really transform their career. When this doesn't materialise, the mentee may feel annoyed and disillusioned. Mentors should ensure from the beginning, therefore, that the mentee has a realistic perspective of what the mentor's role is and what they can and, indeed cannot, do for them. They should never make unrealistic promises or commitments to the mentee that they cannot deliver on.

THE MANAGER AS PERFORMANCE MANAGER

The manager has an important role to play in the performance management process. Line managers typically, but not exclusively, operate most performance management processes. Performance management has a number of important objectives for the business, the line manager and the individual, summarised in **Figure 10.10**.

FIGURE 10.10: OBJECTIVES OF THE PERFORMANCE MANAGEMENT PROCESS

Business Objectives
• Increase focus on key business objectives
• Alignment of organisation, department and individual objectives
• Reduce costs and raise productivity
• Support a total quality management initiative
• Support "Excellence through People"
• Improve or maintain values and standards
• Implement a new project or structure e.g. team working
• Achieve other specific business objectives

Line Manager Objectives
• Improve communication about business objectives
• Increase employee commitment to learn
• Improve managerial capabilities
• Change to a more focused "performance culture"
• Improve retention of staff
• Increase staff motivation and commitment
• Increase focus of training through clearer definition of training needs
• Increase mangers' focus on their "management" and development roles
• Provide better ways of assessing individuals' performance to fit people to roles and careers

Individual's Objectives
• More clarity about what performance is exacted
• More regular feedback on how they are performing
• Understand clearly how managers view their performance
• Define more specific training to meet their needs
• Have an opportunity to discuss how the manger has managed them
• Define more specific development to meet their needs
• Identify career development opportunities
• Increase opportunity for more participation in decision making
• Take ownership for development

The performance management process usually culminates in an appraisal interview in which the manager and subordinate review the appraisal and make plans to remedy differences and develop strengths.

There are a number of issues that you need to be aware of when conducting this discussion:

• **Preparation:** Effective preparation involves three steps. You should first give the direct report sufficient notice to review his/her work. It is also advisable to read his/her job description, analyse problems or development issues and compile questions and comments. Secondly, you will need to study the job role, compare the employee's performance to his/her standards and revisit previous reviews. Finally, you should agree an appropriate time/place to conduct the review

- **Conducting the Interview:** The primary aim of the interview is to reinforce satisfactory performance, to address unsatisfactory performance and to plan for future development. It is important that you check the determinants of performance or behaviour that apply to the performance situation you are analysing. Some of the issues that you need to consider here are presented in **Figure 10.5**. You will need to be direct and specific. You should talk in terms of objective work data, using examples to support your arguments. Before your direct report leaves, you will need to get agreement on how things can be improved.

It is also important that you are conscious of the possible rating errors you can make in a performance appraisal, which have the potential to significantly undermine the effectiveness of your performance discussion. These include:

- **Halo and Horn:** A tendency to think of an employee as more or less good or bad is carried over into specific performance ratings. Stereotypes based on the employee's sex, race, or age also affect performance ratings. In either case, the rater does not make meaningful distinctions when evaluating specific dimensions of performance – all are rated either low (horn) or high (halo)

- **Leniency:** All employees are rated higher than they should be. This happens when managers are not penalised for giving high ratings to everyone, when rewards are not part of a fixed and limited pot, and when dimensions ratings are not required

- **Strictness** All employees are related lower than they should be. Inexperienced raters unfamiliar with environmental constraints on performance, raters with low self-esteem, and raters who have themselves received a low rating are most likely to rate strictly. Rater-training that includes a reversal of supervisor-incumbent roles and confidence building can reduce this error

- **Central Tendency:** All employees are rated as average, when performance actually varies. Raters with large spans of control and little opportunity to observe behaviour are likely to use this "play safe" strategy. A forced distribution format requiring that most employees be rated average also may create this error

FIGURE 10.11: CHECKLIST FOR DIAGNOSING THE CAUSES OF EMPLOYEE PERFORMANCE DEFICIENCIES

Check the determinants of performance or behaviour that apply to the situation you are analysing.

Competencies / Skills
- Does the direct report have the competencies needed to perform as expected?
- Has the direct report performed as expected before?
- Does the direct report believe he or she has the competencies needed to perform as desired?
- Does the direct report have the interest to perform as desired?

Goals of the Direct report
- Were the goals communicated to the direct report?
- Are the goals specific?
- Are the goals difficult but attainable?

Certainty for the Direct report
- Has desired performance been clearly specified?
- Have rewards or consequences for good or bad performance been specified?
- Is the direct report clear about her or his level of authority?

Feedback to the Direct report
- Does the direct report know when he or she has performed correctly or incorrectly?
- Is the feedback diagnostic so that the direct report can perform better in the future?
- Is there a delay between performance and the receipt of the feedback?
- Can performance feedback be easily interpreted?

Consequences to the Direct report
- Is performing as expected punishing?
- Is not performing poorly more rewarding than performing well?
- Does performing as desired matter?
- Are there positive consequences for performing as desired?

Power for the Direct report
- Can the direct report mobilise the resources to get the job done?
- Does the direct report have the tools and equipment to perform as desired?
- Is performance under the control of the direct report?

- **Primacy:** As a cognitive shortcut, raters may use initial information to categorise a person as either a good or a bad performer. Information that supports the initial judgement is amassed, and contradicting information is ignored
- **Recency:** A rater may ignore employee performance until the appraisal data draws near. When the rater searches for cues about performance, recent behaviours or results are most salient, so recent events receive more weight than they should

- **Contrast Effects :** When compared with weak employees, an average employee will appear outstanding, when evaluated against outstanding employees, an average employee will be perceived as a low performer.

The performance management process has a major developmental component. There are a number of important benefits to be gained by the manager and direct report, if performance reviews are used effectively as a development tool.

The benefits that the manager can receive from the process include:

- The opportunity to learn about a direct report's hopes, fears, anxieties and careers related to both the present job and the future career
- The opportunity to clarify and reinforce important goals and priorities so the direct report can see precisely where their contribution fits in
- The opportunity to motivate staff by recognising important achievements
- Performance review provides a basis for discussing and agreeing upon courses of action to develop employee performance and contribute to organisational performance.

From the perspective of the direct report, the benefits include:

- An opportunity to receive feedback from a manager on how the direct report's performance is viewed by the organisation
- A forum for agreeing with a manager a plan for overcoming barriers to performance and for enhancing performance in the future
- An opportunity to communicate views about the job to a manager
- An effective process within which to identify the direct report's training and development needs and agree on appropriate actions to implement these needs.

Where you use performance reviews in a developmental context should be aware of the issues summarised in **Figure 10.12**.

FIGURE 10.12: GUIDELINES FOR USING PERFORMANCE REVIEWS IN A DEVELOPMENTAL CONTEXT

Preparation

Agree date and time for discussion

Too often, performance reviews are left until the last minute and then done in a hurry. This undermines the total process. The results are likely to be negative, with managers feeling rather guilty, and employees feeling unimportant and let down by the process. To avoid this, give employees at least a week's notice before the review meeting. Check your own calendar and agree a time when you will be free. It is unlikely that a performance review can be conducted in less than 45 minutes, if there is to be enough time for the discussion to be effective.

Ask employees to complete a self-appraisal

Traditionally, appraisal systems have put the burden of collecting information on the manager – a burden that has become increasingly heavy as the number of "direct reports" increases. You can delegate more responsibility to your direct reports by asking them to complete the same performance review form that you complete. This ensures that they take the time to think about past performance and future development in a comprehensive and structured way. It also increases the commitment of your direct reports and the quality of the information collected. Ask your direct reports to hand in a copy of the completed form a few days before the discussion, so that you can take it into consideration when you complete your own form. In preparation for the meeting, you might also ask your direct report to consider:

- The **past** in terms of major individual and team contributions, problems and their cause, what they enjoyed and did not enjoy
- The **present** in terms of current workload, strengths, concerns and opportunities for improvement
- **Working relationships** within the organisation and with customers / clients - 360 degree feedback from the direct reports' colleagues can provide useful information here
- The **future** in terms of where the department is going, potential individual / team assignments and goals for next year, what help or training may be needed, employees' own plans and self-development opportunities.

Gather information on employees' performance

The direct report's performance in the current job is the key issue. Therefore look at the job description, job requirements and the established goals or standards. Look back at the previous year's performance review records and consider the objectives and targets that were established then. How has the direct report performed in achieving those targets? How has the direct report worked with others in achieving team goals? Check your records (activity reports, project reports) and check your memory against the information in the direct report's self-appraisal.

Conducting the Discussion

Prepare for the discussion

The most critical factor in the success of a performance discussion is the atmosphere in which it is conducted. Make sure you hold the meeting in private to avoid interruptions or anyone overhearing. Prepare yourself mentally by focusing on what you want to achieve:

- Demonstrate your recognition of the person's achievements
- Recognise that the direct report has detailed experience of the job and potentially useful ideas for improvement
- Involve joint exploration of any performance problems
- Generate mutual feedback
- Focus on future performance, rather than arguing about the past.

Establish a constructive climate and a two-way conversation

When the direct report comes to the meeting, welcome him/her and outline the purpose of the discussion. Avoid giving the impression that the performance review is a meaningless chore, which needs to be completed only for the purpose of satisfying personnel. You might open the discussion on a positive, friendly note by highlighting one of the direct report's recent achievements and discussing it. You should then have your direct report review performance over the past 12 months. Your direct report might do this by referring to the review form he/she has completed. This approach enables your direct report to select where to begin and can lead to a relatively candid assessment of actual performance. While the employee is talking, you should be an interested listener but ask clarifying questions and make brief notes. At this point, you can learn more from listening than from talking, and you have a rare opportunity to find out what your direct report feels about his or her work and your management. When your direct report has completed this review, discuss the information and clarify any points by asking for more detail.

Share your assessment of your direct report's performance over the past year

Discuss your direct report's achievements and strengths in detail to show that you recognise his or her distinctive contribution and to encourage your direct report to build on these strengths. Whenever possible, refer back to the form your direct report completed and indicate any similarities, or points where you think your direct report did not give him or herself sufficient credit.

Discuss areas for improvement

The most difficult part of any performance review is discussing unsatisfactory performance and areas for improvement. Generally, the most effective remedy for poor performance is to focus on the future rather than on the past. Focusing on the past is unproductive for two reasons: first, there is no way that the mistakes of the past can be undone, and second, discussions that focus totally on the past are likely to lead to arguments due to different perceptions of past events.

Plan for next year

Outline the department's goals and objectives for the next 12 months. Discuss the individual's potential contributions, tasks and targets, in a general way. You might also discuss actions that you and the employee need to take towards accomplishing these goals. You should not overload this performance review meeting - more detailed discussion of future work is often best left to another meeting – but this general planning discussion provides an opportunity for linking work requirements with the employee's personal development. You should discuss what learning needs and opportunities arise from future work goals and find out your direct report's thoughts on his or her own development needs. You should also explore your direct report's views and feelings about longer-term development, transfers, promotion and career progression. In this discussion, the emphasis should be on why, and in what way, the person needs to develop. You should avoid discussing possible courses as if training provides a shopping list, but you should not ignore off-the-job training and also self-development opportunities.

Summarise and close the discussion on a positive note

Many performance reviews fail because the manager and the employee end the session with different views about what happened and what was agreed upon. Summarise what has been discussed and agreed. Reinforce the praise for good work. Review and show enthusiasm and confidence in the goals and actions that have been agreed upon and end on a positive note.

Follow-Up

Finalise review form and document the discussion

Complete the final review form, making any changes or additional comments that you think necessary as a result of your discussion. Add a summary of your discussion and give the forms to your direct report for signature and ask him/her to make a copy.

Follow-up on agreements and actions

Without coaching and follow-up, the performance review process will be limited in its effectiveness. Ensure that any training or developmental work experience that was agreed upon is planned for and actually happens during the next year. If you do not do this, the process will lose credibility and the employee is likely to see it as a waste of time.

Created from Pattinson (1999) and Sheal (1999).

Using Multi-source Feedback for Development

The major goal of a multi-source feedback intervention is to facilitate change and development in individual or team behaviour. A multi-source feedback intervention involves the systematic collection of specific information from multiple sources to enhance the self-awareness of individuals and teams. Focus groups, interviews, or paper-and-pencil instruments are used to obtain data from multiple sources that have a relevant perspective to share. These data are summarised quantitatively or qualitatively, and are then shared orally or in writing with one or more members of the organisation.

The most common form of multi-source feedback interventions typically uses an off-the-shelf or in-house designed instrument that measures critical competencies required for competitive performance. Most feedback from these interventions is collected from multiple perspectives (for example, an individual's supervisor, direct reports, peers and team members) and is summarised in the form of a written or computerised report (often including graphic comparisons of the perceptions of the individual and others, written comments, and narrative information.

The interventions based on multi-source feedback that are most commonly used are:

- Executive and management coaching
- Training and development
- Career counselling
- Succession planning and development
- Training needs assessment
- Training evaluation
- Performance appraisal and evaluation.

If your organisation is considering using a multi-source feedback process, then you must be clear concerning the situations in which it is appropriate and not appropriate.

The use of multi-source feedback is a valuable tool in the following situations:

- **Behavioural Change in Individuals and Teams:** A multi-source feedback intervention is useful in providing individuals and team members with specific information from multiple perspectives abut strengths and areas for development. This information increases self-insight and self-awareness and becomes a catalyst for behavioural change efforts.
- **Self-Awareness Issues:** It is not uncommon for an individual to lack insight about the impact that he/she has on others or about the way others perceive him/her. A multi-source feedback

intervention helps individual team members to compare their perceptions of themselves to those of others. Multi-rater feedback has been shown to increase self-awareness and insight for both individual and teams, often resulting in successful behavioural change efforts

- **When Multiple Perspectives Provide a Holistic Picture:** Although research suggests that agreement among multiple sources may be at best modest, different perspectives provide the respondent with information about how he/she is perceived and the impact that he/she has on internal and external stakeholders.

There is evidence that line managers may be anxious about receiving feedback on their performance from peers and subordinates. Coping with criticism is often difficult, and is likely to be particularly so if opportunities for open communication between line managers and their subordinates are not the norm. One method used by organisations to manage feedback is through the use of a "neutral intermediary" – an individual who is skilled in providing such feedback but is not a close acquaintance of either the line manager or his or her assessors. The feedback can be put into context by collecting the multi-source appraisal results for all managers in key areas, and then comparing individual performance against the common findings within that department or across the entire organisation.

There are a number of difficulties that can be associated with multi-source appraisal processes, including:

- Survey fatigue – appraisers may tire of having to complete forms for all of the peers, subordinates and subordinates with whom they are associated
- Friends of appraisees may present a flattering but unrealistic assessment in order to avoid hurt feelings
- Evaluators are not always nice or positive and may use multi-source appraisal as an opportunity to criticise others
- Unless training and briefing are adequate, feedback may not be accurate, reliable or truthful
- Managers ignore the feedback and nothing changes.

You can enhance the effectiveness of multi-source feedback by:

- Anonymous and confidential feedback, often using a specialist external consultant
- Considering the length of time the appraisee has spent in the position; if it is less than six months, consider using the first appraisal as a benchmark only for a follow-up appraisal

- Using a feedback expert to "interpret" the feedback and remove all the jargon and unnecessary statistics so that it can be easily understood by the appraisee
- Following-up and developing action plans for "low scoring" areas; improvements should be assessed six months to a year later
- Using written descriptions, as well as numerical ratings, as feedback because they are likely to be more meaningful to the appraisee
- Ensuring that the feedback data collection method is reliable, valid and based on sound statistical methods
- Avoiding survey fatigue by not using multi-source appraisal on too many employees at the same time.

It is not advisable to use a multi-source feedback process :

- When a high level of defensiveness exists on the part of the feedback recipient
- When individual raters, other than the feedback recipient's supervisor, can be identified (when anonymity cannot be maintained)
- When the feedback results will be used in a manner other than initially intended
- When the intervention would be used by practitioners with limited or no training in handling multi-source feedback
- In organisational cultures that do not support, reinforce, and encourage open and honest two-way feedback.

Some organisational now use multi-source feedback processes as a performance review and development tool. We do not propose to give it major consideration here, although **Figure 10.13** provides a brief summary of the issues concerned with the use of 360-degree feedback as a performance management development tool.

FIGURE 10.13: MULTI-SOURCE FEEDBACK & DEVELOPMENT

Multi-source feedback reveals how successful an individual is in all-important work relationships. The person's manager, supervisor, colleagues and direct reports complete individual questionnaires rating his/her competencies and also give written descriptive feedback, where appropriate. These individual questionnaires are collated. The resulting feedback report gives the employee an opportunity to find out how others "see" him or her at work.

Increasingly, multi-source is being used as a tool in development. The advantages of this are:
- Communication of the core competencies the organisation wants to develop. The multi-source lets people know what behaviours and skills are considered important. For example, organisations launching a change process might emphasise continuous improvement, self-development and teamwork in their multi-source questionnaires
- Multiple levels and sources of data should lead to a more objective assessment of a person's contributions, strengths and development needs
- Higher levels of trust in the fairness of the process. Data from organisations using multi-source indicates that people are more satisfied with ratings from multiple sources than from one person alone. When you hear the same things from different people, you are more likely to change your behaviour
- Making the multi-source part of the performance review gives it some "teeth" – it sends the message that the organisation takes this seriously.

Despite important advantages, there are potential areas for concern:
- Using multi-source can affect trust. Some people fear that a person's manager could misinterpret the consequences if they give negative feedback. The result can be low quality, or not very useful, feedback
- Staff become less ready to accept multi-source feedback if it seems too negative and has possibly damaging consequences in the performance review process
- Multi-source provides more perspectives on an individual's performance and development needs but there may still be bias. Degree of agreement measures can be used in the scoring so that high degrees of agreement between raters are highlighted
- The multi-source process can be expensive and the demands of running 360-degree reviews annually as part of the performance review are considerable. Rating fatigue sets in, when everyone has 10 or more questionnaires to compete and the process quickly loses effectiveness and credibility.

Source: Garavan *et al.* (1997).

PERSONAL DEVELOPMENT PLANS

Development is a lifelong process of nurturing, shaping and improving of skills, knowledge and interests in enhancing effectiveness. It does not necessarily imply upward movement; instead, it is concerned with enabling the individual to improve and realise their potential.

The personal development cycle is one of continuous learning, with a longer time horizon than a specific training need and requires considerable reflection and thought. Successful planning for development is very dependent on the individuals' willingness to develop, as well as having the ability to do so.

Personal development can be explained in terms of four key phases:

- **Understanding Principles:** This first phase is something that individuals experience throughout their lives as jobs change and individuals change with jobs. It is a period in which individuals acquire new knowledge, when they try to understand the details of the job, and when they seek to demonstrate understanding by achieving effectiveness in the role

- **Developing Competence:** The second phase of personal development is concerned with becoming more competent in a role. As an individual's skills develop, his/her concentration tends to focus on delivering work goals. Learners are concerned about planning work, controlling output in terms of reaching a high standard and delivering on objectives. The individual's development focuses on organising resources and working both effectively and efficiently

- **Demonstrating Confidence:** Individuals then move on to focus on developing skills that will enable them to deliver on current work demands and also focus on the future. In this personal development phase, learners demonstrate confidence in performing work roles. They begin to demonstrate an ability to innovate and create, where the focus is on finding new and better ways to deliver on goals

- **Coaching Others:** The final state involves a situation where a learner is competent to coach others. Learners can take decisions confidently. They draw on their experience and skills. They coach others and help them acquire the knowledge that they need for their own personal development.

Defining the Personal Development Plan

A personal development plan involves establishing what a learner wishes to achieve, deciding where they want to go in the short- and long-term and identifying the learning needs in terms of knowledge, skills or competence. The plan also defines the development that is appropriate to meet the perceived needs. Although this is similar in many ways to a performance review, **Figure 10.14** distinguishes the two processes.

FIGURE 10.14: THE PERSONAL DEVELOPMENT PLAN *VERSUS* THE PERFORMANCE REVIEW

Criterion	Personal Development Plan	The Performance Review
Content	• Primarily a plan for personal growth and development • Primary focus is learning and development, rather than reward	• Record of performance against agreed objectives • Identification of specific training and development needs
Time Focus	• Primarily concerned with the future • Development is a continuous process	• Primarily concerned with the current year
Primary Purpose	• To enable the learner to be proactive about development	• To plan performance improvement and acknowledge effective performance
When Conducted	• Reviewed as appropriate, not bound by specific review cycles • It may not be necessary to complete a personal development plan each year • It does not form part of the performance review	• Usually reviewed on a six month or annual basis • It is a mandated process, determined by organisational and HR policy • It feeds into the reward and merit bonus process
Role of Parties	• **Manager:** To facilitate an individual to develop; to encourage learner where appropriate; to provide learner with the business perspective • **Individual:** To take responsibility for assessing and discussing personal development needs; taking ownership for development; taking the initiative in developing a plan • **Human Resources:** Facilitating and improving he effectiveness of the personal development process; designing appropriate initiatives to support staff and the provision of support to line managers	• **Manager:** To review performance and identify strengths and weaknesses; to identify training and development needs • **Individual:** To contribute to an assessment of performance and make inputs on training, development and career • **Human Resources:** To ensure that the process is completed within the agreed review cycle; to monitor the rating process and identify deviations; to collate the T&D needs that arise and devise appropriate initiatives; to provide support to line managers

We will now look at the characteristics of personal development plans (PDPs):

- **Personal Document:** The most significant feature of a PDP is that it is personal and specific to the individual producing it. It represents the goals and ambitions of the individual producing it. While it is personal, it is important that management communicate that they also place value on the plan

- **Individual-Orientated:** The personal development plan is a tailor-made statement. Each element of the plan is specific to individual producing it. It reflects the ambitions, aspirations and learning needs of that person. The individual has full responsibility for producing the plan

- **Individual-Ownership:** The personal development process is the responsibility of the individual, so each employee has ownership of the PDP. If an individual has the responsibility for their own development, they are more likely to learn and develop. The PDP puts the individual learner in control

- **Management Support:** There may be a tendency for line managers to make the mistake of assuming that the introduction of PDPs frees them of responsibility for the training and development of staff. While the PDP is the responsibility of and is owned by the individual, the manager has a key role in supporting the process. The manager should be committed to developing direct reports and be prepared to provide guidance and assistance to help the employee achieve PDP goals. Most best practice advice highlights that manager commitment and support is best illustrated in the provision of T&D resources

- **Time for Reflection:** Personal development planning demands that learners engage in self-reflection. We first must understand ourselves before we can decide what to improve. Thus, in order to prepare a useful PDP, adequate time for self-reflection is crucial

- **Personal Development Planning is a Continuous Process:** The development process is continuous: there is always something to learn and always room for improvement. If the PDP process is to be a success, then it must be viewed as a never-ending process. This requires that it be reviewed on a regular basis

- **A Time-Consuming Process:** Research evidence indicates that employers are often attracted to PDPs because they consider it cheaper and less time-consuming that the alternatives. However, if the process is to succeed, the parties must be dedicated to it. It is more likely that line managers may feel under pressure as more direct reports start producing PDPs, as a great deal of time and effort is required in order to make the process a quality one

- **Provision of Learning Resources:** The T&D resources relevant to the individual's learning needs should be made available. Managers should have the responsibility of setting up suitable T&D, which should be structured and timely. The organisation may not always have the appropriate resources to meet the personal development needs identified, and so must avail of outside resources

- **Balancing the Past and Future:** When an individual produces a PDP, it is essential that they review past achievements as well mistakes. However, although there is a lot to be learned from the past, there must be a strong focus on the future. Learners who over-analyse the past may be expressing a reluctance to change.

Preparing a Personal Development Plan

Personal development planning is a cyclical process. You do not have to start at the beginning, if you have already decided where you are going and what you need to get there. We will consider some of the issues that you need to consider as a trainer or line manager in order to get the PDP process initiated. We also give specific advice on preparing a personal development plan. The steps involved are:

- **Step 1 – Introducing the Idea:** Learners are naturally inclined to shy away from self-organised learning, usually being more comfortable when they are being taught. It is important, therefore, that the concepts of PDPs and of learners taking responsibility for their own development are introduced effectively – you must sell the benefits. If you are to get employees motivated and committed to the plan, they must be clear on what it is exactly and what they will gain from producing the plan. If employees are not motivated towards the idea of developing themselves, the process is useless. The first state of the implementation process should be an information session for employees to grasp the concepts and understand how to design their own PDP

- **Step 2 – Preparing the Individual Plan:** The second step of the process is where the learner starts to take control of his/her own development. The specific tasks involved are:

  ○ *Establish Purpose and Direction:* The learner must identify the purpose of the development cycle. This involves the learner knowing what he/she is good at and interested in; getting a sense of their own potential; taking account of organisational realities; knowing about values and principles and considering the characteristics of work that fit in with their values and priorities

  ○ *Identifying Development Needs:* In order to produce an effective PDP, the learner must consider their strengths and weaknesses. This can benefit the employee through a better understanding of him/herself and of others. Development needs may emerge from intended, or actual, new tasks or responsibilities. Development needs depend on the learner's career goals and other issues such as family, leisure, etc. When a learner takes responsibility for their own development, he/she must be clear on what he/she wants to achieve in life as a whole and not just in the workplace

- ◦ *Identifying Learning Opportunities:* On the basis of a self-assessment, the learner should draw up a list of skills or knowledge that need to be acquired, updated or improved. It is important that the learner considers his/her learning style, the resources available as well as the range of learning options available

- ◦ *Meeting with the Manager:* Although we emphasise that the PDP is owned by, and is the responsibility of, the individual producing it, the role of the manager as adviser and supporter is important. When the learner has documented strengths and weaknesses and has established goals, the next step is to meet with the manager to clarify goals and strategies. This meeting also gives the manager an opportunity to communicate his/her expectations to the individual

- ◦ *Formulating Targets and Action Plans:* The learner should prepare an action plan for each of the gaps or opportunities identified. These actions should be challenging and stretching. Goals, targets and actions should be collaboratively identified, and clear and easy to measure, and few in number (ideally, no more than three development targets. **Figure 10.15** presents examples of learning goals.

FIGURE 10.15: EXAMPLE OF PERSONAL DEVELOPMENT PLANNING GOALS

• Identify a specific area of operation with which you are unfamiliar and seek mentoring from a member of staff regarded as an expert in that area • Plan and organise a full series of "know your business" presentations to be held over a nine-month period, ensuring a wide range of topics and contributors. At the end of the nine-month period, conduct a review of the programme with staff • Chair two/three planned meetings, researching appropriate topics for the agenda, arranging speakers on these topics if required, running the actual meeting and circulating minutes afterwards • Deliver, with the assistance of the local trainer/staff co-ordinator, a series of customer service training modules over a six-month period, ensuring that there is full measurement and evaluation of the training and full participation of all staff	• Design an appropriate meeting around the delivery of business unit results, which will ensure a full understanding, opportunity for questioning and provide meaningful feedback • Lead, or participate in, a small team to improve existing business processes within your particular area of operation, emphasising innovation and customer focus in the redesign • Undertake a professional programme that will develop your further understanding and competence in the management of a particular function • Over a six-month period, act as mentor to at least two junior members of staff, sharing your knowledge of procedures and policy to ensure that these staff members benefit from your experience • Design a programme that will increase the usage and understanding of available technology, track progress, and monitor increased effectiveness within the workplace

° *Initiating Action:* During the meeting with the manager the learner should agree a time period, which is realistic given the targets specified. It is useful for the learner to keep a "learning log", a logbook regularly updated with progress and achievements – the date, the development need identified, the chosen method of development, the dates that development was undertaken, the outcomes and further action. Keeping a record helps the learner to monitor what is done

° *Review and Feedback:* These elements are a vital part of the learning process. Assess what progress has been made and what additional support is necessary. Regular review allows the learner to assess what has been achieved and evaluate what is left to be done. Feedback is useful, if the learner is prepared to listen and take it on board. A line manager or other appropriate individual should give this feedback to provide the learner with an opportunity to reflect on past actions. The review of development activities involves asking these questions:

° What am I better able to do as a result of the development?

° Has this review identified further development needs?

° How well did particular development methods work?

° Could I have gained more from particular development initiatives?

° Would I follow or adopt a particular approach in the future?

The Contribution of Personal Development Plans

Personal development plans have a significant contribution to make to training and development in organisations. They provide a structure, facilitate motivation and offer a useful framework for monitoring and evaluating achievements. An effective PDP process can lay the basis for continuous learning processes in organisations, ensuring that employability issues are addressed and building a learning culture within the organisation.

However, PDPs can also be problematic. It may be difficult to get the process started, because of the need to assign importance to development activities that may not have been considered important in the past. The initial process may be too modest or alternatively too demanding.

Figure 10.16 presents a summary of the benefits for the organisation and the individual learner.

FIGURE 10.16: BENEFITS OF PERSONAL DEVELOPMENT PLANS FOR ORGANISATIONS & LEARNERS

The Organisation	The Learner
• **Reputation of Organisation:** Organisations that adopt PDPs to support the continuous development of employees will gain a reputation as leading edge employers • **Increased Productivity:** An increased concern for an employee's personal development is likely to lead to better performance • **Shifting Responsibility to Employees:** The introduction of PDPs is a strategy to shift responsibility for career management to the employee. It encourages individuals to be independent and proactive • **Retention:** Organisations that place a greater value on employees and demonstrate interest in personal development are more likely to retain high performing employees • **Flexibility:** PDPs are an effective mechanism in producing a more flexible workforce in the organisation • **Developing Competence:** Employers are increasingly seeking individuals who will work hard but also be innovative. Personal development can contribute to producing employees that have initiative, and are proactive and innovative • **Pool of Talent:** Some employers use PDPs to scout for talent and in assessing employee progress and suitability for senior positions. This represents a continuous use of the personal development planning process • **Enhanced Communication:** The personal development planning process is a useful mechanism to enhance communication between manager and subordinate	• **Job Satisfaction:** Individuals who engage in personal development are more likely to experience satisfaction with work. The perception of support and encouragement from management also enhances job satisfaction • **Identifying Learning Needs:** The PDP process enables the learner to focus on learning needs and to influence and shape the priority of these needs • **Employability:** Producing a PDP enables the learner to acquire knowledge and skill that will make him/her more employable in the event of job loss. Learners may have less fear of losing a job because of the potential job opportunities arising from this employability • **Investment in training:** PDPs are more likely to stimulate investment in training. The learner and/or the organisation may resource this • **Self-Awareness:** The PDP allows the learner to identify strengths and weaknesses and to develop self-awareness - a necessary precondition for personal change • **Enhanced Self-Efficacy:** Learners who participate in self-development are likely to gain increased self-confidence. This self-confidence relates to the learner's belief in his/her ability to perform to a high standard • **Net Worth:** PDPs provide evidence of a learner's skills and knowledge and signal important and positive messages to the employer

USING COUNSELLING AS A DEVELOPMENT TOOL

Counselling is a process, very closely related to coaching. In fact, the terms are often paired (coaching and counselling) or used as synonyms.

Counselling is generally considered as an integral part of the coaching process. To be effective coaches, managers have to be able to use some of the techniques and skills associated with counselling. Counselling can be used in a range of human resource management contexts – mentoring, career development and change management.

Workplace counselling is not generally counselling in the modern definition of the term but relates to situations that require the use of counselling skills. Workplace counselling is considered to be any activity in the workplace where one individual uses a set of techniques or skills to help another individual take responsibility of and to manage their own decision-making, whether it is work-related or personal.

The current theory and practice of counselling in organisations owes a good deal to Rogers, who started out from a conventional psychotherapeutic background but abandoned this approach to focus on the quality of the relationship between the counsellor and the client. He advocated that the relationship should be based principally on the counsellor's warmth, genuineness and empathy, operating in an atmosphere of equality and trust. Clients should not be viewed as "patients" needing help from a remote expert, but as responsible people who have freely chosen counselling as a means of tackling problems. Thus, counselling has often concentrated on helping competent people to cope with difficult circumstances.

Counselling has permeated the workplace in that the term "counselling" is regularly used in relation to a number of organisational scenarios: redundancy, career development, discipline, appraisal and coaching, for example. However, professional counsellors would not consider much of this activity as counselling, for the following reasons:

• Much workplace counselling takes place within a power structure and is directed to fulfilling the goals of the organisation, not those of the employee, even though the latter may gain from the process. It cannot be expected that in the manager/subordinate situation there will be complete openness on either side

• Counsellors need training and experience. They should also have a high degree of self-awareness, achieved perhaps through undergoing a prolonged period of self-reflection. They should also subscribe to a professional code of ethics. These requirements may not be appropriate to ask of managers in a workplace setting.

We consider that managers should acquire and practice some of the skills used in counselling, such as listening and empathising, so that they can motivate and develop people rather than control and direct them. Employees must view the process to be genuine and not a relationship based on manipulation.

Counselling works from the assumption that those with problems and anxieties have the resources to deal with them adequately themselves, but help is often needed if these resources are to be activated. Frequently, in a work context, when employees share their problems, they are not seeking advice, solutions to problems or even reassurance. They may wish simply to be listened to, to have a point of view acknowledged and their feelings accepted.

Counselling-type relationships have a highly important role to play in the learning process. Counselling is a tool that is difficult to use well, but rich in returns for the person being counselled if it is successful. It should not be confused with giving advice. The art of counselling is to enable individuals to discover what advice to give themselves.

All counselling, in some sense, can be considered as developmental. It serves to help the individual become aware of problems, to reflect upon their nature and to identify choices and perhaps solutions for themselves. In itself, this is a growth process, but the removal of blocks or difficulties is also developmental. If a person is stuck, feeling trapped or stunted by a personal issue, counselling may provide them with the way out and onwards. Issues may include fear, lack of confidence, inability to cope, emotional crisis, shortage of skill, difficult relationships, lack of clarity.

Counselling cannot be imposed on others. All you can do is to be aware that the other person is troubled and to make an offer of your time, support and your ear. If your offer is accepted, be clear with yourself what your role is to be. If you think you are the judge, you may make the situation worse. Self-assessment of attitude and performance is a powerful prerequisite for learning. Counselling is the means by which individuals can be encouraged to do this.

Attitude influence and change is a part of personal development. Coercion is not likely to achieve this and, even if the manager can produce some modest change by being a respected "significant other" or role model, it may be considered as unethical manipulation. If the attitude is critical, for example, a casual approach to safety or a negative approach to clients, counselling on the issue may lead to the individual unearthing the nature of the difficulty and selling themselves the solution and attitude change. Ownership is once again a key ingredient. Development plans can often be elicited effectively from the individual through a counselling approach, particularly if the learning is in sensitive areas, such as personal skills.

Development blocks constrict ability and limit potential and are a major retardant to growth and learning. Counselling is often the only way to uncover these and to enable the individual to begin the process of removing them. Some of the more common blocks are:

- **Learning Blocks:** Stuck in a "learning style" / Analysis paralysis / Long on ideas; short on action / Takes unevaluated risks / Experience not used for learning

- **Value Blocks:** Beliefs about "right" and "wrong" ways of learning /
  It is essential to make sure that "I am never wrong, so I take no
  chances" / "It is only possible to learn from experience"
- **Feeling Blocks:** Emotional barriers to learning / "I am no good at
  this kind of thing" / "I can't do this on my own"
- **Reward Block:** Development seen as valueless / Development
  involves more costs than benefits.

Qualities of Managers as Counsellors

Three particular qualities are prerequisites for successful
interpersonal helping or counselling. It is taken for granted that active
listening is a key component but the following are also important:

- **Warmth:** This quality manifests itself in a number of dimensions. A
  person comes to you for help. If they are to be helped, they need to
  know that you will respect their experience and understand their
  problems and feelings. Whatever your own feelings about who they
  are and what they have done, you will accept them as they are. If
  they sense you are accepting and understanding of their experience
  and will not be judgemental, they will be more able to disclose their
  concerns and problems and be open to the possibilities of change and
  development. If however, they feel that you, as a manager, have a
  vested interest in their changing and that the relationship is
  conditional upon the change, they may reject the help
- **Genuineness:** This quality refers to the capacity to be open and
  direct with the other person. As a counsellor, you have to be honest
  and open and you should expect the other person to be open also.
  When this happens, genuineness communicates itself and the
  relationship will be positive
- **Empathy:** The concept of empathy is central to effective
  interpersonal communication. It is the ability to convey to other
  people a deep understanding of problems and feelings. It involves
  the sensing of the emotions of the other person and being able to
  communicate this sensing back to them.

Stages in Development Counselling

The development counselling process consists of three key stages:
- Contracting and exploring
- Establishing understanding
- Decision-making and actions.

Figure 10.17 presents a summary of these stages, which involve:

FIGURE 10.17: STAGES OF DEVELOPMENT COUNSELLING

Stage	Client Tasks	Counsellor Tasks
Contracting and Exploring	• Making a preliminary assessment of the suitability of development counselling • Undertaking written preparation • Testing out readiness for, and appropriateness of, counselling • Exploring presenting concerns and influences on development	• Educating and informing each other about development counselling • Evaluating the learner's readiness for, and appropriateness of, development counselling • Building rapport and facilitating exploration • Establishing contract (confidentiality, structures, etc)
Enabling Understanding	• Considering the questions: "Who am I?", "Where am I now?", "What do I want?", "Where do I want to be?" • Completing self-assessment exercises, psychometric tests and questionnaires, as appropriate	• Facilitating exploration of feelings and beliefs associated with development • Helping learner to identify important themes and integrate self-understanding • Making appropriate use of self-assessment exercises and psychometric tests and questionnaires • Helping learners to overcome blocks to action, using challenging skills, if appropriate
Decisions and Actions	• Completing decision-making and action planning exercises • Developing options and choosing between options • Putting decision into action • Agreeing research tasks, if appropriate • Addressing fears of change • Evaluating need for continued support • Reviewing progress made towards objectives during development counselling	• Enabling learner to develop options and choose between them • Supporting learners in developing an action plan • Agreeing research tasks, if appropriate • Helping learners face ambivalence about the future • Exploring learner's need for continued support • Stressing importance of maintaining momentum • Helping learners to identify resources and sources of support

Adapted from Nathan and Hill (1992).

• **Contracting and Exploring:** Contracting is a process by which the line manager and direct report come to a clear understanding about their respective roles in the development counselling process. It focuses on issues related to confidentiality, the establishment of boundaries, the number, length and frequency of meetings and the articulation of objectives. These are typical objectives for development counselling:

  ○ I want to decide on my next development and/or career move

- I want to develop strategies for coping with relationships at work
- I want to increase my awareness and knowledge of different job/career options
- I want to decide on appropriate development opportunities
- I want to develop a personal development plan for the next three years

The process of contracting is inextricably linked with the process of exploration. During the first meeting, you will have the following tasks in mind:

- Building rapport to enable the free discussion of issues
- Helping the leaner to explore what and who has influenced development choices
- Exploring any preparations and thinking required by the learner

- **Establishing Understanding:** This stage takes the issues discussed in the first meeting and addresses more deep-rooted issues such as "Who am I?", "Where am I now?", "What do I want?", "Where do I want to be?" or "What is stopping me from participating in development?" The learner's answers to these questions may be inaccurate, distorted or limited in some way. One of your tasks as a counsellor is to develop a more objective and accurate self-understanding and to deepen the learner's insights. The aim is to move the learner towards a new and more constructive perspective, which can form the basis for decision and action. For many learners, greater self-understanding is all that is required. This may facilitate a change of attitude and renewed energy to participate in learning. Other learners may require more help. Some learners may have self-defeating beliefs or experience ambivalence

- **Decision-making and Actions:** You and your direct report / learner have now reached the final phase of the development counselling process, which involves the analysis of options in terms of pros and cons, and the development of goals and actions. Goals are specific statements of what the learner aims to achieve. Action planning focuses on how the learner will set about achieving these goals. It is important to emphasise that the ending of a development counselling relationship differs somewhat from other types of personal counselling. Five specific features need to be highlighted:

  - Development counselling is usually a short-term process, undertaken because of a particular issue, which may require a decision or action within a relatively short period

- ° A series of meetings is arranged, so the end is in sight from the beginning
- ° The relationship ensures that the meetings are a structured support to the learner's own thinking and working through of the development issues identified
- ° Dependency is never encouraged within the development counselling relationship
- ° The end of the final counselling meeting is not the end of the development process itself. The learner will have an action plan and is likely to be in a position to go forward. There may be dramatic progress, development goals may be in sharper focus and/or the learner will feel more optimistic and energised.

The tasks in the action plan will likely be to the forefront of the learner's mind. Nonetheless, there is a danger that the learner may go back into old patterns. A number of techniques can be used to facilitate the development process after the counselling sessions have concluded. These include the use of a summary, support from others, follow-up meetings, rewards and other reminders.

BEST PRACTICE INDICATORS

Some of the best practice issues that you should consider related to the contents of this chapter are:

- Coaching, mentoring and counselling are important development activities in an organisation
- Managers can perform an effective coaching role, provided they understand fully their developmental role and have insight concerning their coaching style
- When conducting coaching, the manager should listen to direct reports. This requires a process of hearing, understanding, interpreting and responding
- The manager should view mentoring as an opportunity to develop leadership and coaching skills
- The mentoring relationship is most effective when mentees are encouraged to offer and develop their own solutions. The mentor should avoid offering solutions too readily, when problems are discussed
- Use performance reviews for their development potential. Make sure that the purposes of the process are clear. Encourage feedback and ideas. Develop development action plans and monitor progress
- Consider the performance review process in a positive way. Make sure that the performance review meeting is positive throughout,

relaxed and do focus on the need for the direct report to take responsibility and ownership for development

- Personal development plans are personal documents that are owned by the individual. The manager's role is to ensure that options explored are realistic
- Counselling skills can be used in the development context to explore blocks to learning and reenergise the learner.

A Training & Development Scenario

The XYZ experience highlights a number of symptoms of what happens when things go wrong in a performance appraisal process. The system described in the scenario illustrates a number of important issues:

- The system was largely imposed - therefore there is very limited commitment to it
- There is a lack of clear performance review objectives
- Very little training and briefing was provided to managers and employees
- There is very little evidence of a focus on development
- The process is perceived to be unfair
- The criteria used, and the rating process, are considered subjective.

In order to make this system work, we suggest that the company needs to start again. It should pay attention to five core issues:

- The design process needs to be consultative. Employees need to be involved in its design and they need to be clear about its intended purposes
- The aims of the process need to be defined. What is the focus on development? What systems will be put in place to support development? Will managers be trained to cope with this developmental focus?
- The criteria on which performance will be judged need to be agreed. Each criterion needs to be properly defined, so that both managers and employees understand what is to be measured
- A systematic training process will need to be designed in order to ensure the effective implementation of the process. Both managers and employees will need to be trained
- The new system should be implemented on a pilot basis. This will allow the system to be reviewed and modified if necessary.

Chapter 11

COSTING TRAINING & MEASURING RETURN ON INVESTMENT

LEARNING OBJECTIVES

On completion of this chapter, you should be able to:

- Understand the distinction between learning costs, training costs and opportunity costs

- Understand the nature of costs as understood by accountants, and distinguish between direct, indirect and full cost concepts

- Explain the main stages involved in calculating the costs of training

- Use a number of formulae and frameworks to calculate of different categories of training costs

- Develop an appropriate cost classification system to track and keep an accurate record of training costs for budgetary purposes

- Identify the steps you should follow when preparing a training budget

- Calculate the financial return on investment in training

- Publicise the results of training and market the benefits within your organisation.

A Training & Development Scenario

Following a pilot programme, an engineering company decided to replace its former on-the-job training activities for new machine operators with a structured off-the-job programme taught by experienced trainers. The employee development department was charged with designing the new programme and for calculating the return on investment (ROI).

Programme Benefits
Training time: The company was losing more than €65,000 a year because of the lost production of trainees in learning to operate the machines. Based on the pilot programme, it was calculated that trainee losses could be reduced by 50%, saving €33,000 annually.

Machining scrap: Lack of proper training was one of the biggest factors in machining scrap. It was estimated that there could be a 10% reduction in total scrap costs with the new training programme, saving €145,000 annually.

Lower turnover: By reducing the high turnover rate, through providing more effective training, management estimated that savings of €26,000 could be made in recruitment costs annually.

Accidents: It was estimated that accidents in the machining area could be reduced by 25%, saving €8,500 annually.

Maintenance expenses: Improper use of machines caused much of the unscheduled downtime. It was estimated that maintenance expenses could be reduced by 10% through the new training programme, a saving of €97,500 annually.

The total annual savings were estimated to be €310,000.

Programme costs
The programme required an estimated total cost of €195,000, made up as follows:

A new fabricated building for training	€90,000
Equipment and materials	€95,000
Programme development costs	€10,000

In addition, the salaries and overhead expenses of the two trainers were estimated to be €55,000 annually.

INTRODUCTION

Two important skill areas that you will need to acquire competence in to become an effective trainer are:

- Costing your training and preparing a training budget
- Measuring the return on your training investment.

These two issues concern us in this chapter.

Any training and development activity you undertake has an expense (cost) and an asset (benefit) component. It is relatively easy to understand how a training course may be considered as an expense in strict accounting terms. It is less easy to identify and understand how it may be viewed as an asset.

Under strict accounting rules, if the benefits of any T&D activities that you undertake all arise in the current year, the expenditure must be treated as an expense – there is no future benefit to carry forward as an asset. However, if you can demonstrate that expenditure on T&D activities in the current year will give rise to benefits in a future accounting year, the costs of such activities (or part of them) may be carried forward as an asset.

Your skill in costing a learning activity is an important part of your overall effectiveness as a trainer. Inputs to your training process can usually be costed with a significant degree of accuracy, although you will need good information systems to cost your training effectively. You will have to make a judgement about how detailed your costing of training activities should be. It is generally recommended that, at a minimum, you should include:

- The direct personnel costs of participants and trainers
- The development costs of identifying and analysing training needs
- The direct resource and direct accommodation costs.

You should also be concerned with the return on investment that your training provides. There are several ways that this return can be measured.

In many instances, a group of employees are trained together, so the amount invested is the total cost of analysis, development, delivery and evaluation of the whole development programme. The benefits are then calculated by assigning financial data to areas such as improved employee morale or their improved attitudes. This can be difficult, but is not impossible. We will outline later in this chapter how you may go about this task.

DISTINGUISHING LEARNING COSTS, TRAINING COSTS & OPPORTUNITY COSTS

We make a distinction between learning costs, training costs and opportunity costs.

Learning Costs

Irrespective of the type of training activity you undertake, there is still a cost to be borne by the organisation as a result of employees having to learn their jobs. The costs you incur in providing unsystematic or unplanned training are normally termed "learning costs". In the absence of formal training, this learning cost will be incurred, simply because employees are on full pay, at the going rate, when they are first learning their jobs. It is very rare to find that pay is adjusted downward to take account of a reduced level of output. The following are considered the main elements of learning costs:

- Payments to employees when learning on the job
- The costs of materials wasted, sales lost or incorrect decisions made by employees who are less than competent
- Supervision/management cost in dealing with "incompetence" problems
- Costs of reduced output/sales caused by the negative effect on an established team of having members who are less than competent
- Cost attributable to accidents caused by lack of "know-how"
- Cost resulting from employees leaving – either because they find the work too difficult, or resent the lack of planned learning, or feel they have no prospects.

These learning costs can be minimised, or even replaced by new earnings, through expenditure on training and development.

Training Costs

We define training costs as those deliberately incurred to facilitate learning, and with the intention of reducing learning costs. These costs might be aimed not at planned training *per se*, but at the learning system. A training intervention might involve investing in appraisal procedures in order to get better data on learning needs – the act of clarifying learning objectives, in itself, might generate some learning. Most training costs are more directly related to planned training itself and are of two kinds:

- **Fixed costs:** Not expected to change with the amount of training that takes place (salaries of permanent staff)

- **Variable costs:** Vary directly with the level of training activity (materials used or college fees paid).

The following are examples of training costs you might incur:

- **People Costs**: Wages, salaries of trainers and instructors / Managers' or supervisors' salaries while training or coaching / Fees to external training providers / Fees to external assessors / Fees to assessing bodies for in-house courses / Travel and subsistence of trainees and trainers

- **Equipment Costs**: Training equipment and aids / Depreciation of training, building and equipment

- **Admin Costs**: Wages and salaries of admin or backup staff / Telephone and postages / Office consumables / System and procedures (post-training questionnaires) / Hire of rooms

- **Materials Costs**: Films and tapes / Distance learning packages / Materials used in practice sessions / Protective clothing / Books and journals.

The costs of off-the-job training are greater than those of on-the-job training, since on-the job training can incur the costs of additional supervision and the cost of waste or mistakes made by trainees.

Large-scale initial costs relating to buildings or major items of training equipment (a simulator) will normally be "capitalised" – as "fixed assets", the costs of which are spread over a long term via the annual "depreciation" charge in the company's profit and loss account. Additionally, the upkeep of a training centre (a purpose maintained building) will incur all the normal costs usually associated with buildings – for example, insurance, cleaning, heating, lighting, decorating and general maintenance. Training and development departments usually will also be required to carry a proportion of the organisation's overheads.

The relationship between learning costs and training costs should be such that both are minimised, because an expense is justified only if it reduces the costs of unplanned learning. However, the degree of certainty attached to any estimates will vary, and decisions usually have to be made based on incomplete information. This requires that you must set an upper limit in advance – a "budget" on what can be spend in a given period (usually a year).

Opportunity Costs

This is another important cost concept. All T&D activities have associated opportunity costs, equal to the return on capital that could have been gained from investing in other projects. The concept of opportunity cost is relevant to managers who may wish to consider them before they agree to invest in a T&D programme. In order to calculate detailed opportunity costs of training investments you will require detailed financial information. There is also an opportunity cost to be considered when making a choice between two training options. This cost component is the one least likely to be considered by a training specialist on a day-to-day basis, however it is part of the language of senior management and should therefore be considered as senior management frequently have to make choices about alternative investment options.

UNDERSTANDING THE NATURE OF COSTS

We make a distinction between three different types of costs that are commonly used in accounting terminology:

- **Direct Costs:** Expenses that can be traced directly to specific projects or activities. In terms of training, out-of-pocket direct costs include: travel, fees, daily expense allowances, costs for purchased learning materials, contracted consultants, training room rental, and food service. Direct costs are the most obvious and easily tracked costs associated with T&D, although out-of-pocket expenses rarely equal more than 10% of a training programme's total costs. The main cost of training activities relate to people's time – salary costs for people conducting the training, if it is delivered in-house, or of external consultants, as well as participants' salaries

- **Indirect Costs:** Expenses that cannot be directly associated with a specific project or training activity but which are necessary for the organisation to function. Sometimes, the term "overhead" is used to describe all of the indirect costs of conducting training. Examples include costs for interest on organisational debt, general building maintenance and repair, lights, heat, office equipment, and administrative salaries and expenses. Another example of indirect costs is fringe benefits – overhead costs related to the time for which employees are paid but do not work (vacations, sick leave, and holidays) plus employer payments for health insurance, pensions, and other indirect compensation

- **Full Costs:** The total of direct costs plus indirect costs. Full costs are the best measure of how much it actually costs an organisation to deliver a training programme. In particular, recognition of the full cost of an employee's time is a key element for understanding the total costs of training programmes.

Benefits

Best practice makes a distinction between two categories of benefits that are relevant in a training and development context: tangible and intangible.

Tangible benefits include:

- **Increased Revenue:** By impacting the quantity of output or sales per unit of time, training-based improvements can increase revenue. Increased output or sales can be documented and training's share of the increase can be calculated

- **Decreased or Avoided Expenses:** A frequent benefit of a training programme is the reduction (saving) or avoidance of costs. By enhancing employees' skills, training can help improve the quality of a product or service. Other measurements include the reduction of scrap, absenteeism, inaccuracy, grievances, accidents and wasted time or materials.

Intangible benefits are activities, qualities, or conditions that have value but which are extremely difficult, or impossible, to quantify in financial terms. For instance, employee flexibility benefits an organisation, but its contribution is difficult to quantify in cash terms. To keep investment in these benefits in perspective, decision-makers should consider the potential risk of not investing in them and should estimate how substantial intangible benefits might possibly arise.

ESTABLISHING AN ACCOUNTING SYSTEM FOR T&D

We focus in this section on some of the decisions that you need to make when establishing an effective accounting system for training. You will need to consider first what you understand by the term "training and development" for costing purposes, then you will need to determine all of the training cost categories that are relevant. We now explain each of these steps in more detail.

Defining T&D for the Purposes of Costing

Your first step is to reach a decision about what T&D is for the purpose of costing it within your company. We have focused in this book on structured T&D activities with identifiable objectives focusing on knowledge, skills and attitudes and clear learning plans. This definition incorporates the following types of training situations:

- Formal T&D courses offered by the organisation or outside training providers

- Structured on-the-job training conducted by an employee's immediate supervisor or a qualified trainer and supplemented by written learning objectives and schedules
- Open learning programmes, job rotation assignments, and developmental centre activities– if their primary purpose is enhancing the knowledge and skills of the employee
- Participation in conferences and seminars related to the job or professional area
- A training activity, where an employee learns to use a specialist software package in a learning centre.

The definition of T&D does not include activities such as:
- Meetings and performance appraisals – unless development is their primary purpose
- Self-development that an employee carries out on non-work time or using personal resources
- Meetings of a team of managers to introduce a new product
- A performance review that sets new objectives for the employee.

Determining Your Training Cost Categories

You must identify and define training cost categories to track all of your training costs and to keep your training budget in check. We have already briefly defined training costs into two categories: direct and indirect costs.

CALCULATING T&D COSTS: GUIDELINES FOR PRACTICE

We now explain a number of guidelines that you should follow when calculating training costs. It is important to take into account your organisation's accounting policies and conventions when calculating the costs of T&D.

Direct Costs: Personnel

There are four categories of direct personnel costs that you may need to calculate:
- **Training Participant Costs:** Estimate the average salary or wage for training participants and include an organisational overhead rate (this will depend on the accounting practices used in your organisation). The Chartered Institute for Personnel and Development (2001) suggests the methodology in **Figure 11.1** to calculate the cost of an individual learner's participation on a training programme.

FIGURE 11.1: COSTING AN INDIVIDUAL'S PARTICIPATION ON A TRAINING PROGRAMME

Calculating Cost of Individual Participation

This framework can be used to calculate the cost of the time input for any participants in the learning activity (participants, trainer, administrator, coach, line manager, etc).

Start with the annual salary, including any allowances (skills payments). If a substantial part of someone's pay is made up of commission or bonuses, include an average figure.

Add employer's on-costs (PRSI/National Insurance, pensions, and company car). If you want to be extremely rigorous in your calculations, you could also add indirect costs of employment (accommodation, personnel administrative costs, etc). In most organisations, however the information needed to calculate these costs is not readily available, and the effort of attempting to calculate them is probably not justified. An alternative to calculating the exact on-costs of employment is to add on a percentage of salary for on-costs. A reasonable assumption is 35% of salary, although this may vary with seniority and nature of the job (number of "perks", provision of specialist equipment). Your finance department or accountant may be able to provide a more specific percentage figure for your organisation.

Example of calculation of cost of an individual's involvement in learning activity:

Annual salary		
Annual direct on-costs	+	
Annual indirect on-costs (optional)	+	
Total Annual Cost	=	
Annual productive days (253 minus annual and sick leave)	÷	
Daily Employment Cost	=	
Direct learning Costs (travel and subsistence)	+	
Opportunity Cost	+	
Daily Learning Cost	=	
Number of hours in working day	÷	
Hourly Learning Cost	=	

If you are running a programme of learning activities for a large number of people, calculating the individual cost for each one would be time-consuming. Instead, calculate the cost for the average salary level for each grade represented in the activity.

Whether you use individually-calculated or average figures, you do not need to re-calculate them until, or unless, any of the input figures change (salary increases, changes in travel and subsistence rates, change in venue causing changes in travel and subsistence etc.).

Source: CIPD (2001).

- **Training Personnel Costs:** The second direct personnel cost that you will need to calculate is your training personnel costs, which you determine in the same manner as you do your participant costs. If you wish to ascertain the true cost of training personnel, in addition to the time each instructor spends on designing and delivering training programmes, you will also need to factor in the time spent on task analysis, and the identification of training needs, other clerical and administrative support and time spent on training evaluation activities.

- **Other In-House Personnel Costs:** It is quite common for a training department to use the services of other employees in the organisation to design, deliver or in some way support a training programme or activity. Use the same approach as the previous categories to order to calculate the daily and hourly costs of other in-house personnel who contribute.

- **Direct Outside Personnel Costs:** These are easy to identify because you usually agree a fee with the external consultant at the point of contracting.

We now explain three other types of direct costs that you will need to factor in when calculating the cost of your training:

- **Travel, Accommodation and Incidental Expenses:** To establish the total of these costs, multiply the average cost of per participant by the total number of participants. Sometimes, it may be difficult to ascertain the average costs of these items of expenditure, simply because training records are not available. Then, you could survey participants in your organisation and find an appropriate average

- **Outside Goods and Services:** If you use outside goods and services, you will find the total costs for these services simply by adding the sub-costs that make up this category. In some cases, some of these costs are on a per-participant basis, while others are on a per-programme basis

- **Facilities:** If you have to rent out facilities, then you must include this cost. If the rent is a flat fee – the process is relatively simple; however, if it is not, calculate the total by multiplying the daily or weekly fee by the number of days or weeks of rental.

The CIPD recommends the framework in **Figure 11.2** for calculating the direct costs of a training and development activity. This is a very useful matrix because it combines people, accommodation, equipment, material and external costs and considers them for the total training cycle.

Figure 11.3 outlines a "rule-of-thumb" for calculating the costs for the design of different activities.

FIGURE 11.2: COST CLASSIFICATION MATRIX FOR THE TRAINING CYCLE

	Consultation & diagnosis	Needs analysis	Design & development	Delivery of Programme	Admin	Follow-up	Evaluation	Total
People Costs								
Learner time								
Internal trainer time								
Travel & subsistence								
Accommodation Costs								
In-house								
Hire of external facilities								
Catering								
Equipment Costs								
Purchase								
Hire								
Materials Costs								
One-off								
Consumables								
External Training Costs								
Course fees								
Consultancy								
External Facilitation								
Total								

FIGURE 11.3: DESIGN TIME RATIO FOR DIFFERENT TYPES OF LEARNING ACTIVITIES

Design Activity	Content Elements	Design Time Ratio
Face-to-face training course	Familiar, non-technical trainer delivered	**5:1**
Face-to-face training course	Non-familiar, technical trainer delivered	**10:1**
Participant manual	Familiar, non-technical	**3:1**
Participant manual	Unfamiliar, technical	**6:1**
Leader's guide	Familiar, non-technical	**2:1**
Leader's guide	Unfamiliar, technical	**4:1**
Visuals / overheads	Simple, text-based	**1:1**
Visuals / overheads	Complex, graphics-based	**5:1**
Videos	Simple, voice-over, one location	**50:1**
Videos	Complex, live audio, many locations	**150:1**
CBT	Simple, text-based	**50:1**
CBT	Complex, graphics-based	**300:1**
Open Learning	Simple, text-based, non-technical	**100:1**
Open Learning	Complex, text- and graphics-based, technical	**300:1**
Multimedia	Simple, graphics-based	**150:1**
Multimedia	Complex, video-based	**500:1**

Explanation of Terms
- **Familiar – Non-Familiar:** This refers to the degree to which the content area lies within the current expertise of the trainer
- **Technical – Non-Technical:** This refers to the level of technical detail to be found in the training content. Highly technical areas are much more costly to design
- **Simple – Complex:** This refers to the level of complexity in the design process. Does it require specialist input and/or specific technical capabilities?
- **Text – Video:** Is the training material all based on text or does it require the production of graphics and/or video support?

Adapted from Gibb (2002).

Indirect Costs of a Training Activity

Most trainers make systematic attempts to calculate their direct training costs. Indirect training costs can often equal or exceed the direct costs, although they are less likely to be calculated, because they are more problematic to calculate with any degree of precision. The extent and level of accuracy with which you calculate indirect costs will depend on the information available and the accounting policies of the organisation.

There are three sets of indirect costs that you need to consider:

- **Overhead Costs:** The simplest method you can use to estimate overhead costs are to establish a base percentage rate of indirect costs for all training programmes. If you use this approach, the indirect costs are estimated by multiplying the base percentage indirect cost rate by the training programme's total direct cost. A more precise method to capture indirect training costs involves the use of total training department budget information

- **Facilities Costs:** These costs should be accounted for separately from other indirect costs, although they are generally a relatively small percentage of total costs and are often difficult to determine. If your organisation has a well-established accounting function, then it will be easier to ascertain, for example, the costs of electricity, maintenance, building administration and the cost of a mortgage on the premises

- **Equipment and Materials Costs:** Most of these costs will be incurred in off-the-job training, but they may also arise in other training activities. Some of these costs will include:
  - Purchase / subsidy of training material (computer-based training packages or books)
  - Payment / subsidy of external course fees (seminar attendance, evening class fees)
  - Purchase or hire of audiovisual or computer equipment and materials
  - Supply of consumables such as notepads, workbooks, flip-chart pads, etc.

Figure 11.4 outlines the CIPD recommendation for calculating in-house equipment and in-house accommodation costs.

Training Costs: Other Issues

You can make a strong contribution to managing your training department and demonstrate your professionalism to key stakeholders such as senior management if you consider the following training cost issues as part of your overall approach to T&D costs:

- **Target Particular Costs:** If you target particular cost areas for special scrutiny, this can improve your ability to determine how much should be spent on training and where you can make improvements in the management of training

FIGURE 11.4: CALCULATING THE COSTS OF EQUIPMENT & ACCOMMODATION

To calculate the daily costs of using in-house equipment:
- Divide the cost of the equipment by its estimated lifespan
- Divide the annual cost by the average number of days' use per year to produce the daily rate.

Example of Calculation Cost of Using In-House Equipment

Cost of equipment		€540
Estimated life span of equipment		4 Years
Cost per year	÷	€135
Average days use per year	÷	32
Cost per Day	=	€4.22

To calculate the cost of in-house accommodation:
- Obtain the figures for annual accommodation cost per square foot (including heating and lighting if possible)
- Multiply square foot cost by the size of the accommodation to give annual cost
- Divide annual cost of accommodation by 253 working days a year (365 minus 112 days for weekends and bank holidays but could be different for an organisation that works shifts) to give accommodation cost per day.

Example of calculation of cost of in-house accommodation

Annual accommodation cost per square foot		€540
Accommodation Lease		4 Years
Annual accommodation cost	x	€135
Number of working days		32
Daily Accommodation Cost	÷	€4.22

- **Specific Training Populations:** You should consider examining training needs and costs for different groups of employees, such as senior management, technical, administrative and clerical / operative staff. If you can get data from other organisations on how much training and expenditure these groups receive, it should help you to identify priority changes and/or confirm that you have your priorities correct

- **Subject Matter / Training Needs:** It is often a useful exercise to track your training expenditure on different categories of training needs or expenditure on generic courses

- **Training Providers:** If your organisation uses a number of external training providers, it is useful to track expenditure on once-off providers against regular contributors

- **Training Phases:** The CIPD recommends that you analyse training costs for each phase of the training process. You may consider the following:
  - ° Costs related to the analysis of needs
  - ° Resources devoted to the selection of training participants
  - ° Design costs related to the choice of learning objectives
  - ° Preparation of training proposal and developing course content
  - ° Development costs related to instructor guides, workbooks, slides, tapes, etc
  - ° Delivery costs related to personnel, outside goods, services and facilities
  - ° Evaluation costs related to training lists, interactions and analyses
  - ° Administrative costs related to scheduling courses, etc
  - ° Research and development costs related to exploring new training approaches
  - ° Marketing costs related to advertising and publishing training, preparing brochures, etc.

Developing T&D Cost Codes

If you are to keep track of training costs, then you will need to develop a cost coding system. This will enable you to keep accurate records. The codes you develop will be determined by the needs of the organisation – and should be agreed with the accounting function before use.

Figure 11.5: Example of a T&D Budget

The example presented below is for a hotel that employs 119 employees. It has a small managerial team and has made a decision to allocate 3% of its salary budget to training and development during 2003 and 2004.

Budget Allocation	2003	2004
3% Salary Allocation	35,000	40,000
CERT Grant Aid	17,000	15,000
Total	**52,000**	**55,000**
Training Expenditure		
Managerial		
General Manager		
Hotel Management Course (external)	4,000	4,000
Overheads / expenses	500	500
Subtotal	4,500	4,500
Deputy Manager		
Hotel Management Development Course (external)	2,000	2,000
Overheads / Expenses	400	400
Sub Total	2,400	2,400
Assistant Manager (2)		
External Instructor Development Training Course	1,000	1,000
CERT Formal Management Programme	500	700
Overheads / expenses	400	400
Sub Total	1,900	2,100
Trainee Managers (6)		
External Instructor Course	500	600
CERT Junior Manager Programme	3,000	3,500
Overheads / expenses	1,200	1,200
Sub Total	4,700	5,300
Rooms / Reception Manager		
External Instructor Course	500	600
CERT Programme	500	500
Overheads / expenses	200	200
Sub Total	1,200	1,300
Night Club Manager		
External Instructor Course	500	600
CERT Programme	500	600
Overheads / expenses	200	200
Sub Total	1,200	1,400
Supervisory		
Head Barman		
CERT Programme	800	800
Overheads / expenses	200	300
Sub Total	1,000	1,100
Chief Chef		
Professional cookery course (CERT)	1,000	1,000

Overheads / expenses	500	500
Sub Total	1,500	1,500
Restaurant Supervisor		
External Instructor Course	600	600
CERT Programme	600	800
Overheads / expenses	400	400
Sub Total	1,400	1,800
Operational Staff		
Bar (30)		
Internal Training	3,500	3,000
Admin expenses	1,500	1,500
Sub Total	5,000	4,500
Kitchen (15)		
Internal Training (Food safety course, Kitchen Hygiene)	2,000	2,000
Admin expenses	700	800
Sub Total	2,700	2,800
Reception (8)		
Internal Training	800	500
Admin expenses	300	200
Sub Total	1,100	700
Accommodation (15)		
Internal Workshop	1,500	1,700
Admin expenses	700	800
Sub Total	2,200	2,500
Restaurant (26)		
Internal Workshop	3,000	2,500
Admin expenses	1,000	1,000
Sub Total	4,000	3,500
Security (7)		
External Trainer	700	500
Safety Courses	300	200
Sub Total	1,000	900
Ground Maintenance (3)		
Gardening Courses	300	300
Admin expenses	200	200
Sub Total	500	500
EXTERNAL TRAINING ALLOCATION	**36,300**	**36,800**
ON-THE-JOB TRAINING ALLOCATION	**15,000**	**18,000**
TOTAL TRAINING EXPENDITURE	**51,300**	**54,800**

Notes on Training Budget

Through CERT Retain, businesses can receive up to €20,000 in training grants. Individual businesses can obtain grant-aid of 50% towards direct training costs for programmes in management development and human resources. We hope to attain approximately €32,000 overall in grant-aid from CERT over two years.

The Training Budgets for 2003 and 2004 are based on 3% of the projected Labour Costs for both years converted to Euros.

General Manager: The General Manager will be sent on an external Hotel Managerial course at a cost of €4,000 per annum. Appropriate CERT courses identified include: Leadership for results, Managing the personnel function, Trainers in Industry

Deputy Manager: One external course at €3,000 per annum. CERT courses as above would also be identified as appropriate to this position

Assistant Managers: An external instructor will be hired to provide training for this group at a cost of 1,000 per annum. CERT courses, as above, have been identified as appropriate with an outlay of €500 and €700 per annum respectively.

Trainee Managers: The six trainee managers will receive internal training from the General Manager and an allocated assistant. All six should be sent on the CERT approved Coaching and Mentoring course. Other appropriate CERT courses identified include: Developing supervisory skills, Leadership for results, managing the personnel function, Trainers in industry. This would cost approximately €500 per employee.

Rooms / Reception Manager: This employee will receive internal training at a cost of €500 and €600 per year. Appropriate CERT courses identified include: Developing supervisory skills, Leadership for results, Accommodation skills, with an outlay of €500 per annum.

Night Club Manager: This employee will receive internal training at a cost of €500 and €600 per year. Appropriate CERT courses identified include: Developing supervisory skill, Leadership for results, Accommodation skills, with an outlay of €500 and €600 per annum.

Head Barman: The head barman will be placed on a CERT course with an outlay of €800 per annum. Appropriate CERT courses identified include: Introduction to supervision, Leadership for results.

Chief Chef: The chief chef will be placed on a CERT Professional Cookery course with an expense of €1,000 per annum.

Restaurant Supervisors: The two restaurant supervisors will have an external trainer brought in at a cost of €600 per annum. Appropriate CERT courses identified include: Introduction to supervision, Leadership for results, Restaurant advanced skills. We will provide €600 and €800 respectively per annum for the completion of these courses.

Bar Staff: All training will be provided internally. Expenses will be provided to employees who undertake the course.

Kitchen Staff: All training will be provided internally. Expenses will be provided to employees who undertake the course.

Reception Staff: All training will be provided internally. Expenses will be provided to employees who undertake the course.

Accommodation Staff: All training will be provided internally. Expenses will be provided to employees who undertake the course.

Restaurant Staff: All training will be provided internally. Expenses will be provided to employees who undertake the course.

Security Staff and Ground Maintenance Staff: An external trainer will be hired for on-site training.

CALCULATING RETURN ON INVESTMENT IN T&D

The second half of this chapter focuses on some of the issues that you will encounter when evaluating the return on your training investment. Training managers are continually preoccupied by a concern to show that investment in T&D brings tangible benefits to the organisation. They will often resort to methods such as reaction questionnaires, although such questionnaires do not have the capacity to effectively link training activities to financial return. There is evidence of increasing pressures on training specialists to calculate ROI, although the evidence indicates that only a small number of organisations attempt to systematically measure ROI.

We can identify a number of reasons why very few organisations carry out ROI evaluation. Many of them consider it too costly, complex and time-consuming. Seven specific barriers exist:

- Senior management often do not ask for ROI evaluation of training activities. The view often prevails that training, of itself, is a good thing and produces positive outcomes

- Many trainers do not possess the skills to calculate ROI. There is evidence that the collection of ROI data is difficult and time-consuming to collect and analyse

- Training specialists frequently are unsure about what particular dimensions they should evaluate. There is a strong tendency to rely on trainees' reports of improvements rather than seeking to use appropriate measures that can be quantified

- It is sometimes considered a risky activity to undertake. Trainers believe that they will be blamed, if the benefits do not outweigh the costs

- The attribution of benefits to training is very difficult simply because firm or company performance is influenced by a myriad of factors, including markets, interest rates and the efficiency of technology. This results in imprecise ROI figures for T&D

- The costs of training are generally understood to occur up-front, often before the training activity takes place. It is frequently the case that the benefits accrue slowly over time and, in many cases, depend on unpredictable factors such as turnover rates

- Cultural resistance to measurement of the costs and benefits of training may exist in an organisation. Some senior managers may view ROI initiatives simply as promotion and marketing by the training department. Moreover, the "best practice" companies in terms of training are often the most resistant, and accept the value of training as an act of faith.

We believe that the systematic investigation of ROI will bring a number of benefits to the training function:

- It can help to highlight the value of human resources as a significant element of the productivity growth of a company and as a critical component of the adoption of technology
- ROI analysis can be used as a strategy to bring about continuous improvement in T&D practices. It places a greater emphasis on documentation, measurement and feedback processes
- ROI information can provide T&D specialists with critical information to enable them address poor learning transfer
- Finally, ROI analysis can bring greater accountability and enhanced efficacy to the training function.

Figure 11.6 provides examples of the benefits of a number of training interventions.

Starting the Process: Measuring Costs and Benefits

In order to conduct even the most basic analysis of ROI, you will need to ascertain a reliable estimate of costs and benefits.

Return on investment can be used to examine a single isolated training intervention to assess its potential. It has three basic inputs:

- The life or time of a training project
- The amount of investment
- The cash flow after expenses.

We now look at three models that you can use:

- **Compact Cost-Benefit Analysis:** This method measures job performance after training. It is a "compact method", because it uses a formula, not a spreadsheet, to calculate ROI. The result is a monetary amount that describes what the training is worth to the organisation in terms of the performance of employees who have participated in the training. Five steps are calculated to determine the benefits of training using this method:
  - ° Determine the effect of the training
  - ° Determine the monetary value of the effect
  - ° Find out how many people have been trained
  - ° Determine the training cost per person
  - ° Put the information together in the formula and calculate.

Figure 11.7 presents an example of compact cost benefit analysis.

FIGURE 11.6: EXAMPLES OF TRAINING BENEFITS FOR DIFFERENT TRAINING ACTIVITIES

Job	T&D Intervention	Benefits	Measurement	Formula
Construction Job	Initial job training	Reduced time to reach standard and reduced supervisory time	Foreman rating of recent graduate *vs.* crew in terms of productivity and time spent coaching	Productivity gain = trainees x work hours x hourly wage x .5 Time = foreman x hours saved x hourly wage)
Foreman	Attendance administration course	Reduced absence rates	Work groups' absence rates tracked for foreman who were trained *vs.* foremen who were not	(Predicted absences – actual absences) x daily wage
Machine Operators	Re-structure of work group	Reduced turnover and, hence, reduced cost of replacing skilled employees	Factory turnover was monitored before and after creation of "unit work learn"	(Turnover before change – turnover after change) x employees x average replacement cost
Production Managers	Management training programme	Reduced employee turnover (3 other benefits not significant)	Turnover measured before and after for treatment and control groups	Turnover expected – turnover observed x employees x replacement cost
Semi-skilled Machine Operators	Structured *vs.* unstructured (OJT) training	1) Decreased time to achieve job competency 2) Decreased scrap (waste) 2) Increase in problem-solving	1) Mean time to achievement in hours 2) Scrap in lbs, per worker 3) Simulation of problems	1) None 2) Scrap for group S – scrap for group U x employees x cost of material per kilo 3) None
Sewing Machine Operators	Initial job training	Productivity gain due to less time to reach standard, reduced turnover, and increased efficiency	Productivity and turnover of trainees compared to employees hired a) before programme was implemented and b) after it was halted	$(P_2R_2 - P_1R_1) - (W_2R_2 - W_1R_1)$ where: P=productivity R=retention (time with company V=unit value of output W=wages Subscripts 1&2 represent "before" and "after" the programme respectively

Job	T&D Intervention	Benefits	Measurement	Formula
Skilled & Semi-Skilled Manufacturing Employees	Safety training	Increased safety performance	Questionnaire and observation of performance	Compared over four time periods, overall injuries decreased from 84.4/100 to 55.1/100
Supervisors	Speed reading course	Improved reading speed, which makes time available for other activities	Pre- and post-course reading speeds compared	Supervisors x hours saved per day x days x hourly wage
Tax Auditors	Tax audit workshop	Identification of tax payers' errors which led to more tax revenue for State	Trainees were compared to their audit division before and after the workshop	(Post minus pre workshop revenue for trainees) – (post minus pre workshop revenue for audit division)
Truck Terminal Managers	Management training	1) Decreased cost per bill 2) Increased bill/hr, lbs/hr, labour cost/hr 3) Reduced overtime	1) Bill count and cost 2) Bill, lbs, labour 3) Overtime hours	1) Compare to previous 2) Compare to previous 3) Compare over 5 months

FIGURE 11.7: CALCULATING THE RATE OF RETURN ON T&D INVESTMENT

The usual method for assessing the return on investment over a period of time is to compare the return with what would have been earned had the same amount of money been put on deposit at the bank. The expected benefits from the investment and the input costs are discounted by the interest rate over a period of years. If the value of the benefits exceeds the value of the inputs, then there will be a positive return on investment.

The standard equation used in this method is: $S_n = P(1 + r)^n$
The letters used in this equation are:

    P = initial input costs
    r = rate of interest
    n = number of years
    S_n = sum available after n years

Example:

Initial input costs	=	€1,530
Rate of interest	=	0.03 (3% pa)
Number of years	=	2
Sum available after 2 years	=	€1,623.18 = €1530 $(1 + 0.03)^2$

The amount of interest gained after putting the money on deposit would therefore be €1,623.18 - €1,530 = €93.18. So if you want the learning activity to produce a better rate of return than the bank, you need to demonstrate quantifiable benefits worth more than €93.18.

Guidelines

A longer-term return may need to be measured more than once. It is better to measure the return early, even if the full benefits are not yet apparent, so that you can start to see emerging trends. If you leave measuring the return until the point where you expect to see the full benefits, you may have difficulty attributing the benefits to learning and therefore of producing a convincing case.

You should, however, not measure just the early results and impact of the learning. Most people experience a surge of enthusiasm after a learning experience and try to put the learning into practice. That initial enthusiasm usually wears off, and people drift back into their former practices and behaviours. You need to be aware of this and not justify the investment on the basis of the first surge of success, but on the longer-term gain.

When interest rates are low, using a very high rate of interest in the equation could allow you to demonstrate a good rate of return on investment in learning. For example, if €1,530 were invested at the very high rate of interest of 30% for 2 years, the added value would be €1055.70. Investing €1530 in cross-training an individual in computer skills could remove the need to employ a temporary secretary to cover for a colleague's four weeks annual holidays. The cost of one month's temporary support would be approximately €1480. So, in one year, you could produce a better rate of return from investment in learning than two years of placing the same amount of money on deposit at an unobtainable rate of interest.

Source: Phillips (1996) and Phillips (1990).

This compact method has a number of advantages and disadvantages. The advantages are:

- It uses a monetary unit of measure for the analysis. This unit of measurement is usually acceptable to managers because they understand it
- The method is relatively simple to use
- It does not require extensive computer capability or number-crunching power
- It provides results fairly quickly (you don't have to wait for a one-year budget report).

However, it is problematic because:

- It relies on the reports of supervisors and managers concerning the benefits. These reports may not be reliable
- It assumes that the correct training solution was applied in the first instance
- Long-term benefits many not be directly attributable to the training
- It is necessary to make certain assumptions about interest rates and the number of years over which the benefit will accrue
- **The Relative-Aggregate Scores Approach:** This approach compares the relative value of training for different tasks or duties within a job, and for assessing the gain in value for that job after training. When you use it to assess the benefits of training, the difficulty, importance and frequency of various job tasks needs to be assessed. For each of these elements, weights need to be derived. Then, actual performance data are used to show a value for each task, a performance value before and after training, and a performance gain for each task, as well as for the job as a whole. The results of this approach can be used to monitor the results of training and also to plan training so limited resources are invested in the most important or priority areas
- **The Maurice Model:** This model is a combination of numerous ROI models. It consists of the following six steps:

  Estimated figures:

  ° *Step 1:* Calculate the potential for improved performance. A front-end analysis is conducted to determine the purpose of the training request, identify the desired and actual performance after training, and identify the appropriate solutions that are relevant, feasible, and acceptable to the organisation and the targeted employees

- ° *Step 2:* Calculate the estimated training costs. These costs include development costs, implementation costs, and maintenance costs

- ° *Step 3:* Calculate the value analysis. This step verifies the value of training by comparing the cost of training to potential outcomes. First, estimate the highest number and the lowest number of annual deficiencies or improvements. Second, estimate the high and low cost of each deficiency or improvement. Third, calculate the current annual cost of both the high and low deficiencies or improvements. Fourth, estimate the range of expected deficiencies, corrections or improvements obtained from training. Fifth, estimate the high and low annual value of training. Sixth, multiply the high and low annual amounts of training by the length of time the training will last and divide the estimated training costs to obtain the potential worth of a training intervention

Actual figures:

- ° *Step 4:* This step includes design, development, implementation, support, and monitoring/evaluation of training and refers to the actual implementation of the training and the measuring of costs

- ° *Step 5:* Calculate the true costs of training. This step is similar to step 2, but now actual figures are used in place of estimated values

- ° *Step 6:* Calculate the organisational ROI. This step involves estimating the percentage of impact likely due from training and calculating the value of results against training costs. This should be done only on projects where training has been the major performance improvement intervention.

The first three steps are a front-end analysis, based on estimated rather than actual costs; the latter steps are based on actual costs.

SOME ISSUES WHEN PREPARING A COST/BENEFIT ANALYSIS

There are a number of practical decisions you must make in order to conduct an effective ROI analysis.

The Basic Procedure

The basic sequence or approach for calculating a monetary value for any learning benefit, whether hard or soft is as follows:

- Identify one unit of data – for example, one error, one employee grievance, one customer complaint

- Put a monetary value or cost on each unit. Ask people in the line or personnel to help calculate the value, if the management information is not available
- Calculate the change in performance pre- and post-learning
- Calculate the change in performance over a comparable period. Make allowances for any other factors that may have affected performance – for example, reduced equipment breakdowns might be partly due to a new servicing routine
- Calculate the annual change in performance. The most valid way to do this would be to wait till the end of the year, but if you need to produce data sooner, then you could compare shorter periods and extrapolate for annual performance (but beware of any seasonal trends, for instance, does the error rate go up in summer when numbers of casual staff are taken on?)
- Calculate the annual value by multiplying the annual performance change by the unit value. If you subtract the cost of the learning from this figure, it will give you the annual return on investment.

Considering Benefits

When you are considering the benefits of your training, the following may be relevant:

- Output, wastage and sales, which are expressed by value, or by units or amounts, which can be readily converted into monetary value
- There are several indicators of improved quality that can be quantified to produce monetary values, including:
  - *Error rates:* The cost of errors include any materials wasted and time spent correcting the error. There may also be an additional cost of dealing with any resultant customer complaints
  - *Customer complaints:* The costs of customer complaints includes time spent investigating and remedying the cause of the complaint. Some organisations also add in the cost of "shadow" complaints, estimating that for every customer who complains there are others who vote with their feet
  - *Customer satisfaction ratings:* One unit could be represented by a 5% increase in customer satisfaction ratings; if your organisation conducts a customer satisfaction survey, then it should be possible to identify the value to the organisation of an improvement in rating
- You can express employee performance, commitment and morale in terms of the following units:
  - Productivity

○   *Attendance:* The cost of one day's absenteeism will be the cost of a productive day's salary (see calculations for individual participation in learning)

○   *Staff turnover:* If your organisation has a personnel department, they should be able to tell you the average cost of recruitment. Calculation of the cost of staff turnover should also include the value of lost output whilst a job is vacant and the reduced output while the new recruit learns the job.

○   *Equipment breakdown:* If people do not have the correct skills and knowledge to operate the equipment they use at work, there are likely to be more breakdowns. The cost of an average breakdown can be calculated in terms of lost production, time taken to repair the equipment and any spare parts needed

○   *Health and safety incidents:* The cost of a health and safety incident includes lost time and possible sick leave of the employee(s) involved, management time in investigating the incident, and possible management time and legal costs in a resultant court case

○   *Formal grievances:* The cost of dealing with a grievance includes lost employee and management time in the line and human resource department

Other Issues

Other issues that you will need to consider when preparing a cost-benefit analysis include the following:

- You will need to decide over what period you will expect to see full payback from your training investment. This will vary according to the nature and objectives of the learning or training activity. Full payback on an apprenticeship, for example, will take four to eight years, and even after payback is achieved, the benefits of learning may last a lifetime. For sales training on a new product line, payback will be expected much sooner, and the learning may have little or no value after the product line is withdrawn or is modified

- If you find it difficult to calculate a financial value for the organisational benefits, you should ask managers to put their own value on the benefit – but, if you do this, err on the side of caution for the sake of credibility

- You should proceed from the position that not every benefit from learning can be quantified in monetary terms, so do not ignore pay-forward benefits, which we briefly discussed in **Chapter Two**. Qualitative pay-forward benefits are particularly apparent and applicable in organisations that are implementing a programme of change, which includes elements of cultural change. Change programmes include a number of initiatives and it will never be possible to attribute exactly what benefits arose directly from learning activities and what role other factors played in bringing about the changes. Moreover, the aim of change is often to shift perceptions and attitudes rather than develop skills and knowledge to attempt to apply quantitative measures to qualitative benefits is unrealistic and artificial. In such circumstances, you should direct your efforts to identifying pay-forward qualitative benefits such as:

° Improved team working and co-operation
° Increased understanding and awareness of the organisation's purpose and objectives
° Better identification of and focus on strategic priorities
° Development of and/or adaptation of a new organisational culture.

TECHNIQUES & STRATEGIES USED TO QUANTIFY THE BENEFITS OF T&D

The management and training literature is replete with examples of strategies and techniques you can use to quantify the benefits of training and development. Some of them will give you a rough and more subjective measure, others are more precise but may be complicated for you to use. We will consider some of these approaches and techniques and comment on their strengths and weaknesses.

Direct Reports from Participants and Line Managers

You could ask participants and line managers to provide estimates of what improvements have occurred in their performance and how much of this can be attributed to a training and learning activity. This approach has advantages in that it solicits direct feedback from those directly involved in implementing the results of the activity in the workplace. It represents an attempt to quantify a level of improvement in both hard and soft skills.

However, direct reports suffer from two significant limitations: The estimates of benefits derived are subjective and they are likely to vary considerably. Any quantitative data, which you derive from the process, will be at best an estimate.

You could enhance this approach by using a combination of structured interviews and questionnaires. The greater the number of people who contribute estimates, the less likely it is that eccentric responses at the extremes will distort your data and the more confident you will be concerning your findings.

TABLE 11.8: USING DIRECT REPORT EVIDENCE: STRATEGY & EXAMPLE

Strategy	Example
In order to elicit the appropriate information, you will need to ask the following questions: • Has there been an improvement in your performance at work? • What percentage of that improvement do you think can be attributed to the application of the knowledge or skills you acquire in the learning activity? • What is the basis for your estimate? • How confident are you about the accuracy of your estimate? • What other factors might have contributed to improved performance? The question about people's level of confidence about their estimate is key, as it allows you to get a more rounded picture of the possible impact of the learning and to show that you are taking a cautious approach to handling subjective information. The response to the confidence question should be factored into the response about the percentage improvement attributable to learning.	Participants estimate that their performance has improved by 25% (one box marking on a five-box appraisal scale; output up by 25%; error rate reduced by 25% etc) Participants estimate that 50% of this improvement in their performance can be attributed to the learning activity Participant is 70% confident about the accuracy of their estimate Calculate the confidence level. Multiply the confidence percentage by the improvement percentage and divide by 100: (50 x 70) / 100 = 35. The confidence level is therefore 35%. Multiply the confidence percentage by the amount of improvement to isolate the proportion attributable to learning (35 x 25) / 100 = 8.75%.

360° / 180° / 540° Feedback

This method consists of asking those working with participants to assess the participant's behaviour against certain observable criteria. The questionnaires can be sent to peers, boss and subordinates (360°), peer and subordinates (180°), peers, subordinates, boss and other contacts such as customers (540°).

This approach has a number of advantages in the context gathering information about benefits. It is particularly useful when you are attempting to evaluate the impact of learning activities directed at improving less easily evaluated skills such as leadership, management of others, communication and customer service. It allows direct report input for management and leadership skills. It is anonymous, so the feedback is more likely to be objective and it is very useful as a "before" and "after" measure. You could also use it to measure learning over time.

Qualifications Obtained

Qualifications are evidence of achievement, but not all qualifications will be directly related to an individual's current job, nor are they in themselves a guarantee that the individual will apply the certificated skills and knowledge on the job. The types of qualifications that best reflect the impact of learning on performance in the workplace are those qualifications that are assessed on a competency basis in the workplace. Such qualifications can be awarded only when an individual can demonstrate the ability to transfer and apply learning on the job.

Appraisal / Performance Management Reports

If your organisation has a performance management system, this might provide valuable sources of data to enable you to assess the impact of training. The main advantage of this method is that the data already exists and does not have to be specially collected.

It does, however, have a number of inherent weaknesses. Learners may be concerned about the confidentiality of their ratings. It is also a problematic technique in terms of identifying and linking changes in performance to specific learning or training activities. It is possible that the skills and knowledge that are assessed during the performance review process are not the same as the skills and knowledge that the learning activity sought to develop.

This approach will be more effective if your organisation has conducted a learning activity directed at improving the performance of a team or a particular occupational group.

Structured Interview with Senior Managers

This is a similar process as with participants and managers, but repeated at a more senior level in the organisation. It asks managers to focus on the broader picture and the impact on the organisation rather than on individual performance. Its primary strength is that it involves senior management in the evaluation process and, therefore, in the decision-making process concerning T&D.

It has two main disadvantages:

- It requires a significant amount of senior management time
- It may be difficult to get senior managers to engage in the process.

Also, in some organisations, especially larger organisations, senior management may be too far removed from the workplace to observe the direct impact of the T&D intervention.

FIGURE 11.9: USING SENIOR MANAGEMENT EVIDENCE: STRATEGY

Identify which members of the senior management team are most likely to have observed the impact of the training and development activity.

Ask questions that concentrate on business, not learning, objectives and measures – for example, "What changes in output/customer service have you observed?". Top managers' interest is not focused on whether people are better skilled, but whether their performance is adding value to the organisation's overall performance.

You could consider combining the structured interview with the senior managers' evaluation of benefits.

The definition of "senior management" will vary depending on the size and structure of your organisation. In a company employing less than 100 people, it is likely to be director level. In a large company employing 5,000 people, it is more likely to be the level below director.

Send the interviewee a list of the main questions you want to cover, in advance. This will reduce the time needed for the interview and allow for a more considered response.

The level at which you interview will also depend on the depth and breadth of your training and development programme. For instance, if in a large organisation you have targeted only first line managers, then a Board member is unlikely to be able to identify the specific impact of the training and development activity. However, if the learning activity involved every member of staff, then you could expect Board members to be aware of the activity and its impact

Trend Line Analysis

This process involves studying current trends in organisational performance, projecting them into the future and then assessing the impact of learning on those trends. It has two major advantages:

- It possesses the potential to demonstrate a clear link to critical aspects of organisational performance
- It uses existing data.

However, the process assumes that all other factors remain the same.

Impact Analysis

Impact analysis involves representatives of all stakeholder groups likely to be affected by the learning activity in a workshop before the learning activity. It has a number of advantages in that it ensures the involvement of all key stakeholders. It is useful in identifying learning objectives and predicted areas of impact for follow-up evaluation. It helps build stakeholder commitment to the learning activity and it achieves stakeholder consensus on learning objectives. It does however demand a lot of time from each stakeholder.

FIGURE 11.10: TREND LINE ANALYSIS: STRATEGY & EXAMPLE

Strategy	Example
Examine data relating to past and current performance in the area you are targeting for learning – for example, if the learning activity is directed at reducing the number of defective components produced, identify the current trend in component defects	Six month reject rate **before** learning was 5%
	Six month reject rate **after** learning is 2%
Plot past and current trends on a graph	Past trend in reject rate was downwards at 1% every six months
Extend the trend line into the future	
Measure trends post-learning	Percentage reduction attributable to learning is (5 - 2) – 1 = 2%
Calculate the difference between what the trend would have been had there not been a learning intervention, and the actual performance post-learning	
The difference in performance attributable to learning is the difference between the current state and what would have been had the previous trend continued. It is not the difference between what the trend was at the start of the learning programme and the post-learning level of performance.	

The Organisational Elements Model

The Organisational Elements Model (OEM) is designed to demonstrate the relationship between organisational efforts, organisational results, and external payoffs. The aim is to demonstrate the relationship between inputs and results.

The key point of this analysis is the need to show linkages between all the elements of the process, from inputs through to outcomes. If the chain breaks at any point, this indicates there is no connection between the elements – for example, learning inputs are not contributing to the creation of outputs, and therefore there is no return on investment.

It is considered a very useful in identifying areas where evidence of post-learning benefits may be found. It is also useful as a diagnostic tool to identify where there may be a learning need.

It has two major disadvantages:

- It provides no hard data
- It can appear academic.

As a consequence, it is possibly more useful as an aid to discussion rather than persuasion.

FIGURE 11.11: IMPACT ANALYSIS: STEPS

Before the design stage, organise a half-day workshop comprising:
- **Agents:** People who produce, use or implement the learning activity
- **Beneficiaries:** People who will benefit from the activity in some way – for example, participants, their line managers
- Victims: Those who will be negatively affected – for example, colleagues who have to cover for people on day release.

Some people may fall into more than one category, for instance, a line manager could be a beneficiary in the long-term, but a victim in the short-term.

Ask each stakeholder to write down what he or she considers the three most important purposes of the learning activity, one purpose to a piece of paper.

Collect the statements and print them up on a board/fix them on a wall.

In discussion, group the purposes into related clusters and agree a title for each cluster.

Give each stakeholder 10 points to allocate as he/she chooses between the clusters, with the most points to the cluster he/she thinks represents the most important learning objective. There are no restrictions on points allocation; stakeholders can give all the points to one cluster if they wish.

This process should have identified the overall learning priorities for all the stakeholders.

Ask the group to consider each of the learning objectives in turn, and to suggest how they would assess whether or not the objective had been achieved and evaluate its impact on the organisational performance.

Guidelines:

It is most useful in setting up a larger and/or expensive learning programme that is likely to have a major organisational impact.

The clustering process works well using large size "post-it" notes on a wall or flip-chart paper.

You can add in an extra stage between prioritising objectives and identifying evaluation measures, which would be to carry out a force field analysis of factors that will help or hinder the learning activity and process. If you do this, you will need more than a half-day workshop.

You may choose to reconvene the workshop after the learning activity (or perhaps when it is well under way, in a long programme) to see if stakeholders' priorities have changed and if the impact and evaluation measures are proving valid.

FIGURE 11.12: ORGANISATIONAL ELEMENTS MODEL: AN APPROACH

Identify the following elements involved in the learning activity:
- Inputs; numbers and types of participants; organisational resources; policies
- Processes; learning methods; flow of participants etc
- Products: completion of learning activities; tests passed etc;
- Outputs; application of the learning
- Outcomes; longer term and broader payoffs, such as self-confidence and motivation.
- Write this information in the boxes in the OEM table, with the top row showing what your organisation would like the situation to be, and the second row showing the reality of the current situation.

	Outputs	Products	Outcomes	Processes	Inputs
What should or could be done					
What is					

Look at each of the elements and see whether there is a clear link between it and its neighbours. For instance, are inputs used in processes, are outputs the result of the use of inputs in processes?

Missing elements or a lack of clear linkage between elements indicates "disconnects" - areas where there are inefficiencies or lack of the necessary resources and methods to deliver useful results.

An effective learning activity will show clear links between products and outputs and outcomes.

Control Groups and Pilots

This process involves comparing the performance of a group who have undertaken a learning activity, with another group, who have not (the control group). The improved performance in the learning group demonstrates the impact of the learning. When a pilot project is run, those not taking part in the pilot can in effect be used as a control group.

This approach has two major advantages:

- It helps disentangle the impact of learning from the impact of other factors (new equipment)
- It is a useful tool to demonstrate the benefits of learning to a wider sceptical audience.

It is problematic in that it is impossible to exclude effects of other actors; even the fact that people are being observed has been shown to affect their performance (the Hawthorne effect) and it is very difficult to get pilot and control groups that match in terms of composition, experience, etc.

There are a number of issues you need to consider when running a pilot or using a control group:

- If you are running a pilot, and using the rest of the population as a control group and do not tell them in advance that they are the control, then you can prevent the Hawthorne effect. However, this means you will not be able to carry out any pre-learning measures on the control group

- The assessment of performance is of the group as a whole; merely recording that each individual's performance has improved means relatively little

- Use any combination of evaluation tools to evaluate the impact of the learning on the group's overall performance. For instance, compare output and error rates, absenteeism, health and safety incidents, etc. Ask the senior managers responsible for each group to evaluate the group's contribution to organisational success before and after the learning activity

- You should choose a pilot a group whose members are positive toward the idea of learning, but are also as representative as possible of the target population.

PUBLICISING THE RESULTS & MARKETING THE BENEFITS OF T&D

If you conduct a cost-benefit analysis, it is important that you use it to put together a strong case for investing in T&D in the future. You will need to think about your presentation and strategy, as much as about the content of the arguments you make when you communicate your findings to stakeholders.

Presentation Issues

It is important that you consider the following:

- What is the usual style of presentation in your organisation? For example, written report with several appendices, short graphical illustration, executive summary with appendices, or oral presentations?

- Do you want to use the usual presentation style or increase impact by doing something different? What would be the risk of a change of style?

- Look at your terminology: Talk about "investment" not "cost"

- Concentrate your efforts on the activities that will have the greatest organisational impact. Mayer and Pipe put learning activities into three categories: "shoulda", "oughta", "wanna":
  - ○ "Shoulda" are activities that the organisation must undertake, either because of legislation (health and safety procedures) or because they are basic to performance of the job (teaching keyboard users to type)
  - ○ "Oughta" activities are those that there is general agreement are likely to benefit an organisation (management skills, updating professional expertise)
  - ○ "Wanna" activities are those where the benefits are less obvious or are apparent in the longer term (stress management, creativity)
- Make sure your calculations of the up-front investment and expected return on investment are realistic. Where you have had to estimate, say so, and explain the grounds for your estimates. Finally, double-check your figures to make sure the calculations are correct.

Responding to Negative Perceptions about T&D

You need to consider the negative arguments you are likely to come up against in your organisation. Examples include the following:

- "We place no value on training in our organisation."
- "Training stops production and production must never be stopped."

The CIPD makes the following suggestions for pre-empting or countering each of these arguments:

A failure to see the hidden cost of learning by trial and error:

- Cite examples of where mistakes have been made because people were inadequately trained or were thrown in at the deep end
- Identify current mistakes / under-performance and quantify what they are costing your organisation, as well as the value of even a small percentage improvement in individual performance
- Evaluate and compare the performance of a trained or pilot group with an untrained control group.

A belief that effective performance results from innate ability not learning (managers are born not made)

- Quoting individual experience can be powerful in this situation. Find someone who is willing to talk about how they were able to improve their performance following a learning activity. If you are dealing with management skills, get someone's staff to describe the impact of learning on their manager's performance

- Again, evaluating and comparing the performance of control and pilot groups can provide useful evidence.

A lack of an explicit causal link between learning and effective job performance

- The level three (measuring the impact on individual performance, which we explore in the next chapter) evaluation tools will provide the evidence needed to counter this argument.

An inability to distinguish between the effects of training and other factors

- Disentangling the impact of learning from the impact of other factors can be difficult, especially if you are dealing with a situation where there are a number of initiatives taking place at once (reorganisation, new equipment or processes being introduced). A rigorous evaluation process is crucial, involving internal control group comparisons where possible, or eternal benchmarking comparisons
- Data on personal beliefs and attitudes about the relearning may also be effective. In a time of change, maintenance of staff morale is both critical and difficult. Learning often helps by giving people the tools and information to handle the change. A questionnaire and/or programme of interviews will provide information on whether or not people believe the learning is helping them.

A belief that trained staff will be poached and that others will reap the benefits of investment

- Benchmarking research can help in countering this argument; you should look at organisations that have a high reputation for investing in the development of their people and see if you can obtain any information about their staff turnover
- Look at the staff turnover figures for your organisation: Is there a positive or negative correlation between investment in training and staff turnover? Or no obvious correlation?
- Most staff interpret the organisation's willingness to invest in their personal development as a signal of the organisation's loyalty to them, and respond positively; consider conducting an attitude survey by questionnaire and/or interviews in your organisation to obtain staff views about your organisation's investment in learning.

The view that, as long as an individual is performing competently in a current job, the organisation does not need to invest any more in training and development

- This view represents a failure to see the added value benefits of investing in learning; the fact that "with every pair of hands, a brain comes free". Look for individual examples of people who have benefited from learning to advance their careers from an unpromising start to build a case for showing how the organisation is under-utilising its human resources
- Look for spin-off benefits from learning, such as staff suggestions for improvements.

Previous poorly targeted or delivered training

- Examine past learning failures, talk to those who were directly involved and identify why it didn't work. Was the initial business issue correctly identified? Was learning the answer, or was some other action needed? Did the training or learning activity have clearly specified objectives and was it linked directly to the business objectives? Was the nature of the activity appropriate to the organisation's style and culture? Demonstrate why the pervious activity failed to produce the hoped-for results, and show how you will avoid repeating the same mistakes
- Spend time and effort at the front end of the process of linking learning to organisational success, so that you can be confident learning activities are correctly targeted and appropriately designed.

As well as preparing to counter negative arguments, you need to consider how to put together the case for investment, including:

- Identifying: current mistakes and areas of under-performance that are costing the organisation
- Thinking laterally and longer-term about intangible outcomes and pay-forward issues.

Strategy for the Presentation of Your Findings

The following are the issues that you need to consider:

- Think about whom you have to convince - usually senior management
- Whenever possible, speak to the people who need to be persuaded on an informal 1:1 basis before any formal decision-making process. Identify for each of the individuals involved what their position will be (agent, beneficiary or victim). Demonstrate that you have thought about and understand their position. Identify the

benefits to them as individuals and their group; for victims, this may be the long-term overall value to the organisation. Try and think of some parallels – the problems everyone had bedding-in new IT system, but the benefits it brought in the end.

- Is there anyone who would act as a champion in making the case for investment in learning? Your case will be strengthened if you can win the support from people in the line or senior management who are seen as having no axe to grind; best of all, can you win over the Finance Director or budget-holders to support investment in learning? It would also help your case if you can convert an individual who was previously known to be sceptical about the value of investment in learning to the view that learning pays

- Will you have to make your case as a formal presentation, in an informal meeting or in writing? You may want to practise a formal presentation

- What arguments will appeal most to your organization and its managers? Do they want to be seen as on the cutting edge? Are they concerned to stay in step with competitors/parallel organisations?

- Don't neglect the marketing of the benefits during and after the learning activity. Keep everyone informed about progress and publicise success and results of the early evaluation stages. If things aren't going as well as expected, don't' try and hide this; publicise your strategy for dealing with it

- Look for opportunities to get wider publicity and recognition for your successes; a write-up in the local press about learners' successes, consider national award schemes – for example, Investors in People, National Training Awards, Excellence Through People – or articles in trade or specialist press about your activities. If you have one, liaise with your marketing or publicity department over promotional opportunities.

BEST PRACTICE INDICATORS

Some of the best practice issues that you should consider related to the contents of this chapter are:

- A specific proportion of revenue is set aside annually, adequate to resource all planned training and learning activity in the organisation at corporate, unit and operational levels. There is a clear rationale for this proportion, and it is well communicated across the organisation

- An appropriate proportion of the T&D financial investment is targeted on training initiatives and other learning activities that will enhance and continuously improve performance in the workplace

- The T&D budget is not one of the first to be cut in any cost-reduction plan or other contingency. It is treated in the same way as the budgets of other functions and processes that are core to the business
- Top management assesses the added value, as well as the cost, of T&D activity at least annually
- When you are measuring the benefits of training, know your audience and ensure that measures of training impact provide the evidence that is most persuasive, based on their information preferences and priorities.
- Distinguish between organisational results and the financial impact of those results. You should measure the outcomes that make the most sense given the strategic priorities of your organisation.

Reflections on Training & Development Scenario

Calculating the Cost Benefit
A comparison of the costs and savings shows that the first year's savings would be:

Annual gross savings	€310,000
Less annual expenses	€55,000
Net Savings	€255,000

The ROI, assuming a first year total write-off on the building, equipment and the programme development is:

ROI = €255,000 / €195,000 =   130%

Since it would be more correct to spread the investment in the buildings, equipment and development over several years, the true estimate of the ROI would be much higher.

Chapter 12

EVALUATION OF TRAINING & DEVELOPMENT: HAS IT WORKED?

LEARNING OBJECTIVES

On completion of this chapter, you should be able to:

- Provide a justification for the systematic evaluation of training and development

- Define the nature and purpose of the evaluation process

- Evaluate the suitability and appropriateness of a number of evaluation models

- List the steps and issues that you must consider when formulating an evaluation strategy

- Develop both objective and subjective tests to measure learning

- Design an effective questionnaire to measure reactions to the learning event

- Design strategies and methods to measure the impact of the training on performance

- Understand the factors that facilitate transfer to the workforce

- List a set of guidelines that should be followed when conducting evaluation of training.

A Training & Development Scenario

You have been asked to evaluate the impact on individual performance of a training programme on objective setting that you designed and delivered.

The aims of introducing the objective-setting process into the organisation were:

To give individual members of staff:

- A better understanding of what is expected of them, where priorities lie, and where their contribution fits into the organisation
- A better understanding of how he/she is progressing, as a result of regular reviews.

To give managers:

- A basis of allocating responsibility for achieving certain results to individuals, and monitoring achievement of those results
- Solid information that will act as less subjective evidence for assessing individuals' performance

To give the organisation:

- A greater likelihood of strategic and business plans being achieved.

Your task is to prepare a set of questions that you will ask the manager and the participant.

INTRODUCTION

In this book, we have discussed all aspects of the training design process. Although this is the last chapter, evaluation of training is a continuous process and it influences design (the "what") and delivery (the "how") of training interventions. In other words, you do not wait until the training programme is over to start evaluating it! Evaluation should occur therefore before, during, and after a training event.

There are many interpretations of the word "evaluation". In this book, we use the term in its broadest sense. Hamblin (1974) defines evaluation as "any attempt to obtain information (feedback) on the effects of a training programme and to assess the value of the training in the light of that information".

When organisations invest time, money and resources into learning programmes, understandably they will expect to see some tangible benefits. The overall aim of conducting an evaluation is to enable the effectiveness of investment in learning to be appraised. It can be one of the more difficult tasks in the T&D process that you will have to complete, but there are very strong reasons for engaging in systematic evaluation of your T&D activities, including:

- **For Learners**: Evaluation will answer the following questions: Has the training been effective? Was this the best way to address the performance gap or development opportunity?

- **For Trainers:** Feedback is used to take action to improve the design and delivery of the programme and to consider the results of training, rather than focusing simply on activities

- **For the organisation:** Evaluation determines whether or not the programme has achieved its agreed objectives. It can also provide you with information to assess the overall cost-effectiveness and return on investment of the programme. Evaluation also supports the transfer of learning back into the work environment and assists in linking training to performance on-the-job.

If you are still not convinced about the need to evaluate your training, the following are the consequences of not conducting systematic evaluation:

- A trainer's performance is not measured
- A training event's efficiency and effectiveness is not assessed
- Learners' views and/or progress are not recorded
- Changes in knowledge, attitudes or skill levels cannot be linked to the training intervention
- There is no measure of transfer of learning back into the work environment
- The organisation cannot conduct a cost-benefit analysis.

Evaluation is therefore a critical step in the training design process. During the rest of this chapter, we will outline a user-friendly approach to evaluating your training events. We will begin by considering whether you should evaluate. We outline some of the standard models of evaluation used in organisations today, which share many common features although they may use different types of language. We do not advocate that you use one model over another; however, we suggest that you consider who is going to use the outputs from your evaluation efforts.

SHOULD YOU EVALUATE YOUR T&D?

This is a pertinent question to pose. Simply put, any evaluation activity that you undertake will cost you time and money. This means that you have to consider the value of conducting a systematic evaluation. The CIPD recommends that you consider six key questions before you reach your conclusion:

- **How much did the learning activity itself cost?** The greater the investment, the more important it is to be sure it was money and resources well spent. Also, the greater the investment, a smaller proportion of the total cost of the learning activity the cost of evaluation will represent

- **How likely is it that you will run the activity again?** If it is likely that you will run the activity again, then it makes sense to evaluate its impact to avoid any danger of continuing to invest in an activity that is not delivering on its objectives

- **How many people took part in the learning activity?** The higher the percentage of an organisation's staff involved in a learning activity, the greater its potential impact on the business, and therefore the more important it is to evaluate whether the impact was the one intended. Also, the greater the percentage of an organisation's personnel involved, the wider will spread the message from the learning activity; you need to be sure the messages being spread are the ones intended

- **How crucial to your organisation is the successful achievement of the learning objectives?** If the aim of the learning activity was, say, to train people in operating an expensive piece of equipment in a critical business process, then you need to be sure that the result of the training is that people can operate the process correctly

- **Is the method of the learning activity new to your organisation?** It is valuable to assess a new method of learning to see whether it could be applied to other topics and work areas.

Figure 12.1 gives an example of a scoring system that provides a useful indication of whether to evaluate a particular learning activity.

FIGURE 12.1: SCORING SYSTEM FOR MAKING EVALUATION DECISIONS

Rate each of the evaluation factors on a scale of 1 – 10:

Low level of investment									**High level of investment**
1	**2**	**3**	**4**	**5**	**6**	**7**	**8**	**9**	**10**
Small percentage of staff involved									**Large percentage of staff involved**
1	**2**	**3**	**4**	**5**	**6**	**7**	**8**	**9**	**10**
One-off activity									**Activity will be repeated often**
1	**2**	**3**	**4**	**5**	**6**	**7**	**8**	**9**	**10**
Non-critical business objectives									**Critical business objectives**
1	**2**	**3**	**4**	**5**	**6**	**7**	**8**	**9**	**10**
Familiar learning method									**Innovative method**
1	**2**	**3**	**4**	**5**	**6**	**7**	**8**	**9**	**10**

If the total score is more than 25, it will be worthwhile evaluating the learning activity. If any one factor scores 7 or more, you should consider carrying out an evaluation, concentrating on that factor.

For example, if the scores are: Investment – 5; Percentage of staff - 3; Repetition - 4; Criticality – 4; Innovation – 8: Total score 24. Since the score for Innovation was 8, it would be worthwhile carrying out an evaluation of the effectiveness of the new learning method to see if there are useful lessons to be applied to other topics and activities.

EVALUATION MODELS

As a trainer, you will be faced with a number of choices on the type of evaluation model you use to evaluate your training activities. We present six models of evaluation that are good practice models:

- The CIRO Model (1970)
- The Leatherman Model (1996)
- The Hamblin Model (1974)
- The Kirkpatrick Model (1976)
- Jack Phillips Model: An ROI Model (1997)
- The Hodges Model (1999).

The CIRO Model

The CIRO model proposes that evaluation should focus on the content of the training activity, the inputs to the training process and two types of outcomes (reaction outcomes and achievement of objectives):

- **Content evaluation** is the process of deciding whether a particular problem has a learning solution; and if so, what the learning objectives should be
- **Input evaluation** can occur during training, or when there is a review of the resources that were available to meet the learning requirement, the learning structure, and the media and methods used. Another factor would be whether the selection of the learners themselves was valid in the first place
- **Reaction evaluation** covers the reactions to the learning event by the various participants involved in it, especially the employees
- **Outcome evaluation** measures the extent to which the objectives were achieved – the traditional approach to evaluation.

The Leatherman Model

Leatherman suggests a simpler classification of how and when training evaluation can, and should, be conducted. He distinguishes the stages as follows:

- **Within-training evaluation:** In essence, this means planning sufficient time to be able to discuss with the trainees how they view the learning programme – "What should we do more of? Less of?"
- **Terminal evaluation:** This can be carried out by a discussion or through a standard evaluation form that the trainees complete
- **Post-learning evaluation:** This measures the final outcomes of the learning and is the most difficult stage. Some of the problems that can be encountered at this stage are reviewed later.

The Hamblin Model

Hamblin suggests that there are five levels of evaluation that are necessary to be investigated in order to achieve a full picture of the outcomes of the evaluation process:

- **Level 1 – Reaction:** Trainees' reactions during, and immediately after, the learning event to the trainer, other trainees, and to the content and methods of the learning process
- **Level 2 – Learning:** This is conducted before and after the event: Did the trainees learn what was intended?
- **Level 3 – Job Behaviour:** The job behaviour at work at the end of the learning period. Was learning transferred to the job? This level of evaluation is conducted before, and after, the event

- **Level 4 – Functioning:** The effect on the learner's department, preferably identified *via* a cost-benefit analysis
- **Level 5 – Ultimate Value:** Has the learning affected the organisation's well-being? For example: Has it boosted the morale and commitment of the workforce? Has it improved profitability?

The Kirkpatrick Model

Kirkpatrick's model is frequently used in organisations. It proposes that trainers should measure four dimensions of outcome:

- **Reaction:** Measures of reaction typically focus on participants' satisfaction with training received and their perceptions of its quality (structure, content, methods) and relevance. There is debate as to whether reaction criteria actually provide valid standards of training effectiveness – some trainers believe that they only measure satisfaction
- **Learning:** Learning criteria measure whether participants have observed the concepts or content of the training. The concern is with measuring actual learning achieved within the event
- **Behaviour:** Behaviour criteria go a step beyond whether the trainee has learned the relevant concepts. These criteria are concerned with any changes initiated by the learning event in terms of job behaviour and performance.
- **Results:** Measures the business impact of the programme.

Phillips Model: An ROI Model (1997)

The Phillips model of evaluation adds one final level to Kirkpatrick's model of evaluation. Phillips adds level 5, called Return-on-investment. At this level, you seek to measure the monetary value of the results and costs for the program, usually expressed as a percentage. In formula form, the ROI becomes:

$$\text{ROI (\%)} = \frac{\text{Net Program Benefits}}{\text{Program Costs}} \times 100$$

Calculating the ROI from a training programme can be quite time-consuming for you and the organisation. Therefore, in most events that you evaluate, levels 1 to 4 of Kirkpatrick's model will be sufficient.

Hodges Model of Evaluation

Hodges outlines a useful overall evaluation model called *Components for HRD Evaluation,* which uses the following framework:

- **Needs Assessment:** What do they need?
- **Formative Evaluation:** Will it work?

- **Summative Evaluation:**
  - ○ *Reaction Evaluation:* Were they satisfied?
  - ○ *Learning Evaluation:* Did they learn?
  - ○ *Performance Evaluation:* Were they able to use it and were they successful in using it?
  - ○ *Impact Evaluation:* What impact has it had, and was there a financial return?

Needs Assessment

We referred to this process in **Chapter Four**. A needs analysis process produces clarity on the objectives for the programme. It is worth restating the importance of having clear and measurable objectives for a training programme. If objectives are vague, it is very difficult to evaluate the effectiveness of the programme. A useful tool to use, once programme objectives are agreed, is an "objective map Template". This template forces us as trainers to make the links between business, performance and learning objectives. It also encourages us to consider how to measure the achievement of each learning objective.

Formative Evaluation

This stage of evaluation refers to the evaluation that takes place at the end of a pilot programme. Formative evaluation is an important step to complete before the training programme is implemented and ready for general use. You ask yourself such questions as:

- Will this programme fit with the culture of the organisation?
- Will it address the performance gaps identified?
- Has the right learning strategy been employed?
- Has the intervention been pitched at the right level?
- Is the delivery style appropriate to the target audience?

Formative evaluation is a validation of all of your key decisions up to this point (pre-implementation).

Summative Evaluation

This phase combines Kirkpatrick's and Phillips' Models of Evaluation in four steps (see above). Hodges stresses the importance of learning and performance evaluation.

    Figure 12.2 presents a summary of a number of evaluation models relevant to trainers.

FIGURE 12.2: COMPARISON OF SIX EVALUATION PERSPECTIVES FOR TRAINING PROGRAMME EVALUATION

Evaluation Perspective	CIRO Approach: Warr et al. (1970)	Leatherman Model	Five-Level Approach: Hamblin (1974)	Four-level Approach: Kirkpatrick (1959a, 1959b, 1960a, 1960b)	Five-Level ROI Phillips Model	Hodges Model
Context, input, activity before the training	Content evaluation and input evaluation					
Feedback within the training (Level 1)	Reaction	Input & Process	Reaction	Reaction	Reaction & planned action	Reaction
Acquisition within the training	Immediate outcome	Micro	Learning	Learning	Learning	Learning
Performance after the training	Ultimate outcome	Micro	Job behaviour	Behaviour	Job application	Transfer
Organisational pay-offs	Ultimate outcome	Macro	Organisation	Results	Business results and return on investment	Business impact
Social or cultural values			Ultimate			

FIGURE 12.3: CHARACTERISTICS OF DIFFERENT EVALUATION METHODS

	Level 1	Level 2			Level 3								Level 4				
	Q/aire	Pre/Post Tests	Q/aire	I/view	Q/aire	I/view	Est. Ben-efits	360° Feed-back	Quali-fications	Appraisal	I/views	Est. Ben-efits	Trend Line Anal.	Impact Anal.	Org. Elements Model	Controls & Pilots	Mgt Info
Quantitative	H	H	M	L	M	L	H	H	M	H	L	K	H	L	L	H	H
Qualitative	H	H	M	H	M	H	M	H	M	M	H	H	L	H	M	H	M
Can be converted to financial value	X	X	X	X	X	X	H	X	X	M	X	H	H	X	X	H	H
Line Input	L	M	L	H	L	H	H	H	L	L	H	H	L	H	L	L	L
Evaluator Input	L	H	M	H	M	H	H	H	M	M	H	H	M	H	M	H	H
Effort to establish baseline	L	L	L	L	L	L	L	M	M	M	M	M	H	H	M	H	M

Notes: H = High, M = Medium, L = Low, X = None

Quantitative: This refers to numerical and tangible data outputs that are usually expressed in financial terms; *Qualitative:* This refers to more descriptive and more tangible data; *Conversion to Financial Value:* This refers to the extent that it is possible to convert the data collected into a financial type statement; *Line Input:* This refers to the extent of involvement of line managers in implementing the method; *Evaluator Input:* This refers to the involvement of the evaluator in administrating the method; *Baseline:* This refers to the possibility that a baseline benchmark figure can be established for identifying trends over time.

DEVELOPING YOUR EVALUATION STRATEGY

Once you have decided to evaluate the impact of your T&D activities, you have a number of decisions to make relating to the level of evaluation and the methods you use to conduct the evaluation. These decisions need to be made early in the process because many of the evaluation methods require a baseline of current performance (a "before" measure) against which you will evaluate the impact of your training intervention.

In choosing which evaluation tools to use, you need to consider the nature of the output you want to produce – what would be the content, style and presentation of information that would best make your case in your organisation? – and the inputs available.

Outputs:

- What are senior management's and budget holders' requirements for data? Do they insist on having hard financial data, or are they happy to make decisions based on qualitative information?
- How sceptical are the decision-makers – and the target participants – about the benefits of investing in learning?
- Are the objectives and benefits measurable in hard financial terms, or assessable in qualitative terms, or both?
- What type of information and style of presentation is familiar to people in your organisation? You may choose to use a different type of presentation to increase impact, or you may feel that people will be happier with the familiar.
- Is the preference in your organisation for information expressed numerically or verbally?

Inputs:

- What /how much information is already available in your organisation?
- Can you use that information in the evaluation process?
- How much time / resources do you have available for the process?
- How much time and resources do other stakeholders (learning participants, their managers, senior managers, providers of management and performance information) have available to contribute to the evaluation?
- How willing are other stakeholders likely to be to spend time on evaluation?
- Are people in your organisation accustomed to completing questionnaires and/or being interviewed? If not, what will be their likely reaction? Or are they already suffering from "survey fatigue"?

Most of these questions can be answered before you embark on the learning activity – or at least a fair assessment can be made. Therefore, you should be able to select your evaluation tools before the learning activity starts. If you are to have any useful "before" and "after" measures, then you must decide at the beginning of the process what baseline measures you will need for which evaluation tools, and then establish the baseline.

Figure 12.3 will help you identify which tools best meet your evaluation requirements. Note that there is a direct correlation between the detail and rigour of the evaluation output chosen and the amount of time and effort demanded of the line and the evaluator. Also, the more rigorous you want the evaluation process to be, the more time and effort you will need to spend to establish a clear baseline of pre-learning performance. You will need to consider, and possibly negotiate, an appropriate balance between the required evaluation outputs and the related inputs. The four levels of evaluation methodologies have been developed over the years, but they all have their foundation in a model developed by Donald Kirkpatrick in 1959.

DEVELOPING LEARNING MEASURES (PRE- & POST-EVENT)

We begin with learning measures (or tests), because you need to be able to design them. All other results depend on this fundamental factor. An effective learning measure will answer the question: "Did the participants learn?" To answer this question, you will need to construct test materials that measure both knowledge and skills.

Objective Tests of Learning

It is first important to clarify what we mean by an objective test. An objective test consists of a number of items, the response to which is precisely predetermined. The term "item" is used rather than question, because, although some items may be in the form of questions, others may not.

Objective tests have a number of advantages in the context of measuring the learning outcomes of a training event. These advantages include:

- The marking is consistent regardless of who is marking the test
- They are quick to mark
- They are efficient in assessing a wide range of knowledge types
- If written with skill, more than mere facts can also be tested – for example, comprehension of material and the application of knowledge to solve problems can be tested
- They discourage "question-spotting"

- Answers are restricted by the questions asked so that the trainer can assess exactly what s/he wishes to assess
- There is less chance of certain trainees being lucky in that the "right" questions came up in an examination
- Rapid feedback in the form of knowledge of results is provided for both learner and trainer
- They encourage the learner to acquire a solid basis of factual matter
- Scoring is not influenced by the "halo effect" produced by a candidate's ability in written expression.

General Principles in Developing an Objective Test

Whatever test you design should have a clearly stated goal. The most useful tests have a number of limited objectives. Each test question should have a stated purpose, directly related to a minor or major objective of the training.

There are four basic steps in constructing a test:

- **Step 1:** Make a determination of the scope of the test and what it is going to measure.
- **Step 2:** Devise your testing strategy. This will require you to make decisions concerning the types of questions you will use, how the test will be scored and how you will interpret and use the results
- **Step 3:** Write a list of test questions. We propose that you consider the following questions before you begin the task of actually wording test items

PROBLEM	SOLUTION
1. What is to be assessed?	Define the objectives of the teaching and learning, hence the testing (objectives were covered in unit 3)
2. How will the completed test reflect the content of the teaching, learning and testing?	Plan a test-scheme specification in the form of a specification table. This makes use of the stated objectives and also of different levels of questions.
3. What form will the test items take?	Decide after having considered the strengths and weaknesses of the various kinds of items and which are the most appropriate ones for these current purposes
4. How can the trainer be sure that test items are doing the job that he has intended?	He must carry out an item analysis. This means finding out something about the difficulty levels of the test items and also about how effective they are in discriminating between the most able and the least able students
5. How can the trainer be sure that the test as a whole is doing a good job?	Following the item analysis the trainer will be better able to produce a final, balanced test.
6. How can the marking best be accomplished?	The trainer will have to consider whether he/she should correct for guessing and whether he/she could conveniently produce a marking key to speed up the process.

- **Step 4:** Decide whether the trainees will have access to the results of the test. If you do not propose using the list again, it is good learning practice to go over the incorrect responses and reinforce the correct answers. If the test will be used repeatedly in a work situation, for different trainees, it may be appropriate to keep it confidential.

Reliability and Validity of Tests

You should consider the validity and reliability of any tests you use in the evaluation process:

- **Reliability:** This focuses on whether the test is consistent and gives approximately the same results, if administered to the same person or groups of people within a short time period. If similar results are obtained, the test is deemed to be reliable; if not, you will need to review the test

- **Validity:** There are different forms of test validity, the main form relevant to trainers being "face-validity", which means simply that the tests that you design must measure what you state they will measure. Guidelines to help you construct valid tests include:

    ○ Have an equal number of questions on each topic that has been taught

    ○ Phrase your questions in a neutral manner, so that the learners do not respond in a way that they think you want them to respond

    ○ Write clear instructions on how the test is to be administered; so that the conditions are the same each time

    ○ Write clear questions that avoid vague answers being given by the learners.

Types of Knowledge-Based Tests

You have a number of options when designing knowledge-based tests.

Multiple Choice Items
This question format requires the learner to select one answer from a list of possible answers to a question (called a "stem").

> **Example:**
> A customer has returned to your branch with a toaster that he purchased less than a week ago. Would you:
> - Apologise and exchange the toaster immediately?
> - Apologise and examine the toaster to find out the fault and then take appropriate action?
> - Apologise for the inconvenience and give the customer a refund?

- Apologise for the inconvenience and ask the customer if she is prepared to accept goods to the value of the toaster?

Multiple-choice items have the advantage that they can be scored quickly and accurately. The main disadvantage is that can be difficult to construct.

Figure 12.4 presents an outline of the main guidelines in preparing a number of different questions to assess the level of learning achieved.

TABLE 12.4: PREPARING DIFFERENT TYPES OF QUESTIONS FOR EVALUATION & VALIDATION

Multiple Choice

Multiple Choice questions are useful when the training objective requires that the learner recognise, differentiate or describe factual elements. In Multiple Choice questions, the correct answer should be a significantly better choice than the other options available to the trainee. All the answers may be correct to an extent and it is the trainee's task to choose the most accurate or relevant answer. In Multiple Choice questions, the question is called the "stem", while the incorrect answers are called the "distracters". Multiple Choice questions are relatively easy to administer and score, however careful thought must be given to their construction.

Guidelines for the Construction of Multiple Choice Questions

- Use clear, simple language
- Ensure that the intended answer is correct
- Include four or five options
- The distracters should be plausible and attractive
- The correct answer should not be significantly longer or shorter than the incorrect answers
- Do not use "ALL OF THE ABOVE" as an answer, if it is possible
- The items should measure important learning outcomes of your training
- The question should contain one clearly stated problem
- The item should contain as much of the wording as possible.
- Avoid negative items, if possible.
- **Highlight** negative words, if used.
- Avoid verbal clues such as: Repeating the same word in the question and the correct answer but not in the other answers; Ending the item with an indefinite article; Mixing singular and plural nouns between the item and the incorrect ones.

Multiple Response

This type of question consists of an incomplete statement, followed by several responses that are suggested answers to complete the sentence. Multiple Response questions differ from Multiple Choice questions in that there may be one or more correct responses.

Example:

"Over-printing" may be caused by:

> Uneven tension in the paper
> Dirty rollers
> Fluctuations in roller speed
> Wet storage
> Misaligned rollers.

Sequencing

These items test the trainee's ability to list information or a process in the correct sequence.

Example:

Which row below shows the correct order of seniority of staff in a department store?

> Manager, supervisor, assistant manager, departmental manager.
> Supervisor, assistant manager, departmental manager, manager.
> Manager, assistant manager, departmental manager, supervisor.
> Departmental manager, manager, supervisor, assistant manager.

Matching

This is another variety of a Multiple Choice question, in which the trainee is presented with two lists and is required to make the correct link between an entry in list A with one in list B.

Example:

Various transactions are listed in list A. Various forms are listed in list B. Place the letters corresponding to the form (from list B) in the space next to the transaction (in list A) on which it is required.

List A	List B
1. Refund to customer	(a) D72
2. Defective stock	(b) E20
3. Stock transfer	(c) D17
4. Textile recorder	(d) E11
	(e) N4
	(f) M62

True/False (or Yes/No)

The trainee is presented with a statement that is true or false and is asked to underline which answer he/she considers correct.

Example:

True/False - The term shrinkage in retailing refers to losses due to theft or damage.

Simple Recall/Completion

These are common items that demand the recall of a fact.

Example:

Question type: What is the colour of the neutral wire in an electric cable?
Completion type: The colour of the live wire in an electric cable is ...

Check Lists/Rating Scales

These can be objective or subjective. They are particularly useful for practical competence tests and on-the-job assessments.

Example:

Here are some items from one form of checklist used for assessing the practical competence of fork lift truck drivers:

Faults

1. Travels with forks/load too high/low
2. Fails to position mast correctly for travelling
3. Fails to release brake when travelling
4. Accelerates or brakes erratically
5. Etc.

Example:

Here is an example of a rating scale commonly used in appraisal forms for sales floor staff.

Service	*Attitudes to selling*	*General helpfulness to Customers*	*Dealing with Customer Problems and Complaints*
Very good	Very good	Very good	Very good
Good	Good	Good	Good
Satisfactory	Satisfactory	Satisfactory	Satisfactory
Poor	Poor	Poor	Poor

Developing Subjective Tests to Measure Learning

Subjective tests of learning usually provide less valid data, since it is difficult to predict the precise answer and they are difficult to score. The quality of the trainee's response, and the score achieved, depends on your judgement.

We should highlight that the distinction between objective and subjective tests is sometimes difficult to maintain. There are times when the overlap is evident; however the items presented in **Figure 12.5** are usually categorised as "subjective", simply because the trainer is required to judge the quality of the performance, the answer or the attitude displayed.

In this section, we have discussed different forms of testing. Learners' skills and knowledge can be tested before, and after, a learning event to show progress. Being able to measure progress can have a very positive motivational effect on learners. Objective and subjective testing both have their uses in evaluating training programmes. Now, we will discuss how to assess learners during the learning event.

Assessing Learning During Learning Events

As a successful trainer, you will be concerned to assess how the learning event is progressing, either formally or informally.

Formal methods of assessing progress during the event include:

- **Mid-point objective test:** We described this in the previous section
- **Feedback session:** Learners' comments on approach/learning material are recorded on flip-chart or on individual feedback sheets
- **Table Quiz:** Based on knowledge imparted
- **Role-play:** New skills are practised by the learners, observed by the trainer, and feedback is given to the learners. Role-plays tend to be based on real-life scenarios, as described in **Chapter Six**
- **Activity Observation:** New skills are practised during an exercise, observed (by trainer and/or other participants) and feedback is given to the learners
- **End-of-day assessment:** Learners are asked at the end of a day how they think the course is progressing. A useful tool here is to use a traffic-light system as follows: "What should we stop? (RED) What should we start? (GREEN) What should we continue?" It can be useful to do this exercise as a silent brainstorm, using "Post-IT" notes. The feedback can be placed on a board by the trainer and read out at the start of the next day.

TABLE 12.5: EXAMPLES OF SUBJECTIVE TESTS IN THE VALIDATION OF TRAINING

1. Essays

This is the most used form of assessment in examinations, but there are occasions in training evaluation situations when essays can also serve a useful purpose. The distinctive features of the essay question are that no one answer is correct, the answers vary in quality and correctness and the trainee has the opportunity to recall and organise ideas.

2. Logs and Diaries

A log or diary is a very useful device for continuous assessment. It is of particular value for apprentices and trainees who are expected to include in their training programmes experience of a wide range of skills and techniques. A log or diary serves to: Check that a technique or skill has been covered; Provide the learner with an opportunity to describe the techniques involved - a laboratory process; Allow the trainee to comment on the quality or effectiveness of the instruction.

3. Oral Questioning

Oral questioning is frequently used in training to provide informal feedback on the success of instruction and the level of understanding. The advantage is that its impact is immediate. Oral questioning may be used on a more formal basis as a variation of the essay question. It can even be used by the trainer to help assign grades. Some benefits of oral questioning: It permits detailed probing by the examiner; Candidates can ask for clarification of the question; Errors in thinking can be diagnosed and trainees with poor literary skills can succeed.

4. Interviews

Interviews represent one of the means of assessing the suitability of trainees/employees for roles within the organisation. If properly structured, they serve a variety of purposes: Assessing the attitudes, aspirations and commitments of the trainee; Explaining company policy and options available; Assessing knowledge as in oral questioning. It is therefore a useful two-way process for gaining and providing information.

5. Profiles

Profiles are rather different from most of the other techniques we have outlined, in that they are not strictly a form of assessment. They might be better described as a multi-faceted means of recording a learner's skills, capabilities, experiences and achievements. Such a tool both encourages, and supports, a great variety of assessment techniques. The range of achievements and qualities for which profiles are suitable includes: Communication skills, numerical skills, planning, problem solving, learning, creative thinking, manipulative skills and attitudes. Profiles can also be used for self-assessment of the trainee.

6. Observation

There are many important features of a trainee's performance that can only be assessed by direct observation. There is a whole range of techniques available, including: Anecdotal records such as a descriptive account of what the apprentice or salesman does; Checklist or rating scale, where the assessor notes when particular procedures occur or at what standard.

7. Simulations

Simulation describes the context, rather than precise assessment methods. The trainer tries to reproduce conditions, situations or problems that are as close to reality as possible. He/she has then to find a means of assessing the learner's ability to respond. The classic example is the flight simulator for aircrew training.

You could use some of the following informal methods of assessing progress during the event:

- **Discreet questioning during an event:** The trainer will assess levels of understanding from this type of questioning
- **Informal conversations with learners at break-times:** This will usually provide very honest and timely feedback
- **Informal observation of learners:** This can take place during written exercises or skill-practice sessions.

A word of caution for the trainer here: If you engage in formal assessment during a learning event, the learners will expect you to take their feedback on board and change the programme accordingly. Ensure that you have both the skills as a trainer, and authority from the organisation, to make the suggested changes. The Golden rule is: **Once you ask for feedback, you raise expectations of the learners. If you cannot be flexible with the learning event, do not ask for feedback during the event.**

SUMMATIVE EVALUATION (POST-EVENT)

Each stage of the evaluation process provides challenges in terms of the types of data that you wish to collect and the method you use to collect it. We set out in this section some of the options that are available for summative, or post-event, evaluation.

Reaction Evaluation

This basic level of evaluation measures whether your learners perceive that a particular learning event was of benefit to them as individuals. It does not measure whether learning has taken place, whether that learning will be used or whether it will impact on the performance of the participant.

Gathering information about the learner's reactions to the learning event is usually achieved by using a reaction evaluation questionnaire; however, other methods such as interviews and group discussions are equally legitimate.

The reaction evaluation questionnaire seeks to investigate the following dimensions of the training:

- The perceived value of the training
- The enjoyment of the learning experience
- The timelines of the training
- The relevance of the training
- The competence of the instructors / trainers
- Satisfaction with the training facilities

- Changes that could be made to the programme content and/or the methods of learning used.

The main method used for evaluating reaction is a post-learning questionnaire. An alternative, or additional, method is post-learning interviews. However, the time and effort involved in conducting interviews is unlikely to be justified by the small amount of information to be gathered. Interviews to assess reaction to learning would only be worthwhile when language, literacy or physical barriers make it difficult for individuals to complete a questionnaire.

Post-Learning Questionnaires

Pros:

- An immediate indication of the likelihood of trainees implementing what they have learned
- High completion rates, if the questionnaire is distributed immediately after the learning event.

Cons:

- No direct link between reaction to learning and impact on work performance.

How to set about it:

- In the normal course of events, the questionnaire should be administered immediately on completion of the training. You are likely to get a much lower response rate if you allow participants to complete it when they return to work
- Ask questions people can answer. People taking part in a learning experience are, by definition, not experts on the subject. They are therefore not well-qualified to answer questions such as: "Was the course the right length?", "Was the balance between theory and practice right?" until they have the benefit of hindsight some time after the learning. They can, however, respond immediately to questions such as "Did you find it easy to understand the course material?"
- Concentrate on active questions about what individuals felt and learned, rather than passive questions about the skills of the instructor or coach. Passive questions reinforce the view that the individual is not responsible for his or her own learning, especially on a formal training course.

If you intend to use reaction questionnaires, it is important that you consider:

- In a formal course, building in time for completion of questionnaires at the end of the course

- If you have been directing the learning experience, do not collect questionnaires yourself; this may embarrass respondents and lead them to give the responses they believe you want to hear, rather than their true reactions
- Some of the best learning comes from situations in which people are not happy; unsettling and challenging experiences make deeper impressions. This means that people can benefit from learning without enjoying the learning experience, although they must be prepared in advance for a difficult learning experience. Otherwise, if a learning experience does not meet an individual's expectations (it is more challenging than they were prepared for), then the greater the likelihood of adverse reaction and failure to implement the lessons learned.

DESIGNING EVALUATION QUESTIONNAIRES

The design of a questionnaire is not an easy task. It requires that you carefully consider the question content, the wording of questions, the use of an appropriate type and the questionnaire layout.

Deciding on the Content of your Question

When you consider the topic of training evaluation, there are basically four distinct types of question content:

- Behaviour
- Beliefs
- Attitudes
- Attributes.

If you are interested in behaviour as a result of a training course, you should formulate questions to establish what learners do, or have done, as a result of participation on the training programme. This type of question will identify what behaviours have changed as a result of participation in the training.

If you are interested in what learners believe to be true or false, then you will need to ask a very different type of question. The focus of a belief question is on establishing what people think is true rather than on the accuracy of their belief. Belief questions can be distinguished from those that aim to establish the learner's attitude. Belief questions ascertain what the learner thinks is true, whereas attitude questions try to establish what learners think is desirable.

Attribute questions are designed to obtain information about he learner's characteristics – for example, information about the learner's age, job title, gender, education and training history, etc.

It is important that you are clear about the precise type of information you require. If you do not clearly distinguish between the four types of information, then you will lack of clarity on the questions you wish to ask, which will lead to the collection of the wrong type of information.

Wording your Questions

You should put considerable effort into developing clear, unambiguous and useful questions. This requires that you pay attention to their wording. **Figure 12.6** summarises a number of issues that you should consider.

Selecting the Question Type

This is a difficult task, as well as the most technical. Should you use an open or closed format of question? We will briefly evaluate each type and explain when you should use it.

An Open Question

An open question is one in which the respondent formulates his/her own answer. You should use an open question, if you wish to get the general feelings of the respondent. However, if you use a lot of open questions in an evaluation questionnaire, you will make the results of your questionnaire difficult to analyse, since answers to open questions are less easily to categorise. It is also likely that you will reduce the response rate if you require your respondents to do a lot of writing. Nonetheless, open questions are very useful in giving respondents an opportunity to suggest new ideas and to share different perspectives or to give honest insights on learning content and methods.

You should consider including at least one catch-all question in your questionnaire, usually at the end. It is important that you leave enough space so that the respondents can write a full response. It is not advisable to start your questionnaire with an open question.

Example: "What improvements, if any, would you make to the programme content? How relevant did you find the course content to your current work?"

Closed or Forced-Choice Question Format

A closed or forced-choice question is one in which a number of alternative answers are provided, from which respondents must select one or more. Closed or forced-choice questions are easier to code and analyse. In addition, they do not discriminate against the less articulate respondents.

FIGURE 12.6: CHECKLIST FOR WORDING QUESTIONS

Is the language simple?	You should avoid jargon and technical names
Can the question be shortened?	The shorter the question, the less confusing and ambiguous it is likely to be
Is the question double-barrelled?	Double-barrelled questions are those that ask more than one question
Is the question leading?	It is important to ensure that respondents can give any answer without feeling that they are giving a wrong answer or a disapproved-of answer. Do not use phrases such as "Do you agree that ..."
Is the question negative?	Questions that use "not" can be difficult to understand. This is especially the case when you are asking the respondent whether they agree or disagree
Is the learner likely to have the necessary knowledge?	When you pose questions in an evaluation exercise, it is important that the learner has the knowledge to provide the answer
Will the words have the same meaning for everyone?	You will need to be conscious of site-cultural differences. Some words may vary in meaning because of cultural or ethical factors
Is there a prestige bias in your organisation?	When an opinion is attached to a prestigious person and the respondent is then asked to express their own view on the same matter, this type of question can suffer from "prestige bias" in that the person who holds the view may influence the way respondents answer the questions
Is the question ambiguous?	Ambiguity can arise if the question is poorly structured or it uses words with several different meanings
Do you need a direct or indirect question?	If the question area is sensitive, it may be better to ask the question in a more indirect way
Is the frame of reference for the question sufficiently clear?	It is important that the time period is clearly stated
Does the question artificially create opinions?	On certain issues, your learners may have no opinion. You should always offer respondents a "Don't know" or "No opinion" option
Is personal or impersonal wording preferable?	If you use personal wording, you will ask respondents how "they" feel about an issue. You may also use the word "people", if you want a more impersonal style
Is the question wording unnecessarily detailed or objectionable?	Questions that ask precise details such as age or other personal details can create problems for respondents
Does the question have dangling alternatives?	If you use a question that has options such as frequently, sometimes, rarely or never, before you come to the subject matter of the question, then it is confusing for the respondent
Is the question likely to produce a response set?	Where you ask respondents to either agree or disagree with a statement, you run the danger that respondents will simply agree regardless of opinions or attitudes

A set of alternative responses can act as a useful prompt for respondents. However, if you do use a forced-choice or closed format, it is important that you put considerable thought into developing alternative responses.

You can use a closed question to see if the respondent has thought about or is aware of an issue, to get at the specific aspects of an issue or to find out how strongly an opinion is held. The following are the main types of closed or forced-choice formats:

- **Two-Way Closed Question:** This type of question asks the respondent to give a simple yes/no response. This is a good question format to use if you wish to confirm facts or get straightforward answers. They are easy for learners to complete and equally easy to analyse. You can use this type of question format at the start of a questionnaire to motivate the respondent to complete it.

  Example: Did you complete all components of the programme? Yes / No. Would you recommend the programme to your peers? Yes / No.

- **Ticklist Questions:** With this question type, you ask respondents to choose from a list of alternatives. It is useful, and recommended, to include a blank response into which respondents can write in an extra item, if the list does not offer their preferred option. Ticklist questions are often used as follow-up to yes/no questions.

  Example: In what way have you improved as a result of participation on the supervisory development programme? (Tick as many as apply)

My level of self confidence has improved	
I am better able to manage my direct reports	
I am comfortable interacting with customers	
I am confident managing upwards	
Other (please state)	

- **Checklists:** These questions consist of a list of items or words; respondents are asked to circle each relevant word or item. It is common to specify the number of items or words that should be ticked or circled.

  Example: Circle up to four of the words below that best sum up your overall opinion of the trainer:

  Interesting; Challenging; Expert; Participative; Articulate; Professional; Motivating; Flexible; Rigid

- **Semantic Differential Formats:** This format consists of choosing adjectives to represent the two extremes of a continuum and asking respondents to put a mark between the two extremes. This type of question may be used to elicit respondents' views concerning a process, concept, idea, experience or individual. This type of question requires a considerable amount of preparation. *Example:* Using the following set of words, how would you describe the trainer?

Warm	1	2	3	4	5	6	7	Cold
Professional	1	2	3	4	5	6	7	Unprofessional
Structured	1	2	3	4	5	6	7	Unstructured
Expert	1	2	3	4	5	6	7	Amateur
Directive	1	2	3	4	5	6	7	Participating
Dominant	1	2	3	4	5	6	7	Submissive
Open	1	2	3	4	5	6	7	Closed

- **Ranking Question:** You can give your respondents a list of alternative answers but, rather than selecting between them, you ask respondents to rank their importance. For example, you could give respondents a list of 10 qualities thought to be desirable in trainers. The respondents can then be asked to rank these qualities from most to least important by placing a 1 next to the most important, a 2 to the next most important, and so on. Avoid using very long lists; where they are unavoidable, ask the respondents to rank only the top five (you could also ask respondents to rank the two least important items)

- **Likert-Type Rating Scales:** This question format is useful if you wish to measure attitudes, opinions or preferences, or the quality of particular aspects of the training. You can use either a numeric or descriptive scale. The numeric scale may be any number range, although you need to consider whether a longer scale of rating will provide you with any more useful information than a shorter scale.

Example: Rate the effectiveness of the trainer on the following training skills, using the scale: 1 = very ineffective to 7 = very effective. Circle the answer that applies:

1. Delivery of complex information						
1	2	3	4	5	6	7

2. Interaction with the learners						
1	2	3	4	5	6	7

3. Skill to answer questions						
1	2	3	4	5	6	7

4. Skills to listen to learners						
1	2	3	4	5	6	7

You could get similar information using a descriptive scale, in which case, you would re-format the first question as follows:

1. The trainer skilled in delivering complex information						
Disagree Totally	Disagree Broadly	Disagree Slightly	Not Sure	Agree Slightly	Agree Broadly	Agree Totally

If you use a descriptive scale, then you must consider whether you want a mid-point on the scale. If you want to force a response, then you should not use a mid-point. Alternatively, you may take the view that "neutral" is a valid answer

- **Likert-Type Attitude Scales:** This type of question is most appropriate when you wish to find out about participants' attitudes towards learning. The scale used will usually have either five or seven points of agreement, although you may prefer to eliminate the neutral category (see above).

  Example: Please indicate your level of agreement with the following statements concerning the outcomes of the training programme you have completed

A. I intend to use this training to advance my career	Disagree Strongly	Disagree	Not Sure	Agree	Agree Strongly
B. I am confident that I will continue to work as a supervisor	Disagree Strongly	Disagree	Not Sure	Agree	Agree Strongly
C. I have made lots of changes in my behaviour since completing this programme	Disagree Strongly	Disagree	Not Sure	Agree	Agree Strongly
D. I believe strongly in continually developing my career	Disagree Strongly	Disagree	Not Sure	Agree	Agree Strongly
E. I will apply the learning to my job in the near future	Disagree Strongly	Disagree	Not Sure	Agree	Agree Strongly

- *Attitude Choices Rather Agree-Disagree Statements:* The agree-disagree format is one of the most widely used. It is problematic in that people often agree with the statements, regardless of their content. One way of avoiding this problem is to provide a number of alternative views and ask the respondent to select the view that is closest to his/her own. Alternatively, you could use a points distribution system. This involves respondents allocating 10 points amongst a number of statements.

  Example: Please select one of the following statements that expresses your attitude to learning:

Learning is the responsibility of the company	
Learning is my personal responsibility	
Learning is a shared responsibility when you are employed	
Learning is possible when the company provides resources for it	

Questionnaire Layout

There are a number of areas to which you should give attention to when laying out your questionnaire, including: instructions, use of space, order of questions and answering procedures.

Instructions

Most evaluation questionnaires are self-administered. Your instructions should:

- Be clear and concise, in a language understood by the respondents
- Tell the respondent the reason for the questionnaire
- Motivate the respondent to complete the questionnaire by explaining the benefits from the respondents' perspective
- Include an assurance that the data is confidential.

You will most likely include one or more of the following types of instruction:

- **General Instructions:** An introduction to the purpose of the questionnaire, an assurance of confidentiality, and how and when to return the questionnaire
- **Section Introductions:** If you divide your questionnaire into subsections, you should provide a brief introduction to each
- **Question Instructions:** Indicate how many responses the respondent can/should/must tick
- **"Go to" Instructions:** Ensure you make use of these when you use contingency questions
- **Use of Space:** You are more likely to motivate respondents to complete the questionnaire if you avoid cluttering it. Print questions on one side of the page only; if you must print on both sides, make sure you inform participants. Leave sufficient space for answers to open-ended questions and list alternative responses down rather than across the page.

Order of Questions

- A good questionnaire will have a logical flow to the questions
- Start your questionnaire with questions that are factual, then with questions that are easily answered
- Ensure that the initial questions are obviously relevant to the stated purpose of the evaluation
- Go from easy to more difficult questions
- Go from concrete to more abstract questions
- Open-ended questions should be kept to a minimum and, where possible, placed at the end of the questionnaire

- Group questions into sections – this helps your questionnaire structure and provides a flow
- Do not start with demographic questions – leave these to the end of the questionnaire
- If you use Likert-type scale questions, make sure to mix positive and negative items
- Introduce a variety of question formats, so that the questionnaire remains interesting.

Answering Procedures and Contingent Questions

- With open-ended questions, ensure that you leave sufficient space for answers to avoid respondents cramming responses
- With closed questions, ask respondents either to tick appropriate boxes or brackets or circle a number next to the response
- If you use a series of Likert-type questions, present them in a matrix format, as we did in the example given earlier
- Do not waste the time of your respondents reading questions that are not relevant to them – use "filter" or "contingency" questions, as well as arrows and insert boxes to highlight follow-up questions, to avoid confusion.

Figure 12.7 shows a reaction questionnaire, consisting mostly of open questions with one tick-list section.

Figure 12.8 provides a summary of the issues you should consider when designing a reaction evaluation form.

Reaction evaluation methods and instruments are relatively easy to develop. However, there are potential problems that you should be aware of:

- Reactions can be affected by things not directly related to the learning – for example, the standard of food and accommodation
- Reaction can shift over time – the end-of-course euphoria might not last after the trainee has returned to work.

Experienced learning specialists, therefore, learn to interpret reaction feedback information with care and will supplement them with other techniques, including further assessment at an appropriate time after the learning event.

FIGURE 12.7: AN EXAMPLE OF REACTION EVALUATION QUESTIONNAIRE

Title of Training/Development Programme: _____

Trainer(s) _____ Date: _____

Participant _____ Staff No. _____

Manager / Executive _____

We strive continually to improve the quality and usefulness of our training and development. Your comments and suggestions are crucial in this process. Therefore, we would appreciate if you would take the time to complete this form and return it to us. Your views will be used to help us improve the training/development programme for future participants.

Q.1 To what extent do you agree with the following statements in regard to this training?

	Strongly Agree	Agree	Neither Agree nor Disagree	Disagree	Strongly Disagree
It was a good use of my time					
The content was relevant to me					
The objectives were clearly stated					
The stated objectives of the training were fully achieved					
I was encouraged to actively participate in the training					
The training methods used were effective					

Q.2   Circle up to four of the words below which best sum up your overall opinion of this learning experience:

Interesting	challenging	exciting	revealing	fascinating	boring
confusing	difficult	basic	clear	entertaining	easy
realistic	practical	theoretical	irrelevant	useful	new
innovative	complicated inspiring	comprehensive	enjoyable	valuable	
over-ambiguous	thought-provoking	waste of time	stimulating	exhausting	
nothing new	Thorough	changed my life	rushed		

Add your own words:

Q.3 Overall rating of the training programme:

Ineffective				Very Effective
1	2	3	4	5

Q.4 Overall rating of the trainer:

Ineffective				Very Effective
1	2	3	4	5

FIGURE 12.8: DESIGN CRITERIA & STRUCTURE FOR REACTION QUESTIONNAIRE CONSTRUCTION

Design Issues	Meaning
Introductory and closing statements and directions	An **introductory statement** includes the general purpose of the reaction evaluation, an appeal for co-operation, the anonymity or confidentiality procedures, information about the evaluators and debriefings or other procedures for reporting the evaluation findings. A **closing statement** expresses appreciation for completing the reaction evaluation and provides instructions for completing and returning it. **Directions** and instructions specify how to answer various types of items.
Response Format	These are the types of answers required for the questions. There are open- and closed-ended questions. The nature of the information being sought, and practical limitations, will influence how many and what types of response formats are used.
Question Construction	General guidelines for writing questions that avoid errors in grammar, syntax, structure, etc., are important. There are established dos and don'ts for writing good questions. *Do:* <ul><li>Use simple, clear and short words</li><li>Use specific precise words</li><li>Use appropriate language</li><li>Ask one idea per item</li></ul> Don't: <ul><li>Use sensitive wording</li><li>Use ambiguous wording</li><li>Use strange or exotic terms</li><li>Use a double-negative in wording an item</li><li>Use double-barrelled items</li><li>Use overlapping or unbalanced response categories</li><li>Ask about issues outside the respondent's experience</li><li>Ask bias or loaded questions</li><li>Use false premises or future intentions</li></ul>
Layout	Layout guidelines relate to the appearance and arrangement of written material, to make reactions clear in meaning, appear neat and easy to follow. A professional appearance with quality graphics, spaces between questions, easy-to-follow layout and accuracy in grammar usage, spelling, etc, makes it easier to use the instrument and gives it credibility.
Data analysis	The type of data analysis to be used is decided when an evaluation study is planned. Guidelines for analysing data should follow standard procedures for calculating, interpreting and reporting descriptive and inferential statistics.
Content/ Structure	Purposes and Sample Questions
Programme objective(s) / content	To evaluate the objectives of a programme against participants' expectations. Appropriateness, structure, level and up-datedness of the content presented in the programme. <ul><li>Did programme content meet the stated objectives?</li><li>Were topics and learning activities effectively sequenced?</li></ul>

Design Issues	Meaning
Programme materials	To ascertain the effectiveness's efficiency and usefulness of written and other materials used in the programme. • Were the materials consistent with the programme objectives? • Was the course material helpful in understanding the subject?
Delivery methods / technologies	To judge the appropriateness and effectiveness of instructional delivery methods including media technologies. • Were the instructional methods effective for learning the content? • Was the multimedia a useful way to present the material?
Instructor / Facilitator	To relate the presentation skills, leadership and overall effectiveness of the instructor or facilitator. • Was the instructor well prepared for class? • Was the instructor's presentation easy to follow?
Instructional activities	To evaluate the appropriateness and usefulness of in- and out-of-class activities. • Were the instructional activates helpful in learning the course content? • Were the instructional activities well organised?
Programme time / length	To assess the time length of sessions and an entire programme. • Was the allowed time enough for the programme content? • Was the time length of the course enough to learn the programme objectives?
Training Environment	To evaluate the adequacy of the physical training environment, including the classroom, dining facilities, lodging and leisure facilities. • Were the training facilities favourable for learning? • Was the audiovisual equipment available when needed?
Planned Action / Expectation	To evaluate the participants' plans and expectations for applying what was learned upon returning to the job and to identify barriers to applying what was learned on the job. • Was the course content applicable to your present job? • Are there on-the-job barriers that will keep you from applying what you learned when you return to work?
Logistics / Administration	To evaluate the smoothness and effectiveness of scheduling, registration and other logistical and administrative matters associated with the programme. • Was the programme scheduled at a convenient time? • Was it easy to enrol for the course?
Overall Evaluation	To determine overall participant satisfaction with the feeling about the programme. • How would you react this course in comparison to others you have taken? • What was the most valuable thing you learned in the course?
Recommendations for Programme Improvement	To solicit suggestions and recommendations for improving this or similar programmes in the future. • How would you improve the course? • Would you recommend this course to your colleagues? Why or why not?

Adapted from Heum Lee and Pershing (2002).

LEARNING EVALUATION

Learning evaluation can be conducted at two levels:

- Objective evaluation of the level of learning achieved
- Evaluation of the design of the learning programme in terms of whether it achieved the learning objectives set.

We focused earlier in this chapter on the objective measurement of learning. We discussed knowledge and skill tests, which can be designed for pre-course evaluation and post-course testing. In addition to testing knowledge and skills, it can be useful for the trainer to administer a *learning questionnaire*, which focuses on the learning achieved by participants (this can identify unintended learning) and rates the effectiveness of the programme in terms of learning.

There is much debate on when this type of evaluation should take place. Should you insist that learners fill in the learning questionnaires immediately after the event or allow for completion after the learners have returned to work? Our own experience would indicate that it is best for learners to complete questionnaires as soon as possible after the learning.

The methods available for pre- and post-testing of learning are:

- Participant self assessment
- Written tests
- Practical tests.

Evaluation of learning:

- Validates the effectiveness of the learning methods
- Compares the effectiveness of learning methods
- Shows that the acquisition of the new skill or knowledge is directly linked to the learning experience
- Shows changes in attitudes and perspectives, through pre-then-post testing, which could be useful in assessing learning activities aimed at bringing about attitudinal changes

The disadvantages include:

- No evidence that the learning is relevant to, or will be applied on, the job
- Effort must be spent in developing tests and measures that do not assess business benefits
- "Exam nerves" – people can perform well in tests and simulations, but not in reality, and *vice versa*
- Individuals concentrate on "passing the test", rather than absorbing and applying learning.

If you do decide to evaluate the learning, consider these issues:

- Written tests can be either multiple-choice style, or essay type. Multiple-choice questions are easier to score

- Practical tests can be marked either after the tests (as in a typing test) or by observing individual's performance (as in many NVQ assessments)

- If you are using tests that allow more open-ended or a wider range of responses, you will need to prepare a marking grid. You will need to decide what points you are looking for and how many marks will be allocated to each

- A useful refinement on pre- and post- testing is "pre-then-post" testing. What often happens before a learning event is that participants rate themselves as performing acceptably in an area of work. The learning experience then shows that there was much in the subject that they were not aware of, and that they were therefore not as competent as they had precisely believed ("we don't know what we don't know"). Thus someone could rate themselves as an adequate performer before a learning experience and again as adequate after learning. This would appear to show that the activity had no impact, which would not be true. In pre-then-post assessment, individuals are therefore asked to return to their pre-learning assessment and review it in the light of their new knowledge, and therefore show the true change in knowledge or skill (this process is often called to as the response-shift bias).

Tips

- In some circumstances, there will be no need for – or possibility of – pre-testing; for instance, if someone is learning a new language

- The marking system should be as clear and simple as possible. This will reduce the amount of time spent marking and also help standardise marks, if more than one person is scoring

- Whenever possible, the same person should mark an individual's pre- and post-tests

- A thorough testing process should include checking the validity of the tests as a whole and of individual questions. A number of texts cover this subject in some detail.

Designing Questionnaires for Skill assessment

Questionnaires for use in analysing current skills levels, assessing post-learning levels and $360°$ / $180°$ / $540°$ feedback, all follow the same basic principles and methodology.

The process involves:

- Identifying the skills/behaviours or competencies you wish to assess

- Drawing up descriptions of how someone who has those skills will apply them at work (performance criteria)
- Asking people to rate themselves, or others, on the extent to which they display the performance criteria.

You can also ask people to rate how important the application of each skill is in doing a particular job. It is not essential to include this rating but it could be very helpful in making the case for investment in learning – for instance, you would be able to show that the learning activity had most impact on the skills that were most important to effective performance in the job.

If your organisation has a competence framework for the relevant skills, then you can use the performance criteria from that framework as the basis for your questionnaire. If there is no competence framework specific to your organisation, then you may be able to adapt a generic set of competencies produced by, for instance, an industry standards lead body, such as NVQs or MCI.

PERFORMANCE EVALUATION
(INCLUDING LEARNING TRANSFER)

The performance evaluation level, or Level 3 evaluation, is concerned with measuring this dimension of training outcomes: Has the learner's performance in the job actually improved as a result of the training programme?

This is a relatively simple task for operator training, but a much more complicated process for management and supervisory training. We will explore a number of options that you may find useful to achieve this evaluation phase.

Post-Course Interviews

One of the quickest and most cost-effective ways to evaluate the training is for the manager (or trainer) to conduct a debriefing discussion with the learner. A discussion with the manager will help create the right environment for training to be put into practice and help the transfer of learning to the workplace. Having already established interest by conducting a pre-course discussion, this post-course discussion can reinforce the message that the manager and organisation are not merely paying lip-service by treating training as an isolated event.

The interview should focus on how the learner intends to apply the learning in the work situation and should provide the trainee with an opportunity to reflect on the programme now that it is completed. **Figure 12.9** presents a summary of the main questions that should be addressed.

FIGURE 12.9: QUESTIONS TO BE INCLUDED IN THE POST-COURSE EVALUATION INTERVIEW

Intention to Apply the Learning:
- Have their training needs been met?
- Did the course give them a new insight into their role?
- What skills and knowledge have they gained from the course?
- How is this new knowledge relevant to their job?
- How do they intend to apply their learning at work?
- Have they drawn up an action plan on the course?
- What help do they need from their manager or anyone else, to put this plan into action?
- Which areas do they need further information or coaching?
- Any follow-up programmes needed in the future?

Reflections on the Programme of Training:
- What did they think about the course overall?
- Did it live up to the promises in the brochures?
- Were the trainers knowledgeable and competent at delivering the material?
- Was the course pitched at the right level for them?
- What use was made of any pre-course material?
- Had they done enough preparation for the course? Could their manager have helped more?
- Were there any weaknesses in the course? How could these be overcome?
- How appropriate were the training methods used?
- Was there enough variety to suit different styles?
- What efforts were made to relate the topics to their own working environment?
- Would they recommend this course for other members of staff? If, so who would benefit?
- Do they consider the event value for money?
- Are there any follow-up activities planned by the trainers?

The Six Months Evaluation Interview

It is recommended that a further interview should be conducted about six months after the trainee has returned to the workplace. This interview process should have four main purposes:

- To appraise the identified training needs. Were these accurate in their assessment of what was required to improve the individual's performance?

- To explore how successful the jobholder has been in transferring what they learned to the work place

- To review the effectiveness of a particular training event and the methods used. Time passing should help the participant to make a more objective assessment

- To determine whether the training has had any impact on overall organisational goals.

Using Questionnaires to Evaluate Job Performance

This is another method you can use. It is defined as a process asking the same questions as in the interviews, but in a written questionnaire format. It has a number of advantages:

- Allows for the involvement of a larger number of people in the evaluation process
- Less time-consuming than interviews for the evaluator, participants and their managers
- Useful if participants are geographically spread over a range of sites, or travel a lot
- Direct feedback from the workplace
- Reminds participants and line managers about the need to relate learning activity to the workplace
- Immediate demonstration to the line of the value placed on learning activity, and concern to meet learning needs in the most cost-effective way.

The main disadvantages are as follows:

- Possibility of low response rate
- Limited opportunity for open questions; more leads and prompts will be required
- Less qualitative information
- Less opportunity for people to offer direct suggestions for improving learning activity.

Here are some guidelines for using questionnaires to evaluate job performance:

- Shorter questionnaires get better response rates; try to keep your questionnaire to two or three sides of A4
- A good in-house response rate is about 50%
- Allow respondents about three weeks to complete the questionnaire; any longer and it tends to be put on one side, any less and you miss the chance to get responses from people on holiday or off sick
- Only allow one or two open questions, as these are more difficult to analyse.

If you are sending out a large number of questionnaires, consider using a software package to analyse the results. There are a lot of companies that can provide an analysis service for you, including inputting the data.

If you are going to use a processing firm, it is useful to discuss the questionnaire design with them first, to make analysis of the results as easy as possible. For instance, it will help the data inputting, if the answers to questions have code numbers:

In what way has the individual's use of the telephone improved? (tick as many as apply)

Phone answered within five rings	☐ 1
Greeting and clear announcement of department and name	☐ 2
Clear messages taken	☐ 3
Calls not lost in transfer	☐ 4
Other (please write in)_____	☐ 5

Example of a Questionnaire Aimed at Evaluating Impact on Individual Performance

The questionnaire in **Figure 12.10** was used in the same project as the structured interviewing examples.

FIGURE 12.10: REVIEW OF OBJECTIVE SETTING IN TRAINING

Participants:
This questionnaire is for completion by everyone who has agreed a set of objectives and is working towards achieving them during the pilot study.

How to complete this questionnaire
For most questions, you should circle a number. On some questions, there are spaces for you to write in more detailed answers.

Please complete and return this questionnaire by DD MM YY

1. Are you a member of:
   Administration Group   1
   Engineering and Science Group   2
   Other (write in_____)3

2. What is your grade? (if you are not sure what your grade is write in your job title at 'Other' below)
   A   1
   B   2
   C   3
   D   4
   E   5
   Other (write in_____)   6

---

3. How straightforward has objective setting been in practice?
   Very straightforward   -   Very complicated
      1   2   3   4   5

4. How useful have you found the written guidance?
      Very useful   -   No use at all
      1   2   3   4   5

5. In practice, how helpful was the training/briefing you received?
      Very useful   -   No use at all
       1   2   3   4   5

6. Using the scale where 1 = agree and 5 – disagree, to what extent do you agree or disagree with these statements about objective setting?

	Agree			Disagree	
	1	2	3	4	5
It gives me a clear picture of what I need to achieve in the year ahead					
It helps clarify the standards of performance expected of me in terms of:					
Quality of work					
Quantity of work to be done					
Deadlines to be met					
Keeping within budget					

	Agree			Disagree	
	1	2	3	4	5
It helps me to understand how my job fits into the business of my section of the organisation					
It increases my feeling of personal responsibility for the work I do					
My objectives are not specific enough to give me a real sense of direction					
I do a lot of work that is not covered by my objectives					
My objectives take account of the relative priorities of the different parts of my job					
Agreeing personal development objectives has helped me make decisions about my training and development					
Referring to my objectives helps me plan and prioritise my work					
I am able to make my own assessment of my progress towards achieving my objectives					
I have a clearer understanding of the quality of the work I am expected to deliver					
Setting objectives has helped me improve my performance in my job					

7. If you have any comments on objective-setting, including the method of setting objectives, the type and length of training, and how you think it can work in practice in our organisation, please write them below:

Other Performance Evaluation Methods

There are other methods available to help evaluate changes in job behaviour but they are all variants on two themes: watching and asking, or observing and questionnaire/interview. Wherever possible, the two types of technique should be employed together.

Thus, techniques available at this level are:

- **Activity sampling:** This is a work-study technique in which the evaluator records the trainee's behaviour at random intervals in time. Apart from the problem that the method may not be acceptable to some employees, it is also expensive in time/effort
- **Performance records:** For example, sales records may show a sharp increase in sales after a course
- **Diaries:** If these are used before and after a learning event or programme, they can be a very useful starting point for discussions between the trainee and evaluator about the nature of the job and the effect on the learning. There are two types of diary: observer and self-diaries. Self-diaries are cheaper to maintain than observer diaries but the trainees may lack the time, skill and motivation to complete them satisfactorily. Ideally, the two types of diary should be kept together
- **Appraisal:** Before and after discussions between an individual and his/her supervisor about learning needs and the value of the learning programme are another useful technique. Self-appraisal is also important, since the trainee is in the best position to appraise his/her own behaviour.

TRANSFER OF TRAINING TO THE WORKPLACE

An important issue is whether trainees are able to put into practice what they have learned in training. Positive transfer will have taken place if they are able to make the transition from being in a training environment to performing the job in reality. There are two forms of positive transfer:

- **Specific or Pure Transfer:** This is when the skill or task learned in training is performed in precisely the same way in the work environment – for example, operating a circuit printing machine
- **Generalisable Transfer:** This is when the trainee learns to perform skills and tasks in training in ways that are similar, but not identical, to the ways in which they are performed in the work environment – for example, conducting an appraisal interview.

Generalisable transfer is particularly important in training in interpretational skills, for example.

The following factors should be considered in the planning and preparation stages to assist in making learning transfer effective:

- The training environment should be as realistic as possible. This is particularly pertinent to role-playing but, even with "live" enactment, it is important to ensure that the situations that the trainee is exposed to are not "too easy", otherwise the level of transfer will be low

- Ample opportunity should be given to practice and rehearse the key interpersonal skills, to the point where reactions and responses come naturally or with ease

- A variety of contexts in which to learn and practice the key interpersonal skills should be used. In role-playing, this helps the trainee to apply more easily what has been learned in training to the less predictable aspects of the real job

- Sessions in which the trainee is "drilled" in interpersonal skills are best avoided, as rote learning tends to discourage transfer

- Show the value of the interpersonal skills that are learned in training to the problems or issues that occur in the work-setting. A trainee's motivation to succeed in training is strongly influenced by his/her perception of its value. This in turn has a strong effect on transfer.

Tactics to Use during the Learning to Facilitate Transfer

In order to maximise transfer of learning, trainers must give emphasis to practising the skills that are the focus of the programme. This applies specifically to skills training.

Trainers can teach trainees a number of things in order to facilitate transfer of skill:

- How much practice is necessary?
- What criteria to apply to judge their performance?
- What constitutes a practice?
- When to stop practicing? And how to know?
- How to maintain motivation and curbed anxiety throughout practice?
- How to allow the trainee to take risks and to explore possibilities?
- How to practice in a safe environment?

Figure 12.11 presents a set of actions that you can implement to ensure effective learning transfer.

FIGURE 12.11: WHAT A TRAINER MIGHT SAY TO PREPARE TRAINEES FOR PRACTICE

Introduction

- In this lesson, you will practice what you will need to use in real situations ... to carry out such responsibilities as ....
- Because you must learn to perform in real situations, we will have you practice behaviours required in real situations.
- In addition, you will learn how to set up, carry out, and continue practicing once you are on the job.
- I want you to be motivated to practice and to possess the knowledge you need to be efficient in your practice.
- Practice does not only mean performing skills; practice also means acting to see if you have accomplished what you wish. So you may practice using facts, concepts, principles, interpersonal skills, and mental processes. For example, in this lesson you will practice performing....
- **You can think of the 'final' test as the last formal supervised practice. In that final practice you will be asked to ... .**

Explanation and Demonstration

- Here is the information you will need to practice.
- This example illustrates conditions (behaviours, criteria) similar to those you will confront in practice ...
- This demonstration shows the way you should practice. You will practice performing after the demonstration.
- When I demonstrate performance, and when you practice performance, observe the given steps and criteria.
- I will proceed with the demonstration first by noting what I will do and then by doing it. Consider adopting that pattern in your early practice.
- Commit the steps and criteria to memory to use as a template for checking your own practice.

What a Trainer Might Say to Emphasise Practice Before and After Practice Before Practice

- I will coach you closely in early practice, then when you can, you should arrange for similar practices for yourself, first under simulated and then under field conditions.
- In this practice, you should be checking for specific qualities and consequences.
- Here is how to practice ... here is how to check using the criteria ... Here I should stop you (or you should stop yourself) because you have accomplished the goal of the practice .... Otherwise, continue practice ... Observe this ... This is good practice because ....
- You may have to repeat practice traits many times because ... (lots of criteria, lots of steps, need for automaticity).
- There are some small parts of the big task you need to master. Whenever possible, I will arrange conditions so that you will practice these enabling tasks as they are done under real circumstances.
- Here are the payoffs for practicing performance ... (related to course and trainee's objectives and to automaticity). Here are ways to keep up your own

motivation during practice ... (say these things to yourself, take risks, explore possibilities, and create safe simulations in which errors are OK).

- Remember that you are trying to learn to perform tasks so that you can do them automatically. That means that, as you perform, you must look for the most important cues to attend to so that you can respond selectively and quickly. Here are the cues that I use ....

After Practice
- First, check your own practice according to the stated criteria.
- My turn to give feedback. These aspects were fine, good going. Continue to do the same in future performances.
- These aspects don't match the criteria. Here is what should have been done before and during the next practice.
- The final exam is the last and most realistic supervised practice. Think of the exam as your last chance for supervised practice before you have an on-the-job test.
- You will have to keep practicing on the job in the same way.

Created from Kozlowski and Salas (1997) and Mackin (2002).

ORGANISATIONAL ISSUES IN LEARNING TRANSFER

In **Chapter Five**, we outlined a number of learning design issues that were relevant in explaining and facilitating learning transfer. Some of these will be beyond your direct control; nonetheless, it is important that you are aware of them, so we consider them again here in more depth.

Supervisory Support

Supervisory support is very important because, where supervisors provide support for trainees who demonstrate the appropriate behaviour, then it is likely that transfer will take place. This supervisory support may take three forms:

- Support from supervisors for development
- Provision of information concerning the benefits of development
- Alleviation of adverse working conditions that can result from attending training.

Peer Support

If a trainee is the only member from a department who is receiving training, there may be no peers back on the job to support the learner. It is useful for trainees to train with their peers, as peers can provide support to use the training, or can be considered potential coaches.

Trainer Support

You have a major role to play in facilitating learning transfer. Trainers who commit to meet the trainees to discuss learning transfer, and the effective use of the training, facilitate learning transfer. You can be a useful resource in helping trainees work through problems encountered in the workplace.

Figure 12.12 provides a summary of organisational strategies to facilitate learning transfer.

FIGURE 12.12: ORGANISATIONAL STRATEGIES TO SUPPORT LEARNING TRANSFER

	Pre-Training	Within-Training	Post-Training
Goals	• Improve trainees' motivation • Improve trainees' pre-training self-efficacy or knowledge • Show organisational support for training	• Improve trainees' understanding and adaptive expertise • Improve trainees' intentions to transfer • Improve trainees' reactions to training	• Improve the climate for the transfer of training • Improve the vertical transfer of training
Strategies	• Use goal-setting • Allow trainees to participate in decision-making • Provide information on the purpose and intended outcomes of training • Reduce any perceived threat to the trainee • Help the trainee develop better learning strategies • Develop a plan for using the training • Identify external factors that may restrict the trainees' ability to use their training • Assist trainees in identifying organisationally valuable outcomes from training	• Use procedures in training similar to workplace • Use familiar real-life problems • Provide different examples during training; highlight important features • Help trainees develop detailed, well-integrated knowledge structures and self-regulatory skills such as planning, monitoring and evaluation • Set short-term goals for the immediate transfer of training • Set longer-term goals that focus on mastery of the training • Help trainees develop and commit to specific implementation plans • Use relapse prevention to identify where trainees may fail to use training • Create a positive training climate	• Provide trainees with specific goals for improved performance from transfer of training • Ensure supervisors and co-workers are supportive of transfer of training • Ensure trainees have access to resources needed for transfer of training • Positively reinforce better performance • Reduce barriers such as lack of time or opportunity to perform the tasks learned during training • Train all members of a work unit at the same time • Monitor post-training performance • Align training with organisational goals and directions

Source: Mackin (2002).

GUIDELINES FOR EFFECTIVE EVALUATION

Throughout this chapter, we have presented a pragmatic approach to evaluating your training events. It is essential for you as a trainer to try out different approaches to evaluation. At a minimum, we recommend that you measure what learning has occurred.

As an effective trainer, you will no doubt engage in some form of assessment during a learning event. It is your choice whether to adopt a formal or informal approach here. You will also find it useful to obtain reactions at the end of an event. This will help you to decide on the future of this event.

You really begin to add value in your role when you not only measure what learning has happened, but how effective the learning process was. Once you are comfortable with the basics of evaluation, we would encourage you to consider Performance Evaluation. Finally, for training of strategic importance, we recommend that you engage in impact evaluation.

FIGURE 12.13: EVALUATING T&D ACTIVITIES: IMPORTANT QUESTIONS FOR TRAINERS

- What does the word "evaluation" mean to you in the context of a learning event?
- Who do you believe should decide the worth of the events you conduct? Is evaluation, however you define it, your responsibility? Is it the responsibility of individual participants? Is it a joint responsibility? Or someone else's responsibility?
- Apart from the trainer, who contributes to the psychological contract associated with a particular event? Merely the participants? Or others as well? Who, specifically, are the stakeholders? Should all stakeholders be involved in any evaluation? If not, can you justify your stance? On what grounds?
- What should be evaluated in the events that the trainer conducts? All the main elements? Or just some? Or something else? How can you justify this stance? Do you view learning events as part of a continuing process? Or merely as a product? Or does your perspective combine both process and product? Is any distinction drawn between the educational element(s) in the events you conduct?
- How should any evaluation be achieved? Using what particular approach (or approaches) to evaluation?
- When should the evaluation take place? Should the principle be established before the event? Established and conducted afterwards? Within what time frame? Does your answer make sense? To you? To others?
- What do your answers suggest about the way you approach evaluation? How did you come to hold such views? To what extent do your views on this aspect of learning reflect your own personal values and beliefs? How far should they?
- To what extent could your biases and prejudices be actively discouraging, rather than encouraging, learning in others?

- What is your focus of interest in evaluating the learning events in which you are involved? At what level of generality does evaluation take place? Is it genuinely more thoughtful than the "happiness rating" completed at the conclusion of some learning events?

- To what extent are you familiar with the various approaches to evaluation? What evaluation "labels" would you associate with the following questions?
  - What is the worth of this learning event? Should you be concerned with it?
  - Are "end-states" important? Or is the process of discovery and self-discovery, more important? Who should decide?
  - How should the learning methods used during the event be questioned? Should they be questioned? By Whom?
  - In what ways could the questions raised in any evaluation of this event be explored? Who should explore them?
  - How should the different perceptions and needs of those involved be met?
  - Could an evaluator as a team member in this event be used?
  - Does feedback need to be cheap and fast? Is the need realistic? From whose point of view?
  - How much has the event cost? How much would the preferred approach to evaluating the event cost?
  - Could a value-free position be adopted during any evaluation of the unintended results of the event?

- Is the identification of the appropriate label important? If so, why? If identification is not important, again, why?

- What do the answers to these questions suggest about your present involvement in, and commitment to, the process of evaluation? Do you feel that you know enough? Do you practice it? What more could you do?

- What action should you take now to develop your contribution to the learning events in which you are involved?

- What, if anything, do you propose to do? Over what time-scale? How will you evaluate your own progress?

BEST PRACTICE INDICATORS

Some of the best practice issues that you should consider related to the contents of this chapter are:

- There are regular and timely reviews of T&D outcomes at organisational and unit level
- T&D stakeholders work together pragmatically to monitor and review planned learning experiences and events.
- It is standard practice that, before taking part in a developmental activity, learners and their managers discuss the purpose and intended outcomes of the activity; and that, after the activity, there is agreement on outcomes achieved and how best to use the learning
- Performance-related learning targets – qualitative, as well as quantitative – together with performance indicators, strategic milestones and surveys, are used to review the implementation of plans and to evaluate learning events
- A variety of simple, low-cost and effective methods of evaluation are used, and there are regular checks to ensure best practice and innovation
- Review of T&D plans, and evaluation of learning outcomes, are oriented to ensure a focus on their continuous improvement
- Results of evaluation of planned learning experiences critical to the success of T&D plans are fed into the ongoing T&D planning process at organisational and unit level, and also into wider HR policy-making and planning
- Be clear about the expected uses of evaluation data. Where you conduct evaluation to certify employees, it is likely to be more rigorous than where your purpose is to measure performance outcomes
- Recognise that, as you move from reactions to organisational outcomes, you will have to make more assumptions in order to derive the data you require. It is also likely that the results of the evaluation are more likely to be questioned by organisational decision-makers when you attempt higher levels of evaluation.

Reflections on Training & Development Scenario

Interview with Managers

- How long did it take you to agree objectives for your staff? If more than one member of your staff was involved in the project, did the time taken vary? If so, why – for example, type of job/individual's ability?
- How were the objectives drafted – for example, you did first draft /your staff did the first draft / you drafted them on a team basis?
- Did you refer to any unit/branch objectives when you were agreeing your staff's objectives?
- Do your staff's objectives cover routine as well as one-off duties?
- Was it easy for you and your staff to agree on their objectives? If not, what did you disagree about? How did you resolve the disagreement?
- Have you reviewed your staff's objectives at any time? If so, when and why? Did you make any changes? If so, why?
- Have there been any important changes in the workplace/working practices during the period of the pilot – for example, changes in personnel / role / responsibilities?
- With the benefit of practice and hindsight, how helpful was the training / briefing?
- How useful was the written guidance – for example, length, examples, relevance? What did you find most/least helpful?
- Has the objective-setting made you think/ think differently about your job purpose / what you are there for? Do you think it has made your staff think differently about their jobs?
- Did you know any more about your team / section / branch objectives after agreeing individual's objectives? Do you think your staff are now more aware of the section / unit's objectives and priorities?
- Do you think your staff now have a clearer understanding of their own job responsibilities and their role in contributing to the achievement of the team's success?
- Do you and your staff discuss their objectives outside appraisal sessions? If so, do you discuss them when you are: a) planning and organising work? b) prioritising work?
- what type of effect?
- Have you given your staff feedback on their progress towards achievement of their objectives? How often, and in what circumstances?
- Have you observed any change in staff motivation as a result of a desire to achieve objectives – for example, looking for improved ways of working / willingness to complete routine tasks / deadlines met?
- Do you think your staff have a clearer understanding of the standard and quality of work they are expected to deliver?
- Has objective-setting had any influence on the service you and your staff provide to customers?

- Have your staff set personal development objectives? What progress have they made towards achieving them?
- Do you think that your staff's performance in the job has improved during the period of the pilot study? If so, do you think any of this improvement can be attributed to working towards the achievement of objectives?

Interview with Individuals

- How long did it take you to draft your objectives?
- How were the objectives drafted – for example, you did first draft / your line manager did the first draft / you drafted them on a team basis?
- Did you refer to any unit / branch objectives when you were agreeing your own objectives?
- Do your objectives cover routine as well as one-off duties?
- Do your objectives include a personal development objective?
- Was it easy for you and your line manager to agree on your objectives? If not, what did you disagree about? How did you resolve the disagreement?
- Have you reviewed your objectives at any time? If so, when and why? Did you make any changes? If so, why?
- Did you find the objective-setting process easy to follow – for example, clarity, logical structure?
- How useful was the written guidance – for example, length, examples, relevance? What did you find most / least helpful?
- With the benefit of practice and hindsight, how helpful was the training / briefing?
- Has objective setting made you think / think differently about your job purpose / what you are there for?
- Do you have a clearer understanding of your own job responsibility and your contribution not the achievement of the team's success?
- Do you refer to your objectives when organising / prioritising your work?
- Do you and your manager discuss your objectives outside appraisal sessions? If so, do you discuss them when you are: a) planning and organising work? b) prioritising work?
- Does your manager give you any feedback on your progress towards achievement of your objectives? How often, and in what circumstances?
- Has working towards achieving objectives had any effect on your working relationship with colleagues and / or other sections? If so,

BIBLIOGRAPHY

Beard, C. and Wilson, J. (2002): *The Power of Experiential Learning*, London: Kogan Page.

Berne, E. (1964): *Games People Play*, London: Penguin Books.

Bloom, B.S. (1976): *Human Characteristics and School Learning*, New York: McGraw-Hill.

Boydell, T.H. (1997): *Understanding The Process of Learning*, Paper presented at the International Society of Training and Development Conference, Dublin: Trinity College.

Bramley, P. (1991): *Evaluation of Training*, Maidenhead: McGraw-Hill.

Carlopio, J., Andrewartha, G. and Armstrong, H. (1997): *Developing Management Skills*, Sydney: Longman.

CIPD (2001): *Making Training & Development Pay*, London: CIPD.

Delahaye, B.L. (2000): *Human Resource Development*, Sydney: John Wiley and Sons.

Evenden, R. and Anderson, G. (1992): *Management Skills: Making the Most of People*, Wokingham: Addison-Wesley Publishing Company.

Ford, J.K., Kozlowski, S.W.J., Kraiger, K., Salas, E. and Teachout, M.S. (1997): *Improving Training Effectiveness in Work Organisations*, New Jersey: Lawrence Erlbaum Associates.

Gagné, R.M. and Medsker, K.L. (1996): *The Conditions of Learning: Training Applications*, New York: Harcourt Brace College Publishers.

Garavan, T.N., Morley, M. and Flynn, M. (1997): 360° Feedback: Its Role in Management Development, *Journal of Management Development*, 16 (3) 56-71.

Gardner, H. (1999): *Multiple Intelligences for the 21st Century*, New York: Basic Books.

Gibb, S. (2002): *Learning and Development: Processes, Practices and Perspectives at Work*, Basingstoke: Palgrave Macmillian.

Gilley, J.W., Eggland, S.A. and Maycunich Gilly, A. (2002): *Principles of Human Resource Development*, New York: Perseus Publishing.

Gunnigle, P. (Ed.) (1999): *The Irish Employee Recruitment Handbook*, Dublin: Oak Tree Press.

Hamblin, A. C. (1974): *Evaluation and Control of Training*, Maidenhead: McGraw-Hill.

Hardingham, A. (1998): *Psychology for Trainers*, London: CIPD.

Harris, T. (1995): *I'm OK, You're OK*, London: Arrow Books.

Heum Lee, S. and Pershing, J. A. (2002): Dimensions and Design Criteria for Developing Training Reaction Evaluations, *Human Resource Development International*, 5, 2, 175-199.

Honey, P. and Mumford, A. (1995): *Using Your Learning Styles*, Maidenhead: Honey Publications.

Kingsland, K. (1986): *The Personality Spectrum*, London: Self-published.

Kirkpatrick D.L. (1976): Evaluation of Training, in R.L. Craig (Ed.): *Training and Development Handbook: A Guide to Human Resource Development*, New York: McGraw Hill, 2nd edition.

Knowles, M.S., Holton, E.F. and Swanson, R.A. (1998): *The Adult Learner*, Woburn, MA: Butterworth-Heinemann, 5th edition.

Kolb, D.A. (1974): *Organisational Psychology: An Experiential Approach*, Englewood Cliffs, NJ: Prentice Hall.

Kozlowski, S.W.J. and Salas, E. (1997) An Organisational Systems Approach for the Implementation and Transfer of Training, in Ford, J.K., Kozlowski, S.W.J., Kraiger, K., Salas, E. and Teachout, M.S.: *Improving Training Effectiveness in Work Organisations*, New Jersey: Lawrence Erlbaum Associates.

Kraiger, K. (Ed.) (2001): *Creating, Implementing and Managing Effective Training and Development: State of the Art Lessons for Practice*, San Francisco: Jossey-Bass.

Leatherman, R. (1990): *The Training Function: Designing Programmes*, Amherst, MA: Human Resource Development Press Inc.

Lynton, R.D. and Pareck, U. (2000): *Training for Organisational Transformation Part 2*, London: Sage Publications.

Mackin, M.A. (2002): Planning Managing and Optimising Transfer of Training, in Kraiger, K. (Ed.) *Creating, Implementing and Managing Effective Training and Development: State of the Art Lessons for Practice*, San Francisco: Jossey-Bass.

Mager, R.F. and Pipe, P. (1999): *Analysing Problems or You Really Oughta Wanna*, Belmont, CA: David S. Lake Publishers.

Mayo, A. (1998): *Creating a Training & Development Strategy*, London: CIPD.

Megginson, D., Joy-Matthews, J. & Barefield, P. (1993): *Human Resource Development*, London: Kogan Page.

Moorby, B. (1991): *How to Succeed in Employee Development*, London, McGraw-Hill.

Nathan, R. and Hill, L. (1992): *Career Counselling*, London: Sage.

O'Connor, K. (1999): Coaching and Mentoring: Aids to the Development of Performance, in Gunnigle, P. (Ed): *Irish Employee Recruitment Handbook*, Dublin: Oak Tree Press.

Pattinson, B. (1999): Performance Appraisal, in Gunnigle, P. (Ed.): *Irish Employee Recruitment Handbook,* Dublin: Oak Tree Press.

Phillips, J.J. (1997): *Handbook of Training Evaluation and Measurement Methods*, London: Kogan Page.

Rea, L. (1996): *Using Activities in Training & Development*, London: Kogan Page.

Rothwell, W.J. (1996): *Beyond Training and Development: State of the Art Strategies for Enhancing Human Performance*, New York: American Management Association.

Schultz, W. (1958): *FIRO: A Three Dimensional Theory of Interpersonal Behaviour*, London: Will Schultz Associates.

Sheal, P. (1999): *The Staff Development Handbook*, London: Kogan Page.

Silverman, D. (1970): *The Theory of Organisations: A Sociological Framework*, London: Heinemann.

Sloman, M. (2003): *Training in the Age of the Learner*, London: CIPD.

Smith, P.L. and Ragan, T.J. (1993): *Instructional Design*, New Jersey, Merrill.

Stammers, R. and Patrick, H. (1975): *Psychology of Training*, London, Metheun.

Truelove, S. (1997): *Training in Practice*, Oxford: Blackwell Business.

INDEX

OAK TREE PRESS

Oak Tree Press is Ireland's leading business
book publisher, with a wide range of titles
ranging over management, HR, finance, law,
and economics.

Full details of all our titles are available on
our website, www.oaktreepress.com.

Oak Tree Press is also increasingly an
international developer of small business
training and support materials and
methodologies.

www.oaktreepress.com

OAK TREE PRESS
19 Rutland Street, Cork, Ireland
T: + 353 21 431 3855   F: + 353 21 431 3496
E: info@oaktreepress.com
W: www.oaktreepress.com